The Goshenhoppen Registers
1741–1819

The Goshenhoppen Registers
1741–1819

Registers of Baptisms, Marriages, and Deaths
of the Catholic Mission at Goshenhoppen (Bally),
Washington Township, Berks County, Pennsylvania

Reprinted from
*Records of the American
Catholic Historical Society of Philadelphia*

With an Index by Elizabeth P. Bentley

CLEARFIELD

Reprinted for
Clearfield Company, Inc. by
Genealogical Publishing Co., Inc.
Baltimore, Maryland
2002

Library of Congress Catalogue Card Number 84-80489
International Standard Book Number: 0-8063-5077-6
Made in the United States of America

Originally published in *Records of the American
Catholic Historical Society of Philadelphia,* thus:
First Series, Vol. II (1886 – 1888)
Second Series, Vol. III (1888 – 1891)
Third Series, Vol. VIII (1897)
Fourth Series, Vol. XI (1900)
Fifth Series, Vol. LXI (1950)

Note to the Reader

he Goshenhoppen registers of baptisms, marriages, and deaths comprise the sacramental records of the mission church at Goshenhoppen, now Bally, in Washington Township, Berks County, Pennsylvania. They are presumably the oldest extant Catholic church registers in Pennsylvania, and belonged formerly to the old mission church of St. Paul, known since 1837 as the church of the Most Blessed Sacrament.

Beginning in 1741, the year the mission was founded by the Jesuit Theodore Schneider, and extending, with some gaps, to 1819, these registers provide a record of the sacraments administered at Goshenhoppen and outlying missions in southeastern Pennsylvania, particularly in the counties of Berks, Bucks, Northampton, Montgomery, Lehigh, and Lebanon, an area embracing a large proportion of the early German population of Pennsylvania.

Although Goshenhoppen was not the first Catholic mission in Pennsylvania, its registers are believed to be not only the oldest extant Catholic church registers in the state but the oldest in existence of the original thirteen colonies. Hence their special place in the annals of the Catholic Church in America, their overriding importance in Pennsylvania-German history and genealogy, and the reason for their translation and publication in the *Records of the American Catholic Historical Society of Philadelphia*.

Buried for years in the yellowing pages of this journal, however, the registers have been overlooked as a reference source, and it is doubtful that more than a handful of scholars have penetrated their secrets or tested their importance. For this reason we have chosen to reprint the Goshenhoppen registers and to place them in the hard-wearing apparel of a book. So that their contents may be readily accessible we have added an index of names, trusting that the entire work will now take its long-deserved place as a fixture on the reference shelves.

Genealogical Publishing Company

Contents

GOSHENHOPPEN REGISTERS, 1741–1819

First Series (1741–1764)
Tr. by Francis T. Furey, from *Records,* Vol. II (1886–
1888), 316–332 1

Second Series (1765–1785)
Tr. by Thomas C. Middleton, from *Records,* Vol. III (1888–
1891), 295–398 18

Third Series (1787–1800)
Tr. by Thomas C. Middleton, from *Records,* Vol. VIII
(1897), 330–393 122

Fourth Series (1801–1819)
Tr. by Thomas C. Middleton, from *Records,* Vol. XI (1900),
43–60, 196–207, 303–307 186

Fifth Series (1807–1818)
Tr. by John R. Dunne, from *Records,* Vol. LXI (1950),
57–63, 112–123, 185–192, 248–262 221

Index 263

FATHER SCHNEIDER'S

GOSHENHOPPEN REGISTERS,

1741—1764.

[Transcribed for the SOCIETY, and translated and prepared for publication, by FRANCIS T. FUREY.]

THE contents of the oldest Catholic Church register of the original thirteen English colonies now known to be in existence are here given to the public. A brief mention of the book has already been made in this volume: Mr. Philip S. P. Connor[*] describes its form and appearance in a paper which he read last year before our Society.[**] Dr. Shea, too, in his "Catholic Church in Colonial Days," refers to it and gives fac-simile reproductions of its title-page and first entry.[†]

Only a small portion of the book is really Father Schneider's work, by far the geater part of it being taken up with the registers of his successor, Father John Baptist De Ritter, the publication of which is reserved for a future occasion.[***]

It will be noticed with much regret that Father Schneider's registers are far from being a complete record of his missionary labors in America. There is, unfortunately, a very wide gap, beginning with the middle of the year 1747 and extending to 1758; and even then only the list of marriages is resumed. We are, therefore, left without any authentic account of the missionary's journeyings during the years that

---

[*]For *Connor* read *Conner*.
[**]See RECORDS, Vol. II, pp. 22-28.
[***]See pp. 18-121, this volume.

[†] See Shea, pp. 393, 402.

1

were probably the most interesting period of his labors, that of the hostile Indian incursions and massacres in Berks county.

The editor had originally intended to give, along with these registers, geographical and historical annotations; but his investigations have been rewarded with so vast and rich a mass of valuable material that he has been persuaded to utilize it in a separate historical essay covering the territory and time of Father Schneider's mission in this country.* This work is now nearly completed. It is put in the form of a paper, which he intends to read before the American Catholic Historical Society some time in the early part of next year. Until then the uninitiated are left to guess at the location and present name of many of the places mentioned by our pioneer missionary, whose parish embraced all the territory in Pennsylvania north of the Schuykill and the Neshaminy rivers, and had the whole colony of New Jersey as an annexed mission.

We now proceed to give a translation and adaptation of the registers under their separate headings:

I. BAPTISMS.

BAPTISMS FOR THE YEAR 1741.

Kohl, Albertina, of George and Barbara Kohl, born May 6th, baptized August 23d, in John Utzman's house in Falkner's Swamp; sponsors John Utzman and Albertina (Luth.), his wife.

Magudiens, Catharine and Mary, of Patrick and ——— Magudiens (Irish), baptized December 23d, in their parents' house, in the Swedish settlement; sponsor Judith Coners, widow.

Utzman, George, of John and Albertina (Luth.) Utzman, baptized December 26th; sponsor George Kuhn.

Lery, George Henry, of Derby Lery (Irish) and Anna Margaret ———, baptized December 28th, in the house of Henry Michel, who served as sponsor.

BAPTISMS FOR THE YEAR 1742.

Comins, Timothy, of Michael and ——— Comins (Irish), baptized January 13th, in parents' house, in the Swedish colony; sponsors John Larkin and Judith Coners, widow.

*See pp. 18-25, this volume.

Crossby, Thomas, of Farrel and —— Crossby (Irish), baptized the same day, at the same place; sponsor Michael Magdanel.

Mayer, Joseph Caspar, of Caspar and ——— Mayer, baptized January 22d; sponsor Joseph Kuhn.

Lang, Eva Mary, of James (Calv.) and Apollonia Lang, baptized February 28th; sponsors George Kuhn and his sister, Eva Mary.

Frantz, Mary Apollonia, of James and —— Frantz, baptized March 4th, in Wendelin Helffer's house, in Bethlehem country; sponsors Simon Becker and Wendelin Helffer's wife.

Friderich, George Reinold, of Philip (commonly called the stone-breaker) and ——— Friderich, baptized March 9th, near Germantown; sponsors John George Schwartzmann and his wife.

Kuhn, Anna Barbara, of Henry and Margaret Kuhn, baptized March 28th, in John Kuhn's house; sponsors John Kuhn and Anna Barbara, his wife.

Kill, Philip, of George and ——— (P.) Kill, baptized April 18th (Easter Sunday), in John Kuhn's house; sponsor Eva Maria Kuhn.

Canceler, Sara, of John and ——— Canceler (Irish), baptized April 20th, in Henry Guibson's house; sponsors Ambrose Rilay and Judith, his wife.

Pawlitz, Michael, of Jacob and ——— (P.) Pawlitz, baptized May 17th, in parents' house in Allemängel.

Meyer, John, (posthumous child) of John (P.) and Mary (P.) Meyer, baptized the same day at the same place; sponsor John Meyer (P.).

Onan, Denis, of Denis and Rebecca Onan, baptized May 27th, in Christian Haug's house in Dinekum; sponsor Wendelin Helffer.

Maguin, Margaret, of Henry and Mary Maguin; sponsor Mary Apollonia Helffer.

Blayny, John, of Edmund and Ann Blayny; sponsor Patrick Karmick.

McCardy, Nicholas, of Edward and Catharine McCardy; sponsor Edmund Gueréti.

McCardy, Edward, of the same parents; sponsor Lawrence Mair.

Dörm, John, of John and Catharine Dörm; sponsor Denis Onan.

(All of the above were Catholics, beginning with Onan, Denis.)

Spengler, Mary Eva, of Peter (P.) and Mary Eva Spengler, baptized July 25th, in John Kuhn's house; sponsor George Kuhn.

Bricker, Ann Elizabeth, of John and Barbara (P.) Bricker, baptized August 15th, in Jacob Pawlitz's house; sponsors James (P.) and Anna (P.) Lantz.

MaKarmick, Elias, of Patrick and —— MaKarmick, baptized August 29th, in Christian Haug's house; sponsors Lawrence Mair and Ann Blayny.

Schwartz, George James, of John (puddler) and Agnes Schwartz, baptized September 26th, in John Kuhn's house; sponsor James Danckel.

3

[Here Father Schneider makes an entry to the effect that in the latter part of August three persons, whose names were not recorded, were baptized at the New Forge, near Jotter's Mill.]

————, John and David, children of a widow whose husband was a Protestant, baptized October 17th, in the house of William Hall (Irish), near North Wales Meeting House.

Haug, Simon, of Christian and ———— Haug, baptized October 28th, in parents' house; sponsors Thomas McCardy and his wife.

Helffer, Mary Apollonia, of Wendelin and Mary Apollonia Helffer, baptized in the same place; sponsors John Utaman and Anna Barbara Lorentz.

Gust, Rosina, of Henry and Mary Magdalen Gust, baptized November 7th, in the chapel in Philadelphia; sponsor George Esselin.

Arnold, George, of George and ———— Arnold, baptized November 8th, in parents' house, in Germantown; sponsor Catharine Spengler, wife of George Spengler, who stood quasi god-father.

Molitor, Anna Martha, of John and ———— (P.) Molitor, baptized the same day and in the same place; sponsor Anna Martha, wife of John Schmidt, who stood as quasi god-father.

Lechler, John, of George Ernest (weaver) and ———— (P.) Lechler, baptized December 12th, in Mark Schiffer's house, in Oley.

Doeri, John, of James and ———— Doeri, baptized December 13th, in Falkner's Swamp; sponsor John Utzman.

Keffer, John Peter, of Matthew and ———— Keffer, baptized December 19th, in parents' house, at Maxetani; sponsor Ursula Luckenbihl.

Reppert, Mary Apollonia, of Stephen and ———— Reppert, baptized December 25th, the Feast of the Nativity, in John Kuhn's house; sponsor Mary Apollonia Lang.

———

BAPTISMS FOR THE YEAR 1743.

Melchior, George, of Nicholas (P.) and ———— Melchior, baptized February 13th, in Cushenhopen; sponsor John George Gauckler.

Johnson, John, of Patrick and ———— Johnson, baptized February 14th, near New Furnace.

Calver, Patrick, of Philip and ———— Calver, baptized February 27th, in Henry Guibson's house.

Becker, Elizabeth Mary, of Simon and Elizabeth (P.) Becker, baptized March 16th, in Wendelin Helffer's house; sponsors Maurice Lorentz and Eva Mary Immel.

Minime, Anna and Martha, of John and ———— Minime, baptized March 17th, near Dörm Furnace; sponsor Edward Garden.

Leehoffer, Johanna Catharine Albertina, of Ursula Leehoffer and ————

————, baptized March 22d, in the house of John Utzman, who stood sponsor.

Maurer, John, of John (Calv.) and M. Catharine (Calv.) Maurer, baptized April 4th, in the same house and with the same sponsor.

————, James, of a certain married negress, baptized April 17th, in James Hoffman's house, in Philadelphia ; sponsors James Hoffman and his wife.

Pulton, Charles, of Charles and Ruth Pulton (English), baptized May 28th, in parents' house, near Durham Road.

Dörm, Anna, of John and Catharine Dörm, baptized May 29th, the Feast of the Most Holy Trinity, in Thomas Garden's house, at Haycock ; sponsors Patrick Cardy and Catharine, wife of Edward Cardy.

Mair, David, of Lawrence and Mary Mair, baptized May 30th, in Maurice Lorentz's house.

Meyer, Catharine, of John (P.) and Mary Meyer, baptized the same day at the same place ; sponsors, for both Catharine Seibert, and for David Patrick MacKarmick.

Rilay, M. Margaret, of Ambrose and Judith Rilay, baptized June 19th, in parents' house, near New Furnace; sponsors Frank Gibson and Margaret, his wife.

Ridgens, Samuel, of John and Mary Ridgens, baptized May 29th, in Thomas Garden's house ; sponsors Edward Cardy and his wife, Catharine.

————, ————, of Patrick and ———— ———— (an Irish married couple), baptized July 2d, in Handlon's house, in Frankford ; sponsor Cornelius ————.

Fick, Mary Susanna, of Jodoc[?] (P.) and Anna Regina (P.) Fick, baptized July 17th, in Jaacob Pawlitz's house ; sponsor Godfrey Bezel.

Blany, Catharine, of Edmund and Anna Blany, baptized July 31st, in the house of Thomas Cardy, who stood sponsor.

Lorentz, John Wendelin, of Maurice and Barbara Lorentz, baptized August 1st, in parents' house ; sponsors John Wendelin Helffer and A. M. Meyer.

Fitzcharroll, John and Gerald, of Patrick and Elizabeth Fitzcharroll, baptized in the same place ; sponsors Lawrence Mair for John, Wendelin Helffer for Gerald, and A. M. Meyer for both.

MacKarmick, Martha, of Patrick and Johanna MacKarmick, baptized August 2d, in parents' house; sponsor Frank McAgane.

O'Nayl, Thomas, of John and Catharine O'Nayl, baptized on the same occassion ; sponsor John McClaughlen.

Schüssler, John George, of Henry (Calv.) and Catharine Schüssler, baptized at the same place ; sponsor James Frantz.

Stockschlager, John Adam, of John and A. Martha Stockschlager, baptized August 4th, in parents' house ; sponsor John Adam Bender.

5

Kohl, M. Apollonia, of John George and —— — (P.) Kohl, baptized August 14th, in George Gauckler's house; sponsors Wendel Helffer and Mary Apollonia, his wife.

Canceler, Elizabeth, of John and Mary Canceler, baptized August 24th, in Mark Schiffer's house, in Oley; sponsor John Mulcastor and Margaret, wife of Francis Gibson.

Reiss, David, of Valentine and Elizabeth (P.) Reiss; sponsor ———— , commonly known as " the old widow."

Bender, John Peter, of Adam and Margaret (P.) Bender, baptized September 18th, in parents' house; sponsors John Stockschleger and A. Martha, his wife.

Alter, John Martin, of John Martin and Catharine Alter, baptized October 5th, near the Glass Works; sponsor Joseph Walter.

Schwartzmann, Andrew, of John and Anna Maria Schwartzmann, baptized October 6th, in parents' house, near Germantown; sponsors Andrew Engelhard and Walburga, his wife.

Laydon, James, of Maurice and Margaret (Linnert) Laydon, baptized October 16th, in John Mulcastor's house; sponsors Frank Gibson and Margaret, his wife.

Mayer, Peter James, of Caspar and ——— Mayer, baptized December 26th, in John Utzman's house; sponsor James Doeri.

Onan, Mary, of Denis and Rebecca Onan, baptized December 28th, in parents' house; sponsor Ann Blainy.

Rilay, Thomas, of Hugh and ——— Rilay, baptized in Thomas Cardy's house; sponsor Edmund Blany.

BAPTISMS FOR THE YEAR 1744.

Savage, Henry, of Henry and ——— Savage, baptized January 1st, in the chapel in Philadelphia; sponsor Catharine Spengler.

————, Eva Helena, of a certain English married couple, baptized January 8th, in John Kuhn's house; sponsor M. Eva Schmidt.

Stagle, Melon, of Matthew and Anna Stagle, baptized March 18th, in Maurice Lorentz's house, in New Jersey; sponsor Patrick MacKarmick.

Ridgens, John, of John and Mary Ridgens; sponsors James Lorentz and Catharine Seibert.

Riley, John, of Charles and Sarah Riley, baptized March 27th, in Henry Gibson's house; sponsors Frank Gibson and Margaret, his wife.

Cawlvert, William, of Patrick and Margaret Cawlvert; sponsors Philip Cawlvert and Margaret Gibson.

Utzman, Margaret Apollonia, of John and Albertina (Luth.) Utzman, baptized March 28th in parents' house ; sponsors Wendel Helffer and Apollonia, his wife.

Bischof, Paul, of Peter and Charlotta Bischof, baptized April 1st, in the chapel in Philadelphia ; sponsors Paul Müller and Elizabeth Gatringer.

Müller, Charlotte Elizabeth, of Paul and M. Magdalen Müller, baptized April 2d, in the same place ; sponsors Peter Bischoff and Elizabeth Gatringer.

Staab, Eva Catharine, of John Adam and Catharine Staab, baptized April 15th, in parents' house, in Allemängel ; sponsors George Kuhn and Sara Catharine Bewerts.

Koch, Henry, of John Adam and A. Maria (Con.) Koch, baptized April 17th, at Cedar Creek ; sponsors Henry Kuhn and Marg. his wife.

Kuhn, Margaret, of Henry and Margaret Kuhn, baptized April 22d, in John Kuhn's house ; sponsors John Eckenroth and Margaret, his wife.

Schmidt, A. Barbara, of Philip and Eva Mary Schmidt ; sponsors John Kuhn and Anna Barbara, his wife.

Wentzel, Simon, of John William and Catharine (P.) Wentzel, baptized April 25th, at the Glass Works ; sponsors Simon Griesmeyer and Susan, his wife.

————, Margaret Elizabeth, an adult, baptized April 30th, in the chapel in Philadelphia ; sponsor Elizabeth Gatringer.

————, Christina, an adult Negress, slave (or servant) of Dr. Brown, in whose house she was baptized ; sponsors the same Dr. Brown and his wife.

Griesmeyer, Anna Mary, of Simon and Susanna Griesmeyer ; sponsors Caspar Alter and A. M., his wife.

Madin, Margaret, of Patrick and Sarah Madin, baptized May (April) 9th, in Michael Comins' house, at Branson's Iron Works ; sponsors William Sands and Frances Langford.

Maxfield, Margaret, of James and Catharine Maxfield ; sponsor Patrick Madin.

Konlen, Patrick, of Denis and Honora Konlen ; sponsor Susan Hickey.

Comins, Thomas, of Michael and Anna Comins ; sponsor Thomas Connor.

Mair, Helena, of Lawrence and Mary Mair, baptized May 19th, in Jacob Frantz's house, in New Jersey ; sponsors John Murphay and A. M. Meyer.

Buttler, William, of James and Mary Buttler ; sponsors James Toy and Catharine Morgan.

Sauter, Simon, of Philip and Christina Sauter, baptized June 6th, in Matthew Geiger's house, in New Jersey ; sponsors Simon Griesmeyer and A. M. Beitelmann.

Geiger, John Henry, of Matthew and A. Mary Geiger; sponsors William
Wentzel and M. Eva Halter.

Bucher, Elizabeth, of Peter and A. Barbara Bucher, baptized June 17th,
in Jacob Pawlitz's house, in Allemängel ; sponsors Jacob Pawlitz and
M. Elizabeth Seissloff.

Lechler, Martin, of George Ernest and M. Magdalen (P.) Lechler, baptized July 24th, in parents' house, in Oley ; sponsors Martin Reisel
and Catharine Riffel.

Eckenroth, Margaret, of John and Margaret Eckenroth, baptized July
25th, in the priest's house ; sponsors Wendel Helffer and Apollonia,
his wife.

Connely, Peter, of Bernard and Brigid Connely, baptized July 27th, in
Thomas Cardy's house; sponsors Edward Cardy and Catharine
Harvy.

Frantz, Elizabeth, of Jacob and Eva M. Frantz, baptized July 29th, in
parents' house ; sponsors Adam Sommer and Elizabeth Reiffenberger.

Kelsey, Anna, of Bartholomew and —— —— Kelsey, baptized July 30th,
in parents' house, at Bonbrook ; sponsor Nicholas Power.

Chateau, A. Barbara and Catharine, of Nicholas (Calv.) and M. Eva
Chateau, baptized August 7th, in John Molitor's house, near Germantown ; sponsors A. Barbara Fridrich for the former, and Catharine Riffel for the latter.

Groskopff, A. Margaret, of James and Anna Mary (Calv.) Groskopff;
sponsor John Molitor.

Normand, Richard, of John and Johanna Normand, baptized August
19th, in James Darnay's house, near Branson's Iron Works ; sponsors James Darnay and Rose, his wife.

Shay, John, of Edward and Eleanor Shay, in Michael Comins' house ;
sponsors Michael Comins and Sarah, his wife.

Arnold, —— ——, of George and Margaret Arnold, baptized September
2d, in George Arnold's house in Philadelphia ; sponsor Catharine
Spengler.

Fues, Margaret, of John and Dorothea Fues, baptized September 20th,
in George Ernest Lechler's house, in Oley ; sponsors Martin Reisel
and Margaret Gibson.

BAPTISMS FOR THE YEAR 1745.

Ruffener, Jo. M. Eva, of Simon and M. Barbara Ruffener, baptized February 4th, near Croner's Mill ; sponsor M. Eva Lorentz.

McCardy, Thomas, of Patrick and Ann (P.) McCardy, baptized February 17th, at Haycock ; sponsors Matthew Handlon and Ann
Blany.

8

Dörm, Margaret, of John (P.) and Catharine Dörm; sponsors Denis Onan and Ann Blany.

Gibson, Henry, of Frank and Margaret Gibson, baptized March 31st, in Charles Riles's house; sponsors Charles Riles and his wife.

Johnson, Edward, of Patrick and ——— Johnson, baptized April 16th; sponsors John Utzman and Albertina, his wife.

Morgan, Ann, of Francis and Catharine Morgan, baptized April 20th, sponsors John McCray and A. M. Meyer.

Sommer, John Adam, of Adam and ——— Sommer, baptized April 20th, sponsor James Frantz.

Minimay, John, of John and Mary Minimay, baptized April 22d.

Canceler, George Ernest, of John and Mary Canceler, baptized May 23d; sponsors George Ernest Lechler and his wife.

Reppert, Daniel, of Stephen and ——— Reppert, baptized May 26th; sponsors James Lang and Apollonia, his wife.

Halter, Andrew, of Caspar and Anna Eva Halter, baptized June 2d, in Philadelphia; sponsors Martin Gassner and his wife.

Noulen, Ann, of Denis and Honora Noulen, baptized June 16th; sponsors Thomas Donahew and Rose Darnay.

Normand, Joseph, of John and Johanna Normand, baptized June 19th, sponsor James Darnay.

Grismeyer, M. Agnes, of Simon and Susanna Grismeyer, baptized July 9th; sponsors Caspar and Christina Alter.

Alter, A. Margaret, of Martin and Catharine Alter; sponsors Christopher Stumpff and Margaret Schæffer.

Doeri, George Peter, of James and ——— Doeri, baptized August 12th; sponsors George Kuhn and Catharine, his wife.

Pulton, Barbara, of Charles and Ruth Pulton; sponsor Catharine Harvay.

———, Isaac, of a certain Sarah, who said her husband was a Catholic; sponsor Charles Pulton.

Riles, Elizabeth, of Charles and Sarah Riles; sponsor Michael Comins.

Staab, George Adam, of Adam and Catharine Staab; sponsors Adam Koch and Anna Mary, his wife.

Koch, Frederick, of Adam and Anna Mary Koch; sponsor Henry Kuhn.

Væth, Elizabeth, of Adam and Magdalen (Brückner) Væth; sponsors John Peter Högener and Elizabeth, his wife.

Molitor, Elizabeth, of John and ——— Molitor; sponsor Adam Spæth.

Riffel, Anna Barbara, of Matthew and Christina Riffel; sponsors John Kuhn and Anna Barbara, his wife.

Wolflinger, ———, of Bernard and ——— Wolflinger.

Kuhn, M. Ottilia, of Henry and Margaret Kuhn; sponsor Ottilia Meyer.

Schmidt, Catharine, of Philip and Eva Mary Schmidt; sponsors George and Catharine Kuhn.

Krafft, John George and Michael, twins, of Anna Catharine, widow of Frederick Krafft, baptized February 20th; sponsors John George Gauckler and Michael Reiser (Luth.).

Kohl, George Bernard, of George and ————— Kohl, baptized March 9th.

Connely, Mary, of Bernard and ————— Connely, baptized March 16th; sponsor Ann, wife of Edmund Blany.

Castelah, Mary, of Pierce and Sarah Castelah, baptized March 23d; sponsors Thomas Catugn and Mary, wife of Patrick Johnson.

Madin, Elizabeth, of Patrick and Sarah Madin; sponsors James Ryan and Eleanor Püsert.

Flaharty, Margaret, of Patrick and Frances Flaharty; sponsors Charles Riles and A. M. Utzmann.

Kuhn, George James, of George and Catharine Kuhn, baptized March 31st; sponsors Jacob Riffel and Ottilia Meyer.

Ridgens, Margaret, of John and Mary Ridgens, baptized April 11th; sponsor Edward Morpheu.

Meyer, John James, of John and Anna Mary Meyer, baptized April 13th; sponsor Jacob Lorentz.

Onan, Rebecca, of Denis and Rebecca Onan, baptized April 14th; sponsors Matthew Handlon and Ann, wife of Edmund Blany.

Stockschleger, M. Apollonia, of John and A. Martha Stockschleger, baptized April 17th; sponsors John Wendelin Helffer and Apollonia, his wife.

Steyerwald, M. Catharine, of Theobald and A. Marg. Steyerwald, baptized April 20th; sponsor Adam Koch.

Keffer, A. Dorothy, of Matthew and A. M. Kefter; sponsors John Fues and Dorothy, his wife.

Helffer, John Maurice, of John Wendelin and Apollonia Helffer, baptized May 11th; sponsors Maurice Lorentz and John Stockschleger.

Kerck, Mary, of John and Bridget Kerck, baptized June 15th; sponsors Thomas Donahew and Eleanor Shehea.

Ulrich, John Francis, of John and Barbara Ulrich; sponsor Frank Gibson.

Lechler, Anthony, of George Ernest and M. Magdalen Lechler, baptized June 16th; sponsor the priest.

Cognway, Margaret, of John and Mary Cognway, baptized June 29th; sponsors John McCray and Catharine, wife of Francis Morgan.

Stasy, Matthew, of Matthew and Ann Stasy, sponsors John McClaughlen and Gaudentia, his wife.

Mair, John, of Lawrence and ———— Mair; sponsor Edward Morpheu.

Spies, Anna Magdalen, of Wolffgang and Catharine Spies, baptized July 14th ; sponsor A. Mary Bechtl.

Lorentz, Joseph, of Maurice and Barbara Lorentz, baptized July 17th ; sponsors John Wendelin Helffer and Apollonia, his wife.

Fuss, A. Catharine, of John and Dorothy Fuss, baptized July 20th ; sponsors Adam Staab and Catharine, his wife.

Wentzel, Theodore, of William and Catharine Wentzel, baptized August 5th, in Matthew Geiger's house ; sponsor the priest.

Villar, John George, of Anthony and M. Eva Villar, baptized September 14th, in Philadelphia ; sponsors John George Ulrich and Anna Catharine ————.

Shaw, Johanna, of ———— and ————— Shaw, baptized September 21st.

Reppert, James, of Stephen and ———— Reppert, baptized September 28th ;, sponsors James Lang (P.) and Apollonia, his wife.

Schwager, Wolffgang Adam, of Peter and Anna Magdalen Schwager ; sponsors Adam Væth (the bridge builder) and Magdalen, his wife.

Sommer, John Henry, of Adam and ———— Sommer, baptized September 29th, in the priest's house ; sponsor John Henry Pishing.

Gassner, Edward Daniel, of Caspar and Elizabeth Gassner, baptized October 5th, in Philadelphia ; sponsor Edward ————.

Darsey, Daniel and Johanna, of Charles and Elizabeth Darsey, baptized October 6th, in Matthew Geiger's house ; sponsor James Lestrange.

Guill, Peter, of Patrick and ———— Guill ; sponsor Daniel Sulivan.

Sauter, Philip, of Philip and Christina Sauter ; sponsors John Martin Alter and Eva, wife of Caspar Alter.

Bewerts, Henry, of John and M. Ottilia Bewerts, baptized October 19th, in Adam Staab's house ; sponsors Henry Kuhn and Margaret, his wife.

Eckroth, Catharine, of John and Margaret Eckroth, baptized November 17th, in parents' house ; sponsors George Kuhn and Catharine, his wife.

Smith, Philip, af Patrick and Elizabeth Smith, baptized November 30th, at Haycock ; sponsors Edmund Morphey and Catharine Harvey.

BAPTISMS FOR THE YEAR 1747.

Noulen, Denis, of Denis and Honora Noulen, baptized January 8th ; sponsor Edward Hogan.

Hogan, Mary, of Edward and Sarah Hogan ; sponsor Denis Noulen.

11

Cardy, John, of Patrick and Ann Cardy, baptized January 18th, at Haycock.

Handlon, John, of Matthew and Rachel Handlon; sponsors Edward Morpheu and Catharine Harvey.

Ruffener, Adam, of Simon and M. Barbara Ruffener, baptized April 17th, in the preist's house; sponsors Adam Brückner and Magdalen, his wife.

Kuhn, Anna Catharine, of Henry and Margaret Kuhn, baptized April 13th, in parents' house; sponsors Adam Staab and A. Catharine, his wife.

Minimay, William, of John and ——— Minimay, baptized April 25th, in Thomas Cardy's house; sponsors Edward Cardy and Rebecca Onan.

Smith, David, of Patrick and Elizabeth Smith; sponsors Thomas Cardy and Ann, his wife.

Frantz, Simon, of Jacob and Eva M. Frantz, baptized April 26th; sponsors Simon Becker and ——— Immel.

Morgan, M. Elizabeth, of Frank and Catharine Morgan; sponsors David Conaugh and A. M. Meyer.

Pulton, Ruth, of Charles and Ruth Pulton, baptized April 28th.

Alter, Simon, of Caspar and Eva Alter, baptized May 4th; sponsors Simon Griesmeyer and Barbara Bachmann.

Geiger, Simon, of Matthew and A. M. Geiger; sponsors Martin Alter and Christina, his sister.

———, Rachel; sponsor Simon Griesmeyer.

Utzman, Sarah, of John and Albertina Utzman, baptized May 17th, sponsors Frank Gibson and Mary Johnson.

Maxfield, Isabella, of Catharine, widow of James Maxfield; sponsors James Bryan and A. M. Utzman.

Keragan, Thomas, of Manasses [Manus ?] and Johanna (Crames) Keragan; sponsor Thomas Bissit.

[Thus abruptly ends Father Schneider's register of baptisms. Closely following, on the same page, but in a far different hand and much smaller characters, more difficult to read, are recorded three baptisms, dated November 18th, 1764 (which will be found placed in their proper chronological order in this list); and on the next page are two others, of the Bock (Buck) family, one dated October 16th, 1763, and the other of the year 1764, but without mention of month or day. Closely following the last of these is a single line of an unfinished record, which reads, "1740, 10 Julii Ann. Margaretha fil." Then, with two blank pages intervening, there is a whole page of entries of the Hookey family, which look as if they might have been copied in Father De Ritter's time from memoranda that had been kept privately by some interested person. The spelling of the surname may seem peculiar to modern eyes acquainted with the present generation of the family; but it is the same as was used by Father De Ritter thirty years later than the birth of these children. There are a few other records of the year 1764, preceding the death of Father Schneider, which occurred on July 10th of that year; and in these instances Father Farmer came from Philadelphia to officiate. The few scattered registers referred to above are given below in regular chronological order.]

Hucki, Elizabeth, of Nicholas and Catharine (Kleyss) Hucki, born September 29th, 1751, baptized October 17th following in Edward Carty's house; sponsors Anthony Grüsser and Elizabeth, his wife.

Hucki, Catharine, of the same parents, born January 12th, 1753, baptized February 18th following, in the same place; sponsors George Kohl and Barbara, his wife.

Hucki, Anthony,* of the same parents, born April ——, 1755, baptized on the 17th of the same month, *ibid.*; sponsors Anthony Grüsser and Elizabeth Kleyss, his wife.

Hucki, Nicholas, of the same parents, born about the end of March or beginning of April, 1757, baptized in the same place on April 17th of the same year; sponsors Joseph Kohl and Barbara Henrich.

Hucki, John George,† of the same parents, born May 6th, 1759, baptized in the same place June 17th following; sponsors George Kohl and Barbara Kohl.

Bock, Leonard, of Nicholas and Apollonia Bock, baptized October 10th, 1763, sponsors Leonard Beutelman and Salome Fricker.

Bock, Joseph, of the same parents, baptized —— ——, 1764, sponsor Joseph Kohl.

Schmidt, John George, of Philip and Ursula (Zip) Schmidt, born November 23d, 1763, baptized [privately?] when eleven weeks old, by Henry Fredder, the schoolmaster, at Couissahopen; Chrism given by P. Frambachs [ceremonies supplied by Father Farmer?]; sponsors George Zip and Eva Zip.

Ristel, Bernard, of Matthew and Christina (Danner) Ristel, born in Macunshi, May 22d, 1764, baptized June 30th following, at Goshenhoppen, by Father Farmer; sponsors Melchior Ziegler and Catharine, his wife.

Röhr, John Martin, of Martin and Anna Mary Röhr, born this year, baptized in the parents' house the same month as the last named infant by Father Ferdinand Farmer, Father Theodore [Schneider] being then in his last illness; sponsors John Grett and Elizabeth, his wife.

Lorentz, Henry, of Maurice and Mary Lorentz, baptized November 18th; sponsors Henry Fredder and Anna Mary, his wife.

---

* Ancestor of the Drexel family of Philadelphia.
† Ancestor of the present Hookey family of Philadelphia.

Norbudy, John Daniel, of Henry and Mary Norbudy; sponsors Henry Hein and Magdalen, his wife.

Hoffman, Margaret, of Michael and Catharine Hoffman; sponsors Martin and Catharine Moulier.

[The last three entries, which are recorded on the same page with the last of Father Schneider's own records, are so indistinctly written that some of the words can only be guessed at. They are the last in date recorded at Goshenhoppen prior to Father De Ritter's arrival in the Summer of 1765, after which time the registers were kept regularly.]

— · —

II. MARRIAGES.

Laub— ————-: December 8th, 1741, in the chapel in Philadelphia, John Michael Laub to Regina ———, widow; witnesses John Schmidt and several others, Protestants as well as Catholics.

Dubon—Krebs: March 7th [1742], *ibid.*, Lawrence Dubon, widower, to Anna Mary Walburger (Luth.), widow of Jacob Krebs, in the presence of several witnesses.

Magdanel—Welsh : March 9th, *ibid.*, after dispensation and in presence of witnesses, Edmund Magdanel to Sarah Welsh, both Irish.

Rilay— ————- : April 19th, after publication of the banns in the city and in the country, in Henry Guibson's house, in presence of many witnesses, Catholics and non-Catholics, Ambrose Rilay to Judith (O'Nayl) ———, widow.

Schwartz—Fischer : July 12th, in George Zimmermann's house, John Schwartz, puddler, to Agnes Fischer (P.); witnesses George Zimmermann and wife.

Müller—Gärtner : Christmas day, in John Kuhn's house, John Henry Müller (P.) to Anna Margaret Gärtner(P.),in the presence of witnesses.

Högner— ———— : March 8th [1743], in the Philadelphia chapel, Peter Högner, widower, to Elizabeth ———— (P.), widow; in presence of several witnesses.

Staab—Bewerts : April 4th, in John Utzman's house in Falkner's swamp, John Adam Staab to Catharine Bewerts; several witnesses were present.

Gibson—Brodbeck : April 5th, in Henry Gibson's house on the Schuylkill, Frank, son of the said Henry Gibson, to Margaret Brodbeck, a German; witnesses the bridegroom's father and mother and another married couple of the neighborhood.

Müller—Walltrich : April 11th, in the Philadelphia chapel, Paul Müller to Mary Magdalen Walltrich; witnesses the bride's parents and several others.

Beck—Stengler: April 12th, *ibid.*, John Beck to Barbara Stengler, both Lutherans ; witnesses Catharine Spengler and several Protestants.

Schmidt—Kuhn : April 26th, in John Kuhn's house, Philip Schmidt to Eva Kuhn ; witnesses the bride's parents and several others.

Grosskopf—Stumpf: September 5th, in the Philadelphia chapel, Jacob Grosskopf to Anna Mary Stumpf; witnesses a number of Protestants, relatives of the bride's father, who had recently come here with her.

Smith—Sanders : November 8th, in the priest's house, John Smith to Margaret Sanders ; witnesses some English people who came with the young couple, Peter Schwager and Valentine Wildt.

Cardy [McCarty]—Sanderson : February 14th [1744], at Haycock, Patrick Cardy to Ann Sanderson (P.) ; witnesses the bridegroom's parents, brothers and sisters.

Schwager—Schwitz : February 28th, in the priest's house, John Peter Schwager, widower, to Anna Magdalen Schwitz (Luth.) ; witnesses Valentine Wild and several Protestants.

Morgan—Seibert: May 19th, in Jacob Frantz's house in New Jersey, Francis Morgan, an Irishman, to Catharine Seibert ; witnesses Jacob Frantz and his wife, and others.

Fernandez—Leonard : September 24th, in Charles Riles's house, John Fernandez, an Italian, to Margaret Leonard, an Irish girl ; witnesses Charles Riles, James Darnay and others.

Kuhn—Riffel : November 27th, in John Kuhn's house, John George Kuhn to Catharine Riffel ; witnesses the bridegroom's parents and brothers, and others.

Reisel—Bewerts : December 16th, in Jacob Pawlitz's house in Allemaengel, Martin Reisel to Sarah Catharine Bewerts ; witnesses the bride's parents and others.

Hopkins—Roosberry: January 6th, 1745, in Henry Gibson's house, James Hopkins to Mary Roosberry ; witnesses Henry Gibson and Frank Gibson.

Jacks—Herp : December 26th, in Jacob Keller's house, Michael Jacks to Catharine Herp (Luth.) ; witnesses Jacob Keller and Nicholas Schappert.

Schappert—Stockschleger: April 17th, 1746, Nicholas Schappert to Mary Clara Stockschleger ; witnesses the bride's father and Wendel Helffer.

Hecht—Fridrich : January 1st, 1747, William Hecht to Barbara Fridrich ; witnesses several Catholics and some others.

Riffel———— : January 8th, Jacob Riffel to Mary Catharine ————— ; witnesses Maurice Lorentz and his wife.

[Here there is a wide gap of eleven years in the marriage registry. Why this record is resumed at all, while that of baptisms is not, will, most probably, ever remain a mystery. The entries of marriages for the

15

six years beginning with 1758 are in the same handwriting as those we have already given. They are as follows :]

Ehrman—Sigfrid : January 30th, 1758, in George Sigfrid's house in the Oley hills, John Ehrman to Eva Sigfrid ; witnesses George Sigfrid, the bride's father, John Michael and Andrew, her brothers, and others.

Ledermann—Becker : February 6th, in Philadelphia, John Ledermann to Catharine Becker.

Kientz—Geidlinger : at the same time and place, Michael Kientz to Catharine Geidlinger.

Riedacker—Brunner : April 19th, 1759, in the chapel [at Goshenhoppen], Jacob Riedacker (Luth.) to Anna Mary Brunner ; witnesses Maurice Lorentz and Nicholas Frantz.

Fricker—Kohl : April 16th, 1760, in the chapel [at Goshenhoppen], John Fricker, widower, to Salome Kohl ; witnesses Michael Kohl, Maurice Lorenz and others.

Kohl—Becher : in George Kohl's house, Michael Kohl to Elizabeth Becher ; witnesses the bridegroom's father, the bride's father and others.

Zipp—Schreik : June 26th, 1761, in the chapel [at Goshenhoppen], Joseph Zipp to Apollonia Schreik ; witnesses Maurice Lorenz and John Wendel Lorenz.

Müller—Grünewald : April 19th, in Edward Cardy's [McCarty] house, Michael Müller to Elizabeth Grünewald ; witnesses the bride's father and others.

Bock—Kohl : April 21st, in George Kohl's house, Nicholas Bock to Apollonia Kohl ; witnesses the bride's parents and others.

Lorentz—Reppert: May 12th, in the chapel [at Goshenhoppen], Maurice Lorentz to Mary Apollonia Reppert ; witnesses Nicholas Cardy, Wendel Lorentz and others.

Reppert—Peter : June 30th, ibid., Melchior Reppert to Barbara Peter ; witnesses Mathias Reichart, Joseph Lorentz and others.

Eimold—Meck : April 22d, 1762, ibid., Peter Eimold to Marian Meck ; witnesses Maurice Lorentz and Joseph Lorentz.

Egg— ——— : October 26th, ibid., John Egg, Sr., widower, to Mary Magdalen ——— ; witnesses Francis Hartman and Maurice Lorentz.

Keffer—Hartmann : November 7th, in Christopher Henrich's house, Peter Keffer to Barbara Hartmann ; witnesses Joseph Lorentz and Wendel Lorentz.

Sigfrid—Zweyer : November 8th, in Zweyer's house in the Oley Hills, Andrew Sigfrid to Mary Agatha Zweyer ; witnesses Jacob Kuhn and Paul Huck.

Stahl—Kolb : December 13th, ibid., Michael Stahl to Margaret Kolb ; witnesses Paul Huck and Anthony Zinck.

16

Shaw—Carroll: December 20th, in John Faller's house, Denis Shaw to Ann Carroll; witnesses Philip McDeed and his wife.

Huck—Zweyer: April 11th, 1763, in Zweyer's house, Paul Huck to Julianna Zweyer; witnesses the bride's parents and others.

Lorentz—Kauffmann: June 7th, in the chapel [at Goshenhoppen], Wendel Lorentz to M. Eva Kauffmann; witnesses Maurice Lorentz, Joseph Lorentz and others.

Zweyer—Stahl: June 13th, in Zweyer's house, Stephen Zweyer to Anna Mary Stahl; witnesses the bridegrom's parents and others.

Leibig—Kraus: August 2d, in the chapel [at Goshenhoppen], John Leibig to Gertrude Kraus; witnesses George Demand and John Bischoff.

Bewerts—Eckroth: August 14th, in Philip Schmid's house in Magunshi, Conrad Bewerts to Anna Margaret Eckroth.

[Thus ends Father Schneider's marriage register; and before the arrival of Father De Ritter only one more ·marriage is recorded in the book, namely, the following:]

Grünewald—Schmidt: June 18th, 1765, in Macunshi, by Father Farmer, John Grünewald to Barbara Schmidt; witnesses Henry Fredder, Christian Henrich and Mathias Riffel.

III. BURIALS.

[Of these only three are recorded before Father De Ritter came to Goshenhoppen, and none of them are dated; they are:]

Kuhn, Margaret, daughter of Henry and —— Kuhn, died July 19th, from being burnt while her parents were away attending a religious service at Magunshi, buried July 21st, near her father's house at Cedron Creek.

Maguin, Mary, wife of Henry Maguin, buried May 27th at Dinekum [Tinicum].

Bisping, Henry, commonly called "the old Hollander," died December 13th, after having been fortified with the last rites, buried December 15th, near the church used in common by the Calvinists and the Lutherans, above Goshenhopen.

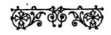

GOSHENHOPPEN REGISTERS.

(SECOND SERIES.)

1765-1785.

[Translated and annotated by Rev. Thomas C. Middleton, D.D., O. S. A.]

With this second series of the Goshenhoppen registers is concluded the publication of presumably the oldest records now extant relating to the Catholic missions of Pennsylvania.*

These registers belonged formerly to the old mission church of St. Paul, known since 1837 as the church of the Most Blessed Sacrament, at Goshenhoppen, now Bally, in Washington township, Berks county, Penna. They contained the records of the baptisms, conversions, marriages, deaths and burials, as kept by the Rev. Theodore Schneider and his successor, Rev. John Baptist Ritter, both Jesuits, who for forty-four years, namely, from 1741 to 1785, were in charge of Goshenhoppen and its outlying missions.

John Gilmary Shea, LL.D., refers frequently to the mission of Goshenhoppen and its two earliest rectors in his valuable "History of the Catholic Church in the United States." In Volume I., at page 447, he gives a picture of the old church at Goshenhoppen.

Mr. Philip S. P. Conner, in his paper on "The Early Church Registers of Pennsylvania," printed in the second volume of the "Records of the American Catholic Historical Society" (Philadelphia, 1889), gives a brief description of the Goshenhoppen registers.

In 1741, the mission of Goshenhoppen was opened by Father Schneider, who attended it until his death, July

---

*Three additional series of Goshenhoppen registers, contained in a second manuscript volume, were also published in RECORDS. See pp. 122-262, this volume.

†Unless indicated otherwise, page references in the text refer to pages in the original Goshenhoppen registers, not to this volume.

10, 1764, and was succeeded by Father Ritter, who continued in charge until toward the close of his life, February 3, 1787.

In the second volume of the "Records" of this Society was published the first part of these Registers as kept by Father Schneider.* It takes up some twenty-five pages in the original.

In this present volume of the "Records" is continued the publication of the registers down to their close. They fill about three hundred and twenty-one pages in the original book.

From 1741 to 1764, the date of Father Schneider's death, all the entries, with the exception of three on page 16 of the register, are in his hand-writing. The exceptions are (as noted in Vol. II. of the "Records," page 327), in an unknown hand, perhaps (this is a mere supposition) by a visiting priest from Philadelphia or from Conewago. [*]

All the remaining entries in the registers, as here published, are in the handwriting of Father Ritter.

These Goshenhoppen registers are believed to antedate all existing mission registers in Pennsylvania. The missions of St. Joseph's church, in Philadelphia, and of Conewago, in Adams county, are both of earlier foundation than Goshenhoppen, but their early records are, it is believed, no longer in existence.

A word now about the book or volume that contains the Goshenhoppen records, which it has been my pleasing task to prepare for publication. It is a small book, six inches long, three and three-quarter inches wide, and about one inch thick. It has been bound twice, as evidently appears, once in skin, and again in strong muslin or canvas. It still wears this double cover, with the exception of the skin or leather back, which is wanting.

The book consists of two parts, or rather the original book of two hundred and seventy-eight pages has had bound into it at the end sixty-eight pages, all at least that now remain, of a larger form, measuring about one inch longer and wider than the original book, of which they

---

*Pages 1-17, this volume.

now form a part. The original book is in an excellent state of preservation, having every page whole and unbroken. The remaining part has suffered considerably from one cause or another. Some of its leaves have been loosened from the binding and then reinserted by pasting in the wrong order. This appears from the inversion of the dates. Moreover, eight of the leaves are even now wholly loose and in danger of being lost, while one of them, namely, pages 289–90, has two-thirds of its length missing. The handwriting in these registers is, as has already been noted, of three different persons, namely, Father Schneider, Father Ritter and the unknown. Father Schneider's writing, though rather close and crabbed, is clear enough to be easily read. Father Ritter writes a neat, running hand, very scholarly and business like, that with few exceptions is as easy to read as copper-plate. Occasionally, on some of the added pages in the back of the book, his writing is hard to make out, partly on account of the inferior quality of the paper and of the ink, which in many places has faded away, either wholly or in part, but chiefly because of the slovenly way in which the broken leaves have been patched together.

Fr. Schneider's signature appears but once in the book. This is on the first page of the baptismal entries, where he has signed, on August 23, 1741, as "Theodorus Schneider, S. J." Father Ritter's name appears frequently in the book, at least, if I have counted rightly, fourteen times, twice as heading a page and twelve times as a signature. Father Ritter signs his family name both Ritter and De Ritter. De Ritter is met with on two occasions only, both in 1765, his first year in the Goshenhoppen missions; at all other times he signs, invariably, Ritter. Besides these signatures of Fathers Schneider and Ritter no other occurs in the registers. But the names of three other Jesuit priests are met with, Father Ferdinand Farmer's, twice in the baptismal records for 1764, and once in the marriage register for 1765; Father Luke Geisler's, twice in the baptismal and marriage entries

20

for 1769, while Father James Frambachs, so his name is written, is recorded as having applied the holy chrism at a baptism in 1764, and once to have been present at a marriage in 1768. Father Ritter records these several facts.

One of the most interesting studies I have found in looking over these old registers, and perhaps the most valuable from a purely scientific point of view, is the mention that every now and then occurs of the many places in eastern Pennsylvania which the above-named missionaries visited to say Mass or confer the sacraments, or where the parties who visited them had their residence. I here subjoin a list of the different places named in Father Ritter's registers. The principal ones, those that most frequently occur, are (1) Goshenhoppen, written "Gosshenhopen," "Gosschenhopen," "Cushenhopen," and "Couissahopen ;" (2) Falkner's Swamp, in Montgomery county, which Dr. Shea, in his "History of the Catholic Church" (Vol. I., p. 393), says is now known as Pottsgrove, near the famous Ringing Hill, in Berks county. In Father Ritter's registers it is spelled variously as "Falksner Schwam," "Falckner's Swamp, "and "Falkoner Swam ;" (3) Sharp Mountain, which I take to be the English rendering of a name that occurs very frequently in the registers as "*Asperum Collem*," or "*Collem Acutum*," or "*Montem Acutum.*" The only place where I have seen this name in the above English form is in Bishop Neumann's MS. visitation-book. Referring to the mission of Reading, the venerable bishop says that prior to 1787 Reading was attended by Father Ritter, who also visited Makunzie [*sic*], Cedar Creek, and Sharp Mountain. This is presumably the "*Asperum Collem*" of Father Ritter. (4) Oley, in Berks county, which is very frequently met with under the Latin forms of Mt. Olivet, Olivetan mountains, or hills, or even in the vernacular as Oley and Ol ; (5) Cedar Creek, which Father Ritter Latinizes as "*ad torrentem Cedron* ;" (6) Easton, in the registers "*Ostonia*," in Northampton county ; (7) Haycock, in Bucks county ; (8) Reading, written once in the registers as "Readingtown," in Berks county, and (9) Macungie, in Lehigh county, which is variously written in the registers as "Macunski," "Magungi," "Magunshi," "Macungi," "Magunchi," "Makunshi," and "Macunhi." Then occur more or less frequently the names of these places in Berks county, namely, Allemängel, a place in Albany and Linn townships, a barren spot, which Dr. Shea styles in his history (*ut supra*, Vol. I., p. 394) "Lackall ;" District township ; Hereford township, written "Herford" and "Hertford ;" Long Swamp, which in the registers appears only as "Langerschwamm ;" Maiden creek ; Ruscombmanor, written "Roskemainor," and Windsor. The places in Bucks county that are named are as follows : Nockamixon, in the registers written "Nocanixom ;" Rockhill ; Tinicum, written "Denikum" and "Denickom," and Warwick. Among the places in Lehigh county the following are named : Linn township, written "Linen," in the Blue Mountains, and perhaps meant by Father Ritter in his "Lecha" and "Leche" township, which he locates in the Blue Mountains ; Allentown, written always "Allenstown ;" Weissenburg, which Father Ritter gives as another name for Macungie ; Weithendael, or Saltzburg, so they are written in the registers.

The following places are in Northampton county : Saucon, at least this is what I take "Sacone" in the registers to mean, and Bethlehem.

The names of some other places occur that I cannot venture to locate, as Springforge, Frankford, the Forks in the Blue Mountains, Mayburry Furnace, "Mebris" Furnace, "*Missillem torrentem*," Paint Forge, Pine Township, perhaps in Berks county, Providence, maybe the one in Montgomery county, Rich Valley, and "*Longo prato*," which I suppose was used to designate Long Meadow. New Jersey is occasionally named, usually as Jersey, "*Jersia.*"

Not to mention the various places, which can easily be seen for themselves in the register, where Father Ritter frequently said Mass, he names distinctly a chapel (*sacello*) in Philadelphia, another in Reading (see baptism June 8, 1766), and a third, which he styles chapel, or church, at Goshenhoppen (see the marriage register, for June 30, 1766). He also makes mention of two Catholic grave-yards, in the year 1765, one at Goshenhoppen and the other at Reading.

From these registers one discovers that there were some customs of the olden time rather peculiar, that will bear mention here. For instance:

(1) It was an almost universal practice for the subjects at baptism to receive the Christian name of one or the other of the sponsors, either the godfather's or the god-mother's, according as the recipient was a boy or a girl.

(2) At baptisms it was not unfrequently the case that one or the other of the sponsors was a non-Catholic, and,

(3) In one instance, 1773, August 15, both the sponsors were non-Catholics.

(4) Marriages were commonly solemnized in church at Mass.

(5) Father Ritter, as appears from an entry (see marriage, December 30, 1770), had large powers of dispensing in the impediment of consanguinity.

(6) In several instances, Father Ritter marries parties in church when one of them was a non-Catholic, and Father Schneider, as appears from an entry in 1741, marries two non-Catholics, during Mass, on Christmas day, in John Kuhn's house. There is another instance in the marriage register for April 12, 1742, of his marry-ing two non-Catholics.

(7) Sometimes bonds of indemnity were required by the priest before witnessing a marriage contract. This was the case where the parties were slaves, or indentured.

(8) From the inversion of the dates, it appears to have been a common practice to make the various entries in the register weeks, and sometimes months, after the performance of a ceremony. It seems from this that the registers were not carried around by the missionaries on their journeys, but that on their return home to Goshen-

hoppen they entered their proceedings, either from memory, or, much more probably, from memoranda they had made at the time.

It is also interesting to note the presence of Catholic schoolmasters in the Goshenhoppen missions. The names of four are found recorded, namely, Henry Fretter (once only, I believe, written Fredder); a certain Breitenbach; John Laurence (or, more frequently, simply Laurence) Gubernator, and Ferdinand Wagner. There is mention made, too, of a surgeon, "*Chirurgus noster*" Father Ritter styles him, by name Nicholas Schmitt, which goes far to attest that cultured Catholic laymen were not wholly wanting in the rural districts of Pennsylvania.

Before closing this paper it is only right to add a line or so on the difficulty met with in copying various family names. The variations of geographical names have already been sufficiently treated of. The family names that are found written in various ways are chiefly : (1) Beverts, Bevertz, Bewertz, Bebers, Bibers and Biberts ; (2) Brück, Brücks and Brucx ; (3) Eck and Egg ; (4) Käs and Käss ; (5) Meckler, Meckeler and Meckl ; (6) Offer, Ofer, Affer and Ufer; (7) Strubbel, Strubel, Strubl and Struppel, and (8) Dabber and Tapper. Others will be found noted in the text. In copying down the above names I have invariably followed the form of spelling given in each instance in the registers, although it was obvious that the various forms of spelling referred to the same families.

The only case that has caused a real doubt is a party, at least I take him to be one and the same person, whom I have found named three times in the registers in three such different ways as to render it somewhat venturesome to express an opinion. This is a man of the name of Lochely Miclaine, whose daughter Catharine Elizabeth was baptized on October 16, 1774. Her mother's name is given as Catharine Connelly. So far there is no doubt, but on November 21, 1783, I find recorded the baptism, at Nicholas Carty's house, near Haycock, of Elizabeth, daughter of Lothi MacMalone and his wife Catharine, and again, un-

24

less I am deceived, he is named in another baptismal entry, for February, 1782, as Lothi MacMalowne. Now neither Lochely nor Lothi is a Christian name, but may they not stand for Laughlin, a Christian name, sometimes pronounced, I believe, Loughy, and misunderstood by Father Ritter through his unfamiliarity with Celtic or Gaelic sounds? For the same reason I take it that he has so variously spelled the family name Miclaine, MacMalone and MacMalowne, and that in all three instances one should make the true spelling of the father's name Laughlin Malone.

The Christian names, with the above exception, offer no difficulty. I have translated *Susanna* as Susan, and sometimes have left it in its Latin form ; so with *Maria*, *Anna* and *Helena*, which I have commonly rendered Mary, Ann and Ellen. *Jacobus* I have, as a rule, translated James, and only in a few cases Jacob.

It is also to be observed that certain family names, given in the text with a double f, seem to have been so written by Father Ritter, yet there is a bare possibility that these two letters are really st. I am unable to determine the point, so I will now merely observe that the names Krafft, Seiffert, Hoffmann, Riffel, Keffer, Ruffner and Schäffer may after all be really Krast, Seistert, Hostmann, Ristel, Kester, Rustner and Schäster.

The entries in the several registers of Father Ritter, here printed, comprise nine hundred and twenty-three baptisms, sixteen conversions, one hundred and thirty marriages, and one hundred and twelve deaths and burials. In the registers the baptisms from May 21, 1780, to the end of the same year are missing ; so are the marriages from May 4, 1779, to April, 1784.

The annotations, which I have thought it well to embody in the text, will be found enclosed in square brackets.

    FATHER THOMAS C. MIDDLETON, *O. S. A.*
VILLANOVA COLLEGE, *August* 10, 1891.

I. BAPTISMS.

BAPTISMS FOR THE YEAR 1765.

[Father Ritter heads the baptismal records for this year as follows :—"*Ego Joannes Baptista de Ritter Soct'is Jesu baptizavi !*" Then immediately follows this entry, namely.]

Miller, Margaret, of Henry Miller, farmer, and his wife Anna Mary Reiter, of Roske mainor township, born on the feast of the Ascension, May 16, 1765, baptized in Reading, July 14 ; sponsors, Joseph Algayer and Anna Mary Stahl,

Burkhard, John Phillip, of Martin Burkhard and his wife Gertrude, baptized when eight days old, July 28, in the church ; sponsors, Philip Weismiller and Mary Elizabeth Weismiller.

Eck, Mary Magdalen, of John Eck and his wife Mary Eva, four weeks old, baptized at the same time and place ; sponsors, John Peter Eck and Elizabeth Weibel.

Reppert, Mary Catharine, of Stephen Reppert and his wife Mary Barbara, seven weeks old, baptized at the same time and place ; sponsors, Joseph Lorenz and Mary Catharine Wetzler.

Geri, Philip James, of Philip Geri and his wife Eva Bernard, born July 15, 1765, in Herford township, baptized August 4, in the church ; sponsors, Jacob Kuhn and Elizabeth Adams.

Kohl, Joseph, of John Michael Kohl and his wife Elizabeth Becker, born July 22, in Denickom township, baptized August 18, in Edward Carty's house at Haycock ; sponsors Joseph Kohl and Elizabeth Tapper.

Hönig, Mary Salome, of Jacob Hönig and his wife Catharine Weisbecher, the same place and date of nativity and baptism as the preceding ; sponsors, Nicholas Macarty and Mary Salome Fricker.

Kropf, John Joseph, of Peter Kropf and his wife, Claudina Zeyer, born October 7, 1765, in Denikum township, baptized October 20 in Edward Carty's house in Haycock ; sponsors, Joseph Rösner and Catharine, his wife.

Ruffner, Anna Margaret, of Christian Ruffner and his wife Odilia Kuhn, born October 2 in the Forks of the Blue Mountains, baptized October 22, in Widow Kuhn's house, at Cedar Creek ; sponsor, Anna Margaret Kuhn, grandmother of the child. [Signed, "J. B. Ritter."]

Geyer, Mary Eva, of Conrad Geyer and his wife Mary Elizabeth, baptized November 1, in the church at Couissahopen ; sponsors, Phil. Gerich and Mary Eva, his wife.

Baur. Henry and John James, twins of Leonard Baur and his wife Ursula Haffner, born November 28, Henry at about 8 A. M. and John James at about 9:30 A. M., baptized December 14, in their parents' house, near Mebris [?] furnace ; sponsors for the former, Henry Norbeck and his wife Mary Ann, and for the latter, John James Norbeck and Margaret Norbeck. [This entry is signed "J. B. Ritter."]

Deprè, Andrew, of James Deprè, farmer, and his wife Barbara Ackermann, born November 7, 1765, baptized privately the same day on account of danger of death ; ceremonies supplied December 15, in Edward Carty's house; sponsors, Andrew Hamerstein and Elizabeth Houcki [elsewhere written also Hucki].

Leutner, Anna Margaret, of Matthias Leutner and his wife Eva Barbara, baptized by a Lutheran minister when three days old ; ceremonies supplied December 8, 1765, when nine weeks old, in Kuhn's house, at Cedar Creek. [The baptisms for this year are numbered fourteen.]

BAPTISMS FOR THE YEAR 1766.

Grett, George Adolph, of Andrew Grett and his wife, born December 8, 1765, baptized January 1, 1766, in the church in Couissahopen, or rather Hertford township ; sponsors, George Adolph Mayer and his wife.

Ruffner, Simon, of Philip Ruffner and his wife Catharine Kuhn, born December 28, 1765, baptized January 12, 1766, in widow Kuhn's house near Cedar Creek ; sponsors, Simon Ruffner and his wife Mary Barbara Schiltz, the child's grandparents.

Fricker, Henry George, of Anthony Fricker and his wife, baptized when two weeks old, February 9, in the parents' house ; sponsor, Henry 'Fretter.

Gibbins, Mary, of James Gibbins and his wife Eleanor Sulivan, born January 15, baptized February 9, in the chapel ; sponsors,——Breitenbach, the schoolmaster, and his wife Susan.

Mayler, Mary, of Robert Mayler and his wife Catharine, born October 28, 1765, baptized February 9, in the chapel ; sponsors, Michael Rode [?] and Mary Gibson.

[Father Ritter here notes that these three last-named baptisms were administered without ceremonies because he had no ritual at hand.]

Hauck, Andrew, of George Hauck, baker, and his wife Jacobina, of upper Hanover, baptized February 25, in Christopher Schuhmann's house ; sponsors, Andrew Schuhmann and Catharine Griffonson.

27

Bisschof, Simon, of Peter Bisschof and his wife Mary Charlotte, born March 5, 1766, baptized March 17, in Kuhn's house; sponsors, Simon Leydekker and his wife.

Laibig, Henry, of John Laibig and his wife Gertrude, born March 12, 1766, baptized March 23, in the church; sponsors, Henry Fretter and Eva Stoll.

Grass, Regina, of Christopher Grass and his wife Catharine, born March 31, 1766, baptized April 13, in Reading; sponsors, Joseph Schif and Regina Gibson.

Corrent, Samuel, of Fairis Corrent and his wife Rose, nine months old, born in Warwick township, had been baptized privately by George Kohl; ceremonies supplied April 20, in Edward Carty's house, in Haycock.

Miller, Nicholas, of Nicholas Miller and his wife Catharine, born August 9, 1763, baptized April 20, in Edward Carty's house, in Haycock; sponsors, James Spring and Mary Barbara Spring.

————, Abigail, of Louis and Felicitas, married slaves of Judge Jonas Sedli [or Seelli], born March 3, baptized May 11, in the chapel at Reading; sponsors, Anthony Bluhm, Sr., and Margaret Gibson.

Keffer, Mary Magdalen, of Peter Keffer and his wife Mary Barbara, born March 5, baptized May 18, in the church [in templo nostro]; sponsors, Joseph Lorenz and Mary Magdalen Hartmann.

Eckenroth, Henry, of Henry Eckenroth and his wife Barbara, born April 12, 1766, baptized May 19, in P. Schmidt's house, in Magunshi; sponsors, Henry Fretter and Anna Mary Eckenroth.

Both, Eva Catharine, of John Both and his wife Eva, born March 28, 1766, baptized with the above; sponsors, Melchior Zieger, non-Catholic, and Catharine Zieger.

Eckenroth, Adam, of Peter Eckenroth and his wife Elizabeth, born February 28, 1766, baptized with the above; sponsors, Adam Stahl and Elizabeth Eckenroth.

Killenberger, George Adam, adult, admitted this day, June 1, to the sacraments [of penance and eucharist], born in Creutz-Steinach, in the Upper Palatinate, of a Catholic mother and a Calvinist father; instructed in Lutheranism by his step-father, but never professed this heresy; emigrated with his parents to Halifax seventeen years ago; came to Pennsylvania last year, and is now staying in Falkner's Swamp.

Matthys, Joseph, of Martin Matthys and his wife Catharine, born June 2, 1766, baptized June 7, in his parents' house; sponsors, John Grett and Anna Elizabeth.

Martin, Anthony, of Henry Martin and his wife Ellen, Irish, born April 2, 1766, baptized June 8, in the chapel at Reading ; sponsors, Anthony Fricker and his wife.

Daily, Mary and Helen, of Charles Daily and his wife Margaret, born January 13 and 14, 1766, baptized June 15, in Edward Carty's house ; sponsors, Edward and Catharine Murphi [sic] for Mary, and Henry and Margaret Magloski [perhaps better McCloskey for Helen.

Schäffer, Elizabeth, of William Schäffer and his wife Susanna, born October 20, 1765, baptized the same day and place ; sponsors, Jacob Lenzinger and Elizabeth Kohl.

Horn, John Peter, of John George Horn and his wife Anna Margaret Rose, born June 11, 1766, baptized June 16, in John Faller's house ; sponsors, John Peter Heins and Mary Glass.

Hucki, Mary Juliana, of Paul Hucki, workman in Paint Forge, and his wife Mary Juliana, born May 13, 1766, baptized July 14, in the church ; sponsors Balthasar Zweyer for his father John George Zweyer, and Mary Juliana, grandmother of the child.

Jung, Anna Christina, of Ferdinand Jung and his wife Catharine Götz, born July 24, 1766, baptized July 27 ; sponsors, John Weibel and Ann Lorenz.

Schorb, Joseph, of Joseph Andrew Schorb and his wife Anna, born June 23, 1766, baptized August 3, in the church ; sponsors, Philip Piri, non-Catholic, and Mary Ann Meyer.

Muller, Eva Margaret, of Philip Muller and Anna Mary, baptized August 17, in the Gosschenhopen church ; sponsors, Henry Fretter and Eva Margaret Stoll.

Jung, Mary Johanna, Ann and John, of Ferdinand Jung and his wife Catharine Götz, all three of whom had been baptized without ceremonies in Jersey ; ceremonies supplied in the church August 18.

Röhr, Anna Margaret, of Martin Röhr and his wife Anna Maria, born ——, 1776, baptized August 24, at the same place as above; sponsors, Peter Egg and Margaret Matthes.

Bluhm, Mary Catharine, of Anthony Bluhm, Jr., a citizen, and his wife Barbara, born October 8, 1766, baptized October 12, in Reading ; sponsors, Peter Bluhm and Catharine Huber.

Sigfried, Mary Ann, of John Michael Sigfried and his wife Justina, born October 6, baptized October 18, in Mount Olivet ; sponsors, George Sigfried, the grandfather, and Anna Mary Fuchs.

Hoffman, Martin, of Michael Hoffman and his wife Catharine, born October 10, in Gosshenhopen, baptized October 26, in the church ; sponsors, Michael Hoffman Hartman and Magdalen, his wife.

Scot, Petronilla, of William Scot and Mary Wulsin, born May 3, 1763. [written "1663"] baptized November 9, in Reading; sponsors, Andrew Kirschweiler and Catharine, his wife.

Ehrman, Henry, of John Ehrman and his wife Mary Cecelia, born October 28, baptized November 10, in the Oley mountains; sponsors, Henry Fretter and Anna Mary, his wife.

Grünewald, Philip Joseph, of John Grünewald and his wife Anna Barbara, born September 22, 1766, baptized November 16, in *Monte Acuto*, in Christian Henrich's house; sponsors, Philip Schmitt, the child's grandfather, and his wife, Ursula.

Schmidt, Mary Eva, of Philip Schmidt and his wife Ursula, born November 1, 1766, baptized November 17, in the parents' house, in Macunshi; sponsors, John Becker, non-Catholic, and Anna Mary, his wife, Catholic.

Sigfried, Joseph, of Andrew Sigfried and his wife Agatha, baptized November 23, in the church; sponsors, —— Zweyers and Eva Kuhn.

Keycher, Mary Elizabeth, of Ignatius Keycher, and his wife, born June 30, 1766, baptized at the same place as above; sponsors, Leonard Litzinger and Magdaleñ, his wife.

Eck, Mary Teresa, of John Eck and his wife Magdalen, born October 28, 1766, baptized November 26, in her parents' house, near Rich valley; sponsors, her brother Conrad for Joseph Kohl, and her sister Anna for Mary Teresa Fricker.

Käs, Peter Anthony, of Peter Käs and his wife Anna Margaret, born October 7, 1766, baptized November 30, in his parents' house, near Cedar creek; sponsors, Caspar Schmit and Anna Margaret Jedel.

Keffer, Elizabeth, of John Keffer and his wife Regina, residing in Allentown, born ——, 1766, baptized December 21, in Haycock; sponsors, Nicholas Bock and his wife.

[The number of baptisms for the year is forty-two.]

BAPTISMS FOR THE YEAR 1767.

Offer, Francis Joseph, of Francis Offer and Mary Ann, born November 26, 1766, baptized January 12, in Sigfried's house, in the Oley mountains; sponsors, Joseph Zweyer and Catharine Hild.

Bibers [Bevertz], Mary Magdalen, of Conrad Bibers and Elizabeth Eckenroth, born November 22, 1766, baptized January 18, in Christian Henrich's house, in *Monte Acuto;* sponsors, Christian Henrich and Magdalen Bibers.

30

Stahl, Joseph, of Michael Stahl and ———, born December 23, 1766, baptized February 2, in the church ; sponsors, John Egg and his wife.

Ruffner, Peter, of Christian Ruffner and his wife Mary Odilia, born January 24, 1767, baptized privately by its father on account of danger of death ; ceremonies supplied in the church February 22 ; sponsors, Peter Käss and his wife.

Ulrich, John Michael, of Adam Ulrich and his wife Catharine, born March 6, 1767, baptized March 8, in Reading ; sponsors, John Michael Altkayer and Mary Anselm.

Keller, Frances, of John Keller and his wife Barbara, born March 2, 1767, baptized with the above ; sponsor, Frances Schorb, born Fricker.

Keffer, Mary Magdalen, of Martin Keffer and his wife Mary Eva, born the eve of Epiphany, baptized March 13, in *Colle Acuto ;* sponsors, Philip Henrich and Mary Magdalen Hartman.

Zip, Matthias, of Joseph Zip and his wife Apollonia, baptized March 14, in Philip Schmitt's house, in Magunshi, when eight weeks old ; sponsors, Matthias Riffel and his wife, non-Catholic.

Killenberger, James, of George Adam Killenberger and his wife, baptized in the church April 12 ; sponsor, Stephen Rudolf.

Grett, John James, of John Grett and his wife Elizabeth, baptized with the former ; sponsors, James Matthes and Eva Margaret Kuhn.

Miller, Catharine, of Michael Miller and his wife Elizabeth, baptized with the above ; sponsors, Theobald Miller and Catharine, his wife.

———, John Michael, baptized in the church April 19.

Gallon, Andrew, of John Joseph Gallon and his wife, had been baptized by a certain minister of the Reformed church named Michel ; ceremonies supplied in the church April 28, when six months old.

Hirtsman, John, of George Hirtsman, non-Catholic, and his wife Mary Catharine, born September 31 [*sic.*], 1766, in Libanum [Lebanon ?] township, in Georgia, baptized May 3, in Haycock ; sponsors, John George Kless and Elizabeth Kuhnz [*sic*].

Kuhns, John, of William Kuhns and his wife Elizabeth, born ———, 1766, baptized with the above ; sponsor, John Kuhns.

Sanders, Anna Mary, of the late Peter Sanders and his wife, baptized May 10, when six weeks old, in Reading ; sponsors, Joseph Schiff and Anna Mary Schorb.

Lorenz, Anna Catharine, of Jacob Lorenz and his wife, born May 3, 1767, baptized in the church May 24 ; sponsors, Patrick Griffith and Anna Catharine Weibel.

Kuss, George Adam, of Peter Kuss and his wife, born May 24, 1767, baptized May 28, in the house of its grandfather, John Fuss, near *Monsacutus ;* sponsors, George Adam Fuss and Mary Henrich.

Burger, Joseph, of Michael Burger and his wife Anna Mary, born February 2, 1767, baptized June 6, in the church ; sponsors, Joseph Rapp and Ursula Rapp.

Litzinger, Simon, of Leonard Litzinger and his wife Magdalen, born May 29, 1767, baptized with the above ; sponsors, Simon Adams and Catharine Litzinger.

Schämfessel, Elizabeth, of John Louis Schämfessel and his wife Catharine Mayer, born September 22, 1766, baptized June 14, in Reading ; sponsors, John Welsch and Elizabeth Welsch.

Machel, Joseph, of Christopher Machel and his wife Magdalen, born December 22, 1766, in Rockhill township, baptized June 21, in Haycock ; sponsors, Thomas Yedler and Elizabeth Kohl.

Ruppel, Anna Maria, of Jacob Ruppel and his wife Barbara, born in [New] Jersey, June, 1766, baptized in Haycock, June 21 ; sponsors, Jerome Grünewald and Anna Mary Grünewald.

Lambin, James, of Christopher Lambin and his wife Anna Maria, born June 19, 1767, baptized July 19, in Philip Schmitt's house in Magunshi ; sponsors, Jacòb Kuhn and Maria Riffel.

Lenzinger, Elizabeth, of Jacob Lenzinger and his wife Mary Salome, born July 14, baptized August 20, in Edward Carty's house in Haycock ; sponsors, William Schäffer and Elizabeth Kohl.

Miller, George James, of Theobald Miller and his wife Catharine, born September 4, 1767, baptized September 6, in the church ; sponsors, Jacob Kuhn and Margaret Matthes.

Ruffener, Anna Mary, of Philip Ruffener and his wife Catharine, born August 28, 1767, baptized September 8, at Cedar creek ; sponsors, George Adam Ruffener and Mary Kuhn.

Holstein, George James, of Michael Holstein and his wife Anna Mary, had been privately baptized, ceremonies supplied September 8, when eleven years old.

Felix, Nicholas Laurence, of Nicholas Felix and his wife, born September 11, 1767, baptized September 12, in Reading ; the sponsors were the child's grandfather, Lawrence Lepler, and his wife.

Sullivan, Solomon and Rebecca, twins, of John Sullivan and his wife, born May 12, baptized September 12, in Reading ; sponsors for Solomon, N. Brady and his wife, and for Rebecca, —— and —— Schorb.

Bock, Nicholas, of Nicholas Bock and his wife Elizabeth, residents of Haycock, born August 20, 1767, baptized October 4, in the church ; sponsors, Peter Keffer and his wife.

Dietrich, Mary Eva, of N. Dietrich and wife, of Windsor township, in the Blue mountains, baptized October 11, in Reading, when eight weeks old ; sponsors, Lawrence Leple and his wife.

Hönig, Elizabeth, of Jacob Hönig and his wife Catharine, born September 13, 1767, baptized October 18, in Edward Carty's house at Haycock ; sponsors, Nicholas Bock and his wife.

Thum, Valentine, of Caspar Thum and his wife Eva, born September 3, 1767, baptized November 9, in George Sigfried's house, in Oley ; sponsors, Valentine Uhlein and Catharine Altkayer.

Lorenz, Barbara, of Maurice Lorenz and his wife, baptized November 6, in the church ; sponsors, Jacob Kuhn and Anna Eva Keffer.

Hild, Anna Cecilia. of Joseph Hild and his wife, born November 21, 1767, baptized with the above ; sponsors, Christian Schumacher and Anna Mary, his wife.

Leutner, Anna Mary, of Matthias Leutner and his wife Barbara, baptized in John Kuhn's house, near Cedar creek, December 8, being then six weeks old ; sponsors, Thomas Yedler and Anna Mary Bischofl.

Fricker, Catharine Elizabeth, of Anthony Fricker and his wife, born on St. Elizabeth's day, baptized December 13, in Reading ; sponsors, Conrad Finck and his wife.

Carty, Catharine, of Nicholas Carty and his wife Albertina, baptized December 20, in her parents' house, in Haycock ; sponsors, George Kohl and Catharine Carty.

[Forty baptisms are recorded for this year.]

BAPTISMS FOR THE YEAR 1768.

Sigfried, Catharine Elizabeth, of John Michael Sigfried and his wife Justina, born March 10, 1868, baptized March 14, in George Sigfried's house, in the Oley hills; sponsors, John George Wantz and Catharine Hild.

Reiger, John Simon, of George Simon Reiger and his wife Anna Margaret, born March 9, 1768, baptized with the above ; sponsors, John Erman and Mary Cecilia, his wife.

Schnabel, Mary Elizabeth, of Andrew Schnabel and his wife Eva, born January 6, 1768, baptized with the above ; sponsors, Michael Kuhn and Eva, his wife.

Eckenroth, Eva Mary, of the late Peter Eckenroth and his wife Elizabeth Margaret, born December 2, 1767, baptized March 19, in Christian Henrich's house, at *Collis Acutus;* sponsor, Eva Mary Henrich.

Keffer, John Louis, of Matthias Keffer and his wife Mary Eva, born February 25, 1768, baptized with the former ; sponsors, John Louis Keffer and Catharine Weismiller.

Riffel, Catharine Elizabeth, of Matthias Riffel and his wife Christina, born December 7, 1767, baptized March 25, in John Kuhn's house, at Cedar creek; sponsors, Augustine Isinger and Elizabeth, his wife.

Burchard, James, of Martin Burchard and his wife Gertrude, born January 14, 1767, baptized April 1, in the parochial house; sponsors, Jacob Kupser and Elizabeth Weismiller.

Keffer Joseph, of Peter Keffer and his wife Barbara, born March [?] 28, 1768, baptized April 3, in the church; sponsors, Francis Joseph Hartman and Anna Eva Keffer.

Grass, Mary Barbara, of Christopher Grass and his wife Catharine, born April 8, 1768, baptized April 24, in the Reading chapel; sponsors, Joseph Schiff and Barbara Ritner.

Huck, Susanna Margaret, of Paul Huck and his wife Juliana, baptized in the church May 1, when fifteen weeks old; sponsors, John Huck and Margaret Kuhn.

Schmitt, John Melchior, of Philip Schmitt and his wife Ursula, born April 29, 1768, baptized May 2, in the parents' house; sponsors, John Melchior Ziegler and Catharine, his wife.

Egg, Elizabeth, of John Egg and his wife Magdalen, born April —, 1768, baptized May 12, in the parents' house; sponsors, Anthony Grieser and his wife.

Hauck, John George, of George Hauck and his wife Jacobina, born April 12, 1768, baptized May 22, in the church; sponsors, Andrew Schumann and Catharine Griffith.

Gibbins, James, of James Gibbins and his wife Ellen, born May 18, 1768, baptized at Reading, June 12; sponsors, Francis Gibson and Frances Schorb.

———, Rosina, of John and Felicitas, married negro slaves, born March 15, 1768, baptized with the above; sponsors, John Palm, non-Catholic, and Margaret Gibson.

Kuhn, Magdalen, of Michael Kuhn and his wife Eva, born April 24, 1768, baptized June 13, in Mount Olivet; sponsors, Andrew Schnabel and Eva Schnabel.

Erman, Catharine, of John Erman and his wife M. Cecilia, born May 13, 1768, baptized with the above; sponsors, John Michael Sigfried and Justina Sigfried.

Glass, Anna Catharine, wife of James Glass, farmer, of New Georgia, made profession of faith in Edward Carty's house, in Haycock, June 19.

Russ, Elizabeth, wife of James Russ, farmer, of the same neighborhood, did likewise in the same place on the same day.

Lynn, Mary, of Hugh Lynn and his wife Anna, born April 11, 1768, baptized June 19 in Edward Carty's house in Haycock; sponsors, William Minimay and Mary Maclaski [McCloskey?].

Malsberger, Jacob, of Jacob Malsberger and his wife Catharine, born June 2, baptized June 26, in the church; sponsors, James Matthes and Anna M. Schöner.

Grünewald, James, of John Grünewald and his wife Barbara, baptized in Philip Schmitt's house, in Weissenburg (otherwise Macungi), July 17, when six weeks old; sponsors, Jacob Arents and Margaret Schmitt.

Henrich, Christian, of Christian Henrich and his wife Magdalen, born June 11, 1768, baptized July 31, in Christian Henrich's house, at *Mons Acutus;* sponsors, Christian Henrich and his wife, the child's grandparents.

Gibson, Margaret, of Henry Gibson and his wife Catharine, born July 30, 1768, baptized August 7, in the church; sponsors, James Matthes and Margaret Schmitt.

Bisschof, Philip James, of Peter Bisschof and his wife Charlotte, born May 1, 1768, baptized privately by its father in danger of death, baptized conditionally August 28; sponsors, Henry Fretter and Mary Bisschof.

Eckenroth, John, of Henry Eckenroth and his wife Anna Barbara, born August 4, 1768, baptized September 18, in Philip Schmitt's house in Macunhi [sic]; sponsors, John Kuhn and Mary Kuhn

Krafft, Catharine, of Michael Krafft and his wife Magdalen, born September 11, 1768, baptized September 20, in the church; sponsors, Nicholas Röhr and Catharine Adams.

Mayer, Francis Michael, of Michael Mayer and his wife Catharine, born September 24, 1768, baptized October 9, in Reading; sponsors, Francis Gibson and Margaret, his wife.

Schönfessel, Mary Ann, of Louis Schönfessel and his wife Catharine, born September 5, 1768, baptized with the above; sponsors, Stephen Fütterer and Mary Ann Huber.

Loggeri [Loughery?], daughter of Philip Loggeri [Loughery?] and ——, baptized October 16, in Edward Carty's house.

Rose, Anna Mary, of James Rose and his wife Elizabeth, born August 16, 1768, baptized October 17, in Nicholas Hucki's house, near Easton; sponsors, Anthony Grüsser and Elizabeth, his wife.

Mogorni [?], Anna Mary and Daniel, three years and one year old respectively, of Michael Magorni [?] and his wife, baptized November 6, in the church; sponsors, James Norbeck and Anna Egg for the former, and John Jodocus Riffel and Margaret Matthes for the latter.

Matthes, Apollonia, of Martin Matthes and his wife Catharine, born November 8, baptized November 10, in the church ; sponsors, Martin Röhr and his wife.

Lambin, George James, of Christopher Lambin and his wife Mary Ann, born November 11, 1768, baptized November 20, in Philip Schmitt's house in Macungi ; sponsors, George Jacob Riffel and Elizabeth Tapper.

Ruffner, Simon, of Christian Ruffner and his wife Odilia, born November 9, 1768, baptized December 8, at Cedar creek ; sponsors, Simon Ruffner and Mary Kuhn.

Lorenz, John, of Wendelin Lorenz and his wife Mary Eva, born about the beginning of November, 1768, baptized with the above ; sponsors, John Faller and Mary Eva Keffer.

[Thirty-seven baptisms are recorded for this year.]

BAPTISMS FOR THE YEAR 1769.

Jütz, John Anthony, of Anthony Jütz, shoemaker, and his wife Catharine, born January 1, 1769, baptized January 5, in Simon Leydecker's house ; sponsors, John Faller and Mary Bischoff.

Myler, Anna Mary, of —— Myler and his wife, baptized January 8, at Reading; sponsors, Henry Miller and Anna Mary Moritz.

Egg, John Peter, of John Egg and his wife Eva, born January 5, 1769, baptized January 15, in Christopher Schuhmann's house, in Falkoner's swamp ; sponsors, Valentine Weibel and his wife.

Stahler, Catharine, of Adam Stahler and his wife Mary, seven weeks old when baptized, January 15, in Christian Henrich's house, at *Mons Acutus;* sponsors, George Eckenroth and Margaret Henrich.

Kuhn, Henry, of John Kuhn and his wife Catharine, born January 8, 1769, baptized January 17, in his parents' house, at Cedar creek; sponsors, Henry Kuhn and Margaret Schmitt.

Hofman, Magdalen, of Michael Hofman and his wife Catharine, five weeks old when baptized, January 22, in the church ; sponsors, Francis Hartman and Margaret Matthes.

Röhr, Frances, of Martin Röhr and his wife Anna Mary, born January 24, 1769, baptized January 28, in the church ; sponsors, Martin Matthes and Catharine, his wife.

Keffer, Mary Barbara, of John Keffer and his wife Regina, born December 4, 1768, baptized February 19, in Edward Carty's house in Haycock ; sponsors, Peter Keffer and Barbara, his wife.

36

Zip, Mary Elizabeth, of Joseph Zip and his wife Apollonia, born January 22, 1769, baptized March 5, in Philip Schmitt's house, in Macungi; sponsors, Louis Mechle, non-Catholic, and Mary Elizabeth, his wife, Catholic.

Bevertz, Henry, of Conrad Bevertz and his wife Margaret, born February 3, 1769, baptized March 6, in Christian Henrich's house, at *Mons Aculus;* sponsors, Henry Bevertz and Elizabeth Eckenroth.

Miller, John, of Philip Miller and his wife Anna Mary, baptized March 19, in the church; sponsors, Michael Hofman and Catharine his wife.

Sigfried, Mary Agatha, of Andrew Sigfried and his wife Mary Agatha, born January 31, baptized the same day and date as the preceding; sponsors, Paul Huck and Juliana, his wife.

Schuhmacher, Christian Joseph, of Christian Schuhmacher and his wife Anna Mary, born February 26, 1769, baptized with the last named; sponsors, Joseph Hild and Catharine.

Chaffet, Henry, of Michael Chaffet and his wife Catharine, baptized March 23, in the church; sponsors, Henry Gibson and Catharine, his wife.

Litzinger, Catharine, of Leonard Litzinger and his wife Magdalen, born March 29, 1769, baptized April 2, in the church; sponsors, Henry Litzinger and Catharine Litzinger.

Grett, Michael, of John Grett and his wife Ann Elizabeth, born March 13, 1769, baptized the same day and place as the preceding; sponsors, Adolph Mayer and Anna Mary, his wife.

Horn, Elizabeth, of John George Horn and his wife Anna Margaret, born September 12, 1768, baptized April 16, at Haycock; sponsors, William Schaffer and Elizabeth Grusser.

Deprè, Mary Barbara, of James Deprè and his wife Barbara, born April 1, 1769, baptized the same day and place as above; sponsors, Anthony Grüsser and Barbara Ruppels.

Schuhmann, Andrew, Elizabeth, John, Adam, William, Barbara and Conrad, of Christopher Schuhmann and his wife ———; had been baptized privately; ceremonies supplied April 31 [*sic*], in Langerschwamm.

Kemp, John, of John Kemp and his wife Anna [?] Christina, born December 4, 1769 [*sic*], baptized May 4, in John Egg's house, in Rich valley; sponsors, John Egg and Magdalen, his wife.

Finck, Mary Christina, of Conrad Finck and his wife Catharine, born December 1, 1769 [*sic*], baptized May 7, at Reading; sponsors, Anthony Fricker and Margaret, his wife.

Affer, Mary Ann Eva, of Francis Affer and his wife Mary Ann, born April 1, baptized May 8, in Sigfried's, at Mount Olivet; sponsors, Joseph Zweyer and Eva Becker.

Lentzinger, Mary Barbara, of James Lentzinger and his wife Mary Salome, born June 14, baptized June 18, at Haycock ; sponsors, George and Mary Barbara Kohl, the child's grandparents

Gless, John George, of James Gless and his wife Anna, born March 17, 1769, baptized the same day and place as the foregoing ; sponsors, John George Heitsmann and Agatha, his wife.

Heitsmann, James, of George Heitsmann and his wife Agatha, born September 23, 1768, baptized with the preceding ; sponsors, James Gless and Ann, his wife.

Horn, Philip and Caspar, twins, of John Horn and his wife Anna Mary, born June 13, 1769, baptized June 28, at Cedar creek ; sponsors, Philip Schmitt, Jr., Caspar Schönenbusch and Anna Mary Kuhn.

Reider, Susanna, of Fr. Joseph Reider and his wife Anna M., born May 12, 1769, baptized July 9, at Reading ; sponsors, Joseph ———— and Susanna Weibel.

Keffer, Francis Joseph, of Peter Keffer and his wife Barbara, born July 11, 1769, baptized July 23 ; sponsors, Francis Hartmann and Barbara Weibel.

Keffer, Martin, of Martin Keffer and his wife Mary Eva, born June 29, 1769, baptized July 30, at *Mons Acutus ;* sponsors, Maurice Lorenz and Mary Apollonia, his wife.

Schneider, John George, of John Schneider and his wife Mary Bisschoff, born St. James' day, in July, 1769 ; baptized August 15, at Cedar creek ; sponsors, John Kuns, and Elizabeth Bisschoff.

Ruffner, Henry and Peter, twins, of Philip Ruffner and Catharine, his wife, born March 8, 1769, ceremonies of baptism supplied August 16, 1769, in Lecha township, near the Blue mountains ; sponsors, Henry Kuhn, Anna Maria Holstein, Peter Käss and Anna Margaret Kuhn ; up to this time three children had been born to the above-named parents and baptized by a Protestant minister ; of these, Christian, the oldest, died when six weeks and four days old.

Cremer, Elizabeth, of Matthias Cremer and Mary Catharine, his wife, born April 24, 1769, baptized at Haycock, August 21 of same year ; sponsors, Anthony Grüser and Elizabeth, his wife.

Magel, Elizabeth, of Christopher Magel and Magdalen, his wife, born June 23, 1769, baptized with the above ; sponsors, John Dideraff and Elizabeth Kohl.

Wagner, John Baptist, of Matthias Wagner and Anna Maria, his wife, born April 20, 1769, near the Blue mountains, baptized at Nicholas

Hucki's house, August 21 ; sponsors, Edward Maccarty and Elizabeth Hucki.

Egg, Mary Magdalen, of John Egg, farmer, and his wife, of Rich valley, born June 9, 1769, baptized in her father's house, September 8 ; sponsors, Henry Norbeck and wife.

Kientz, Mary Eva, of Matthias Kientz and his wife, born August 12, 1769, baptized in the house of John Egg, September 10 ; sponsors, George Kohl and M. Eva Hönig.

Miller, John, of Henry Miller and Anna Maria his wife, born August 13, 1769, baptized in the Oley hills, September 18 ; sponsors, John Baur and Catharine, his wife.

Schmitt, Mary Dorothy, of John Adam Schmitt and Margaret his wife, born September 14, 1769, baptized in the church, October 1 ; sponsors, Caspar Schmitt and M. Dorothy.

Fricker, M. Catharine, of An'hony Fricker and Margaret, his wife, born August 15, 1769, baptized in Reading, October 8 ; sponsors, Joseph Chaumont and M. Catharine, his wife.

Tapper, Elizabeth, of Andrew Tapper and Anna Maria, his wife, born October 13, 1769, baptized in the church, by Rev. Luke Geisler, November 5 ; sponsors, George James Riffel and Elizabeth Tapper.

Hauck, Matthias, of John George Hauck and Mary Jacobina, his wife, born September 26, 1769, baptized in the church, November 25 ; sponsors, Christopher Schuhmann and Mary Elizabeth, his wife.

Miller, John Michael, of Theodore Miller and Catharine, his wife, born November 14, 1769, baptized December 24 ; sponsors, John Michael Miller and Elizabeth, his wife.

[Forty-nine baptisms are recorded for this year.]

BAPTISMS FOR THE YEAR 1770.

Gaucker, John, of Louis Gaucker and Ann, his wife, 22 years old, baptized February 11, 1770 ; witnesses, Valentine Weibel and Nicholas Walter.

Krafft, Magdalen, of Michael Krafft and his wife, born March 8, 1770, baptized March 11 ; sponsors, Leonard Litzinger and wife.

Huck, Johanna Margaret, of Paul Huck and Juliana his wife, born ——, baptized April 15 ; sponsors, John Huck and Margaret Kuhn [written "Khun"].

Stahl, Joseph, of Michael Stahl and Margaret, his wife, born April 4, 1770, baptized at Sigfried's, April 23 ; sponsors, Joseph Zweyer and Anna M. Fraul [?].

Felix, Stephen, of Nicholas Felix and his wife, born ——, baptized April 24 ; sponsors, Stephen Federer and Barbara Rittner.

Henrich, Elizabeth, of Christian Henrich and Magdalen, his wife, born March 11, 1770, baptized April 26, at *Monte Acuto* ; sponsors, George Eckenroth and Elizabeth Henrich.

Käss, Caspar, of Peter Käss and Margaret, his wife, born April 15, 1770, baptized at Cedar creek, May 2 ; sponsors, Caspar Schmitt and Anna Margaret Weidner.

Henley, Elizabeth Barbara, of Dennis Henly and Anna Martha, his wife, born October 8, 1769, baptized in the church, May 20; sponsors, John Michael Sigfried and Barbara Berger.

Bock, James, of Nicolas Bock and Elizabeth, his wife, born May 1, 1770, baptized in the church, June 3; sponsors, James Kohl and Elizabeth Grüsser.

Miller, John George, of Nicholas Miller and Catharine, born eight days before Christmas, baptized June 18, in the house of Nicholas Hucki; sponsors, John George Spring and Barbara [perhaps Spring].

Burchard, John, of Martin Burchard and Gertrude, his wife, born June 2, 1770, baptized June 24 ; sponsors, John Walter and Susanna Weismiller.

Groner, Mary Catharine, of John George Groner and M. Margaret, his wife, born May 8, 1770, baptized July 8, at Sigfried's house, in the Oley hills ; sponsors, Stephen Zweyer and Mary Zweyer.

Zipp, M. Elizabeth, of Joseph Zipp and Apollonia, his wife, born May 28, 1770, baptized at the house of Philip Schmitt, at Magunshi, July 15 ; sponsors, Augustine Isinger and his wife, Elizabeth.

Schorb, Stephen, of John Adam Schorb and Elizabeth, his wife, born August 4, 1770, baptized August 12, at Reading ; sponsors, Stephen Fiderer and Barbara Ritner.

Thum, Magdalen, of Caspar Thum and Eva, his wife, born July 28, 1770, baptized in the house of Andrew Grett, in Windsor township, August 13 ; sponsors, Andrew Grett and Magdalen, his wife.

Kropf, George Tobias, of Peter Kropf and Claudina, his wife, born August 1, 1770, baptized at Haycock, August 19, 1770 ; sponsors, George Lanzel and Elizabeth Hucki.

Monroy, Rebecca, of Henry Monroy and M[ary] Ann Carty, thirteen months old, baptized September 2 ; sponsors, Henry Flower and his wife Rosina.

Riffel, Augustine, of Matthias Riffel and his wife Christina, born July 25, 1770, baptized at Philip Schmitt's, at Magunshi, September 16 ; sponsors, Augustine Isinger and his wife Elizabeth.

Miller, John, of Martin Miller and his wife Anna, born August 20, 1770, baptized October 7 ; sponsors, John Norbeck and Mary Ann Walter.

Hert, Magdalen Margaret, of John Hert and his wife Elizabeth, baptized at Reading October 14 ; sponsors, Anthony Fricker and wife.

Gless, Mary Agatha, of James Gless and his wife, born in [New] Jersey, July 25, 1770, baptized at Haycock, October 21 ; sponsors, John George Heitsman and Mary Agatha Gless.

Ruffner, M[ary] Barbara, of Philip Ruffner and his wife Catharine, born October 18, 1770, baptized in Lehigh township [written " Leheig "], October 22; sponsors, Simon Ruffner and M[ary] Barbara, the child's grandparents.

Schrunck, Louis, of John William Schrunck, non-Catholic, and his wife, Elizabeth Weismiller, Catholic, born August 21, 1770, baptized October 28 ; sponsors, Louis Keffer and his sister Susan.

Eckenroth, George, of Henry Eckenroth and his wife Anna Barbara, born September 3, 1770, baptized at *Monte Acuto*, November 18 ; sponsors, George Eckenroth and Mary Kuhn.

Spring, Conrad, of James Spring and his wife Catharine, born September 3, 1770, baptized with the above ; sponsors, Conrad Bever [*sic.*] and his wife Margaret.

Kupser, Catharine, of James Kupser and his wife Catharine, born November 23, 1770, baptized November 25 ; sponsors, Joseph Hild and Catharine Adams.

Gibson, George, of Henry Gibson and his wife Catharine, born November 25, 1770, baptized December 2; sponsors, George James Riffel and Regina Gibson.

Ufer, Susan Juliana, of Francis Ufer and his wife M[ary] Ann, born November 28, 1770, baptized December 8, at Sigfried's in *Collibus Olivetanis*, that is, Oley hills; sponsors, Joseph Zweyer and the child's grandmother, Juliana Zweyer.

Gibbins, Frances Margaret, of James Gibbins and his wife Helen, born November 25, 1770, baptized Demember 9, at Reading ; sponsors, Francis Gibson and Margaret Fricker.

Schnabel, Rosina, of Andrew Schnabel and his wife Eva, born November 5, 1770, baptized December 30, at Christopher Schuhmann's, in *Longo prato* [maybe Long meadow ?] ; sponsors, Michael Kuhn and his wife Eva.

[Thirty baptisms recorded for this year.]

Lambin, Anna Margaret, of Christopher Lambin and his wife Anna M(aria), born January 19, 1771, baptized February 17 ; sponsors, Simon Mayer and Elizabeth Kohl.

Grass, Elizabeth Catharine, of Christopher Grass and his wife, Catharine, born January ——, 1771, baptized March 3, at Reading ; sponsors, George Langhammer and Catharine Stahl.

Kuhn, John, of John Kuhn and his wife Catharine, born ——, baptized privately, in case of necessity, ceremonies supplied at John Kuhn's, at Cedar creek (*torrente Cedron*) ; sponsors, Joseph Eckenroth and Elizabeth, cousins.

Leibig, Leonard, of John Leibig and his wife Gertrude, two months old, ceremonies supplied March 19, in the chapel ; sponsors, Leonard Litzinger and his wife Magdalen.

Litzinger, Magdalen, of Leonard Litzinger and his wife Magdalen, born two weeks ago, ceremonies supplied March 19, in the chapel ; sponsors, James Kupser and his wife Catharine.

Popp, Abraham, the son, it is said, of Abraham Popp and Catharine Fisher, both non-Catholics, born ——, baptized April 1, in the church ; sponsor, Margaret Stoll.

Sigfried, Mary Eva, of Andrew Sigfried and his wife Agatha, born March 19, 1771, baptized in the church, March 31 ; sponsors, John Zweyer and his wife Eva.

Sigfried, Mary Catharine, of John Michael Sigfried and his wife Justina, born April 1, 1771, baptized April 13, in the Oley hills ; sponsors, John George Wantz and Catharine Baur.

Fricker, John Frederic, of Antony Fricker and his wife Margaret, born on Good Friday, April 29, 1771 [*sic*], baptized at Reading, April 14 ; sponsors, Frederic Haffner and his wife, Catharine.

Russ [or Rose,] Elizabeth, of James Russ [or Rose,] of Georgia, and his wife Elizabeth, born six weeks ago, baptized April 22, near Easton, at Nicholas Hucki's ; sponsors, William Schaffer and Elizabeth Hucki.

Tapper, John, of Andrew Tapper and his wife Anna M., born and baptized on the night of April 11, 1771, ceremonies supplied April 16 [?] at a farm house [*domo villici*] ; sponsor, Elizabeth Tapper, John Tapper, the godfather, being absent. [Then follow certain words in the register, viz., "*cum in eadem nte* (i. e. *nocte*) *perseveraret parvulus*, which I am unable to understand, unless they were added by Father Ritter to account for the godfather's absence.]

Arents, John, of Jacob Arents and his wife Margaret, born April 20, 1771, baptized May 9, at Magungi, at Philip Schmitt's house ; sponsors, John Henrich and Gertrude Schmitt.

Flower, John Henry, of Henry Flower and his wife Rachel, born two months ago, baptized at Reading, May 12 ; sponsors, John Grett and —— Flower.

Krafft, Michael Henry, of Michael Krafft and his wife Elizabeth, born May —, 1771, baptized May 19 ; sponsors, Henry Litzinger and —— Adams.

Egg, Sabina, of John Egg and his wife Magdalen, born four weeks ago, baptized May 30 ; sponsors, Andrew Tapper and Barbara Berger.

Schneider, John, of John Schneider and his wife Mary, born April 29, 1771, baptized June 2 ; sponsors, John Bisschoff and his wife Anna Barbara.

——, at Edward Carty's house, baptized June 16 [the rest blank] ; sponsors, John Rössner and Mary Anne Fricker.

Horn, M. Magdalen, of George Horn and his wife Anna Margaret, born January 26, 1771, baptized June 17, at Nicholas Hucki's house ; sponsors, Anthony Hucki and Margaret Flower.

Kuntz, John, of John Kuntz and his wife Catharine, born July 12, 1771, baptized July 14, at Peter Käss's house, at Cedar creek ; sponsors, Joseph Brenner [?] and Mary Kuhn.

Kefer, John Philip, of Matthias Kefer and his wife Mary Eva, born May 9, 1771, baptized July 20, at *Aspricollem;* sponsors, Philip Weis miller, non-Catholic, and his wife Elizabeth, grandparents of the child.

Molsberger, Catharine, of James Molsberger [*ante* Malsberger] and his wife Catharine, born June 28, 1771, baptized July 28 ; sponsors, John Joseph Riffel and Anna Maria Schöner.

Kemp, M. Magdalen, of John Kemp and his wife Anna, born April 5, 1771, baptized August 18, at Haycock; sponsors, Christopher Magel and wife.

Heitzmann, John William, of John George Heitzmann and his wife M. Magdalen, born June 23, 1771, baptized August 18; sponsors, George Gless and wife.

Kuhns, Elizabeth, of William Kuhns and his wife Elizabeth, born July 10, 1771, baptized at Nicholas Hucki's house, August 19 ; sponsors, James Rose and his wife Elizabeth.

Fisher, Henry, of Joseph Fisher, and his wife, born February —, 1770, baptized September 15, 1771, at *Asperum Collem* ; sponsors, Henry Eckenroth and wife.

MacDivet, Michael, of Michael MacDivet and his wife Catharine, born five weeks ago, baptized in the church, September 22; sponsors, Michael Hoffman and wife.

Egg, M[ary] Eva, of John Egg and his wife, born six weeks ago, baptized September 22; sponsors, Andrew Schnabel and his wife, M. Eva.

Lorenz, Martin Stephen, of Maurice Lorenz and his wife, born October 2, 1771, baptized November 17, at Christian Henrich's house, at *Asperum Collem;* sponsors, Martin Keffer and Mary Ann Lorenz.

Bevertz, John George, of Conrad Bevertz and his wife, born September 1, 1771, baptized on the same date and at the same place as above; sponsors, John George Spring and M. Eckenroth.

Schäffer, Susan, wife of William Schäffer, farmer in [New] Jersey, the woman seems to be thirty years old, baptized November 20, at Carty's house, at Haycock. [No sponsors named.]

Ruffner, Anna Margaret, of Simon Ruffner and his wife Catharine, born November 16, 1771, baptized December 8, at Cedar creek; sponsors, George Adam Ruffner and Anna Margaret Wider.

Gaucker, John, of John Gaucker and his wife Anna Barbara, born November 30, 1771, baptized December 25, in the church; sponsors, John Hartman and Regina Weibel.

Schmitt, Margaret, of John Adam Schmitt and his wife Margaret, born November 23, 1771, baptized at the same time and place as above; sponsors, John Norbeck and Margaret Matthes.

Miller, James, of Michael Miller and his wife Elizabeth, born———, baptized December 13, 1771; sponsors, James and Barbara Miller, grandparents of the child.

[Thirty-four baptisms are recorded for the year.]

BAPTISMS FOR THE YEAR 1772.

Ufer, Balthasar, of Frank Ufer and his wife M[ary] Ann, born December 11, 1771, baptized January 13, 1772; sponsors, Balthasar Zweyer and Catharine Sigfried.

Grünewald, Catharine, of John Grünewald and his wife Barbara, born———, baptized January 18, at John Both's house, in Magungi; sponsors, Henry Gibson and his wife Catharine.

Burchard, Martin, of Martin Burchard and his wife Gertrude, born January 10, 1772, baptized March 1; sponsors, Mart. Matthes and his wife Catharine.

44

Miller, Anna Mary, of Philip Miller and his wife Anna M., born January 31, 1772, baptized at the same time and place as above; sponsors, Matthias Rohr and Anna M. Matthes.

Küss, Henry, of John Küss and his wife Magdalen, born February 5, 1772, baptized March 29, at John Both's house, in Macungi; sponsors, Henry Eckenroth and Elizabeth Schmitt, step-daughter of John Both.

Käss, Mary Magdalen, of Peter Käss and his wife Margaret, born March 4, 1772, baptized at the same time and place as above; sponsors, Michael Morloch and his wife Magdalen.

Carty, Elizabeth, of Nicholas Carty and his wife Albertina Kohl, born December 22, 1771; sponsors, Joseph Kohl and Elizabeth Hucki.

Lentzinger, John, of James Lentzinger and his wife M. Salome Kohl,. born January 3, 1772; sponsors, Nicholas Hucki and his daughter Catharine for her mother.

Mayer, Catharine, of Simon Mayer and his wife Elizabeth Kohl, born March 5, 1772; sponsors, John Rösner and Catharine Carty.

[The mothers of the three children named immediately above were sisters, and the three children were baptized April 5, at Edward Carty's house, at Haycock.]

Hönig, Joseph, of Eva Hönig and ———, born March 31, 1772, baptized April 5, at the grandfather's of the child; sponsor, Joseph Hild.

Schrunck, Mary Eva, of William Schrunck, non-Catholic, and his wife, Elizabeth, a Catholic, born February 27, 1772, baptized April 19, in the church; sponsors, Matthias Kester and M. Eva Weismiller.

Langhammer, Ann Mar., of George Langhammer and his wife Barbara, born April 17, 1772, baptized May 10, at Reading; sponsors, Frederic Haffner and Anna M. Rittner.

Thum, Joseph, of Caspar Thum and his wife Eva, born March 8, 1772, baptized May 11, at Sigfried's house, in the Oley hills; sponsors,. Joseph Zweyer and Catharine Sigfried.

Zweyer, John Adam, of John Zweyer and his wife Eva, born March 11,. 1772, baptized at the same time and place as above; sponsors, John Adam Zweyer and Eva Thum, Jr.

Lorenz, Anna Maria, of Wendelin Lorenz and his wife Eva, born February 26, 1772, baptized May 18, at Christian Henrich's house, at *Aspricollem;* sponsors, Joseph Lorenz and his wife Anna Maria.

Finck, Conrad Andrew, of Conrad Fink and his wife Catharine, born August —, 1771, baptized May 18, at Andrew Grett's, in Windsor;. sponsors, Andrew Grett and his wife.

Miller, Peter, of Theobald Miller and his wife Catharine, born May 4, 1772, baptized May 24, in the church ; sponsors, James Matthes and Anna M. Kuhn.

Zip, Joseph, of Joseph Zip and his wife Apollonia, born May 21, 1772, baptized June 18 ; sponsors, Joseph Hild and his wife.

Bock, Catharine, of Nicholas Bock and his wife Elizabeth, born May 28, 1772, baptized June 21, at Edward Carty's, at Haycock ; sponsor Bernard Kohl and his wife Catharine.

Auf, Frederic, of Theodoric Auf and his wife Elizabeth, born November 28, 1771, baptized at the same time and place as above ; sponsors, Frederic Brant and Magdalen Kientz.

Ruffner, Henry, of Philip Ruffner and his wife Catharine, born June 4, 1772, baptized July 5, in Christian Ruffner's house in the Blue mountains ; sponsors, Henry Kuhn and Ann M. Wieder.

Fischer, James, of Joseph Fischer and his wife Anna Barbara, born January 16, 1772, baptized July 19, at Christian Henrich's house, at *Asperum Collem* ; sponsors, Henry Eckenroth and his wife Anna Margaret.

Muthart, James, of Frederic Muthart and his wife Magdalen, born July 13, 1772, baptized July 26, in the church ; sponsors, Peter Keffer and his wife Barbara.

St. Jean, Anthony, of Louis St. Jean, a black slave owned by D. Seelly, and his wife, born two years and two months ago, baptized August 9, at Reading ; sponsor, Anthony Bluhm.

Kuhn, Andrew, of Michael Kuhn and his wife Eva, born July 19, 1772, baptized August 30, at Seigfried's in the Oley hills ; sponsors, Andrew Schnabel and his wife.

Zweyer, Mary Magdalen, of Stephen Zweyer and his wife Eva, born August 16, 1772, baptized at the same time and place as above ; sponsors, Joseph Eck and M. Margaret [Magdalen] Kuhn.

Spring, M. Margaret, of James Spring and his wife Catharine, born September 4, 1772, baptized October 20, at Christian Henrichs, at *Aspricollem* ; sponsors, Christian Henrich and his wife M. Margaret.

Rogers, John, of James Rogers and his wife M. Margaret [Magdalen], born September 20, 1771, baptized at the same time and place as above; sponsors, Thomas Thum and Elizabeth [Catharine] Weibel.

Eckenroth, Catharine, of Peter Eckenroth and his wife Eva, born September ——, 1772, baptized at the same time and place as above ; sponsors, Christ. Eckenroth and Catharine [Scandal ?] Eckenroth.

Tapper, Andrew, of Andrew Tapper and his wife Anna Mary, born five weeks ago, baptized September 27, 1772, in the chapel ; sponsors, John Tapper and Agatha Riffel.

Kupser, Magdalen, of James Kupser and his wife Catharine, born September 26, 1772, baptized October 4, in the chapel; sponsors, Leonard Litzinger and his wife Magdalen.

Schorb, Andrew, of Adam Schorb and his wife ——, born five weeks ago, baptized October 11, 1772, in the chapel at Reading; sponsors, —— Both and his wife Eva.

Cremer, Anna Maria Gertrude, of Matthias Cremer and his wife ——, born September 30, 1772, baptized October 19, at her father's house at Haycock; sponsors, George Lantzel and Gertrude Sicken.

Kuhn, James, of John Kuhn and his wife Catharine, born ——, baptized October 15, at Christian Henrich's at *Asperum Collem;* sponsors, James Kuhn, the father's brother, and Elizabeth Eckenroth Jr., unmarried.

Keffer, Catharine, of Peter Keffer and his wife Barbara, born November 28, 1772, baptized December 1, at the father's house among the hills in what is known as " District township ; " sponsors, Michael Hartman and Catharine Hartmann.

Schmitt, John Michael, of Philip Schmitt and his wife Ursula, born——, 1772, baptized December 6, at the house of Peter Käss at Cedar creek ; sponsors, Michael Morloch and his wife.

Arents, James, of James Arents and his wife Margaret, born ——, 1772, baptized at the same time and place as above ; sponsors, John Grünewald and his wife Barbara.

Schneider, Elizabeth, of —— and Mary Schneider, born December 3, 1772, baptized at the same time and place as above ; sponsors, Henry Kuhn and Elizabeth Bisschof.

Fiderer, James Michael, of Stephen Fiderer and his wife Catharine, born December 5, 1772, baptized December 13, in the chapel at Reading ; sponsors, Michael Rittner and Cathalina Stahl.

Kohl, Anthony, of George Bernard Kohl and his wife Catharine, born October 20, 1772, baptized December 20, at Haycock ; sponsors, Anthony Grüser, Jr., and Catharine Hucki.

Lambin, Catharine, of Christopher Lambin and his wife Anna Maria, born November 26, 1772, baptized at the same time and place as above ; sponsors, John Rösner and Catharine Carty.

[Forty-one baptisms are recorded for the year.]

BAPTISMS FOR THE YEAR 1773.

Bevertz, Margaret, of Conrad Bevertz and his wife Margaret, born five weeks ago, baptized January 21, 1773, at her father's house at Allemängel ; sponsors, George Eckenroth and Margaret Henrich.

Huck, Anna Mary, of Paul Huck and his wife Juliana, born eight days ago, baptized January 26, 1773, at her father's house near Paint Forge; sponsors, Juliana Zweyer, grandmother of the child, and her son Balthassar Zweyer.

Gaucker, Anna Mary, of John Gaucker and his wife Barbara, born January 7, 1773, baptized February 2, 1773, in the priest's room on account of the cold ; sponsors, Joseph Egg and Anna Mary Weibel.

Gibson, Joseph, of Henry Gibson and his wife Catharine, born January 23, 1773, baptized at the same time and place as above ; sponsors, Joseph Lorenz and his wife Mary Ann.

Langhammer, George Michael, of George Langhammer and his wife M. Barbara, born February 4, 1773, baptized February 14, at Reading ; sponsors, Michael Rittner and Frances Fricker.

Sigfried, Francis Joseph, of John Michael Sigfried and his wife Justina, born January 23, 1773, baptized February 15, at his father's house in the Oley hills ; sponsors, Francis Joseph Ofer and his wife M. Ann.

Rohr, Theresa, of Martin Rohr and his wife Anna Maria, born December 16, 1772, baptized February 24, 1773, in the chapel ; sponsors, John Adam Schmitt and his wife Margaret.

Felix, John, of Nicholas Felix and his wife Catharine, born February 26, 1773; baptized March 14, at Reading ; sponsors, John Felix and M. Ann Altgayer.

Schuhmacker, M. Dorothy, of Christian Schuhmacker and his wife Anna Maria, born March 11, 1773, baptized March 28, in the church ; sponsor, Simon ———.

Krafft, Simon John, of Michael Krafft and his wife Magdalen [Elizabeth], born March 8, 1773, baptized April 11 ; sponsors, Simon Adams and Margaret Wider.

Litzinger, John James, of Leonard Litzinger and his wife Magdalen, born March 29, 1773, baptized at the same time and place as above ; sponsors, John James Norbeck and Anna M. Adams.

Flower, Joseph, of Henry Flower and his wife Rosina, born March 19, 1773, baptized May 9, at Reading ; sponsors, John Joseph Gallon and his wife Margaret.

Grass, John, of Christopher Grass and his wife Catharine, born April 8, 1773, baptized at the same time and place as above ; sponsors, John Felix and Regina Stahl.

Schlosser, M. Margaret, of Joseph Schlosser and his wife Anna Margaret, born May 1, 1773, baptized May 16, at Christian Henrich's house, near *Asperumcollem;* sponsors, Michael Morloch and his wife Magdalen.

Magel, Susanna, of Christopher Magel, Catholic, and his wife Magdalen, non-Catholic, born January 31, 1775, baptized May 20, at John Egg's house at Rock hill; sponsors, Anthony Grüser and his wife.

Ruffner, M. Eva, of Christian Ruffner and his wife M. Odilia, born February 7, 1773, baptized May 24, at Peter Kass's house at Cedar creek; sponsors, John Kleintop, non-Catholic, and his wife M. Eva, Catholic.

――――, Mark, of Louis and his wife Felicitas, black slaves of N. N. Löscher, born January 1, 1773, baptized May 30, in the chapel; sponsors, Francis Gibson and his wife.

Eck, John Baptist, of John Eck and his wife Magdalen, born May 29, 1773, at Rockhill, baptized June 19, 1772 [evidently an error for 1773], at his father's house; sponsors, the priest and Mary Norbeck.

Ruppel, John, of John Ruppel and his wife ――――, born in Georgia, December 14, 1772, baptized June 20, at Edward Carty's house; sponsors, John Miller and his sister Catharine.

Stahl, Catharine, of Michael Stahl and his wife Anna Maria, born March 30, 1773, baptized July 11, 1773, at Reading; sponsors, Catharine Sigfried and Balthasar Zweyer.

Ruffner, John, of Simon Ruffner and his wife Catharine, born June 30, 1773, baptized July 31, in his grandfather's house in Leche township, in the Blue mountains; sponsors, Patrick Griffin, Jr., and Mary Ermann.

Heitsman, Anna Barbara, of N. Heitsman, non-Catholic, and his wife Anna Barbara, Catholic, of Georgia, born July 27, 1773, baptized August 15, at Edward Carty's house; sponsors, N. Brechtel and his wife, non-Catholics.

Kuhns, John Adam, of John Kuhns and his wife Catharine, born June 9, 1773, baptized August 29, at Cedar creek; sponsors, John Adam Widder, non-Catholic, and his wife, Catholic.

Schönebruck, John, of Caspar Schönebruck and his wife Anna Margaret, born June 13, 1773, baptized at the same time and place as above; sponsors, Peter Käss and Elizabeth Meckler the child's grandmother.

Moor, Anthony, of James Moor and his wife Sophia, born July 25, 1771, baptized September 19, 1773, at Christian Henrich's house at *Asperum Collem*; sponsors, James Arents and his wife Margaret.

Thornbach, Nicholas, of ―― Thornbach and Catharine ――――, born five weeks ago, baptized October 10, 1773. in the chapel at Reading; sponsors, Nicholas Felix and his wife, Anna Maria.

Kemp, John George, of John Kemp and his wife Susanna, born August 12, 1773, baptized October 17, at Edward Carty's house at Haycock ; sponsors, Matthias Kientz and his wife.

Käss, Matthias, of Peter Käss and his wife Anna Margaret, born December 15, 1773, baptized privately in danger of death, ceremonies supplied December 31, at the father's house ; sponsors, Matthias Brucx and his wife Mary.

[The number of baptisms for the year is twenty-eight.]

BAPTISMS FOR THE YEAR 1774.

Litzinger, Magdalen, of Henry Litzinger and his wife, Anna Maria, born December 29, 1774 [an error for 1773], baptized January 1, 1774, in the chapel ; sponsors, Leonard Litzinger and his wife, Magdalen.

Fricker, Thomas, of Anthony Fricker and his wife Margaret, born on his patron saint's day [*i. e.* December 21], 1773, baptized January 9, in Anthony Fricker's house ; sponsors, Frederic Haffner and M. Theresa Fricker.

Lorenz, Mary Eva, of Maurice Lorenz and his wife Mary, born November 17, 1773, baptized January 18, 1774, at Christian Henrich's house at *Asperum Collem* ; sponsors, Wendelin Lorenz and M. Eva, his wife.

Spring, John, of James Spring and his wife Anna Catharine, born January 8, 1774, baptized January 29, 1774, at his father's house in Allemängel ; sponsors, John Füss, his maternal grandfather, and Anna M. Spring, his paternal grandmother.

Wagner, Mary Salome, of Matthias Wagner and his wife, born December 29, 1773, baptized February 20, 1774, at Edward Carty's house at Haycock ; sponsors, Nicholas Carty and his wife Albertina.

Haiss, M. Catharine. of William Haiss and his wife Mary, born February 3, 1774, baptized at the same time and place as above ; sponsors, John Girard and his wife Mary.

Schnabel, John, of Andrew Schnabel and his wife M. Eva, born December 21, 1773, baptized February 27, in the priest's room [*in cubiculo meo*] ; sponsors, John Egg, Jr., and Magdalen Kuhn.

Schimpfessel, John Michael, of Louis Schimpfessel and his wife———, born December 8, 1773, baptized March 13, in the chapel at Reading ; sponsors, John Michael Altgayer and his wife.

Henrich, Joseph, of Philip Henrich and his wife Elizabeth, born March 4. 1774, baptized March 20, in Christian Henrich's house at *Asperum Collem ;* sponsors, Joseph Weibel and Magdalen Henrich.

Henrich, John Adam, of Christian Henrich and his wife Magdalen, born January 23, 1774, baptized at the same time and place as above; sponsors, John Adam Stahler and his wife Mary.

Keffer, John, of Matthias Keffer and his wife Eva, born sixteen weeks ago, baptized at the same time and place as above; sponsors, Philip Weismiller and his wife Anna Maria.

Dapper [elsewhere written Tapper], Christian, of Andrew Dapper and his wife Mary, born March 5, 1774, baptized March 25, at Francis Cooper's house at Allenstown; sponsors, Christian and Barbara Dapper, the child's grandparents.

Offer, Magdalen, of Frank Offer and his wife Mary Ann, born March 19, 1774, baptized April 10, in the chapel at Reading; sponsors, Joseph Zweyer and Mary Sigfried, daughter of Andrew.

Schimpfessel, Louis, of Andrew Schimpfessel and his wife Margaret, born February 24, 1774, baptized at the same time and place as above; sponsors, Louis Schimpfessel and Margaret Becker, grandparents of the child.

Kohl, Elizabeth, of Bernard Kohl and his wife Catharine, born February 28, 1774, baptized April 17, at Edward Carty's house at Haycock; sponsors, James Kohl and his wife Elizabeth.

Carty, M. Salome, of Nicholas Carty and his wife Albertina, born April 7, 1774, baptized at the same time and place as above; sponsors, James Lentzinger and his wife Mary Salome.

Keffer, Anna Catharine, of Peter Keffer and his wife Barbara, born April 4, 1774, baptized May 1, in the church; sponsors, Michael Hoffman and Catharine Hartman.

Gaucker, Joseph, of John Gaucker and his wife Anna Barbara, born April 23, 1774, baptized at the same time and place as above; sponsors, Joseph Egg and Anna Maria Weibel.

Riffel, Daniel, of John Joseph Riffel and his wife Margaret, born April 8, 1774, baptized May 1, about five o'clock in the evening, in the chapel; sponsors, Melchior Riffel and Mary Matthes.

Molsberger, John, of James Molsberger and his wife Catharine, born April 9, 1774, baptized May 22, in the church; sponsors, James Kuhn and his wife Magdalen.

Schrunck, M. Elizabeth, of William Schrunck, non-Catholic, and his wife M. Elizabeth, Catholic, born March 22, 1774, baptized at the same time and place as above; sponsors, Philip and M. Elizabeth Weismiller, grandparents of the child on the mother's side.

Riffel, Anna Magdalen, of George James George [sic] Riffel and his wife Elizabeth, born May 20, 1774, baptized May 29, at Joseph Riffel's house at Magungi ; sponsors, Matthias Riffel, Jr., and Magdalen Henrich.

Schmitt, Henry, of John Adam Schmitt and his wife Margaret, born May 7, 1774, baptized June 2, in the church ; sponsors, Henry and M. Anna Norbeck, grandparents.

Schäfer, John, of William Schäfer and his wife Susanna, born March 13, 1774, baptized June 19, at Edward Carty's house ; sponsors, George Bernard Kohl and Elizabeth Kohl.

Lambin, John, of Christopher Lambin and his wife Anna Maria, born April 19, 1774, baptized at the same time and placed as above ; sponsors, John Rösner and M. Barbara Grünewald.

Krafft, John George, of Michael Krafft and his wife Elizabeth, born June 14, 1774, baptized June 29, at Francis Cooper's house at Allenstown ; sponsors, Henry Kuhn and Margaret Wider.

Kupser, Anna Mary, of James Kupser and his wife, Catharine, born July 9, 1774, baptized July 24, in the church ; sponsors, Joseph Hild, Jr., and Anna Mary Adams.

Baur, Mary, of Francis Baur and his wife, Elizabeth, born July 13, 1774, baptized August 7, in the church ; sponsors, James Matthes and Mary Both.

——, Daniel, son of an Irishman, about two years old, baptized privately, ceremonies supplied August 14, at Reading. [Sponsors not named.]

La Fleur, John, of John La Fleur and his wife Catharine, born June 3, 1774, baptized August 15, at Sigfried's in the Oley hills ; sponsors, John Becker and Mary Baur.

Zweyer, John Thomas, of John Zweyer and his wife Eva, born July 7, baptized at the same time and place as above ; sponsors, Matthias Kuhn and Catharine Sigfried.

Putz, Mary Sophia, of John William Putz and his wife Magdalen, born July 16, 1774, baptized August 21, at Edward Carty's house ; sponsors, Peter Welcker and Mary Sophia Strubl.

Fischer, Mary Barbara, of Joseph Fischer and his wife Anna Mary, born March 14, 1774, baptized at Christian Henrich's house at *Asperum Collem* ; sponsors, Henry Eckenroth and M. Barbara Eckenroth.

Brücks, Henry, of Matthias Brücks and his wife Mary, born September 1, 1774, baptized at Francis Cooper's house at Allentown, September 29 ; sponsors, Henry Kuhn and Margaret Wider.

Sigfried, John George, of John Michael Sigfried and his wife Justina, born September 14 1774, baptized October 10, at George Sigfried's house in the Oley hills ; sponsors, John George Wantz and Mary Magdalen Kuhn.

Kroner, Matthias, of John George Kroner and his wife Mary Margaret, born August 14, 1774, baptized at the same time and place as above; sponsors, Matthias Kuhn and Mary Miller.

Arents, Joseph, of Joseph Arents and his wife Margaret, born September 25, 1774, baptized October 14, in the church; sponsors, Joseph Erman and his wife Catharine.

Miclaine, Catharine Elizabeth, of Lochely Miclaine and Catharine Connelly, born July 7, 1774, baptized October 16, at Edward Carty's house; sponsors, Joseph Rittner [?] and his wife Catharine.

Ruffner, M. Eva, of Christian Ruffner and his wife M. Odilia, born August 1, 1774, baptized October 18, at her father's house near the Blue mountains; sponsors, John Kleintop and his wife M Eva.

Miller, Catharine, of Philip Miller and his wife Anna M., born September 29, 1774, baptized October 23, in the church; sponsors, James Matthes and Catharine Hoffmann.

Grünewald, Anna Maria, of John Grünewald and his wife Barbara, born September 23, 1774, baptized October 30, at Joseph Riffel's house at Macungi; sponsors, Matthias Brücks and his wife Anna Maria.

Zipp, Anna Catharine, of Joseph Zipp and his wife Appolonia, born July 24, 1774, baptized November 6, in the church; sponsors, James Spring and his wife Anna Catharine.

Schlosser, George, of Joseph Schlosser and his wife, Anna M., born October 19, 1774, baptized November 20, at Christian Henrich's house at *Asperum Collem*; sponsors, Joseph Lorenz and his wife Anna Maria.

Ruffner, Anthony, of Philip Ruffner and his wife Eva, born October 18, 1774, baptized November 30, at Francis Cooper's house at Allenstown; sponsors, Anthony Hönig and Eva Wider.

Ruffner, Barbara, of Simon Ruffner and his wife Catharine, born November 5, 1774, baptized at the same time and place as above; sponsors, Simon and Barbara Ruffner, grandparents of the child.

Kuhns, Elizabeth, of John Kuhns and his wife Catharine, born October, 31, 1774, baptized at the same time and place as above; sponsors, James Kuhn and Elizabeth Wider.

Norbeck, M. Magdalen, of James Norbeck and his wife Mary, born October 30, 1774, baptized in the church December 4; sponsors, Theodore Egg and M. Magdalen Norbeck.

Chaumont, John Bernard, of John Bernard Chaumont and Susanna Zinn, born December 1, 1774, baptized December 11, at Joseph Rüttner's house in Reading; sponsors, James Stahl and his wife Catharine.

Kropf, Anthony, of Peter Kropf and his wife Claudina, born October 22, 1774, baptized December 18, at Edward Carty's house at Haycock ; sponsors, Anthony Grüser and Catharine Carty.

Hönig, John Joseph, of James Hönig and his wife, Catharine, born November 14, 1774, baptized at the same time and place as above ; sponsors, Joseph Rösner and his wife Catharine.

[The baptisms for the year number fifty.]

BAPTISMS FOR THE YEAR 1775.

Schorb, Barbara, of Adam Schorb and his wife Anna Elizabeth, born December 13, 1774, baptized January 8, 1775, at Joseph Rüttner's house at Reading ; sponsors, Sebastian and Barbara Altgayer.

Kuhn Joseph, of John Kuhn and his wife Catharine, born December 10, ' 1775 [sic], baptized January 15, at Christian Henrich's house at *Asperum Collem* ; sponsors, Henry Kuhn and M. Elizabeth Eckenroth.

Eckenroth, M. Elizabeth, of Henry Eckenroth and his wife Anna Barbara, born January 13, 1775, baptized January 16, at James Spring's house at *Asperum Collem* ; sponsors, the same as yesterday [*i. e.* " *susceperunt hesterni*"].

Muthart, Catharine, of Frederic Muthart, non-Catholic, and his wife Magdalen, born January 16, 1775, baptized February 2, in the priest's room ; sponsors, Michael Hartman and Catharine Grett.

Marx, Anthony, of Thomas Marx and his wife Eva, born December 22, 1774, baptized February 19, at Edward Carty's house ; sponsors, Anthony Grüser and his wife Elizabeth.

Ruffner, Christian, of George Adam Ruffner and his wife Mary, born January 5, 1775, baptized February 24, at Francis Cooper's house at Allenstown ; sponsors, Christian Ruffner and his wife Mary.

Eck, Veronica, of John Eck, a farmer (*coloni*) in Rich valley, and his wife Magdalen, born March 6, 1775, baptized March 8, at her farther's house ; sponsors, John Norbeck and Catharine Eck.

[Four pages ahead the record of this baptism is entered in the same handwriting with the additional memorandum of the mother having died in childbirth.]

Stahler, Elizabeth, of Adam Stahler and his wife Mary, born January 19, 1775, baptized March 19, at Christian Henrich's house at *Asperum Collem ;* sponsors, John Weibel and Margaret Henrich.

Lorenz, John, of Maurice Lorenz and his wife Apollonia, born February 28, 1775, baptized at the same time and place as above ; sponsors, John Henrich and Barbara Spring.

Lorenz, Catharine, of Wendelln Lorenz and his wife M. Eva, born January 29, 1775, baptized at the same time and place as above ; sponsors, Joseph Spring and Catharine Keffer.

Litzinger, John, of Leonard Litzinger and his wife Magdalen, born March 16, 1775, baptized March 26, in the church ; sponsors, John Norbeck and Anna M. Adams.

Gerschweiler, Louis, of Philip Gerschweiler and his wife Catharine, born January 28, 1775, baptized April 2, at Joseph Rüttner's house at Reading ; sponsors, Louis Schimpfessel, the child's maternal grandfather, and Margaret Schimpfessel [sic], daughter-in-law of the same.

Thum, Mary Elizabeth, of Caspar Thum and his wife Mary Eva, born January 21, 1775, baptized April 3, at Michael Sigfried's house in the Oley hills ; sponsors, George Wantz and Mary Miller.

Bock, John, of Nicholas Bock and his wife Elizabeth, born February 19, 1775, baptized April 23, at Edward Carty's house at Haycock ; sponsors, James Hönig and his wife.

Miller, Anna Mary, posthumous child of Michael Miller and his wife Elizabeth, born March 8, 1775, baptized at the same time and place as above ; sponsors, Anthony Hönig and Barbara Grünewald.

Kämperling, John George, of John Kämperling and his wife Mary Cecily, born April 29, 1775, baptized May 7 ; sponsors, George Schrör and Elizabeth Uhlein.

Huck, John James, of Paul Huck and his wife Juliana, born January 12, 1775, baptized June 4 ; sponsors, Joseph Zweyer and Mary Ermann.

Gaucker, John Peter, of John Gaucker and his wife Anna Barbara, born May 31, 1775, baptized June 5 ; sponsors, John Weibel and Margaret Henrich.

Zweyer, Matthias, of Stephen Zweyer and his wife Anna Maria, born May 27, 1775, baptized June 11, at Michael Sigfried's, in Oley hills ; sponsors, Matthias Kuhn and Catharine Sigfried.

———, Salome, of Louis, a black slave of John Löscher, and Salome, born April 9, 1775, baptized at the same time and place as above ; sponsors, Mart. Burchart and his wife Gertrude.

Ruppel, John William, of John James Ruppel and his wife Barbara, born March 28, 1775, baptized June 18, at Edward Carty's house at Haycock ; sponsors, John William Schäffer and Susanna Schäffer, his wife.

Bevertz, Christopher, of Conrad Bevertz and his wife Margaret, born June 4 [?], 1775, baptized July 16, at *Asperum Collem;* sponsors, Christopher Eckenroth and Eva Weibel.

Gibson, Catharine, of Henry Gibson and his wife Catharine, born July 30, 1775, baptized August 6, in the church ; sponsors, John Adam Schmidt and his wife Margaret.

Schneider, Peter, of John Schneider and his wife Mary, born May 26, 1775, baptized August 15, at Francis Cooper's house at Allenstown ; sponsors, Maurice Bisschof and Benigna Cooper.

Lentzinger, James, of James Lentzinger and his wife M. Salome, born June 13, 1775, baptized August 20, at Edward Carty's house, at Haycock ; sponsors, James Kohl and his wife Catharine.

Finck, Anna M., of Nicholas Finck and his wife Agnes, born May 30, 1775, baptized at the same time and place as above ; sponsors, William Schäffer and Anna Maria Schlaut.

Käss, Mary, of Peter Käss and his wife Margaret, born September 8, 1775, baptized September 10, at Christian Ruffner's house in Lehigh [written " Leheig]," township, near the Blue mountains ; sponsors, Matthias Brücks and his wife Maria.

Grett, Michael, of Michael Grett and his wife Catharine, born September 8, 1775, baptized September 17, at Christian Henrich's house at *Asperum Collem;* sponsors, Michael Hartmann and Magdalen Muthart.

Spring, James, of James Spring and his wife Catharine, born September 13, 1775, baptized at the same time and place as above ; sponsors, John Henrich and Mary Barbara Spring.

Billich, Mary Barbara, of Arnold Billich, non-Catholic, and his wife Petronilla, born September 1, 1775, baptized at same time and place as above ; sponsors, Henry Eckenroth and his wife.

Schnabel, Andrew, of Andrew Schnabel and his wife Eva, born September 10, 1775, baptized October 8, at Sigfried's house in the Oley hills ; sponsors, Michael Kuhn and Eva Kuhn.

Flower, Thomas Christopher, of Henry Flower and his wife, born September 23, 1775, baptized at the same time and place as above ; sponsors, Thomas Thum and Mary Miller.

Schimpfessel, John George, of Andrew Schimpfessel and his wife Margaret, born September 26, 1775, and baptized rightly in case of necessity, ceremonies supplied at the same time and place as above ; sponsors, John George Wantz and Catharine Sigfried.

Grünewald, M. Barbara, of John Grünewald and his wife Barbara, born October 1, 1775, baptized October 29, at John Joseph Riffel's house at Macungi ; sponsors, Matthias Brücks and his wife Mary.

Riffel, Elizabeth, posthumous child of George James Riffel and his wife Elizabeth, born October 4, 1775, baptized November 19, at

Christian Henrich's house; sponsors, George Riffel and Margaret Henrich.

Tapper, James, of Andrew Tapper and his wife Mary, born October 27, 1775, baptized November 30, at Francis Cooper's house at Allenstown; sponsors, James Kuhn and his wife Magdalen.

Schönebruch, Andrew, of Caspar Schönebruch and his wife Margaret, born November 7, 1775, baptized at the same time and place as above; sponsors, Matthias Wiber and Margaret Wider.

Grass, Magdalen Catharine, of Christopher Grass and his wife Catharine, born October 2, 1775, baptized December 10, at Reading; sponsors, Francis Bock and Catharine Rüttner.

Croner, Mary Eva, of John George Croner and his wife Margaret, born ———, baptized December 11, at Michael Sigfried's house in the Oley hills; sponsors, Matthias Kuhn and M. Eva Thum.

Hammerstein, Anna Margaret, of Andrew Hammerstein and his wife Anna Barbara, born November 6, 1775, baptized December 18, at Edward Carty's house at Haycock; sponsors, Ant. Grüser Jr., and Anna Margaret Hammerstein.

Ulmer, Frederic, on December 26, 1775, made his profession of Faith in my [the priest's] room; had been brought up a Lutheran; the same day he publicly received the Holy Eucharist; witnesses, Nicholas Carty and Thomas Marx.

[The baptisms for the year number forty-one.]

BAPTISMS FOR THE YEAR 1776.

———, Catharine, step-daughter of the above Frederic Ulmer, a little child [*puellula*] about eight years old, answered fearlessly through God's wonderful grace all the questions put to her on the Christian doctrine. Not long before, despite her Catholic mother, her Lutheran step-father tried in vain to draw her over to his belief and had already taught her some heretical prayers, when, lo! he himself of his own accord embraced the faith of his step-daughter and her mother and brought the little child himself to be baptized according to the Catholic rite. The ceremonies of baptism were supplied January 6, in the chapel.

Spring, M. Barbara, of George Spring and his wife Barbara, born December ———, 1775, baptized January 21, at Christian Henrich's house at *Asperum Collem*; sponsors, Matthias Riffel, Jr., and M. Barbara Spring.

Kohl, John, of Joseph Kohl and his wife Barbara, born January 22, 1776, baptized February 18, at Edward Carty's house; sponsors, John and Catharine Maccarty.

Rösner, Catharine, wife of John [Rösner], farmer "at the Haycock," previously of no religion, publicly makes her profession of faith on February 18. [Apparently at Edward Carty's house.]

Ufer, John Adam, of Francis Ufer and his wife Mary Ann, born September 18, 1775, baptized March 10, at Joseph Rüttner's house at Reading; sponsors, Joseph Rüttner and his wife Barbara.

Kuhns, Mary, of John Kuhns and his wife Catharine, born January 3, 1776, baptized March 25, at Francis Cooper's house at Allenstown; sponsors, Francis Cooper and Catharine Miller.

Miller, Catharine, of Theobald Miller and his wife Catharine, born December 1, 1775, baptized at the same time and place as above; sponsors, John Kuhns and his wife Catharine.

Rüffner, Philip, of Philip Rüffner and his wife Eva, born December 7, 1775, baptized at same time and place as above; sponsors, Peter Käss and his wife Margaret.

Kupser, Barbara, of James Kupser and his wife Catharine, born April 1, 1776, baptized April 12, in the chapel; sponsors, Joseph Hild, the maternal grandfather, and his wife Catharine.

Lambin or Langbein, Matthew, of Christopher Lambin or Langbein and his wife M. Ann, born April 12, 1776, baptized April 21, at Haycock; sponsors, Matth. Seiffert and Catharine Wagner.

Meschel, Anna, of Adam Meschel and his wife Elizabeth, born January 4, 1776, baptized April 22, at Nicholas Hucki's house near Easton; sponsors, Matthias Wagner and Magdalen Wagner.

Carty, Nicholas, of Nicholas Carty and his wife Albertina, born April 21, 1776, baptized April 23, at Edward Carty's house; sponsors, Anthony Grüser and his wife Elizabeth.

Kohl, George, of George Bernard Kohl and his wife Catharine, born April 22, 1776, baptized at the same time and place as above; sponsors, George and Barbara Kohl, grandparents of the child.
[These two infants had three grandfathers and two grandmothers living]

Riffel, Catharine Barbara, of John Joseph Riffel and his wife Margaret, born April 11, 1776, baptized May 5; sponsors, George Riffel and Mary Barbara Spring.

Rüffner, George Adam, of Simon Rüffner and his wife Catharine, born April 27, 1776, baptized May 12, at Christian Rüffner's house in Lecha township near the Blue mountains.

Rüffner, George Adam, of Christian Rüffner and his wife M. Odilia, born May 5, 1776, baptized at the same time and place as the above; sponsors for both children, George Adam Rüffner and his wife Mary.

Stahler, Christian, of John Adam Stahler and his wife Mary, born May
1, 1776. baptized May 9, at his grandfather's house at *Asperum
Collem*; sponsors, Christian Henrich and his wife Magdalen.

Hartmann, John, of Francis Hartmann and his wife Angela, born April
2, 1776, baptized May 26, in the chapel ; sponsors, John Gaucker
and his wife Barbara.

Kuhn, Catharine, of John Kuhn and his wife Theresa, born May 24, 1776,
baptized May 27, in the church ; sponsors, Joseph Fricker and
Mary Ermann.

Kreiss, Joseph, of Martin Kreiss and his wife Catharine, born April 8,
1776, baptized June 2, in the church ; sponsors, Joseph Hild and his
wife Catharine.

Fricklinger, Christian, twenty years of age, a Calvinist, makes publicly
his profession of faith in the chapel on June 6.

Keffer, M. Barbara, of Peter Keffer and his wife M. Barbara, born May
27, 1776, baptized June 6, in the chapel ; sponsors, Michael Hartmann and Catharine Hofmann.

Rösner, John Joseph, of John Rösner and his wife Catharine, born
June 8, 1776, baptized June 16, at Edward Carty's house, at Haycock ; sponsors, Joseph Rösner and Catharine Rösner, grandparents
of the child.

Machel, Anna, of Christopher Machel and his wife Magdalen, born July
8, 1775, baptized at the same time and place as above ; sponsors,
George Bernard Kohl and his wife Catharine.

Halter, Catharine, of James Halter and his wife Margaret, born April
27, 1776, baptized at the same time and place as above ; sponsors,
Peter Maison and Catharine Kientz.

Schäffer, Anna Margaret, of William Schäffer, of [New] Jersey and his
wife Susanna, born February 1, 1776, baptized at the same time
and place as above ; sponsors, Anthony Grüser, Jr. and Anna Barbara Hammerstein.

Röhr, John, of Martin Röhr and his wife Anna M., born May 14, 1776,
baptized June 23, in the chapel ; sponsors, John Norbeck and his
wife Rosina.

Lafleur, Henry James, of John Lafleur and his wife Catharine, born
May 18, 1776, baptized July 7, at Sigfried's house, in the Oley hills ;
sponsors, Henry Finck and Mary Baur.

Fischer, Catharine, of Joseph Fischer and his wife Anna Maria, born
November 14, 1775, baptized July 21, at Christian Henrich's house,
at *Asperum Collem;* sponsors, John Weibel and Catharine Dietrich.

Gerschweiler, John, of Philip Gerschweiler and his wife Catharine, born
July 9, 1776, baptized August 4, at Reading ; sponsors, Louis

Schimpfessel and his wife, Catharine, maternal grandparents of the child.

Molsberger, John George, of James Molsberger and his wife Catharine, born June 28, 1776, baptized August 11, in the chapel ; sponsors, John Joseph Riffel and his wife Margaret.

Onel [O'Neill ?], John, of Henry Onel and his wife, born four weeks ago, baptized August 15, at Edward Carty's house at Haycock ; sponsor, Edward Carty.

Weibel, Mary Margaret, of John Weibel and his wife Margaret, born August 16, 1776, baptized September 15, at Christian Henrich's house at *Asperum Collem*; sponsors, George Riffel and Mary Weibel.

Henrich, Mary Magdalen, of Christian Henrich, Jr., and his wife Magdalen, born September 7, 1776, baptized at the same time and place as above ; sponsors, Christian Eckenroth and Magdalen Henrich.

Braun, Catharine, of Andrew Braun and his wife Rachel, or Regina, born September 15, 1776, baptized September 22, in the church ; sponsors, Henry Gibson and his wife Catharine.

Arents, Henry Peter, of James Arents and his wife Margaret, born September 21, 1776, baptized October 13 ; sponsors, Henry Gibson and his wife.

Norbeck, M. Anna, of James Norbeck and his wife Mary, born September 10, 1776, baptized at the same time and place as above ; sponsors, Henry and Mary Ann Norbeck, grandparents of the child.

Strunk, M. Gertrude, of William Strunk [elsewhere Strunck] and his wife Elizabeth, born September 11, 1776, baptized at the same time and place as above; sponsors, Mart. Burchart and his wife, Gertrude.

Keffer, M. Elizabeth, of Matthias Keffer and his wife Eva, born October 3, 1776, baptized November 17, at Christian Henrich's house ; sponsors, William Strunck, non-Catholic, and his wife, M. Elizabeth.

[The following three entries are here given after the baptism as above of November 17, in the order in which they are found recorded in the register at page 160.]

Kemp, Susanna, of John Kemp and his wife Anna, born July 20, 1776, baptized October 19, at Matthias Kientz's house ; sponsors, Matthias Kientz and his wife Margaret Kientz.

Bradley, William, of William Bradley and his wife Margaret Grün [perhaps better Green], born September —, 1771, baptized October 20, at Edward Carty's house ; sponsors, James Kohl and his wife Elizabeth Kohl.

Gaucker, Anna Maria, of John Gaucker and his wife Barbara, born November [error for October] 24, baptized November 1, in the church ; sponsors, Valent. Weibel and his wife.

Adams, John, of Simon Adams and his wife Catharine, born November 22, 1776, baptized November 24, in the church ; sponsors, John Eck and Mary Adams.

Felix, Barbara, of Nicholas Felix and his wife Anna Maria, born November 2, 1776, baptized December 1, at Reading ; sponsors, Frederick Haffner and his wife Barbara.

Haffner, Catharine, of Frederick Haffner and his wife Barbara, born November 5, 1776, baptized at the same time and place as above ; sponsors, Frederick and Catharine Haffner, grandparents of the child.

[The baptisms for the year number forty-five.]

BAPTISMS FOR THE YEAR 1777.

Sigfried, Thomas, of John Michael Sigfried and his wife Justina, born December 30, 1776, baptized January 5, 1777, at Sigfried's house in the Oley hills ; sponsors, Thomas Thum and Mary Sigfried.

Henrich, Philip, of Philip Henrich and his wife Elizabeth, born December 18, 1776, baptized January 19, at Christian Henrich's house ; sponsors, Valent. Weibel and his wife.

Eckenroth, Conrad, of Henry Eckenroth and his wife Barbara, born December 29, 1777 [error perhaps for 1776], baptized at the same time and place as above ; sponsors, Conrad Bevertz and his wife Margaret.

Lorenz, Christian, of Maurice Lorenz and his wife Anna Maria, born January 11, 1777, baptized at the same time and place as above ; sponsors, Christian Henrich and his wife.

Kropf, Anna Maria, of Peter Kropf and his wife Claudina, born on the Feast of the Holy Innocents [i. e. December 28], 1776, baptized February 16, at Edward Carty's house ; sponsors, Christopher Lambin and his wife Anna Mary.

Ruffner, Mary Barbara, of George Adam Ruffner and his wife Mary, born January 18, 1777, baptized February 21, at Peter Käss's house beyond the river Lehigh [written "Leheig"], in the Blue mountains ; sponsors, Michael Holstein and Mary Barbara, maternal grandparents of the child.

Ruffner, Catharine, of Philip Ruffner and his wife Eva, born ——, baptized at the same time and place as above ; sponsors, Catharine Hönig and Michael Holstein, Jr.

Schmitt, of John Adam Schmitt and his wife Margaret, born January 12 [1777], baptized February 23, in the church ; sponsors, Henry Gibson and wife.

Kuhn, Catharine, of John Kuhn and his wife Catharine, born February 5, 1777, baptized March 16, at Christian Henrich's house at *Asperum Collem* ; sponsors, John Fuss and Catharine Eckenroth.

Grett, John, of John Grett and his wife Elizabeth, born January 20, 1777, baptized March 17, at Andrew Grett's house in Windsor township ; sponsors, John Finck and Barbara Grett.

Finck, Magdalen, of Conrad Finck and his wife Catharine, born August 10, 1777 [error for perhaps 1776], baptized at the same time and place as above ; sponsors, John Grett and Magdalen Grett.

Krafft, Anna Maria, of Michael Krafft and his wife Elizabeth, born March 10, 1777, baptized March 30, in the chapel ; sponsors, Joseph Egg and Anna Maria Adams.

Fowler, Thomas and Peter, of Edward Fowler and Elizabeth (said to be his wife) ; they are homeless [*vagi*] ; Thomas was born three years ago ; Peter, three months ago ; baptized April 4, in the chapel; sponsors, Thomas Marx and his wife Eva, and Peter Langbein alone [*solus*].

Lampert [perhaps better Lambert, as in entry for February 2, 1783], Anna Margaret, of James Lampert and his wife Dorothy, born February 16, 1777, baptized April 6, at Reading ; sponsors, Joseph Gallon and his wife Anna Margaret.

Huck, Joseph, of Paul Huck [perhaps better Hucki], and his wife Juliana, born November 17, 1776, baptized April 7, in the Oley hills ; sponsors, Joseph Zweyer, uncle of the child, and Juliana Zweyer, its grandmother.

Bieger, Magdalen, born of a Catholic father and a non-Catholic mother, was brought up a Lutheran and was a communicant of that church ; she made her profession of faith, at Magungi, in John Joseph Riffel's house, on April 13, "I, J. B. Ritter," receiving it in the presence of Joseph Riffel, Philip Ruffner, John Hofman and Michael Holstein, Jr.

Kuhns, Margaret, of John Kuhns and his wife Catharine, born January 20, 1777, baptized at the same time and place as above ; sponsors, Caspar Schönebruch and his wife Margaret.

Burchart, M. Magdalen, of Martin Burchart and his wife Gertrude, born April 8, 1777, while its mother was at the point of death from pleurisy, baptized April 15, at her father's house ; sponsors, Philip Burchart and —— Weismiller, brother and grandmother of the child.

Lenzinger, M. Magdalen, of James Lenzinger [elsewhere Lentzinger] and his wife Salome, born April 5, 1777, baptized April 21, at Nicholas Hucki's house near Easton ; sponsors, Matth. Wagner and his wife Anna M.

Muthart, Anna Maria, of Frederick Muthart, non-Catholic, and his wife Magdalen, Catholic, born April 1, 1777, baptized April 27, in the priest's room.

Lörschbach, Magdalen, of John Lörschbach and his wife Magdalen, born April 3, 1777, baptized at the same time and place as above ; sponsors for both children, James and Magdalen Hartmann.

[Father Ritter here observes in the Register of Baptisms, at page 168, that he has by mistake recorded four baptisms belonging to this year among the marriages further on, namely, at pages 242–3. They are as follows :]

MacHill, Mary and Margaret, twins, of Arthur MacHill and his wife Anna Maria, born January 1, twenty-two years ago, baptized February 2, in the priest's room [*i. e. in cubiculo meo*].

Norbeck, Mary Magdalen, of John Norbeck and his wife Rosina, born January 27, 1777, baptized at the same time and place as above ; sponsors, Joseph Schmitt and Magdalen [the last name is ill-written but looks something like] Rorbusy [or perhaps Norbeck].

Brücx, Peter, of Matthias Brücx and his wife Mary, born January 4, 1777, baptized at the same time and place as above ; sponsors, Peter Käss and Margaret Käss.

Miller, Henry, of Philip Miller and his wife Anna Maria, born January 11, 1777, baptized at the same time and place as above ; sponsors, Henry Gibson and his wife Catharine.

Struppel, Peter, unmarried, formerly a Lutheran, makes public profession of faith in the chapel, May 11 ; witnesses, Conrad Welsch and John Oeltz.

Spring, George, of James Spring and his wife Catharine, born March 10, 1777, baptized June 1, 1777, at Christian Henrich's house at *Asperum Collem;* sponsors, George Ristel and Barbara Spring.

Tapper, or Dabber, John Henry, of Andrew Tapper, or Dabber, and his wife Maria, born May 18, 1777, baptized June 7, in the chapel ; sponsors, Joseph Riffel and his wife Margaret.

Neuman, James, of Henry Neuman and ——, born a year and three months ago, baptized June 21, in the chapel ; sponsors, James Walter and Margaret Eck.

Butz, William Peter, of John William Butz and his wife Magdalen, born July 1, 1777, baptized July 13, in the chapel ; sponsors, Peter Struppel and Magdalen Norbeck.

Drexel, James, of Anthony Drexel and his wife Catharine, born July 27, 1777, baptized July 30, in the chapel; sponsors, James Kuhn and Theresa Kuhn.

Butz, John Henry, of Christian Butz and his wife Catharine, born August 1, 1777, baptized August 3, in the chapel; sponsors, John Henry Els and Elizabeth Strubbel.

Käss, Henry, of Peter Käss and his wife Margaret, born July 31, 1777, baptized August 31, at Joseph Riffel's house, at Macungi; sponsors, Henry Kuhn and his wife Margaret.

Bock, Barbara, of Nicholas Bock and his wife Elizabeth, born at the beginning of August, 1777, baptized September 5, at her father's house, at Haycock hill (*in monte Haycock*); sponsors, George Kohl and his wife Barbara by Catharine Bock.

Ruffner, Christian, of Christian Ruffner and his wife M. Odilia, born six weeks ago, baptized September 6, at the town of Lehigh ["Leheig (*sic*) *vico*], near the Blue mountains; sponsors, Simon Ruffner, grandfather of the child, and his wife Barbara.

Reichart, John Adam, twenty-five years of age, millwright [*molendinorum artifex*], makes publicly his profession of faith on [September] 9, in the church.

Kemperling, Barbara, of John Kemperling and his wife M. Cecily, born August 23, 1777, baptized September 9, in the chapel; sponsors, Francis Uhlein and Barbara Meckeler.

Stahler, Eva Maria, of Adam Stahler and his wife Eva Maria, born July 29, 1777, baptized September 22, at Christian Henrich's house, at *Asperum Collem*; sponsors, Christian Henrich and M. Margaret, grandparents of the child.

Bevertz, Anna Margaret, of Conrad Bevertz and his wife Anna Margaret, born August 1, 1777, baptized at the same time and place as above; sponsors, Andrew Braun [?] and Anna Margaret Eckenroth, grandmother of the child.

Litzinger, John [?] Leonard, of Leonard Litzinger and his wife Magdalen, born September 20, 1777, baptized September 28, in the chapel; sponsors, John Kuhn and his wife Theresa.

Lorschbach, Catharine, of Henry Lorschbach and his wife Catharine, born July 28, 1777, baptized at the same time and place as above; sponsors, Joseph Eck and Barbara Spring.

Zweyer, Catharine Frances, of Stephen Zweyer and his wife Anna M., born September 15, 1777. baptized October 5, at Michael Sigfried's house in the Oli [*sic*] hills; sponsors, John Eck, Jr., and Catharine Sigfried.

——, George, of Louis, a black slave of Löscher's, and Cecily, born more than six months ago, baptized October 12, in the chapel; sponsors, Philip Burchart and Mary Butz for Gertrude Burchart.

Edelblut, William Peter, of James Edelblut and his non-Catholic wife, Catharine Elizabeth, born in Georgia August 12, 1777, baptized October 15, in the chapel; sponsors, William Peter Strupel and Magdalen Butz.

Hammerstein [the first three letters are blurred, but in the Marriage Register, 1775, February 20, they are clear enough], Catharine Elizabeth, of Andrew Hammerstein and his wife Anna Barbara, born August 18, 1777, baptized October 19, at Edward Carty's house at Haycock; sponsors, Joseph Rösner and his wife, maternal grandparents of the child.

Kreyss, William Peter, of Martin Kreyss and his wife Catharine, born September 27, 1777, baptized November 1, in the chapel; sponsors, Peter Struppel and Margaret Schmitt.

Gibson, M. Gertrude, of Henry Gibson and his wife Catharine, born November 21, 1777, baptized November 23, in the chapel; sponsors, Nicholas Röhr and Gertrude Schmitt.

Fiderer, Peter, of Stephen Fiderer and his wife ——, born November 30, 1777, baptized December 7, at Reading; sponsors, Peter Rüttner and Susanna Haffner.

Schimpfessel, M. Elizabeth, of Andrew Schimpfessel and his wife Margaret, born May 9, 1777, baptized at the same time and place as above; sponsors, John Grett and M. Elizabeth Schimpfessel [sic].

Zweyer, Joseph, of Anthony Zweyer and his wife Catharine, born November 30, 1777, baptized November [ought perhaps to read December] 8, at Michael Sigfried's house in the Oli [sic] hills; sponsors, Joseph Zweyer, the father's brother, and Juliana Zweyer, grandmother of the child.

Flower, Catharine, of Henry Flower and his wife Rosina, born November 27, 1777, baptized at the same time and place as above, sponsors, John La Fleur and his wife Catharine.

Derham, John, of Catharine Derham [father's name not given], born May 11, 1777, baptized December 21, at Edward Carty's house at Haycock; sponsors, Nicholas and Albertina Carty.

Kohl, Maria Barbara, of Joseph Kohl and his wife Margaret, born December 16, 1777, baptized at the same time and place as above; sponsors, George Kohl and his wife M. Barbara, grandparents of the child.

[The baptisms for the year number fifty-five.]

BAPTISMS FOR THE YEAR 1778.

Haffner, John Michael, of Frederick Haffner and his wife Barbara, born during Mass and a little before he was baptized, baptized February 10, at his father's house at Reading ; sponsors, John Michael Rüttner and his wife Catharine.

Rösner, Anna Elizabeth, of John Rösner and his wife Catharine, born January 28, 1778, baptized February 8, at Edward Carty's house at Haycock hill ; sponsors, Simon Hönig and Anna Elizabeth Ziegenfuss.

Kuhn, Elizabeth, of Henry Kuhn and his wife Margaret, born March 1, during the dinner hour, baptized March 2, 1778, in her father's house at Weithendael or Saltzburg ; sponsors, Joseph Kuhn and Elizabeth Wider.

Walker, Susanna, wife of William Walker, a blacksmith, twenty years of age, both belonging, it is said, to the Pietists [that is Presbyterians], lying ill of the small-pox, but in the full use of her senses, she desired baptism and received it March 3, in her husband's house at Christian Butz's iron mines [*ferrifodina*].

Walker, George Christian, of William Walker and his wife Susanna, born March 27, 1777, baptized at the same time and place as above ; sponsors, Christian Butz and his wife.

Hartmann, Abraham Frederick, of Francis Hartmann and his wife Angela, born January 6, 1778, baptized March 8, in the chapel ; sponsors, Fred. Brand and his wife Magdalen.

Kuhn, Anna Margaret, of John Kuhn and his wife Catharine, born February 21, 1778, baptized March 15, at Christian Henrich's house at *Asperum Collem* ; sponsors, George Eckenroth and Anna Margaret Eckenroth, grandmother of the child.

Henrich, Anna Magdalen, of John Henrich and his wife Mary Barbara, born February 26, 1778, baptized at the same time and place as above; sponsors, Louis Keffer and Magdalen Henrich.

Braun, John Conrad, of Andrew Braun and his wife Rachel, born February 26, 1778, baptized at the same time and place as above ; sponsors, Conrad Bevertz and his wife Anna Margaret.

Chaumont, John, of John Chaumont and his wife Anna Maria, born January 16, 1778, baptized April 5, at Reading ; sponsors, Thomas Thum and Catharine Rüttner.

Grett, Magdalen, of Michael Grett and his wife Catharine, born January 13, 1778 baptized April 12, in the chapel ; sponsors, John Hartmann and Magdalen Keffer.

Allen, William John, of John Allen and his wife Eleanor, born February 1, 1778, baptized April 21, at the "villa" [country seat?] of Mr. Joseph Caüffmann; sponsors, Mr Joseph Caüffman and his wife Mary Caüffmann [perhaps more correctly Kauffman].

Kohl, Catharine, of George Bernard Kohl and his wife Catharine, born March 20, 1778, baptized April 25, at Edward Carty's house at Haycock ; sponsors, Nicholas Carty and his wife Albertina.

Wingert, Theresa, of Joseph Wingert and his wife Anna Elizabeth, born February 22, 1778, baptized April 26, at Edward Carty's house ; sponsors, Matt. Krämer and Anna Catharine Demùth,

Krämer, Joseph, of Matthias Krämer and his wife M. Catharine, born January 22, 1778, baptized at the same time and place as above ; sponsors, Joseph Wingert and Anna Catharine Demùth.

Demuth, M. Catharine, of James Demuth and his wife Anna Catharine, born November 8, 1777, baptized at the same time and place as above ; sponsors, Joseph Wingert and M. Catharine Krämer.

Schmitt, John William, of William Schmitt and his wife Mary, six years old, baptized April 27, 1778, at Nicholas Hucki's house ; sponsors, John William Miller and Elizabeth Miller.

Weber, Matthias, of Matthias Weber and his wife Magdalen, born April 17, 1778, baptized May 17, at Christian Henrich's house at *Asperum Collem* ; sponsors, Matthias Riffel and Magdalen Henrich.

Derr, James, of John Derr and his wife Margaret, born March 7, 1778, baptized at same time and place as above ; sponsors, James Spring and his wife Catharine.

Gaucker, Anna Barbara, of John Gaucker and his wife Anna Barbara, born May 18, 1778, baptized May 28, in the chapel ; sponsors, John Eck and Anna Barbara Heitz.

Kuntz, John Henry, of John Kuntz and his wife Catharine, born April 6, 1778, baptized June 1, at Henry Kuhn's house ; sponsors, Henry Kuhn and his wife Margaret.

Schot, Joseph, of Philip Schot and his wife Catharine, born November 21, 1778 [error for 1777?], ceremonies supplied June 7 ; sponsors, Joseph Wingert and Catharine Butz.

Keffer, John Louis, of Peter Keffer and his wife Barbara, born May 26, 1778, baptized June 7 ; sponsors, Louis and Margaret Hoffmann.

Kupser, M. Elizabeth, of James Kupser and his wife Catharine, born June 5, 1778, baptized June 8 ; sponsors, George Kientz and Maria Fraul.

Kuhn, Mary Magdalen, of John Kuhn and his wife Theresa, born May 22, 1778, baptized at the same time and place as above; sponsors, James Kuhn and his wife Magdalen.

Rüttner, John, of Michael Rüttner and his wife Catharine, born May 22, 1778, baptized June 14, at Reading; sponsors, Sebastian Altgayer and Catharine Rüttner.

Ofer, M Elizabeth, of Frank Ofer and his wife Mary Ann, born November 24, 1778, baptized at the same time and place as above; sponsors, Adam Zweyer and Eva Zweyer.

Fasser, William, of Charles Fasser and Margaret Walter, born October 9, 1777, baptized June 15, at James Walter's house, at the iron mines at Readingtown [sic] furnace [fornace]; sponsors, James Weissenburger and his sister Anna M. Weissenburger.

Johns, Joseph, of Edward Johns and his wife Mary, born November 13, 1777, baptized at the same time and place as above; sponsors, James Weissenburger and his sister Catharine.

Foy, James, of Henry Foy and his wife Sarah, born January 16, 1778, baptized at the same time and place as above; sponsors, James Walter and Frances Walter.

Wurtzer, Elizabeth, of George Wurtzer and his wife Eva, born January 20, 1777 [?], baptized June 21, at Ed. Carty's house; sponsors, George Bernard Kohl and his wife Catharine.

Strunck, Henry, of William Strunck, non-Catholic, and his wife Elizabeth, Catholic, born July 27, 1778, baptized August 9, in the chapel; sponsors, Henry Gibson and his wife Catharine.

Ruffner, Magdalen, of Christian Ruffner and his wife M. Odilia, born August 11, 1778, baptized August 30, at his father's house near the Blue mountains; sponsors, Peter Käss and his wife Margaret.

Norbeck, Catharine, of John Norbeck and his wife Rosina, born August 19, 1778, baptized September 13, in the chapel; sponsors, Stephen Reppert and Catharine, maternal grandparents of the child.

Eck, Anna Maria, of Joseph Eck and Anna M. Eck, born August 17, 1778, baptized September 15, in the chapel; sponsors, Andrew Deprè and Anna M. Eck.

Henrich, John, of Philip Henrich and his wife Elizabeth, born August —, 1778, baptized September 20, at Christian Henrich's house at *Asperum Collem;* sponsors [space blank].

Hild, John, of Joseph Hild and his wife, Albertina, born September 25, 1778, baptized September 27, in the chapel; sponsors, John Kientz and his sister, Catharine (*germani*).

Gerschweiler, M. Elizabeth, of Philip Gerschweiler and his wife Catharine, born August 15, 1778, baptized October 4, at Reading ; sponsors, John Becker and M. Elizabeth Schimpfessl.

Arentz, Magdalen, of James Arentz and his wife Margaret, born October 2, 1778, baptized October 12, in the chapel ; sponsors, Caspar Schmitt and Margaret Kuhn.

Adams, Anna Maria, of Simon Adams and his wife Catharine, born September 30, 1778, baptized October 14, in the chapel ; sponsors, Theodore Eck and Anna Maria Adams.

Els, M. Frederica, of John Frederick Els and his wife M. Elizabeth, born October 12, 1778, baptized October 17, in the chapel ; sponsors, John William Butz and Catharine Butz, wife of Christian Butz.

Carty, Mary Albertina, of Nicholas Carty and his wife Albertina, born September 26, 1778, baptized October 18, at her father's house, at Haycock ; sponsors, Anthony Grüser, Jr., and Mary Carty.

Finck, Elizabeth, of Nicholas Finck and his wife Agnes, born January 6, 1778, baptized at the same time and place as above ; sponsors, George Bernard Kohl and his wife Catharine Kohl.

Riffel, George James, of John Joseph Riffel and his wife Margaret, born October 9, 1778, baptized October 25, in the chapel ; sponsors, Matthias Riffel and Ann M. Matthes.

Schönebruck, Elizabeth, of Caspar Schönebruck and his wife Margaret, born October 6, 1778, baptized November 8, at Matthias Brück's house, at Cedar creek ; sponsors, John Wider and Elizabeth Meckler.

Brück, Joseph, of Matthias Brück and his wife Anna M., born November 7, 1778, baptized at the same time and place as above ; sponsors, Joseph Kuhn and Anna M. Käss.

Reichart, Anna Mary, of John Adam Reichart and his wife M. Eva, born September 27, 1778, baptized November 15, at Christian Henrich's house, at *Asperum Collem* ; sponsors, Joseph Schnable and Ann M. Thum.

Lorenz, Christian, of Maurice Lorenz and his wife Apollonia, born October 14, 1778, baptized at the same time and place as above ; sponsors, Christian Henrich, Sr., and his wife.

[On this same page, 190, after the preceding entry there is what seems to be part of a record of a third baptism, conferred at the same time and place as above ; but with all in blank except three disjointed parts of sentences, namely, "fil" . . ., which may mean either son or daughter, "of Petronilla his wife, born," and then, that "this Petronilla was not present."]

69

Butz, Lawrence, of John William Butz and his wife Magdalen, born November 17, 1778, baptized November 21, in the chapel; sponsors, Laurence Gubernator and Mary Kuhn.

Strupel, John Henry, of Peter Strupel [*sic*, but elsewhere Struppel.] and his wife Magdalen, born December 4, 1778, baptized December 8, in the chapel; sponsors, Henry Norbeck, Sr., and Catharine Betz, Sr.

[The baptisms for the year number fifty-one.]

BAPTISMS FOR THE YEAR 1779.

Röhr, Henry, of Catharine Röhr, born December 27, 1778, baptized January 2, 1779, in the chapel; sponsors, Henry Gibson and his wife Catharine.

Grett John Adam, of Andrew Grett and his wife Elizabeth, born November 29, 1778, baptized January 17, at Christian Henrich's house in *Aspricolle;* sponsors, John Adam Finck and Magdalen Grett.

Billich, Petronilla, of Arnold Billich and his wife Petronilla, born October 10, 1778, baptized at same time and place as above; sponsors, John Henrich and his wife Barbara.

Grünewald, Anna Margaret, of John Grünewald and his wife Barbara, born December 7, 1779 [error for perhaps 1778], baptized January 31, at Matthias Brück's house at Cedar creek; sponsors, Peter Kass and his wife Anna Margaret.

Hert, John, of Frederic Hert and his wife Elizabeth, born eight weeks ago, baptized February 7, at Reading; sponsors, John Hert and his wife Elizabeth.

Felix, Catharine, of Nicholas Felix and his wife Anna M., born February 1, 1779, baptized at the same time and place as above; sponsors, Martin Felix and his wife Barbara.

Eckenroth, Christopher, of Henry Eckenroth and his wife Anna Barbara, born February 17, 1779, baptized March 21; sponsors, Christopher Eckenroth and Margaret Weibel.

Spring, Anna Maria, of James Spring and his wife Catharine, born February 2, 1779 baptized at the same time and place as above; sponsors, Joseph Schlosser and wife.

Fischer, Andrew, of Joseph Fischer and his wife Anna M., born March 1, 1779, baptized at the same time and place as above; sponsors, Andrew Grett and his wife Elizabeth.

Walker, Mary Juliana, of William Walker and his wife Mary, born April 2, 1779, baptized April 4, in the church; sponsors, John Becker and Juliana Sigfried.

Burchart, John Peter, of Martin Burchart and his wife Gertrude, born March 13, 1779, baptized April 5, in the church ; sponsors, Peter Keffer and his wife Barbara.

Altgayer, Joseph, of Sebastian Altgayer and his wife Catharine, born April 1, 1779, baptized April 11, in the chapel at Reading ; sponsors, Joseph Rüttner and Barbara Rüttner, maternal grandparents of the child.

Westemayer, John, of John Westemayer and his wife M. Odilia, born about Pentecost, two years ago, baptized at the same time and place as above ; sponsors, John Hert and his wife Mar. Elizabeth.

Sigfried, M. Agatha, of John Michael Sigfried and his wife Catharine, born April 9, 1779, baptized April 12 at her father's house ; sponsors Andrew Sigfried and his wife M. Agatha.

Zweyer, John Thomas, of Anthony Zweyer and his wife Catharine, born ——, 1779, baptized at the same time and place as above ; sponsors, Thomas Zweyer and ——.

Pike, Johanna, of Henry Pike and his wife Martha, born December 15, 1778, baptized April 19, at Edward Carty's house ; sponsors, Nicholas Carty, Jr., and Margaret Carty.

Langbein, M. Barbara, of Christopher Langbein and his wife Anna M., born March 12, 1779, baptized at the same time and place as above ; sponsors, Matth. Seiffert and Barbara Grünewald.

Sep, Regina, of Michael Sep [sic, may be Zip, or Zipp, as elsewhere], and his wife Margaret, born nine weeks ago, baptized April 25, in the church ; sponsors, Hillard Klee and Regina Kemmel.

Dapper [perhaps better Tapper, as elsewhere frequently], Catharine, of Andrew Dapper and his wife Maria, born April 2, 1779, baptized at the same time and place as above ; sponsors, Bernard Riffel and Margaret Gibson.

Norbeck, John Henry, of James Norbeck and his wife Maria, born April 3, 1779, baptized May 2, at Michael Sigfried's house, in the Oley hills ; sponsors, Henry Norbeck and his wife, grandparents of the child.

Hill, Christina, of Jeremias Hill and his wife Susan, non-Catholics, born February 24, 1777, baptized May 16, at Christian Henrich's house, at *Aspricollem ;* sponsors, Andrew Grett, Sr., and his wife Magdalen.

Muthart, John, of Frederick Muthart, non-Catholic, and his wife Magdalen, Catholic, born April 30, 1779, baptized May 21, in the church; sponsors, John Hartman and his wife [?] M. Deprè.

Keffer, M. Barbara, of Matthias Keffer and his wife M. Eva, born April 29, 1779, baptized May 13, in the church ; sponsors, Peter Keffer and his wife M. Barbara.

71

Meyer, John James, of Caspar Meyer and his wife Catharine, born May 3 [or 13 ?], 1799, baptized at the same time and place as above; sponsors, Frederick Nester and his wife, grandparents of the child.

Maison, Peter, of Peter Maison and his wife Elizabeth, born February 21, 1779, baptized June 20, at Edward McCarty's house; sponsors, Christopher Machel and wife.

Wurtzer, Regina, of George Wurtzer and his wife Eva, born October 28, 1778, baptized at the same time and place as above; sponsors, Nicholas Carty and his wife Albertina.

Kemp, John Frederick, of John Kemp and his wife Anna, born March 2, 1779, baptized at the same time and place as above; sponsors, Frederick Brand and his wife Magdalen.

Ruffner, George Adam, of Philip Ruffner and his wife M. Eva, born February 6, 1779, baptized July 5, at Christian Ruffner's house; sponsors, George Adam Ruffner and his wife Mary.

Schlosser, George James, of Joseph Schlosser and his wife Anna Margaret [or Mary ?], born June 6, 1779, baptized June 18 [then follow the figures "1778" an error evidently for 1779], in Christian Henrich's house; sponsors, George Riffel and his wife Barbara.

Lampert, John James, of James Lampert [perhaps better Lambert], and his wife Dorothy, born July 29, 1779, baptized August 1, at Reading; sponsors, James Reiter and wife.

Miller, M. Magdalen, of Philip Miller and his wife Catharine, born August 11, 1779 baptized August 14, in the church; sponsors, Joseph Riffel and his wife Margaret.

Gibson, Henry, of Henry Gibson and his wife Catharine, born August 14, 1779, baptized August 22, in the chapel; sponsors, Henry Norbeck and his wife Catharine.

Kuntz, Susan, of John Kuntz and his wife Catharine, born June 24, 1779 [? the last numeral in the year is indistinct], baptized August 29, at Cedar creek; sponsors, Matthias Brück and his wife Mary.

Käss, Joseph, of Peter Käss and his wife Margaret, born August 3, 1779, baptized at the same time and place as above; sponsors, Joseph Khun [error for Kuhn?] and Anna M. Adams.

Litzinger, Anna Maria, of Leonard Litzinger and his wife Magdalen, born September 8, 1779, baptized September 12, in the chapel; sponsors, Joseph Uhlein and M. Eck.

Finck, John, of Henry Finck and his wife Magdalen, born July 24, 1779, baptized September 19, at Christian Henrich's house at *Asperum Collem*; sponsors, John Henrich and his wife Barbara.

Beverts, Catharine Margaret, of Conrad Beverts and his wife Margaret, born August 7, 1779, baptized at the same time and place as above; sponsors, James Spring and his wife Catharine.

Struppel, John Daniel, of Henry Struppel and his wife, born August 27, 1779, baptized September 27, in the chapel; sponsors, Daniel Norbeck and Catharine Butz.

Braun, Francis, of Andrew Braun and his wife Regina, or Rachel, born September 12, 1779, baptized at the same time and place as above; sponsors, Frederick Brand and his wife Magdalen.

Chaumon [but seems it should read Chaumont, as in entry for April 5, 1778], Elizabeth, of John Chaumon and his wife Anna Maria, born July 17, 1779, baptized October 3, at Reading; sponsors, Joseph Rüttner and Barbara, grandparents of the child.

————, Louis, of Louis, a black slave, and his wife Cecily, born on Ascension Day, 1779, baptized October 13, at Michael Sigfried's house, in Oley hills; sponsors, Michael Sigfried and his wife Justina.

Hammerstein, Albertina, of Andrew Hammerstein and his wife Barbara, born September 17, 1779, baptized October 17, at Edward Carty's house at Haycock; sponsors, Nicholas Carty and his wife Albertina.

Ruffner, M. Magdalen, of George Adam Ruffner and his wife Mary, born September 3, 1779, baptized October 18, at Nicholas Hucki's house; sponsors, Philip Ruffner and his wife Eva.

Kugler, John, of John Kugler and Mary Schneider, born two years and a half ago, baptized at the same time and place as above; sponsors, James Depre and his wife Elizabeth.

Molsberger, Susanna, of James Molsberger and his wife Catharine, born on St. Matthew's Day, 1779, baptized November 1, in the chapel; sponsors, Joseph Riffel and his wife Margaret.

Schärtel, Catharine, of Rosina Schärtel, born — weeks ago, baptized at the same time and place as above; sponsors, Michael Hofman and his wife Catharine.

Kuhn, Henry Matthias, of Henry Kuhn and his wife Margaret, born November 6, 1779, baptized November 7, in his father's house; sponsors, Matthias Brück and his wife Mary.

Krafft, James, of Michael Krafft and his wife Elizabeth, born November 12, 1779, baptized November 14, in the chapel; sponsors, James Kupser and his wife Catharine.

Butz, Augustine, of John William Butz and his wife Magdalen, born December 10, 1779, baptized December 15, in the priest's room on account of the cold; sponsors, Henry Godfrey and M. Elizabeth Struppel.

Hild, Joseph, of Joseph Hild and his wife Albertina, born December 9, 1779, baptized December 17, in the priest's room on account of the cold ; sponsors, Joseph Hild, grandfather, and Margaret Kientz, maternal grandmother of the child.

Lanzinger [elsewhere written Lenzinger, as in entry for April 21, 1777], Nicholas, of James Lanzinger and his wife Salome, born November 4, 1779, baptized December 19, at Edward Carty's house at Haycock ; sponsors, Nicholas Bock and his wife Elizabeth.

Kohl, John James, of Joseph Kohl and his wife Margaret, born December 4, 1779, baptized at the same time and place as above ; sponsors, James Deprè and his wife Elizabeth.

Rösner, John Joseph, of John Rösner and his wife Catharine, born October 23, 1779, baptized at the same time and place as above ; sponsors, Joseph Kohl and his wife Margaret.

Klée, James, of Frederick Klée and his wife Christina, born November 23, 1779, baptized December 26, in the priest's room ; sponsors, James Walter and his wife Catharine.

[At the close of this entry Father Ritter notes that during the year, 1779, fifty-four children had been baptized.]

--- ---

BAPTISMS FOR THE YEAR 1780.

Schmitt, James, of John Adams [sic] Schmitt and his wife Margaret, born December 21, 1779, baptized February 2, in the chapel ; sponsors, James Arents and his wife Margaret.

Riffel, Magdalen, of George Riffel and his wife Barbara, born November 17, 1779, baptized March 5, at her father's house at Magunchi ; sponsors, Joseph Egg and Agatha Riffel.

Weber, Elizabeth, of Matthias Weber, and his wife Magdalen, born January 23, 1780, baptized at the same time and place as above , sponsors, Melchior Riffel and Elizabeth Dabber [perhaps better Tapper].

Henrich, Philip, of Christian Henrich, Jr., and his wife Magdalen, born December 18, 1779, baptized March 12, at his grandfather's house at *Asperum Collem;* sponsors, Christopher ·Eckenroth and his wife.

Henrich, Mary Barbara, of John Henrich and his wife M. Barbara, born December 14, 1779, baptized at the same time and place as above ; sponsors, Christian Henrich, Sr., and Margaret Henrich, grandparents of the child.

Grett, M. Magdalen, of Andrew Grett, Jr., and his wife Elizabeth, born January 15, 1780, baptized at the same time and place as above ;

sponsors, Andrew Grett and M. Magdalen, grandparents of the child.

Kientz, M. Magdalen, of George Kientz and his wife Anna Maria, born March 18, 1780, baptized March 21, in the chapel; sponsors, Frederick Brand and his wife M. Magdalen.

Gaucker, Catharine, of John Gaucker and his wife Barbara, born ———, baptized March 27, in the chapel ; sponsors, John Uhlein and Catharine Eck.

Schimpfessel, Margaret Barbara, of Andrew Schimpfessel and his wife Margaret, born December 4, 1779, baptized March 31, at her maternal grandfather's house in the Oley hills ; sponsors, Laurence Leple and his wife Margaret, grandparents of the child.

Hert, John Frederick, of John Hert and his wife M. Elizabeth, born February 11, 1780, baptized April 2, at Reading ; sponsors, John Westermayer [ante Westemeyer] and his wife Odilia.

Zweyer, Thomas, of Joseph Zweyer and his wife Catharine, born November 15, 1779, baptized April 3, at Sigfried's house in the Oley hills ; sponsors, Thomas Zweyer and Catharine Butz.

Henrich, Anna Maria, of Philip Henrich and his wife Elizabeth, born March 15, 1780, baptized at the same time and place as above ; sponsors, George Dietrich and Anna M. Weibel.

Kemperling, Elizabeth, of John Kemperling and his wife M. Cecily, born April 3, 1780, baptized April 9, in the chapel ; sponsors, Joseph Uhlein and Elizabeth Meckler.

Wingert, Susan, of Joseph Wingert and his wife Anna Elizabeth, born February 1, 1780, baptized April 16, at Nicholas Carty's house ; sponsors, Anthony Hucki and Catharine Hucki.

Klee, John Adam, of John Hilary Klee and his wife Regina, born April 5, 1780, baptized April 23, in the church ; sponsors, John Adam Schmitt and his wife Margaret.

Kuhn, George, of John Kuhn and his wife Catharine, born March 11, 1780, baptized April 30, at Matthias Brück's house at Cedar creek ; sponsors, Henry Kuhn and his wife Margaret.

Ruffner, Anna Maria, of Simon Ruffner and his wife Catharine, born October 12, 1780 [an error for perhaps 1779?], baptized April 30, 1780, at her maternal grandmother's house in the Blue mountains ; sponsors, Philip Ruffner, for his brother Christian, and the latter's wife M. Odilia.

Grett, Anna Barbara, of Michael Grett and his wife Catharine, born April 23, 1780, baptized May 4, in the church ; sponsors, John Gaucker and his wife Anna Barbara.

Reppert, John, of James Reppert and his wife Christina, born April 23, 1780, baptized May 14, in the church ; sponsors, John Norbeck and his wife Rosina.

Eckenroth, Peter, of Christopher Eckenroth and his wife Anna Margaret, born April 7, 1780, baptized May 21, at Christian Henrich's house ; sponsors, Henry Eckenroth and Elizabeth Eckenroth.

[With the above entry, on page 208 in the original, the baptismal records for this year come to a close, and are followed by the marriage registers, beginning with Father Schneider's, the first of whose is dated December 8, 1741. These have already been published in the second volume of the " Records " of this Society.] *

[The baptisms for 1780, as given above, number twenty.]

BAPTISMS FOR THE YEAR 1781.

[On page 295, Father Ritter begins his register of baptisms for the year 1781, as follows:—"*Baptizatorum a° 1781 a me Joanne Baptista Soc'tis quondam Jesu Sacerdote et Missionario per Americam Borealem,*" that is, " A registry of those who have been baptized by me, John Baptist, Priest of the former Society of Jesus and Missionary for North America." They are as follows :]

Huth, Elizabeth, of George Huth and his wife Elizabeth, blacks, born seven months ago, baptized January 14, 1781, at John Michael Sigfried's house in the Oley hills; sponsors, William Strack and his wife.

Huth, Elizabeth, negress, wife of George Huth, negro, twenty four years of age, baptized at the same time and place as above. [No sponsors named.]

Weibel, M. Theresa, of Joseph Weibel and his wife Margaret, born January 20, 1781, baptized January 21, at Christian Henrich's house at *Aspricollem*; sponsors, Philip Henrich and his wife Elizabeth Weibel.

Muthart, James, of Frederick Muthart, non-Catholic, and his wife Magdalen Hartmann, Catholic, born January 5, 1781, baptized January 28, in the priest's room [*in cubiculo meo*], on account of the cold; sponsors, Michael Grett and his wife Catharine Hartmann.

Huth, Benedict, negro, of George Huth and his wife Elizabeth, four years old, baptized February 3, at the " villa " [country seat?] of Mr. John Löscher at Oli; sponsors, Benedict Stalten [*sic*] and his mother Elizabeth Stalt.

MacGuchin, Henry, of John MacGuchin and Anna Maria Schmitt, born December 30, 1781 [*sic*], baptized February [day obliterated], 1781, at Reading in the chapel. [No sponsors named.]

---

*Pages 1-17, this volume.

Fricker, Mary Eva, of Anthony Fricker and his wife Eva Mary, born December 31, 1780, baptized at the same time and place as above ; sponsors, Laurence Leple and his wife Margaret, grandparents [?] of the child.

Felix, Regina, of Martin Felix and his wife Barbara, born December 31, 1781 [*sic*], baptized at the same time and place as above ; sponsors, Nicholas Felix and his wife Anna Margaret.

Adams, James, of Simon Adams and his wife Catharine Eck, born February 6, 1781, baptized February 11, in the priest's room, on account of the cold ; sponsors, James Kupser and his wife Catharine Hild.

Hoffmann, John, of Michael Hoffmann, Catholic, and his wife Catharine Barbara, non-Catholic, born January 28, 1781, baptized at the same time and place as above ; sponsors, John and Margaret Hoffmann, the brother and sister of the child's father.

Norbeck, Mary Apollonia, of John Norbeck and his wife Rose Reppert, born January 1, 1781, baptized at the same time and place as above ; sponsors, Maurice Lorentz, Jr., and his wife Apollonia Reppert.

Riffel, John, of John Joseph Riffel and his wife Margaret Matthes, born February 5, 1781, baptized at the same time and place as above ; sponsors, John Matthes and Anna M. Molsberger.

Kauffmann, Anna, of Joseph Kauffmann and his wife Barbara, born November 11, 1781 [*sic*], baptized February 12, at her father's house in the village [*pago*] of Providence ; sponsors, Frederick Brand and his wife Magdalen Kientz.

Walker, John, of William Walker and his wife Mary Sigfried, born February 17, 1781, baptized February 25, in the priest's room on account of the cold ; sponsors, John Hofmann and M. Elizabeth Struppel.

Flood, Anna Catharine, of Bernard Flood and his wife Mary, born February 19, 1781, baptized at the same time and place as above ; sponsors, James Weber and his wife Anna Catharine.

Walker, Daniel, 18 years of age, born in [New] Jersey, of no religion, knows nothing of any former baptism, baptized conditionally February 27, 1781.

Schönebruck, James, of Caspar Schönebruck and his wife Margaret Meckler, born a short time before, and just as his mother had left the chapel ; baptized March 4, at the house of one Bartholomew Kuhns, at Magunshi ; sponsors, James Spring and Barbara Meckler.

Ruffner, Elizabeth, of Philip Ruffner and his wife M. Eva, born November 24, 1780, anointed with the holy chrism and the ceremonies supplied on the same day as above, in George Riffel's house; sponsors, Matt. Brück and his wife.

Tapper, Christian, of John Tapper and his wife Elizabeth Wider, born December 30, 1780, anointed with the holy chrism and ceremonies supplied at the same time and place as above; sponsors, Christian Tapper and his wife Barbara, grandparents of the child.

Strunck, Philip, of William Strunck, non-Catholic, and his wife Elizabeth Weismiller, Catholic, born [number illegible, it looks like twelve] years ago ; ceremonies supplied February 27, 1781.

Braun, M. Barbara, of Andrew Braun and his wife Regina Gibson, born March 2 [?], 1781, baptized March — [figure obliterated], in the chapel; sponsors, John Gaucker and his wife M. Barbara Weibel.

Spring, John and Joseph, twins, of James Spring and his wife Catharine Fuss, born February 25, 1781, baptized March 18, at Christian Henrich's house at *Aspricollem ;* the sponsors for John were John Henrich and his wife Catharine Spring, and for Joseph, John Durr and his wife Margaret.

Lafleur, George, of John Lafleur and his wife Catherine Baur, born December 30, 1780, baptized April 1, in the chapel at Reading ; sponsors, James Lambert and his wife Dorothy.

Schluys, Thomas, a married man, twenty-four years of age, baptized April 2, in Michael Sigfried's house in Oley hills, he previously having made his profession of faith.

Keffer, John James, of Matthias Keffer and his wife M. Eva, who died April 15, on Easter Sunday, having given birth to her child on Good Friday, April 13, baptized April 19, in the chapel; sponsors, William Strunck and his wife Elizabeth Weismiller, sister of the deceased.

[In the register the following record is entered after the baptism of John James Kohl, on September 2 ; here it is placed where it belongs.]

Klee, Nicholas, of Ernest Frederick Klee and his wife Christina, born March 24, 1781, baptized April 15, in the church ; sponsors, Nicholas Hucki and his wife Catharine Demuth.

Langbein, Michael, of Christopher Langbein and his wife Anna Maria, born April 3, 1781, baptized April 22, at Nicholas Carty's house at Haycock ; sponsors, Nicholas Carty and his wife Abertina Kohl.

Butz, Magdalen, of Christian Butz and his wife Catharine Struppel, born April 24, 1781, baptized April 27, in the chapel; sponsors, John Cobele and Magdalen Butz.

Käss, Nicholas, of Peter Käss and his wife Margaret, born March 28, 1781, baptized April 29, at Joseph Kuhn's house at Cedar creek ; sponsors, Joseph Kuhn and his wife Elizabeth Tapper.

Kuhn, Margaret, of Henry Kuhn and his wife Margaret Wider, born April 26, 1781, baptized at the same time and place as above ; sponsors, James Käss and Mary Elizabeth Wider.

Ruffner, Elizabeth, of Christian Ruffner and his wife M. Odilia Kuhn, born December 6, 1780, baptized at the same time and place as above ; sponsors, Philip Ruffner and his wife Eva Hönig.

Burchart, John William, of Martin Burchart and his wife Gertrude Weismiller, born April 5. 1781, baptized May 3, in the chapel ; sponsors, William Strunck and his wife Elizabeth Weismiller.

Sigfried, Michael, of Michael Sigfried and his wife Justina, born May 1, 1781, baptized May 6, at his father's house, in the Oley hills ; sponsors, Thomas Thum and Anna M. Fraul.

Els, Sophia Maria Juliana, of John Els and his wife ——— Welker, born May 3, 1781, baptized May 8, in the chapel ; sponsors, Theophilus Welker, the grandfather, and M. Sophia Struppel.

Jung, John Adam, of ——— and Anna Jung, born eight months ago, baptized May 13, in the chapel ; sponsors, John Adam Schmitt and his wife Margaret.

Grett, James, of Andrew Grett and his wife Elizabeth Henrich, born April 20, 1781, baptized May 20, at Christian Henrich's house, near *Aspricollem;* sponsors, Henry Finck and his wife Magdalen.

Stahl, Bernard, of Adam Stahl and his wife Eva Mary, born April 7, 1781, baptized at the same time and place as above ; sponsors, John Henrich and his wife Barbara.

Röhr, Matthias, of Matthias Röhr and his wife Catharine Sigfried, born May 27, 1781, baptized June 10, at Reading ; sponsors, Joseph Röhr and Barbara Sigfried.

Everard, Elizabeth, of Philip Everard, soldier in the Third Pennsylvania Regiment, and his wife Margaret Peraut [or Perant], born May 22, 1781, baptized at the same time and place as above ; sponsors, Joseph Saintgerard and Elizabeth Settel.

Altgayer, Catharine, of Sebastian Altgayer and his wife Catharine, born June 10, 1781, baptized June 20, at Reading ; sponsors, Joseph Rüttner and his wife Anna Maria, grandparents of the child.

Felix, Anthony, of Nicholas Felix and his wife Anna Maria Stahl, born July 29, 1781, baptized August 5, at Reading ; sponsors, Ant. Fricker and his wife Eva.

Stantigel, Matthias, of Anthony Stantigel and his wife ———, born three weeks ago, baptized August 12, in the chapel ; sponsors, Matthias Weber and his wife Magdalen Büger.

Kluzki [Closkey?], M. Magdalen, of Anthony Kluzki [?] and his wife Eva Schnabel, born eight weeks ago, baptized at the same time and place as above; sponsors, Thomas Thum and ―― Schnabel.

Fricker, Nicholas, of Joseph Fricker and his wife Catharine Hucki, born June 21, 1781, baptized August 19, at Nicholas Carty's house; sponsors, Nicholas Hucki and his wife Catharine.

Keffer, Elizabeth, of Peter Keffer and his wife Barbara Hartmann, born August 18, 1781, baptized August 26 in the chapel; sponsors, Nicholas Bock and his wife Elizabeth Hartmann.

Reichart, John, of Stephen Reichart and his wife Mary Gauch or Gerich [?], born August 3, 1781, baptized August 27, in the chapel; sponsor, Eva Danckel, the grandmother.

Kohl, John James, of George Bernard Kohl and his wife Catharine Grüsser, born September 2, baptized September 6 [or 16 or 26], at Nicholas Carty's house; sponsors, John James Kohl and his wife Elizabeth Grüsser.

Williams, Peter, of Peter Williams and his wife Rebecca Croner, born August 12, 1781, baptized September 8, at Sigfried's, in the Oley hills; sponsors, Peter Würff and his wife Eva Kuhn.

Arents, George Adam, of James Arents, and his wife Margaret Schmitt, born September 2, 1781, baptized September 9, in the church; sponsors, John Adam Schmitt and his wife Margaret Norbeck.

Kientz, Catharine, of George Kientz and his wife Anna Maria Matthes, born September 2 1781, baptized at the same time and place as above; sponsors, John Matthes and Catharine Kientz.

Eck, Daniel, of John Eck and his wife Charlotte Knaus, born July 20, 1781, baptized September 23, in the church; sponsors, Joseph Eck and his wife Agatha Riffel.

Ruffner, Margaret, of George Adam Ruffner and his wife Maria, born September 9, 1781, baptized September [day obliterated], at Joseph Kuhn's house, at Cedar creek; sponsors, Margaret Käss and her husband Peter Käss.

Rüttner, M. Barbara, of Michael Rüttner and his wife Catharine, born the same day as above [September 9], baptized October 7, 1781, at Reading; sponsors, Joseph Rüttner and his wife M. Barbara, grandparents of the child.

Schimpfessel, M. Catharine, of Andrew Schimpfessel and his wife Margaret Becker, born August 18, 1781, baptized at the same time and place as above; sponsors, Louis Schimpfessel and his wife M. Catharine, grandparents of the child.

Hild, Frederic, of Joseph Hild and his wife Albertina, born October 3, 1761, baptized October 14, in the church; sponsors, Fred. Brand and his wife Magdalen Kientz.

Walker, Henry, of Daniel Walker and his wife Gertrude Schmitt, born October 10, 1781, baptized at the same time and place as above; sponsors, Henry Gibson and his wife Catharine Schmitt.

Canada, Anna, wife of Patrick Mac—gan, now living in Georgia in the town of Ringwood, in the county [?] [*Satrapia*] of Hunterdon, born nineteen years ago, baptized October 21, at Nicholas MacCarty's house at Haycock.

Maison, Adam, of Peter Maison and his wife Anna Elizabeth Straüss, born November 21, 1780, baptized at the same time and place as above; sponsors, Adam Machel and Catharine Machel.

Hammerstein, M. Magdalen, of Andrew Hammerstein and his wife Barbara Rosner, born September 18, 1781, baptized at the same time and place as above; sponsors, Joseph Kohl and his wife Margaret Depre.

Helffer, Mary Apollonia, of Christ. Helffer and his wife ———, born about eighteen years ago, baptized October 28, in the church; sponsor, Catharine Butz.

Gabriel, John and Mary Magdalen, twins, of ——— Gabriel and Mary Jung, born October 13, 1781, baptized at the same time and place as above; sponsors, for John, John Gaucker and his wife Barbara Weibel, and for Mary Magdalen, Maurice Lorenz and Eva Wagner, Widow Heitz.

Röhr, John, of Nicholas Röhr and his wife Mary Eysenbeiss [?], born November 10, 1781, baptized December —, at Reading; sponsors, Henry Norbeck and his wife Catharine Röhr.

Meyer, John Frederick, of Caspar Meyer and his wife Catharine Nester, born October 18, baptized December 9, in the priest's room on account of the cold; sponsors, Frederick Nester and Catharine, grandparents of the child.

Henrich, Mary Magdalen, of Peter Henrich and Catharine Wagner, born November 29, 1781, baptized December 16, at Nicholas MacCarty's, near Haycock; sponsors, Christopher Langbein and his wife Anna Maria.

Hartman, Simon, of Michael Hartman and his wife Margaret Hammerstein, born December 17, 1781, baptized December 23, in the priest's room on account of the cold; sponsors, Francis Hartman and his wife Angela.

[For this year there are sixty-six baptisms. In the register, at page 305, Father Ritter has numbered the last entry "69", but by reference to the numbers which he has affixed to the margin, one will note that he has omitted in his count the numbers 32, 33 and 60.]

81

BAPTISMS FOR THE YEAR 1782.

[The baptisms for the preceding year ended on page 305. The baptismal registries for 1782 begin on page 379, and are as follows, namely:]

Gibson, M. Barbara, of Henry Gibson and his wife Catharine Schmitt, born January 6, 1782, baptized January 13; sponsors, John Grünewald and his wife Anna Barbara Schmitt.

Eck [?], Catharine, of Joseph Eck [?] and his wife Agatha Riffel, born December 13, 1781, baptized at the same time and place as above; sponsors, Catharine Eck and Matthias Riffel Jr., ———.

Bevertz, John and Christian, twins, of Conrad Bevertz and his wife Margaret, born December 14, 1781, baptized January 20, at Christian Henrich's house; sponsors, Matthias Keffer and his wife M. Elizabeth Eckenroth, and Christian Eckenroth and Barbara Lorenz.

Schmitt, John James, of John Adam Schmitt and his wife Margaret Norbeck, born January 5, 1782, baptized ———; sponsors, Jac. Jacobus [sic] Norbeck and his wife Maria.

Litzinger, Anthony, of Leonard Litzinger and his wife Magdalen Kupser, born February 3, 1782, baptized February 3 [?]; sponsors, John Uhlein and Catharine Kemp.

Kohl, John George, of Joseph Kohl and his wife Barbara, born January 27, 1782, baptized February 7 [?], at Nicholas Carty's house; sponsors, J. George Hucki and M. Depre.

MacMalowne, Mary, of Lothi MacMalowne and his wife Elizabeth Hoffman, born January 25, 1782, baptized February 8 [?], at the same place as above; sponsors, Th. Carty and Catharine Carty.

Keffer, John, of Martin Keffer and his wife Anna M. Adams, born ———, baptized February 24, in the priest's room on account of the cold; sponsors, John Gaucker and his wife Barbara Weible.

Butz, Anna Sophia Juliana, of William Butz and his wife Magdalen Kuhn, born February 16, 1782, baptized at the same time and place as above; sponsors, Michael Kuhn and Anna Sophia Juliana Strubel [but written Strubl].

Hartmann, John Peter, of Jonn Hartmann and his wife Susanna Schartle, born December 24, 1781, baptized at the same time and place as above; sponsors, Peter Keffer and his wife Barbara Hartmann.

Tapper, Anna Maria, of John Tapper and his wife M. Elizabeth Wieder, born February 12, 1782, baptized March 3, at George Riffel's house at Magunshi; sponsors, Andrew Tapper and his wife Mary [or Margaret?].

Weber, Margaret, of Matthias Weber and his wife Magdalen Büger, born December 28, 1781, baptized at the same time and place as above ; sponsors, Christopher Büger and M. Elizabeth Isinger.

Finck, Benjamin, of Henry Finck and his wife Magdalen Henrjch, born November 8, 1781, baptized March —, at Christian Henrich's house at *Asperum Collem;* sponsors, Th. Thum and Magdalen Grett.

Henrich, John, of John Henrich and his wife Barbara Spring, born February 1, 1782, baptized at the same time and place as above ; sponsors, Jacob Spring and his wife Catharine.

Thum, Mary Eva, of Thomas Thum and Anna Margaret Eckenroth, born February 15, 1782, baptized at the same time and place as above ; sponsors, Christian Eckenroth and Magdalen Schlosser.

Bryan, ——, daughter of —— Bryan and his wife ——, born seven weeks ago, baptized March 31, in the chapel ; sponsors, William Butz and Margaret Stoll.

Ufer, John, of Frank Ufer and his wife M. Anna Zweyer, born September 13, 1781, baptized April 7, in the chapel at Reading ; sponsors, James Lambert and his wife Dorothy.

Gerschweiler, John Michael, of Philip Gerschweiler and his wife Catharine Schimpfessel, born March 25, 1782, baptized at the same time and place as above; sponsors, Louis Schimpfessel and his wife Catharine, grandparents of the child.

Zweyer, Daniel, of Anthony Zweyer and his wife Mary Driess, born February 25, 1781, baptized April 8, at Michael Sigfried's house in the Oley hills ; sponsors, Adam Zweyer and Barbara Sigfried.

Wurst [or Wurff], Anna Maria, of Peter Wurst [or Wurff], and his wife Eva Kuhn, born March 18, 1782, baptized at the same time and place as above ; sponsors, John Becker and Anna Maria Kuhn.

Zweyer, Justina Elizabeth, of Stephen Zweyer and his wife Anna Maria Stahl, born March 19, 1782, baptized at the same time and place as above ; sponsors, Michael Sigfried and his wife Justina.

Gaucker, James, of John Gaucker and his wife Barbara Weibel, born March 31, 1782, baptized April 14, in the chapel ; sponsors, James Welsch and Maria Eck.

Grieser, Elizabeth, of Anthony Grieser and his wife Rachel Gordon, born March 29, 1782, baptized April 21, at Haycock ; sponsors, George James Kohl and his wife Elizabeth.

Rösner, Magdalen Eva, of John Rösner and his wife Catharine Ziegenfuss, born April 8, 1782, baptized at the same time and place as above ; sponsors, Joseph Langbein and Eva Lorenz.

Ruhl, M. Anna, of Frederick Ruhl, and his wife Anna Maria Schorb, born April 26, 1782, baptized April —, in the chapel ; sponsors, John Els and M. Anna Schorb, grandmother of the child.

Ruffner, Elizabeth, of Simon Ruffner and his wife Catharine Grist [or Griff], born November 23, 1781, baptized May 5, at Christian Ruffner's house, in the town of Lehigh [spelled " Leheig "] ; sponsors, Philip Ruffner and his wife Eva.

Kuntz, Joseph, of John Kuntz and his wife Elizabeth, born March 27, 1782, baptized May 9, at Joseph Kuhn's house, at Cedar creek ; sponsors, Joseph Kuhn and his wife Elizabeth.

Hartmann, George, of Francis Hartmann and his wife Angela· Herb, born April 6, 1782, baptized May 12, in the chapel ; sponsors, Mich. Hartmann and his wife Margaret.

Kupser, Elizabeth Theresa, of James Kupser and his wife Catharine, born May 10, 1782, baptized May 14, in the chapel ; sponsors, Michael Krafft and his wife Elizabeth.

Klee, Anna Elizabeth, posthumous child of Hilary Klee and his wife Regina Cammel, born three weeks ago, i. e., April 28, 1782, baptized May 19, in the chapel, before Mass ; sponsors, Nicholas Hucki and his wife Catharine.

Becker, M. Magdalen, of John Becker and his wife Maria Kuhn, born April 21, 1782, baptized at the same time and place as above ; sponsors, William Butz and his wife Mary Magdalen.

Fischer, Anna Margaret, of Joseph Fischer and his wife Anna Maria Paul, born December 3, 1781, baptized May 26, at Christian Henrich's house, at *Asperum Collem* ; sponsors, Christ. Eckenroth and his wife Anna Margaret.

Keffer, M. Magdalen, of Matthias Keffer and his wife M. Elizabeth Eckenroth, born May 20, 1782, baptized at the same time and place as above ; sponsors, John Adam Eckenroth and Anna Magdalen Bevertz.

Lorenz, Eva Rose, of Maurice Lorenz and his wife M. Apollonia, born April 20, 1782 [or 1781 ?], baptized at the same time and place as above ; sponsors, John Norbeck and his wife Eva Rose.

Norbeck, William Peter, of Henry Norbeck and his wife Catharine Röhr, born May 2, 1782, baptized June —, in the chapel, at Reading ; sponsors, William Peter Struppel and his wife M. Magdalen.

Hert, John Frederick, of Frederick Hert and his wife Elizabeth Horn, born April 15, 1782, baptized at the same time and place as above ; sponsors, Frederick Haupt and Dorothy Haupt.

Penington, M. Anna, of Daniel Penington and Apollonia Hönig, born May 27, 1782, baptized June 16, at Nicholas Carty's house ; sponsors, Matthias Cremer and Anna Maria Creutzer.

Kemp, James, of John Kemp and his wife Anna, born ——, baptized June 23, in the church ; sponsors, Peter Keffer and his wife Barbara.

Molsberger, Margaret, of James Molsberger and his wife Catharine Schöner, born May 15, 1782, baptized June 23 in the church ; sponsors, Joseph Riffel and his wife Margaret.

Riffel, George James, of George Riffel and his wife Barbara Keffer, born June 2, 1781, baptized July 1, at his father's house, at Macunhi [sic]; sponsors, Joseph Lorenz, Jr., and Elizabeth Riffel.

Grett, Catharine, of Michael Grett and his wife Catharine Hartmann, born July 2, 1782, baptized July 15, in the church ; sponsors, James Hartmann and Catharine Kemp.

Krafft, Magdalen, of Michael Krafft and his wife Elizabeth, born June 27, 1782, baptized at the same time and place as above ; sponsors, Leonard Litzenger and his wife Magdalen.

Hess, George, of George Hess and his wife Anna Maria Baur, born May 20, 1781, baptized July 28, in the chapel, sponsors, Nicholas Grett and Anna M. Molsberger.

Reichart, Michael, of Adam Reichart and his wife, M. Eva[?], born July 6, 1782, baptized August 4, at Reading ; sponsors, Robert Kuhn and his wife Eva.

——, Elizabeth, of Louis, a black slave, and his wife Sarah, born one month and —— weeks ago, baptized at the same time and place as above ; sponsors, Conrad Welsch and his wife Elizabeth.

Grünewald, Elizabeth, of John Grünewald and his wife Barbara, born July 16, 1782, baptized at the same time and place as above; sponsor, Elizabeth Oppolt.

Usden, John, of William Usden and his wife Susanna, born March 11, 1782, baptized August 11, in the church ; sponsors, William Walker and his wife Maria.

Brück, Maria, of Matthias Brück and his wife Maria Kuhn, born August 25, 1782 [sic], baptized August 15, in the church ; sponsors, Matthias Riffel and Maria Käss.

Pycke [perhaps better Pike see baptism, April 19, 1779], John, of Henry Pycke [or Pike?], and his wife Martha Welsch, born February 28, 1782, baptized August 18, at Haycock at Nicholas MacCarty's house. [No sponsors named.]

[Two-thirds of the next leaf in the register, between pages 288–291, have been torn out straight down from top to bottom. On the remaining part are clearly distinguishable on one side fragmentary entries of six baptisms, which are as follows :]

85

(1.) ceremonies were supplied over George Wurtzer, son of George, born 1781.

(2.) on August 25, was baptized in the church a child of George Huth, born about the Feast of ———.

(3.) on September 1, 1782, baptized a child of Adam ———, born June 19.

(4.) baptized Anna [Mary?] daughter of ——— Ruffner and M———, born May, 1782.

(5) on September 15, 1782, baptized M. Eva, daughter of ——— and M. Eva Kan——— ; sponsor, Joseph Lorenz.

(6.) on September 24, baptized son of John ——— and his wife ———, born ——— 22, ———.

[On the opposite side of this fragmentary page are part entries that I am wholly at a loss to explain. What there is can clearly enough be read, namely, proper names with after some of them the letters "p. m.," and under some of them the numerals "1, 2, 3, or 4," sometimes singly and sometimes one under the other.

The names are Mart. Jos. Kuhn, Conr. Welsch, Eliz. Depre, Ant. Grieser, Eliz. Grieser, Ant. Langbein, Georg. Ruppel, Marg. Matthes, [the word] Majus, the widow Schmitt, Ann. M. Keffer, Jun., George Ruppel, Ant. Grüser, Barb. Reynart, John George Hucki, Ant. Hucki, Julii, Nicholas Hucki, Deprè and Grunewald.]

Everling, Anna Catharine. of Henry Everling and his wife Anna Fè, born September 26, 1782, baptized October 7, at the chapel in Reading ; sponsor, Stephen Fiderer.

Zweyer, John, of Joseph Zweyer and his wife Catharine Schorck ———, born July 5, 1782, baptized October 8, at Michael Sigfried's house in the Oley hills ; sponsors, Joseph Sigfried and M. Anna Ufer.

Reppert, Anna Christina, of Stephen Reppert and his wife Ursula Barbara, born October 8, 1782, baptized October 13. in the chapel; sponsors, John Kemp and his wife Anna Margaret.

Strunck, Margaret, of William Strunck and his wife M. Elizabeth, born August 31, 1782, baptized at the same time and place as above ; sponsors, John Joseph Keffer and Margaret Gibson.

Welker, John Theophilus, of John James Welker and his wife Helen Reicharts, born November 8, 1782, baptized November 10, in the church ; sponsors, Theophilus Welker, grandfather of the child, and Magdalen Kuhn.

Spring, John Adam, of James Spring and his wife Catharine Füss, born November 12, 1782, baptized November 17, at Christian Henrich's house near *Asperum Collem* ; sponsors, Conrad Bevertz and his wife Margaret.

Billich, John Arnold, of John Arnold Billich and his wife Petronilla Dupont, born October 17, 1782, baptized at the same time and place as
above ; sponsors, Conrad Spring and Magdalen Bevertz.

Edelblut, John Ferdinand, of James Edelblut and his wife Anna Catharine Strubl [sic], born November 22, 1782, baptized November 24, in
the church ; sponsors, James Welsch and M. Catharine Strubl.

Fiderer, Stephen, of Stephen Fiderer and his wife Catharine, born
November 2, 1782, baptized December 1, at Reading ; sponsors,
Sebastian Altgayer and his wife Catharine.

Sigfried, Anthony, of Michael Sigfried and his wife Justina, born November 7, 1782, baptized December 2, at Michael Sigfried's house
in the Oley hills ; sponsors, Anthony Zweyer and his wife Maria.

Röhr, Justina Magdalen, of Matthias Röhr and his wife Catharine, born
October 30, 1782, baptized at the same time and place as above ;
sponsors, Michael Sigfried and his wife Justina. [Some words here
worn away.]

Cobele, John James, of John Cobele and his wife Catharine, born December 1, 1782, baptized December 8, in the church ; sponsors,
James Welsch and Catharine Butz.

Spahn, Mark William, of Mark William Spahn and his wife Anna
Margaret, born October 28, 1782, baptized December 15, at Nicho-
las Carty's house ; sponsors, Joseph Fricker and his wife Catharine
Hucki.

[In the registry for this year the several entries have been correctly
numbered in order ; the last one is numbered " 69."]

BAPTISMS FOR THE YEAR 1783.

Cobele, Anna Catharine Philippina, of Daniel Cobele and his wife
Maria, born December 28, 1782, baptized January 1, in the priest's
room on account of the cold ; sponsors, Laurence Gubernator and
Catharine Butz.

Muthart, Anna Maria, of Frederick Muthart and his wife Magdalen, born
December 17. 1782, baptized January 6, at the same place as above;
sponsors, Michael Grett and his wife Catharine.

Adams, Catharine, of Simon Adams and his wife Catharine, born
January 4, 1783, baptized January 17, at the same place as above ;
sponsors, Joseph Hild and his wife Catharine.

Borge, Joseph, of Joseph Borge and his wife Anna M. Weibel, born
November 19, 1782, baptized January 19, at *Asperum Collem ;*
sponsors, Joseph Lorenz and M. Eva Weibel.

Röhr, M. Barbara, of Joseph Röhr and his wife Juliana, born December 30, 1782, baptized January 25, in the priest's room at home ; sponsors, Martin Röhr and M. Sigfried.

Lambert, John, of James Lambert and his wife Dorothy, born October 2, 1782, baptized February 2, at Reading ; sponsors, John Flower and his wife Catharine.

Walker, William Bartholomew, of William Walker and his wife Mary Sigfried, born February 21, 1783, baptized February 23, in the church ; sponsors, Bartholomew Cobele and Barbara Sigfried.

Walker, William, of Daniel Walker and his wife Gertrude, born February 20, 1783, baptized February 24, in the chapel ; sponsors, Caspar Schmitt and his wife Elizabeth.

[At this point in the register, follow the baptismal records for 1781 ; then, at page 307, the baptisms for 1785, and, on page 319, a list of converts for the years 1781-5, while on page 323 are continued the baptisms for 1783, as follows :]

Braun, Margaret, of Andrew Braun and his wife Rachel Gibson, born March 7, 1783, baptized March 13, in the chapel ; sponsors, Charles Struppel and Margaret Gibson.

Eckenroth, John, of Christopher Eckenroth and his wife Margaret, born November 24, 1782, baptized March 16, at Christian Henrich's house at *Asperum Collem;* sponsors, Christian Henrich and his wife M. Margaret.

Henrich, Elizabeth, of Philip Henrich and his wife Elizabeth, born February 9, 1783, baptized at the same time and place as above ; sponsors, Andrew Grett, Jr., and his wife Elizabeth.

Flower, Margaret, of Henry Flower and his wife Rose, born December 16 1783 [error for perhaps 1782], baptized at the same time and place as above ; sponsors, John Joseph Gallon and his wife Margaret.

Eckenroth, Anna Catharine, of George Eckenroth and his wife Anna Maria, born February 13, 1784 [*sic*], baptized at the same time and place as above ; sponsors, Christopher Eckenroth and his wife Margaret.

Schmitt, Catharine, of Joseph Schmitt and his wife Catharine, born ——, 1782, baptized March 19, in the chapel ; sponsors, Henry Gibson and his wife Catharine.

Kuhn, George Joseph, of Henry Kuhn and his wife Margaret Wider, born March 15, 1783, baptized March 30, at Joseph Kuhn's house near Cedar creek ; sponsors, Joseph Kuhn and his wife Elizabeth Tapper.

Chaumont, John, of John Chaumont and his wife Anna M., born December 14, 1782, baptized April 6, in the chapel at Reading ; sponsors, Joseph Chaumont and his wife Catharine, grandparents of the child.

Zweyer, James, of Thomas Zweyer and his wife Maria Schröder, born March 1, 1783, baptized April 7, at John Michael Sigfried s house in the Oley hills ; sponsors, Adam Zweyer and Barbara Sigfried.

Gordon, Maria, of John Gordon and his wife Sarah, twenty years of age, of no religion, baptized April 27, at Nicholas Carty's house. [No sponsors named.]

Hönig, John, of Anthony Hönig and his wife Salome, born March 1, 1783, baptized at the same time and place as above ; sponsors, Anthony Grüser and his wife Rachel.

Ruffner, Christian, of Christian Ruffner and his wife M. Odilia, born March 2, 1783, baptized May 4 [?], at Christian Ruffner's house in the Blue mountains ; sponsors, Peter Käss and his wife.

Ruffner, George Adam, of George Adam Ruffner and his wife Anna M.,· born February 7, 1783, baptized at the same time and place as above; sponsors, George Adam Ruffner, son of Christian, and Anna M. Ruffner, grandmother of the child.

Kientz, James, of George Kientz and his wife Anna Maria [elsewhere named Magdalen], born April 28, 1783, baptized May 12, in the church ; sponsors, James Matthes and Margaret Hofmann.

Hammerstein, M. Barbara, of Andrew Hammerstein and his wife Catharine, born April 18, 1783, baptized May 21, at the father's house in Nocanixon [sic] ; sponsors, Christopher Langbein and Barbara Grünewald.

Kuhn Anna Maria, of John Kuhn and his wife Theresa Fricker, born May 18, 1783, baptized May 25, in the church ; sponsors, Anthony Butz and Maria Butz.

Walton, John Joseph, of George Walton and Anna Rogers, born June 3, 1783, baptized June 13 in the church ; sponsors, Joseph Butz and Catharine Kuhn.

MacCarty, Margaret, of Nicholas MacCarty and his wife Albertina, born May 24, 1783, baptized June 15, at her father's house near Haycock; sponsors, Michael Hönig and Margaret MacCarty.

Kuntz, Christian, of John Kuntz and his wife Catharine Eysenhütt, born April 15, 1783, baptized June 29, at Joseph Kuhn's house near Cedar creek ; sponsors, Christ. Künstler and his wife Anna Elizabeth Schönebruch.

Hartmann, M. Magdalen, of Michael Hartmann and his wife Margaret Hammerstein, born July 6, 1783, baptized July 27, in the church ; sponsors, James Hartmann and Magdalen Muthart.

Reppert, Anna Catharine, of Stephen Reppert and his wife Magdalen Keffer, born July 4, 1783, baptized at the same time and place as above ; sponsors, James Keffer and Catharine Kemp.

Lafleur, Valentine, of John Lafleur and his wife Catharine, born June 11, 1783, baptized August 3, at Reading; sponsors, Valentine Gruber and his wife Margaret.

Schimpfessel, Peter. of Andrew Schimpfessel and his wife Margaret, born June 28, 1783, baptized [apparently, at the same time and place as above] ; sponsors, Peter Wurf and his wife Eva.

Fricker, William, of Anthony Fricker and his wife Eva, born April 9, 1783, baptized [apparently at the same time and place as above] ; sponsors, Peter Struppel and his wife Magdalen.

Strubel, Maria Anna, of Peter Strubel [perhaps better Struppel] and his wife Magdalen, born April 17, 1783, baptized [apparently with the above] ; sponsors, Anthony Fricker and his wife.

Lentzinger, Catharine, of James Lentzinger and his wife Salome Wagner, born July 26, 1783, baptized August 7 [or 17], at Nicholas Carty's house ; sponsors, Nicholas Hucki and his wife Catharine.

Fricker, John, of Joseph Fricker and his wife Catharine Hucki, born August 14 1783, baptized at the same time and place as above ; sponsors, Nicholas Hucki and Catharine Carty.

Carty, John, of Nicholas Carty, Jr., and his wife Elizabeth MacLone, born June 18, 1783, baptized at the same time and place as above ; sponsors, John Sweetmann and Catharine Carty.

Wurtzer, John, of George Wurtzer and his wife M. Eva Brennig, born May 10, 1783, baptized at the same time and place as above ; sponsors, John Carty and Catharine Hönig.

Eck, M. Margaret, of Joseph Eck and his wife Agatha, born August 8, 1783, baptized August 25, in the chapel ; sponsors, Matthias Riffel and M. Eck.

Riffel, Barbara, of Melchior Riffel and ———, born July 24, 1783, baptized at the same time and place as above ; sponsors, George Riffel and his wife Barbara.

Geyger, Catharine Frederica, of Conrad Geyger and his wife Philippina, born July 17, 1782, baptized at the same time and place as above ; sponsors, Christ. Butz and his wife Catharine.

Kuhn, Joseph, of Joseph Kuhn and his wife Elizabeth Dapper [elsewhere written Tapper], born August 10, 1783, baptized August 31, at his father's house at Cedar creek ; sponsors, Christian Dapper and his wife, grandparents of the child.

Hofmann, Michael, of Michael Hofmann and his wife ———, born September 6, 1783, baptized September 14, in the church; sponsors, George Kientz and his wife.

Els, John, of John Els and his wife———, born September 11, 1783, baptized at the same time and place as above; sponsors, John Cobele and Helen Welker.

Burchart, John Joseph, of Martin Burchart and his wife Gertrude, five weeks old, baptized September 28; sponsors, William Strunk and his wife Elizabeth.

Wurf, Michael, of Peter Wurf and his wife Eva, born September 21, 1783, baptized September 29, in the Oley hills; sponsors, Michael Kuhn and his wife Eva, grandparents of the child.

Bock, Magdalen, of Nicholas Bock and his wife Elizabeth, born September 24, 1783, baptized October 19, at Nicholas Carty's house at Haycock; sponsors, John Hofmann and Elizabeth Hönig.

Tapper, Elizabeth, of John Tapper and his wife Elizabeth, born October 12, 1783, baptized October 25, at Joseph Kuhn's house at Cedar creek; sponsors, Joseph Kuhn and his wife Elizabeth Tapper.

Lorenz, George, of Maurice Lorenz and his wife M. Apollonia Reppert, born October 26, 1783, baptized November 16, at Christian Henrich's house at *Asperum Collem*; sponsors, Joseph Schlosser and his wife Anna W.

Keffer, M. Elizabeth, of Matthias Keffer and his wife M. Elizabeth Eckenroth, born October 6, 1783, baptized at the same time and place as above; sponsors, Frederick Lutz and his wife M. Elizabeth.

Schönebruck, Mary Barbara, of Caspar Schönebruck and his wife Margaret, born October 25, 1783, baptized November 29, at Joseph Kuhn's house near Cedar creek; sponsors, James Käss and M. Barbara Meckler.

MacMalone, Elizabeth, of Lothi MacMalone and his wife Catharine, born fifteen weeks ago, baptized November 21, at Nicholas Carty's house near Haycock; sponsors, James Kohl and his wife Elizabeth.

Grüser, Anthony, of Anthony Grüser and his wife Regina, or Rachel, born November 17, 1783, baptized at the same time and place as above; sponsors, George Bernard Kohl and his wife Catharine.

Keffer, Elizabeth, of Peter Keffer and his wife Barbara, born December 11, 1783, baptized December 24, in the church; sponsors, James Welsch and Elizabeth Kemp.

[The baptisms for this year are fifty-three. In the register Father Ritter has numbered his entries on the margin as usual, the last one, on page 332, being marked "56." This is an error, as he has omitted number 28, and has counted number 35 as 37].

Eck, Anna Maria, of John Eck, Jr., and his wife Charlotte Kraus, born November 13, 1783, baptized January 11, 1784, in the church ; sponsors, Christian Kraus, non-Catholic, and Anna M. Eck.

Künstler, Anna Elizabeth and Margaret, twins, of Christopher Künstler and his wife Anna Elizabeth Schönebruck, born January 3, 1784, baptized February 27, at Joseph Kuhn's house at Cedar creek ; sponsors, for Anna, Matthias Riffel and Anna Elizabeth Mechl [perhaps better Mechler], and for Margaret, Caspar Schönebruck and his wife Margaret.

Bevertz, John, of Conrad Bevertz and his wife Margaret, born March 2, 1784, baptized March 21, at Christian Henrich's house near *Montem Acutum ;* sponsors, James Spring and his wife Catharine.

Hartman, James, of James Hartman and his wife Catharine Kemp, born February 29, 1784, baptized March 25, in the church ; sponsors, Stephen Reppert and his wife Magdalen.

Ruhl, Conrad, of Frederick Ruhl and his wife Margaret, born March 3, 1784, baptized at the same time and place as above ; sponsors, Conrad Welsch and his wife.

Zweyer, Adam, of Anthony Zweyer and his wife, born October 6, 1783, baptized April 2 [or 12], at John Michael Sigfried's house in the Oley hills ; sponsors, Adam Zweyer and Barbara Sigfried.

Hartmann, Daniel, of Francis Hartmann and his wife Angela, born February 25, 1784, baptized April 4 [or 14], in the church ; sponsors, Keffer and Susan Herb.

Rösner, Simon, of John Rösner and his wife Catharine, born January 30, 1784, baptized April 18, at Nicholas Carty's house at Haycock ; sponsors, Simon Hönig and Mary Ann Lorenz.

———, Charles, of ——— and Catharine Carty, born March 4, 1784, baptized at the same time and place as above ; sponsors, John Carty and Maria Creutzer.

Hess, George James, of George Hess and his wife Maria, born October 26, 1783, baptized April 25, in the church ; sponsors, George Molsberger and his wife Catharine.

Strunck, Catharine, of William Strunck and his wife Elizabeth, born March 23, 1784, baptized at the same time and place as above ; sponsors, Fr. Gibson and his wife.

Käss, Margaret, of Peter Käss and his wife Margaret, born March 6, 1784, baptized May —, at Christian Ruffner's house in the town of

Lehigh [written as usual " Leheig "] ; sponsors, Christian Ruffner and his wife M. Odilia.

Grett, Daniel, of Andrew Grett and his wife Elizabeth, born February 16, 1784, baptized May 16, at *Mons Acutus;* sponsors, Philip Henrich and his wife Elizabeth.

Weibel, Margaret, of Joseph Weibel and his wife Margaret, born April 30, 1784, baptized at the same time and place as above ; sponsors, Christian Ohrendorf and M. Eva Weibel.

Zweyer, M. Juliana, of Joseph Zweyer and his wife Catharine, born February 14, 1784, baptized May 17, at Michael Sigfried's house in Oley hills ; sponsors, Anthony Zweyer, uncle of the child, and Juliana Zweyer, grandmother.

Weber, Mary Barbara, of Matthias Weber and his wife Magdalen, born March [?] 2, 1784, baptized May 20, at Caspar Schönebruck's house, near Cedar creek ; sponsors, George Riffel and his wife.

Huth. Catharine, of George Huth and his wife Elizabeth, born December 2, 1784 [error for perhaps 1783], baptized May 30, 1784, in the church ; sponsors, Michael Hofman, Sr., and his wife Catharine.

Klitz [?], Mary Catharine, of Anthony Klitz [?] and his wife Maria Schnabel, born June 2, 1784, baptized June 6, in the church ; sponsors, Joseph Schnabel and Maria Busch.

Aaf [or perhaps better Auf, as in baptism, June 21, 1772], of Theodoric Aaf and his wife Elizabeth, born April 28, 1782, baptized June 20, at Nicholas Carty's house at Haycock ; sponsors, Joseph Kohl and Elizabeth Boch.

Gaucker, ———, of John Gaucker and his wife Anna, born June 24, 1784, baptized June 27, 1783 [an error], in the church ; sponsors, John Uhlein and Elizabeth Eck.

Reichart [?], Catharine, of Stephen Reichart [?] and his wife Maria Gerich, born May 28 [the only figures of the year that can be made out are 17—], baptized at the same time and place as above ; sponsors, William Reichart and Catharine Butz. [In the register the father's name is wholly rubbed out at this place, but seems to be the same as in the baptismal entry for August 27, 1781. An unknown party, in his desire perhaps to keep the loose folios in the old register from perishing, has at some time or other pasted them together and has done it very unskilfully. The paste has been allowed to overrun the manuscript and harden, then the effort to separate the leaves has resulted in wholly obliterating the writing. Moreover the pages have been misplaced as is evident from, first, the improper order of sequence in the baptismal entries and, secondly, from the non-correspondence of the numbers which Father Ritter has carefully and uniformly put on the margins of the several records. The preceding baptism is on page 336, the following one on page 341.]

Schmitt, Joseph, of Joseph Schmitt and his wife ——, born May 2, 1784, baptized July ——, at George Ruffner's house at —— in Macunshi ; sponsors, Joseph Jung and his wife Eva.

Hartmann, Catharine Frederica, of John Hartmann and his wife —— Schartl, born June 13, 1784, baptized July ——. in the church ; sponsors, Christ. Butz and his wife Catharine Strubl.

Keffer, M. Elizabeth, of Louis Keffer and his wife Magdalen, born July 19, 1784. baptized July ——, at Christian Henrich's house near *Asperum Collem ;* sponsors, Matt. Keffer and his wife M. Elizabeth.

Bur —— [?], Catharine, of Jacob Bur —— [?] and his wife M. Eva Weibel, born —— S, baptized at the same time and place as above ; sponsors, Conrad Allwein and his wife Catharine.

Fischer, Anna Maria, of Joseph Fischer and his wife Anna Maria Fischer, born March 5, baptized at the same time and place as above ; sponsors, Andrew Grett and his wife Magdalen.

Kupser, John James, of James Kupser and his wife Catharine Hild, born July 18, 1784, baptized July 25 [?], in the church ; sponsors, Andrew Braun and his wife Rachel, or Regina.

Ruffner, Maria, of George Adam Ruffner and his wife Maria Holstein, born May 16, 1784, baptized August 1, at Chr. Ruffner's house in Linn, near the Blue mountains ; sponsors, Simon Ruffner and Maria Käss.

Riffel, John, of George Riffel and his wife Barbara Keffer, born July 9, 1784, baptized August ——, in George Riffel's house ; sponsors, Bernard Riffel [or maybe Keffer], and Mary Keffer.

Schorb, Mary Magdalen, of John Schorb and his wife Elizabeth, born July 18, 1784, baptized August ——, in the church ; sponsors Joseph Eck and his wife Agatha.

Kohl, Michael, of George Bernard Kohl and his wife Catharine, born June 23, 1784, baptized August ——, in Nicholas Carty's house at Haycock ; sponsors, Michael Hönig and Catharine Carty.

[The following entries are found on pages 337–340 of the original :]

Cremer, Mary Ann, of Matthias Cremer and his wife Mary Schul, born June 24, 178-, baptized at the same time and place as above ; sponsors, William Strack and his wife Anna.

Kuntz, Helen, of John Kuntz and his wife Catharine, born June 21, 1784, baptized August ——, at Caspar Schönebruck's house near Cedar creek ; sponsors, John Tapper and his wife Elizabeth.

Brück, Theresa, of Matthias Brück and his wife Mary, born August 24, 1784, baptized at the same time and place as above ; sponsors Matthias Riffel and his wife Christina.

Kohl, Joseph, of Joseph Kohl and his wife Margaret Deprè, born August 31, 1784, baptized September 5, at his father's house near Haycock ; sponsors, James Kohl and his wife Elizabeth Grüser.

Reppert, James, of James Reppert and his wife Christina, born July 2, 1784, baptized September 26, in the church ; sponsors, James Keffer and M. Kemp.

Butz, Charles, of William Butz and his wife Magdalen, born September 29, 1784, baptized October 6, in the church ; [after the date " October 6 " follow two abbreviations, that seem to be " ined. 6tae," that I am unable to make out] ; sponsors, Charles Struppel and Elizabeth Kuhn.

Grett, Elizabeth, of Michael Grett and his wife Catharine Hartmann, born September 29, 1784, baptized October 10, in the church ; sponsors, Nicholas Bock and his wife Elizabeth.

Röhr, M. Agatha, of Matthias Röhr and his wife Catharine Sigfried, born October 5, 1784, baptized at the same time and place as above ; sponsors, Charles Struppel and M. Agatha Sigfried.

Power, Anna, of James Power and his wife Rachel, born May 25, 1775, baptized October 17, 1784, at Nicholas Carty's house at Haycock ; sponsors, Nicholas Carty and his wife Albertina.

Power, John, of the same parents, born March 3, 1778 [?] ; sponsors, John Sweetman and Elizabeth Carty.

Power, Catharine, of the same parents, born August 20, 1779 ; sponsors, Catharine Carty and Thomas MacCarty.

Power, Samuel, of the same parents, born October 31, 1782 ; sponsors, Simon Hönig and Mary MacCarty.

[These four children, as above, were baptized at the same time and place.]

Henrich, Anna Maria, of John Henrich and his wife Barbara Spring, born September 30, 1784, baptized November 21, at Christian Henrich's house ; sponsors, Conrad Spring and Catharine Sthaler [sic].

Reichart, John Philip, of John Adam Reichart and his wife Eva Thumm, born September 21, 1784, baptized at the same time and place as above ; sponsors, Phil. Henrich and his wife Elizabeth.

Luth, Henry, of Frederick Luth and his wife Elizabeth, born August 20, 1784, baptized at the same time and place as above ; sponsors, Christ. Eckenroth and his wife Anna Margaret.

Arentz, Philip Caspar, of James Arentz and his wife Margaret Schmitt, born December 2, 178-, baptized December 5, in the church; sponsors, Caspar Schmitt and his wife Elizabeth.

Langbein, Nicholas, of Christopher Langbein and his wife Anna M., born October 19, 1784, baptized December 19, at Nicholas Carty's house ; sponsors, Nicholas Carty and his wife Albertina.

Hönig, Elizabeth, of Anthony Hönig and his wife Sarah, born December 14, 1784, baptized at the same time and place as above ; sponsors, John Carty and Elizabeth Hönig.

Kerenz, Margaret, of John Kerenz and his wife Christina Cole, born November 11, 1784, baptized at the same time and place as above ; sponsors, James MacKuki [sic] and Catharine Carty.

[The number of baptisms for the year is given correctly by Father Ritter as fifty-one.]

BAPTISMS FOR THE YEAR 1785.

[The baptisms for this year are in the register at page 307.]

Braun, Henry, of Andrew Braun and his wife Rachel Gibson, born December 26, 1784, baptized January 1, in the church ; sponsors, Henry Gibson and his wife Catharine.

Gruber, Henry, of Valentine Gruber and his wife Margaret, born December 18, 1784, baptized January 9, 1785, at John Michael Sigfried's house in the Oley hills ; sponsors, John Joseph Gallon and his wife Margaret.

Zweyer, Anthony, of Thomas Zweyer and his wife Anna Maria, born October 27, 1784, baptized January 10, at the same place as above ; sponsors, Anthony Zweyer and his wife Anna M.

Kuhn, George James, of Henry Kuhn and his wife Margaret, born December 8, 1784, baptized January 30, at Caspar Schönebruck's house near Cedar creek ; sponsors, George Schmitt and Eva Käss.

Röhr, Frances, of Joseph Röhr and his wife Juliana, born February 4, 1785, baptized February 6, in the priest's room, on account of the cold ; sponsors, Joseph Sigfried and Frances Röhr.

Adams, John James, of Simon Adams and his wife Catharine Eck, born February 2, 1785, baptized February 13, in the priest's room, on account of the cold ; sponsors, James Hönig and Mary Eva Eck.

Kohl, James, of James Kohl and his wife Elizabeth, born February 5, 1785, baptized February 20, at Nicholas Carty's house at Haycock ; sponsors, Anthony Grüser and his wife Rachel.

Riffel, Bernard, of Melchior Riffel and his wife Margaret, born February 13, 1785, baptized March 6, at George Riffel's house at Magunshi; sponsors, Bernard Riffel and Mary Fries.

Dietrichs, Mary, of John Dietrichs and his wife Elizabeth, born March 7, 1785, baptized March 8, at her father's house; sponsors, John Kemperling and his wife Mary.

Eckenroth, Elizabeth, of Christian Eckenroth and his wife Anna, born February 25 1785, baptized March 13, at Christian Henrich's house at *Aspricollem*; sponsors, Joseph Schlosser, grandfather of the child, and Margaret Eckenroth.

Matthes, Catharine, of James Matthes and his wife Elizabeth, born March 7, 1785, baptized March 20, in the priest's room, on account of the cold; sponsors, George Kientz and his wife Anna Maria.

Korb, Catharine, of Adam Korb and his wife Margaret Luther, born October 28, 1784, baptized March 27, in the church; sponsors, John Dieterichs [*sic*] and his wife Elizabeth.

Reppert, John James, of Stephen Reppert and his wife Magdalen Keffer, born March 9, 1785, baptized March 28, at the same place as above; sponsors, James Keffer and Elizabeth Bock.

Krafft, John Samuel, of Michael Krafft and his wife Elizabeth, born March 3, 1785, baptized April 10, in the church; sponsors, John Uhlein and Elizabeth Kemp.

Walker, Agatha, of William Walker and his wife Mary Sigfried, born April 3, 1785, baptized at the same time and place as above; sponsors, George Fricker and Agatha Sigfried.

Fricker, Catharine Albertina, of Joseph Fricker and his wife Catharine, born February 24 1785, baptized April 17, at Nicholas Carty's house; sponsors, Nicholas Carty and his wife Albertina.

Spahn, M. Elizabeth, of William Spahn and his wife Anna Margaret Geyer, born March 24, 1785, baptized at the same time and place as above; sponsors, George Kohl and his wife Catharine.

Carty, Edward, of Nicholas Carty and his wife Albertina, born April 4, 1785, baptized at the same time and place as above; sponsors, John Sweetman and Maria Magel [or may be Mogel].

Duf, Catharine, of Cornelius Duf and his wife Maria Fernan, born April 1, 1773, baptized at the same time and place as above; sponsors, Catharine Carty and Anthony Langbein.

Duf, Samuel, of the same parents.

Duf, Anna, of the same parents.

Duf, Margaret, of the same parents; sponsors, Nicholas Schmitt and Catharine Fricker.

Gibson, John, of Henry Gibson and his wife Catharine Schmitt, born April 16, 1785, baptized April 24, in the church ; sponsors, John Kuhn and his wife Theresa Fricker.

Hert, Christopher, of Frederick Hert and his wife Elizabeth, born April 7, 1785, baptized May 8, at Christian Henrich's house at *Aspricollem;* sponsors, Christopher Flower and his wife Magdalen.

Schmitt, Johanna, of Nicholas Schmitt, surgeon, and his wife Elizabeth Fischer, born May 8, and being in danger of death was baptized at the same time by the father ; ceremonies supplied May 15, in the church ; sponsors, Laurence Gubernator, our schoolmaster, and his wife Johanna Darham.

Julein, Margaret, of Joseph Julein and his wife Magdalen, born May 19, 1785, baptized May 22, at the same place as above ; sponsors, James Hönig and Margaret Gibson.

Cobele, Henry Daniel, of Daniel Cobele and his wife Anna Maria, born May 29, 1785, baptized June 12, at the same place as above ; sponsors, Henry Gibson and his wife Catharine.

Zweyer, M. Apollonia, of Stephen Zweyer and his wife Anna Maria, born June 3, 1785, baptized June 26, at the same place as above ; sponsors, Peter Eck and Apollonia Matthes.

Schmitt, John Joseph, of Joseph Schmitt, weaver, and his wife Regina, born June 25, 1785, baptized July 10, at the same place as above ; sponsors, John Gaucker and his wife Anna Maria.

Hartmann, John, of James Hartmann and his wife Catharine, born July 16, 1785, baptized August 14, at the same place as above ; sponsors, John Kemp and his sister Elizabeth.

Muthart, M. Barbara, of Frederick Muthart and his wife Magdalen, born July 17, 1785, baptized at the same time and place as above; sponsors, Peter Keffer and his wife Magdalen.

Tul [the same apparently as Duf *supra*], Anna, of Cornelius Tuf and his wife Mary Ann, seven years old, baptized August 21, at Nicholas Carty's house ; sponsor, Elizabeth Krämer.

Tuf, John, of the same parents, ten years old, baptized at the same time and place as Anna ; sponsor, Juliana Kremer.

Hammerstein, Nicholas, of Andrew Hammerstein and his wife Catharine, born July 28, 1785, baptized with the two Tufs above ; sponsors, Nicholas Carty and his wife Albertina.

Aaf [perhaps Auf, as in baptism, June 21, 1772], Magdalen, of Theodore [elsewhere Theodoric, see baptism June 20, 1784] Aaf and his wife Elizabeth, born October 22, 1785 [an error for perhaps 1784], baptized along with the above ; sponsors, Leonard Bock and Magdalen Hönig.

Eck, Anna Maria, of Joseph Eck and his wife Agatha Riffel, born August 14, 1785, baptized September 4, at Joseph Kemp's house ; sponsors, John Uhlein and Elizabeth Eck.

Els, Elizabeth, of John Els and his wife Elizabeth, born September 2, 1785, baptized September 11, in the church ; sponsors, Bartholomew Cobele and Elizabeth Kuhn.

Keffer, Eva Rose, of Matthias Keffer and his wife M. Elizabeth, born August 10, 1785, baptized September 18, at Christian Henrich's house at *Asperum Collem ;* sponsors, Michael Hartmann and his wife Margaret.

Kemperling, Anthony, of John Kemperling and his wife M. Cecily, born September 25, 1785, baptized September 29, in the chapel ; sponsors, John Uhlein and Catharine Kupser.

Fricker, Magdalen, of Anthony Fricker and his wife Eva, born July 21, 1785, baptized October 2, at Widow Sigfried's house in the Oley hills ; sponsors, Laurence Lepplè [elsewhere more frequently Leplè] and his wife Margaret.

Zweyer, M. Margaret, of Anthony Zweyer and his wife Anna M., born September 3, 1785, baptized with the above ; sponsors, Balthasar Zweyer and Margaret Sigfried.

Kuhn, Judith, of John Kuhn and his wife Theresa, born September 28, 1785, baptized October 9, in the church ; sponsors, George Kientz and his wife Anna Margaret [or Maria].

Carty, Thomas, of Nicholas Carty and his wife Elizabeth, born August 31, 1785, baptized October 16, in Nicholas Carty's house ; sponsors, Thomas Carty and Margaret McCarty.

Bock, Mary, of Nicholas Bock and his wife Elizabeth, born September 15, 1785, baptized with the above ; sponsors, Andrew Grett and his wife Catharine Grett.

Matthes, M. Catharine, of John Matthes and his wife Anna M. Eck, born October 9, 1785, baptized October 23, in the church ; sponsors, Peter Eck and Apollonia Matthes.

La Fleur, Louis Henry, of John La Fleur and his wife Catharine Baur, born October 10, 1785, baptized October 25, in his father's house in the town of Maidencreek ; sponsors, Louis Henry Flower and his wife Rose.

McDoffee [Duffy?], Daniel, of Daniel McDoffee and his wife Dorothy, born October 17, 1785, baptized October 30, in Nicholas McCarty's house ; sponsors, Daniel ——— and Elizabeth Hönig.

Keffer, Mary Elizabeth, of Martin Keffer and his wife Anna Maria, born October 17, 1785, baptized November 2, in the church ; sponsors, Peter Keffer and his wife Anna Maria.

Henrich, John, of Philip Henrich and his wife Elizabeth, born October 11, 1785, baptized November 20, at Christian Henrich's house near *Aspricollem;* sponsors, Andrew Grett and his wife Elizabeth.

Spring, John George, of James Spring and his wife Catharine, born November 18, 1785, baptized with the above; sponsors, John Henrich and his wife Barbara.

Kientz, John George, of George Kientz and his wife Anna Maria, born November 13, 1785, baptized November 27, in the church; sponsors, John Kuhn and his wife Theresa.

Hofman [more frequently Hoffmann], James, of Michael Hofman and his wife Christina, born November 6, 1785, baptized December 8, in the chnrch ; sponsors, James Matthes and his wife Elizabeth.

Strunck, John, of William Strunck, and his wife M. Elizabeth, born October 22, 1785, baptized December 11, in the church ; sponsors, John Kemp and Margaret Gibson.

[Fifty-three baptisms are entered in the register for this year. Father Ritter counts only fifty-two, but has omitted the one at the bottom of page 312.]

[The sum total of the baptisms for the years 1765–1785 is nine hundred and twenty three.]

CONVERSIONS.

1781—1785.

[In the register the page is headed "*Conversi.*"]

Hamilton, John, and his wife Frances, Irish, and formerly members of the Church of England, make public ˙profession of faith, in the chapel, January 6, 1781.

Walker, Daniel, eighteen years of age, makes public profession of faith, in the chapel, February 17, 1781, and is afterwards baptized conditionally, since neither he nor his brother William remembers having been baptized.

Schlings [or may be Schluys], Thomas, a married man, twenty-four years old, makes public profession of faith, in Michael Sigfried's house, at Oley, April 12, 1781, and is afterwards baptized.

Schuhmacher, Catharine, betrothed to Joseph Schmitt, makes public profession of faith, in the chapel, April 14, 1781.

Klee, Christina, wife of Ernest Klee, makes profession of faith, in the church, April 15, 1781.

Schul, M., wife of Matthias Cremer, makes profession of faith, at Edward Carty's house, April [or June] 15, 1781.

Gordon, Rachel, wife of Anthony Grüsser, makes profession of faith, at the same place, August 19, 1782.

Stoll, Edward, laborer [*mercenarius*], and a married man [a word or two is here illegible, but seems to read, "rather an elderly man," *i. e.* "*prope senex* "], having renounced the Lutheran heresy, makes public profession of faith, in the church, December 22, 1782.

Strubel, or Struppel, Charles, unmarried, makes public profession of faith, January —, 1783.

Lusl [or maybe Lasl], Elizabeth, twenty years old, betrothed to John Schorb, to whom she is married the same day, makes public profession of faith, February 24, 1783.

Strunck, William, a Lutheran, father of several children, makes public profession of faith, March 16, 1783, the ceremonies of baptism being afterwards supplied. [This entry is signed "*Ego Jo'es B'p'ta Ritter.*"]

Hönig, Salome, wife of Anthony Hönig, born of church of England parents, makes public profession of faith, in Nicholas Carty's house at Haycock, April 27, 1783.

Schlauer, Cecily, makes public profession of faith, February 6, 1784.

Uhlein, Margaret, wife of Joseph Uhlein, makes public profession of faith, January 17, [1785?].

Reichert, John, makes public profession of faith, in the church July 25, 1785.

[Many conversions will be found recorded in the baptismal register, where Father Ritter entered them. Above under the specific heading "Conversions" there are mentioned only sixteen.]

MARRIAGES.

1765—1779; 1784—1785.

Litzinger—Kupser : October 8, 1765, in the church, Leonard Litzinger to Magdalen Kupser, both single ; witnesses, James Kuhn and James Kupser. [The entry of this marriage is signed "J. B. DeRitter," and is in the same hand as the entry ahead, for June 18, 1765, published at page 332 of Volume II. of the " Records."]

Hartman—Altendorff: October 29, 1765, in our church, Francis Hartman to Mary Eva Altendorff, the second marriage for both, residents of Rich valley hills; witnesses, John Eck and Henry Norbeck [signed "J. B. De Ritter"].

Lentzinger—Kohl : January 6, 1766, in the church at Gosschenhopen, James Lentzinger to Mary Salome Kohl, Widow Fricker; witnesses, Joseph Kohl, John Adam Schmidt, Albertina Kohl and Elizabeth Adams.

Gutlan [?]—Flower : February 12, in the church at Gosshehopen, John Joseph John [*sic*] Gutlan [?] to Margaret Flower, widow; four months previous had been married civilly by a justice of the peace.

Roth—Cremer : April 14, 1766, at Sigfrieds at Oley, Michael Roth to Anna Maria Cremer (Krebler), single, residents of the same place [Oley hills]; witnesses, John Ehrman, John Baur, Jacob Kuhn and Henry Gibson.

Bock—Hartmann : May 12, 1766, in the church at Gosschehopen, Nicholas Bock, widower and farmer, at Haycock, to Elizabeth Hartmann, single, daughter of Michael; witnesses, Joseph Lorenz, Jacob Kuhn, Magdalen Hartmann and Barbara Kuhn.

Lambin, or Langbein—Wanner : May 19, 1766, at the same place, Christopher Lambin, or Langbein, widower, to Mary Ann Wanner, single; witnesses, John Adam Schmidt, Michael Kraft, Anna Maria Riffel and Eva Kuhn.

Lorenz—Gibson : June 30, in the chapel, or church, at Gosschenhopen, Joseph Lorenz, carpenter, to Maria Gibson, single; witnesses, Jacob Kuhn, Henry Gibson, Barbara Kuhn and Mary Barbara Fischer.

Keffer—Weismiller : September 7, Matthias Keffer to Eva Margaret Weismiller, both single; witnesses, Theobald Miller, Louis Keffer, Elizabeth Miller and Eva Keffer.

Gibson—Schmitt : September 22, Henry Gibson, blacksmith, to Catharine Schmitt, both single; witnesses, Theobald Miller, John Adam Schmitt, Margaret Schmitt and Magdalen Bevertz.

Miller—Wenig : October 14, Theobald Miller, carpenter, to Catharine Wenig, both single; witnesses, Jacob Krupser [*sic*], Jacob Kuhn and Barbara Kuhn.

Kuhn—Eckenroth: January 18, 1767, at *Monte Acuto*, John Kuhn to Catharine Eckenroth, both single; witnesses, Christian Henrich, Adam Stahl, Magdalen Bibers [Bevertz] and Elizabeth Eckenroth.

[Father Ritter here observes, in a note, that all marriages are celebrated in the chapel [*Sacello*], unless otherwise noted, and that the preceding marriage at *Monte Acuto* was performed at Christian Henrich's house.]

Krafft—Adams: April 28, 1767, Michael Krafft to Elizabeth Adams, both Catholics and single ; witnesses, Simon Adam [sic] and Cathaiine Litzinger.

Löchler—Kuhn: June 9, in our church, John Löchler, of Philadelphia, to Barbara.Kuhn, both single ; witnesses, Henry Löchler, Jodocus Riffel, Eva Löchner and Eva Kuhn.

Tapper—Riffel: September 8, 1767, at Cedar creek, Andrew Tapper, of Sacone [sic, maybe Saucon], to Mary Riffel, of Makunshi, both single ; witnesses, Jacob Kuhn, Jodocus Riffel, Eva Kuhn and Magdalen Tapper.

Henrich—Beverts: September 20, at Magunshi, Christian Henrich to Magdalen Beverts, both single and residents of Allemängel ; witnesses, Adam Stahler and Maria Henrich.

Jütz—Grübler: November 9, 1767, at Sigfried's, in the Oley hills, Anthony Jütz, widower, to Anna Grübler, single ; witnesses John Adam Schmitt, John George Wants, Margaret Norbeck and Catharine Hild.

Schmitt—Nordbeck [perhaps better Norbeck]: January 12, 1768, in the church, John Adam Schmitt, twenty years of age, to Margaret Nordbeck, about seventeen years old ; witnesses, Philip Schmitt, James Norbeck, Margaret Schmitt and Mary Norbeck.

Kuhn—Tapper : May 3, Jacob Kuhn to Magdalen Tapper, both single ;. witnesses, Jacob Kupser, John Jodocus Riffel, Eva Kuhn and Elizabeth Tapper.

Stahler—Henrich : May 15, at Ph. Schmitt's house at Weissenberg alias Macungi, John Adam Stahler to Eva Mary Henrich, both single : witnesses, Phil Schmitt, Jr., Phil. Henrich, Margaret Schmitt and Margaret Henrich.

[On the same page (222) of the register at the top is recorded that Stahler on April 30, 1768, in the church, made public profession of faith and confirmed it by oath. Then follow the signatures of "Johan Adam Stahler," "Marten Matis" and "Antonia Gutz."]

Walter—Kuhn : September 13, 1768, in the church, by Rev. James Frambachs, Nicholas Walter to Mary Eva Kuhn, both single ;. witnesses, the groom's father, the bride's mother and step-father, etc.

Gruss—Nester : September 20, 1768, in the church, Jacob Gruss, widower, to Catharine Nester, single and fifteen years of age ;. witnesses, Andrew Nester, James Matthes [or Maerten], Margaret Mathes [or Maerten].

Kupser—Hild : October 11, 1768, in the church, Jacob Kupser to Catharine Hild, both single ; witnesses, Simon Kupser, Peter Wantz and Margaret Matthes.

Spring—Fuss: May 1, 1769, at Christian Henrich's house at *Monte Acuto*, James Spring to Catharine Fuss, both single; witnesses, John Adam Fuss, John George Spring and Margaret Schmitt.

Miller—Egg: November 6, 1769, by Rev. Luke Geisler, Martin Miller to Anna Egg, both single; witnesses, James Norbeck and Catharine Egg.

Miller—Rupert: at the same time, John Miller to Apollonia Rupert, non-Catholic, the second marriage for both; witnesses, John Grett and Anthony Grüser, with their wives.

Kamperling— ——: November 30, John Kamperling, shoemaker, to Anna Maria —— [it seems from the term "*conjugum*" after their names, that they had been previously married to one another]; witnesses, John Walter, Frederick ——, Margaret Matthes and Christina Weiler.

Gaucker—Weibel: February 27, 1770, John Gaucker to Mary Barbara Weibel, both single; witnesses, John Walter and Elizabeth Weibel.

Arents—Schmitt: April 22, 1770, in the church, Jacob Arents to Margaret Schmitt, both single; witnesses, Jodocus Riffel, Margaret Matthes, Gertrude Schmitt, etc.

Zweyer—Becker: April 23, at George Sigfried's house; John Zweyer to Eva Becker, both single; witnesses, all that were present.

Kuntz—Eysenhutt: October 9 in the church, John Kuntz to Catharine Eysenhutt, both single; witnesses, Philip Ritter and Mary Elizabeth Mensch.

Schuhmann— ——: December 30, 1770, in the father's house, Andrew Schuhmann to his cousin, in the third degree touching on the second; witnesses, the father, mother and whole family, together with some Catholics.

[Father Ritter observes that the above parties had previously been married civilly by a Protestant minister, and that he (Fr. Ritter) dispensed them from this said impediment in virtue of faculties accorded to him by his Reverend Father Superior, to use only in regard to those, who were converts to the faith, and that the bride in the above marriage was yet non-Catholic.]

Ruffner—Griffin: January 8, 1771, Simon Ruffner to Catharine Griffin, both single; witnesses, George Adam Ruffner, Simon Kupser, Margaret Kuhn and Maria Ermann.

Mayer—Kohl: April 22, at Nicholas Hucki's house near Easton, Simon Mayer to Elizabeth Kohl, both single; witnesses, all that were present.

Owings—Kuhn: May 14, 1771, Robert Owings of Conywaga [*sic*, may be Conewago] to Margaret Kuhn of this place [*qu.* Goshenhopen?], both single; witnesses, Joseph Riffel, John Kuhn, Margaret Matthes and Anna Maria Schöner.

Langhammer—Rittner : June 9, at Reading, George Langhammer to M. Barbara Rittner, both single ; witnesses, all that were present.

Danckel—Gerich : July 25, 1771, in the church, Jacob Danckel to Eva Gerich, the second marriage for both ; witnesses Jacob Kuhn, Joseph Hild and their wives.

Weissenburger—Carlin : October 15, 1771, the usual banns having been published for this marriage as well as the one that follows, Christian Weissenburger, single, to Anna Carlin, widow and non-Catholic ; witnesses, Jacob Weissenburger and the bride's sister.

Gantz—Miller: at the same time, John Gantz to Catharine Miller, non-Catholic, both single ; witnesses, Balthaser and Jacob Gantz and Margaret Walter.

Kohl—Grusser : November 20, at Carty's house, George Bernard Kohl to Catharine Grusser, both single ; witnesses, the groom's brothers and some others [the text has it, *" et non tot quin plures "*].

Schönebruck—Meckler : April 27, 1772, in the chapel, Caspar Schönebruck to Anna Margaret Meckler, both single ; witnesses, Elizabeth Schmitt and three other heretics [*Heterodoxi*].

Litzinger—Schmitt: April 28, in the chapel, Henry Litzinger to Anna Maria Schmitt, both single ; witnesses, Simon Adams and Francis Hartmann.

Riffel—Matthes : February 16, 1773, John Joseph Riffel to Margaret [a middle name here illegible] Matthes, both single ; witnesses, George Jacob Riffel, James Matthes, Catharine Hartmann and —— Reppert.

Schimpfessel—Becker: April 19, 1773, at Gossenhoppen, Andrew Schimpfessel to Margaret Becker, both single ; witnesses, Thomas Thum, Matthias Kuhn, Anna Maria Fraul and Catharine Sigfried.

Baur—Schmitt: May 3, 1773, Francis Baur to Elizabeth Schmitt, both single ; witnesses, John Adam Both and Maria Ermann.

Heitz—Wagner: May 6, 1773, Michael Heitz to Eva Wagner, for both the second marriage ; witnesses, Fr. Uhlein, Patrick Griffith, Mar. Griffith and Ursula Uhlein.

Riffel—Henrich: May 16, 1773, at Christian Henrich's house, at *Asperum Collem*, George Jacob Riffel to Elizabeth Henrich.

Henrich—Weibel: at the same time and place, Philip Henrich to Elizabeth Weibel.

Allwein—Weibel: at the same time and place, Conrad Allwein to Catharine Weibel.

[Father Ritter observes that all the parties to the above three marriages were single, and that the witnesses to the contracts were the brothers and sisters of both the grooms and the brides.]

Lafleur—Baur: August 17, 1773, in the chapel, John Lafleur to Catharine Baur, both single ; witnesses, all that were present.

Felix—Stahl: August 22, 1773, at the same place, Nicholas Felix, widower, to Anna Maria Stahl, single, both of Reading; witnesses, all that were present.

Spring—Keffer: September 19, 1773, at *Asperum Collem*, George Spring to Barbara Keffer, both single ; witnesses, Louis Keffer, John Henrich, Ann M. Keffer and M. Barbara Spring.

Fühler—Christ: October 17, 1773, at Haycock, Ulric Fühler to Barbara Christ, for both the second marriage ; witnesses, Anthony Grüser and many others.

Brücks—Kuhn: November 7, 1773, at John Joseph Riffel's house, at Magungi, Matthias Brücks to Mary Kuhn, both single, witnesses, John, Henry and Mary Kuhn and Anna Wider.

Brand—Ulrich: November 14, 1773, at Reading, at Mass, Peter Brand to Catharine Ulrich, both single ; witnesses, all that were present at the cermony.

Kohl—Grüser : November 24, during Mass, at John Eck's house in Rich valley, Jacob Kohl to Elizabeth Grüser.

Norbeck—Hornecker : at the same time and place, James Norbeck to Mary Hornecker.

Hornecker—Norbeck: at the same time and place, John Hornecker to Mary Norbeck.

[None of these couples had previously been married ; the witnesses were all that were present at Mass.]

Felur [or Felue]—Jund: January 9, 1774, John Felur [or Felue] to Anna Maria Jund, both single ; witnesses, the groom's brother and the others that were present at Mass.

Ruffner—Hönig : January 11, 1774, in the mission chapel [*Sacello Missionis*], Philip Ruffner, widower, to Eva Hönig, single ; witnesses, Anthony Hönig and Maria Ermann.

Brand—Kientz : February 8, 1774, in the mission chapel, Frederick Brand to Magdalen Kientz, both single and residents of Rockhill, Bucks county ; witnesses, Adam Schäffer, Adam Nagel, Catharine Egg and Albertina Kientz.

Schindler—Weissenburger : February 13, 1774, in the chapel, at Reading, Henry Schindler to M. Catharine Weissenburger, both single ; witnesses, the bride's brothers and sisters.

Gerschweiler—Schimpfessl : April [the numeral indistinct], 1774, in the chapel at Reading, during Mass, Philip Gerschweiler to Catharine Schimpfessl, both single.

Gantz—Miller : at the same time and place, Balthasar Gantz to Salome Miller, non-Catholic, both single ; witnesses to both marriages, the brothers and sisters of the several parties besides all that were present at Mass.

Schmitt—Meyer : May 12, 1774, during Mass, in the church, Anthony Schmitt, widower, to Catharine Meyer, widow ; witness, Peter Keffer.

Kohl—Deprè : May 23, 1774, in the church, during Mass, Joseph Kohl to Margaret Deprè, both single ; witnesses, all that were present.

Kemperling—Uhlein : June 28, 1774, in the church, during Mass, John Kemperling, widower, to Mary Cecily Uhlein, single ; witnesses, all that were present.

Dorst—Holler : July 10, 1774. in the Reading chapel, during Mass, Frederick Dorst, widower, and non-Catholic, to Catharine Holler, widow and Catholic ; witnesses, all that were at Mass.

[In a note Father Ritter adds that the groom tricked him with a forged license [syngrapho] bearing his employer's name, and that he [Ritter] was sentenced by the court [rerum capitalium Praefecto] to pay a fine of fifty pounds, which, however, was remitted on his showing the deceit practised, and, in a subsequent note, he relates that in the month of January, 1775, Dorst was found in the public square, at Reading, with his neck broken.]

Finck—Braun : August 21, 1774, John Michael Finck, widower, to Agnes Braun, single. [John William Pütz gives a bond of indemnity, Father Ritter observes, for the groom, who had been in his employ, but was now for two years freed from his service.]

Grett—Hartmann : November 15, 1774, in the church, Michael Grett to Catharine Hartmann, both single ; witnesses, Francis Hartmann, Andrew Grett, Jr., Anna M. Grett and —— Keffer.

Hammerstein—Rösner : February 20, 1775, at Edward Carty's house, at Haycock, Andrew Hammerstein to Anna Barbara Rösner, both single ; witnesses, Anthony Hönig, etc.

Kuhn—Fricker : April 25, 1775, in the chapel, John Kuhn to Theresa Fricker, both single ; witnesses, Henry Kuhn and Catharine Erman.

Haffner—Stahl : at the same time and place, Frederick Haffner to Barbara Stahl, both single ; witnesses, George Kientz, George —— and M. Ermann. [Signed] Jo'es Bapt'a Ritter.

Braun—Gibson: May 9, 1775, in the chapel, Andrew Braun to Regina Gibson, both single. [Witnesses not named.]

Weber—Zerfass: June 5, 1775, Matthias Weber to Catharine Zerfass, both single; witnesses, Henry Stättler, Henry Rösch and Catharine Hailmann.

Deprè—Hucki : October 16, 1775, during Mass, in the house of the bride's father, James Deprè to Elizabeth Hucki, both single; witnesses, Anthony Hucki, Anthony Grüser, Catharine Hucki and Christina Deprè.

Rösner—Ziegefuss : November 5, 1775, in the chapel, John Rösner to Catharine Ziegefuss, non-Catholic, both single; witnesses, the bride's two brothers and Catharine and Margaret Eck.

Weibel—Henrich : November 20, 1775, at Christian Henrich's house at *Asperum Collem*, John Weibel to Margaret Henrich, both single; witnesses, John Egg, John Weibel, Magdalen Henrich and Eva Weibel.

Leple—Becker : November 27, 1775, Laurence Leple to Margaret Becker, the second marriage for both; witnesses, Michael Kuhn and wife and Andrew Schimpfessel.

Hartman—Herb : December 28, 1775, Francis Hartman to Angela Herb, both single, with the condition that they do not celebrate their marriage solemnly [*"ne solemnes nuptias celebrent"*] ; witnesses, the brothers and sisters of the contracting parties.

Kuhn—Wider : January 16, 1776, Henry Kuhn to Margaret Wider, both single ; witnesses, Jacob Kuhn, —— Wider and Elizabeth Wider, brothers and sister of the two parties, respectively.

Grett—Seiffert: January 30, 1776, John Grett to Elizabeth Seiffert, both single ; witnesses, the brothers and sisters of both parties.

Adams—Eck [Egg] : February 13 1776, Simon Adams to Catharine Eck [Egg]. both single ; witnesses, Joseph Hild, Matthias Seiffert, Mary Egg and Anna Maria Adams.

Drexel—Ermann : at the same time and place, Anthony Drexel to Catharine Ermann, both single ; witnesses, all that were present.

Norbeck—Reppert: April 16, 1776, John Norbeck to Rose Reppert, both single ; witnesses, Henry and Catharine Norbeck.

Lentzinger—Wagner : June 16, 1776, at Edward Carty's house at Haycock, Jacob Lentzinger, widower, to Salome Wagner, single; witnesses, all that were at Mass.

Butz—Kuhn : August 13, 1776, William Butz, widower, to Magdalen Kuhn, single. [No witnesses named.]

Bradley—Grün [Green?] : November 1, 1776, William Bradley to Magdalen Grün [perhaps better Green], both single ; witnesses, Anthony Grüser, and Nicholas Carty with their wives.

Henrich—Spring : January 19, 1777. John Henrich to M. Barbara Spring; witnesses, Henry and Adam Finck and Magdalen Henrich.

Weber—Büger : April 27, Matthias Weber, widower, to Magdalen Büger, single, of Macungi ; witnesses, Matthias Riffel, Nicholas Röhr, Agatha Riffel and Catharine Röhr.

Zweyer—Dries : May 6, 1777 Anthony Zweyer to —— Maria Dries, both single, of the Oley hills ; witnesses, Balthasar Zweyer and Catharine Sigfried.

Reichart—Thumm : September 9, 1777, John Adam Reichart to Mary Eva Thumm, both single, residents of near Missill [?] creek [in the text written " *Missillem Torrentem*] ; witnesses, Th. Thum, George Wantz, M. Thum and Catharine Sigfried.

Struppel—Norbeck : October 30, 1777, during Mass, Peter Struppel to Magdalen Norbeck, both single; witnesses, Henry Norbeck, Catharine Bütz and M. Elizabeth Struppel.

Grett—Henrich : November 17, 1777, during Mass at Christian Henrich's house at *Asperum Collem*, Andrew Grett, single, to Elizabeth Henrich, Widow Riffel. [No witnesses named.]

Hild—Kientz : November 25, 1777, in the chapel, solemnly, Joseph Hild to Albertina Kientz, both single ; witnesses George Kientz, George Wantz, Catharine Kientz and Anna M. Fraul.

Felix—Haffner : May 24, 1778, during Mass, Martin Felix, single, to Elizabeth Haffner, widow. [No witnesses named.]

Finck—Henrich : June 7, 1778, during Mass, Henry Finck to Magdalen Henrich, both single. [No witnesses named. Before the word "single" i. e, *Coelibum*, in the text, Fr. Ritter has the abbreviated term " *Conj.*" i. e. married, which I am at a loss to understand.]

Eck—Schäffer : June 16, 1778, during Mass, in the chapel, John Eck, twice a widower, to Dorathy Schäffer, non-Catholic and single ; witnesses, all that were at Mass.

Walker—Sigfried : June 30, 1778, in the chapel, William Walker, widower, to Mary Sigfried, single ; witnesses, all that were present.

[Father Ritter subjoins that this Walker who had formerly belonged to the Church of England, or rather was of no belief, made this same day public profession of the Catholic faith.]

Altgayer—Rüttner : July 2, 1778, at Mass, in John Michael Sigfried's house among the Oley hills, Sebastian Altgayer to Catharine Rüttner, both single ; witnesses, all that were at Mass.

Hucki—Demuth: August 16, 1778, in Edward Carty's house, near Haycock, in full accordance with the rites of the Church, Nicholas
Hucki, widower, to Catharine Demuth, widow. [Witnesses not
named.]

Riffel—Spring: November 8, 1778, at Matt. Brück's house near Cedar
creek, George Riffel to Barbara Spring, widow, born Keffer. [No
witnesses named.]

Fowler—MacAlister: April 5, 1779, in the chapel, Edward Fowler to
Elizabeth MacAlister, widow; witnesses, Francis Uhlein, John
[Michat?] and Andrew Deprè.

Zweyer—Scharg: April 11, 1779, during Mass, in Michael Sigfried's
house, Joseph Zweyer to Catharine Scharg, both single; witnesses,
all that were at Mass.

Norbeck—Röhr: April 22, 1779, at Mass in the chapel, Henry Norbeck
to Catharine Röhr, both single.

Walter—Drollinger: also, at the same time and place, James Walter to
Catharine Drollinger, both single; witnesses, the entire congregation.

[Father Ritter observes that Catharine Drollinger not being Catholic,
previous to her marriage, made public profession of faith.]

Eckenroth—Weibel: April 27, 1779, Christopher Eckenroth to Anna
Margaret Weibel, widow, born Henrich; witnesses, all that were
present.

Röhr—Sigfried: May 3, 1779, in the church, Matthias Röhr to
Catharine Sigfried, both single; witnesses, Nicholas Röhr, two sons
of the Widow Zweyer, Catharine Butz and Barbara Sigfried.

Röhr—Schorb: May 4, 1779, in the church, Martin Röhr, widower,
to Anna Maria Schorb, single; witnesses, all that were present at
Mass.

[With this entry at the bottom of page 248 in the register closes the
list of marriages down to 1784.

After the marriages copied above follows, on page 249, the list of
deaths and burials, three of them in Father Theodore Schneider's
handwriting; these have already been published in the "Records;"
see Vol. II., page 332; the remaining ones are in Father Ritter's handwriting. *

On page 343 the record of marriages is continued as follows:]

Eckenroth—Schlosser: April [date obliterated], 1784, according to the
rites of the church, Christian Eckenroth to Catharine Anna Schlosser, both single.

---

*Page 17, this volume.

Flower—Schlosser : at the same time and place, Christopher Flower to Magdalen Schlosser, both single ; witnessess, the brothers of the groom.

Gubernator—Derham : May 2, 1784, John Laurence Gubernator, our schoolmaster [*Ludimagistri nostri*], to Johanna Derham, widow ; witnesses, all that were present.

Schmitt—Kemmel : June 16, 1784, Joseph Schmitt, single, to Regina Kemmel, Widow Klee ; witness, John Gaucker.

Wagner—Creutzer : July 11, 1784, at Mass, Ferdinand Wagner, our schoolmaster at Haycock, to Anna M. Creutzer, widow, born Grandjean ; witnesses, all that were present at Mass.

Riffel—Weibel : August 3, 1784, Matthias Riffel to Eva Weibel, both single ; witnesses, Bernard Riffel, Bernard [Fries?] and M. Elizabeth ——— [last name too much blurred to be read. The same is to be said in regard to the date and the grooms' names in the three following entries].

Eckenroth [?] — Schimpfessl : ———, at Mass, ——— Eckenroth [?] to Elizabeth Schimpfessl.

Mild —[?] — Schorb : August 2, at Mass, Charles Mild—[?], widower, to Anna Schorb, widow ; witnesses, all that were present at Mass.

Rüttner [?] — Martin [?] : September—, 1784, Joseph Rüttner [?], widower, to Eva Martin [?], widow.

Seiffert—Grett : November 2 [?], 1784, at Christian Henrich's house near *Asperum Collem*, Philip Seiffert to Barbara Grett, both single.

Zweyer—Sigfried : January 10, 1785, during Mass in Michael Sigfried's house in the Oley hills, Adam Zweyer to Barbara Sigfried, both single ; witnesses, all that were present at Mass.

Matthes—Eck : January 11, 1785, during Mass, in the church, John Matthes to Anna Maria Eck, both single ; witnesses, George Fricker, John Tren [or Treu] and the two sisters of the bride.

Schmitt—Fischer : March 19, 1785, in the priest's room, Nicholas Schmitt, surgeon, to Elizabeth Fischer, for both the second marriage.

Chevin—Thum : May 3, 1785, in the church, Peter Chevin to Catharine Thum, both single ; witnesses, Peter Thum, Joseph L'eveillè, Maria Thum and Rose Thum.

Hartman—Eckenroth : May 8, 1785, before Mass, in Matthias Keffer's house at Allemängel, Michael Hartman, widower, to Margaret Eckenroth, Widow Beverts ; witnesses, Matthias Keffer, Henry Eckenroth and Margaret Eckenroth, the mother of the [bride?].

[The last two words of this entry present some doubt. As they now stand they read "*Matre spon*"; the final syllable of *spon* being wholly rubbed out, I am unable to determine whether they should read the mother of the bride "*sponsæ*" or of the groom "*sponsi.*"]

Bauman—Grett : May 24, 1785, in the church, John Bauman, non-Catholic, to Magdalen Grett, both single. The groom promised to allow his wife and their children free practice of their religion ; witnesses, Peter Bauman, Laurence Gubernator, our schoolmaster, and Nicholas Schmitt, our surgeon.

Käss—Meckler : May 29, 1785, in Caspar Schönebruck's house, Jacob Käss to Mary Barbara Meckler, both single ; witnesses, Simon Ruffner, Peter Käss, Mary Ruffner and Mary Käss.

Uhlein—Eck : June —, 1785, during Mass, Francis Uhlein to Catharine Eck, both single ; witnesses, the brothers and sisters of the parties.

Schnabel—Bussch : June 28, 1785, Joseph Schnabel, Catholic, to Anna Maria Bussch, non-Catholic ; witnesses, Th. Thum and Michael Schnabel.

Shepperd—Keffer : June [maybe better July] 11, 1785, during Mass, in the church, James Shepherd to Elizabeth Keffer, both single ; witnesses, Edward Gainer, Elizabeth Stoll and Maria Butz.

Reintzel—Nester : November 15, after the three banns, in the church, Conrad Reintzel, widower and farmer [*coloni*] of Pine township, Berks county, to Catharine Nester, widow of this town of Herford ; witnesses, Jacob Gruss, William Strunck, Michael Hartmann and Joseph Schmitt, weaver, who all bound themselves under their seal and signature that no attempt would be made to break this marriage. [This entry the last in the book is dated "15, Nov. 1785," and signed "J. B. Ritter, Miss.", that is to say, "John Baptist Ritter, Missionary."]

[The number of marriages is one hundred and thirty.]

DEATHS AND BURIALS.

1765—1785.

Hartman, Mary, wife of Francis Hartman, farmer [*coloni*], in Rich valley, fell from a rock, broke her arm and died of dysentery, was buried August 28, 1765, in the church graveyard, at Gosshenhopen.

Eck, Magdalen, daughter of John Eck, farmer in Rich valley, had been aiding Mary Hartman [above named] during her illness and, having contracted the same ailment during her labor of charity, died of the same ; buried September 12, 1765, in the graveyard, used by Lutherans, near her father's house.

112

Both, John Leonard, lawful son of John Both, farmer of Magunshi, less than two years old; buried [September] 23, in the graveyard at Gosschenhopen.

Chaumont, Anna Maria, born Fricker, wife of Joseph Chaumont, a Savoyard, died November 10, 1765, seven days after child birth, her infant dying at birth or rather perishing [*occisus*] through unskilful handling; buried November 11, in the Catholic graveyard at Reading.

Lorenz, ———, infant son of Jacob Lorenz, had scarcely been born when it was baptized and died; buried December —, 1765, in the graveyard at Couissahopen [Goshenhoppen].

Bergmans, Christopher, died January 6, 1766, in Linen [better Linn] township in the Blue mountains; buried January 8, in the same graveyard [as above] alongside the choir.

Baur, N——, son, six years old, of Leonard Baur, workman at Mebris furnace; buried April 24, in the same graveyard [as above].

Matthys, Joseph, son of Martin Matthys, ten years old, died June 12, in the mountains; buried June 13, in the graveyard at Gosschenhopen.

Wenig, Anna, wife of George Wenig, a poor laborer on my farm [*praedii mei*], was ill of dropsy for some months and died June 15, 1766; buried June 17, in the same graveyard [as above].

Baur, ———, daughter of Leonard Baur, workman, at Mebris furnace.

Bisschop, Simon, son of Peter Bisschop, tailor, at Allenstown.

[No date, or other particulars, is given with the above two entries.]

Carty, Catharine, wife of Edward Carty, over seventy years of age, died October 16, 1766, of old age and a contagious fever; buried October 19, on her husband's farm at Haycock.

Becker, George, weaver, died two days ago of dysentery; buried September 13 [this date however, has been crosssed over with the pen and underneath it another date, September 1, also crossed over], on his own farm in the Olivet [Oley] mountains.

Wenig, George, a poor laborer on my farm, died of old age, after having received in his full senses all the sacraments of Holy Roman Church, and having had a short agony; buried November 15, in the church graveyard [*coemeterio templi*] alongside his wife Anna, deceased during the past summer.

Geyer, Conrad, died April 19, 1767, after having received in due season all the aids of the dying; had been for many years ill of dropsy and finally died of apoplexy; buried April 21, in the church graveyard.

Strohm [?], Anna Maria, widow, died yesterday morning [the month is blurred, it looks like October], of old age and a long illness, after having received in due season all the sacraments of Holy Roman Church ; buried October [?] 7, in the church graveyard.

Hild, ——, infant daughter, a few days old, of Joseph Hild and his wife, buried December —, 1768, in the church graveyard. [This entry of a death at the close of the year 1768 is followed in the text by entries of several deaths that occurred in the beginning of the same year.]

Z'p, Mary Eva, wife of George Zip, seventy-five years of age, and of married life fifty ; this truly pious old woman had long prayed God and besought Him to take her from life before her husband, and to end her life by a short illness ; she died before her husband, and was ailing barely three days ; buried, February 2, in the church graveyard.

Zipp, George, survivor of his wife by only eleven days ; he, too, had prayed God not to keep him long separated from his wife ; buried, February 13, 1768, alongside her grave.

Geri, Philip, workman, died March 27, 1768, of consumption ; he was beloved by all for his uprightness ; he left a widow and several small children ; buried, March 28, in the graveyard.

Hartman, Francis, died yesterday, in the school-room, of dropsy ; buried, June 3, 1768, alongside his wife in the church graveyard.

Ziegler, Catharine, wife of Melchior Ziegler, non-Catholic, mother of six children, all dead, died July 18, 1768, about eight o'clock in the morning ; buried July 21, in the church graveyard.

Keffer, ——, son, six months old, of Peter Keffer and his wife Barbara; buried, September, 13, 1768, in the church graveyard.

Rittner, Regina, lawful daughter of Joseph and Barbara Rittner, died September 7, 1768, of small pox [*variolis*], aged three years ; buried, September 9, in the church graveyard.

Hartman, Michael, carpenter, had been ill for a long while and finally died November 20, 1768, of dropsy ; buried November 22 in the graveyard near the church.

Seiffert Anna Maria an aged widow long ailing, and twice within the last few months refreshed with the sacraments of holy Roman Church, died yesterday July 24, 1769 unexpectedly and suddenly, at a neighbor's house, where she had gone in good health ; buried July 25, in the church graveyard.

Baur, John Jacob, aged four years, son of Leonard Baur, died of dysentery : buried September 8, 1769, in the public [*communi*] graveyard near Mayburri [perhaps better Maybury] furnace.

Kupser, ———, infant son, one hour old, of Jacob Kupser and his wife Catharine, was baptized before death; buried September 25, 1769, in the church graveyard.

Zweyer, George, a resident of the Oley hills [*Montium Oliveti*], died December 30, 1769, of old age and asthma; buried January 1, 1770, in the church graveyard.

Schmitt, Michael, lawful son, two months old, of Philip Schmitt; buried February 2, 1770, in the church graveyard.

Burchard, ———, the little son of Martin Burchard; buried February 26, 1771, in the graveyard.

Bisschoff, Peter, fifty-six years of age, died March 15, 1771, of pleurisy; buried March 18 in the graveyard, near John Bergmann's grave.

Kemperling, Anna Maria, wife of John Kemperling, died suddenly, August 27, 1771; buried August 28, in the graveyard.

Matthes, ———, infant son of Martin Matthes, died last night, without having been baptized; buried September 6, 1771, without ceremonies.

Schmitt, Mary Dorothy, daughter, three years old, of John Adam Schmitt and his wife Margaret, died February 8, 1771; buried February 10 in the graveyard.

[No deaths are recorded for the year 1772.]

Keffer, Catharine, daughter, six months old, of Peter Keffer and his wife Barbara; buried March 27, 1773.

Jung, Catharine, wife of Ferdinand Jung, died of dropsy, after having been fortified with all the sacraments, on the 7th inst.; buried, August 8, in the church graveyard.

Kuhn, Margaret, widow, died November 22, 1773, of hysteria, at Cedar creek, after having been fortified with all the sacraments of holy Roman Church; buried November 24, in the church graveyard.

Gaucker, Anna Maria, infant daughter, eleven months old, of John Gaucker and his wife Barbara Weibel, died of convulsions; buried December 10, 1773 [place not named].

Schmitt, Rose, wife of Anthony Schmitt, not quite sixty years of age, died yesterday [December 23, 1773], of dropsy; buried December 24 in the chapel [*sacelli*] graveyard.

Linch [perhaps better Lynch], John, unmarried, over twenty years of age, had not been brought up a Catholic. Two months before death, he, of his own accord, came to the priest and said that he desired to embrace the true faith, in the meantime having been stricken with the smallpox he signified his wish for a priest and his desire for the faith. On perceiving that he had suddenly gone out of his mind I did all I could for him—I baptized him, absolved him and anointed him. He had always lived most uprightly. He died March 16, 1774, and was buried March 18, in the chapel graveyard.

Gibson, Francis, an old man, suffered from pain in the bowels—of his own accord desired to be fortified in due season with all the sacraments of holy Roman Church; buried March 27, 1774, in the very spot in the chapel graveyard where he stood while attending the funeral of John Linch.

Litzinger, Magdalen, widow, over seventy years of age, for six years had been afflicted with various ailments and lastly with asthma— yesterday [April 4, 1774], while all were rising for the day, she was found dead, though apparently resting in a most peaceful slumber ; she had frequently been refreshed with all the sacraments of holy Roman Church ; she died of dropsy, and was buried April 5, in the same graveyard as above.

Burchart, Cornelius, a youth, fifteen years of age ; for one year had been ailing of a lung disease ; had received the sacraments not so very long ago ; was stricken down suddenly with apoplexy ; did not receive the holy oils ; died the day before yesterday ; buried April 14, 1774, in the chapel graveyard.

Freudenberger, Conrad, a rather old man, had been ailing from a slow and lingering wasting away [*tabe*] ; received in due season all the aid of the dying ; died October 18, 1774; buried October 20, in the graveyard. [This entry is signed "J. B. Ritter."]

Grünewald, Anna Maria, lawful daughter of John Grünewald, died October 31, 1774 ; was baptized the day before ; born September 23 ; buried November 1, in the church graveyard.

[At the head of the page that follows, marked in the register as page 263, is the record of the death "in the Lord," on February 14, 1751, of John Kuhn, carpenter, with whom Rev. Theodore Schneider, the founder of the Goshenhoppen missions, was wont to lodge. The writing is in Father Ritter's hand.]

Heitz, Michael, died November 30, of old age and a short illness ; buried December 1, 1774, in our graveyard here [*coemeterio nostro hic*].

Eck, Magdalen, wife of John Eck, died March 6, 1775, in child birth ; was the mother of eight children, of whom she left six living ; an excellent woman—a loving-hearted wife ; esteemed by all for her truly Christian traits ; buried March 8, in the public graveyard at Rich valley, a short distance from her husband's farm.

[In the list of baptisms is recorded the birth of Veronica Eck, on March 6, 1775, and her baptism on March 8. The little daughter, in giving birth to whom, Magdalen Eck died, was born on the day of her mother's death, and baptized on the day of her mother's burial.]

Noel, Ignatius, ninety years of age, a native of Lorraine, resident of Pennsylvania for more than thirty years, had once been rich, but died in poverty, where his drunken son-in-law had brought him ; died March 23, 1775 ; buried March 25, in the church graveyard.

Riffel, George Jacob, more than twenty years of age ; married two years ago ; a certain Daniel Stärr taking him, so he said, for a deer, shot him dead ; may this victim be the last in these most fateful times ! Buried May 23, 1775.

Schmitt, Philip, the father by his two marriages, of a large number of children, all living ; died yesterday [July 17], after having been fortified in due season with all the sacraments of holy Roman Church; buried July 18, 1775, in the chapel graveyard.

Riffel, Augustine, the six year old son of Matthias Riffel, and brother of George Jacob Riffel, who was slain [by Daniel Stärr] ; had been ill for several months ; buried October 2, 1775, in the chapel graveyard.

Hofman, Magdalen, daughter of Michael Hofman, seven years old, died January 29, 1776 ; buried, January 31, in the chapel graveyard.

Buchart, Martin, son of Martin Buchart, four years old, died yesterday, [September 5, 1776] ; buried September 6, in the chapel graveyard.

Baur, Leonard, carter [auriga], at Spring forge iron mines ; buried December 12, 1776, in the graveyard.

Schmitt, Catharine, wife of Anthony Schmitt, formerly widow of Caspar Meyer, a Catholic, who died without the sacraments which he had always neglected ; she imitated his life but not his death, for of her own accord she begged the sacraments with great piety and received them ; died yesterday [December 30, 1776] ; buried December 31, in the chapel graveyard.

Norbeck, Catharine, a maiden about seventeen years old, had received in due season all the sacraments of holy Roman Church ; buried January 8, 1777, in the chapel graveyard.

Schmitt, Frederick, an old widower, in Allenstown, died February 8, after a short illness ; buried February 10, in the graveyard.

Schmitt, Anthony, an old man, died February 14, 1777; buried February 16, in the graveyard, while I was away.

Uhlein, Valentine, about twenty years of age, died February 21, 1777, of disease ; buried February 23, in the same graveyard.

Weibel, Valentine, the truly Christian parent of a numerous offspring, died, February 28, 1777; buried March 2, in the same graveyard.

Jung, Ferdinand, widower, rather aged, died on the same day and of the same disease ; buried at the same time and in the same place, with the above Weibel. [Father Ritter, whose words (*eadem die et morbo*) I translate, has failed to state of what disease Weibel died.]

Kientz, Matthias, died April 6, 1777; buried April 8, in the chapel graveyard.

Hofmann, Catharine, fifteen years of age and in my service [*ancilla mea*] for eight days, died August 15, 1777, of dysentery; buried August 17, in the chapel graveyard. [This entry is signed "J. B. Ritter, S. J."]

Butz, William Peter, an infant, three months old; buried October 6, 1777, in the chapel graveyard

Röhr, ——, infant son of Martin Röhr, was what is known as "a seven months' child," died six hours after birth, baptized by its father; buried December 24, 1777.

Röhr, Anna M., mother of the foregoing infant, and wife of Martin Röhr, died yesterday [December 27, 1777], of dysentery, during childbirth, leaving eleven children to her surviving husband, and nearly all under age [*impuberibus*]; buried, December 28, in the same graveyard.

Walker, Susanna, wife of William Walker, blacksmith, baptized by me, March 3, 1778, died yesterday [March 4], of smallpox; she was twenty years of age, had been brought up a Presbyterian, had eagerly desired baptism and received it: buried March 5, in the chapel graveyard. [This entry is signed "J. B. Ritter, S. J."]

Röhr, John, lawful son of Martin Röhr, three years old, died three days ago of smallpox; buried March 13, 1778, in the chapel graveyard. [This entry is signed the same as the preceding.]

Butz, Laurence, son of William Butz, born November 21, 1778, died, February 6, 1779; buried, February 8, 1779, in the chapel graveyard.

[Then follows a part merely of an entry, that reads:] "I buried an infant child of Martin Burchard."

Norbeck, Henry, infant son, four months old, of James Norbeck, died of contagious cough [*tussi contagiosa?* maybe croup,]; buried August 19, 1779.

Welker, Mary Barbara, wife of Peter Welker, brought some months ago from Jersey to the iron works [*officina ferraria*] of Mr. Butz, died April 7, 1780, of dropsy; buried April 8.

Grünewald, John, an infant, a few months old; buried September 8, 1780, in the graveyard.

Keffer, Mary, an infant, a few days old; buried September 10, [1780].

118

Walter, James, an old man, hammerer [*malleator*] in Mayburri [perhaps better Maybury] iron mines, died yesterday [October 24, 1780], of dysentery ; buried October 25, in the chapel graveyard.

Weber, John James, an infant, one month old, died of a cough [*tussi*, croup?] ; buried January 25, 1781, in the chapel graveyard.

Brück, Joseph, infant son of Matthias Brück ; buried February 2, 1781, at the same place.

Schmitt, James, infant son of John Adam Schmitt ; buried February 5, 1781, at the same place.

Adams, Anna Maria, widow, formerly Kupser, an excellent old woman after the apostolic model ; buried March 5, 1781, in the chapel graveyard.

Röhr, Martin, shoemaker [*sutor*], had been twice married, died April 2, 1781, after being for ified in due season with all the aids of the dying ; buried April 4, in the chapel graveyard.

Matthes, Nicholas, a most worthy old man, eighty years of age, full of days ; had seen his daughters' children unto the third generation ; died May 25, 1781 ; buried May 27, in the chapel graveyard.

Adams, ———, an infant son, one year old, of Simon Adams ; buried March 4, 1782, in the chapel graveyard.

Sigfried, George, a most worthy old man, aged eighty-two years, died March 21, 1782, in the Oley hills [*Collibus Olivetanis*] ; buried March 23, at the same place.

Matthes, Margaret, relict of Nicholas Matthes, deceased, in the preceding year ; had received all the sacraments of holy Roman Church ; buried March 29, 1782.

Braun, Magdalen, the little daughter, one year old, of Andrew Braun ; buried March 30, 1782.

Klee, Hilary, hammerer at Mayburri [perhaps better Maybury] forge [*officina*], died yesterday [April 9, 1782], of a quick epidemic ; had been married only a few years ; was barely thirty years of age ; left a widow with a child two years old, and also a child born after his death ; had received the sacraments, while in good health on last Easter day, March 31 ; buried April 10, in the chapel graveyard.

[In the baptismal register is the record of the baptism of John Adam Klee, son of John Hilary Klee, and his wife Regina, born April 5, 1780, baptized April 23, and of Anna Elizabeth, posthumous child of Hilary Klee and his wife Regina Cammel, born April 28, 1782, and baptized May 19. By reference to the birthday of Anna Elizabeth, who was the posthumous child of Hilary Klee, it seems that Father Ritter did not make any note of the father's death until at least nineteen days after it occurred.]

Welsch, Juliana, daughter of Conrad Welsch, hammerer at the above named forge, fourteen years of age, died within two days, of the same epidemic; was anointed; had received the Easter sacraments on Palm Sunday; buried April 5, 1782, in the chapel graveyard.

Welsch, Elizabeth, died of the same epidemic, though had been ill of consumption; buried April 21, alongside her sister, in the same graveyard.

Nester, Frederick, an old man, seventy-three years of age, died April 21, 1782; buried April 23, at the same place.

Butz, Magdalen, infant daughter, one year old, of Mr. Christian Butz and his wife [Catharine Struppel], died of smallpox; buried September 5, 1782, in the chapel graveyard.

Edelblut, Anna Catharine, daughter of NN. Edelblut, non-Catholic, hammerer in Christian Butz's iron works [officina ferraria], died September 15, of smallpox; buried September 17, in the chapel graveyard.

Strunck, Barbara, daughter of William Strunck, two years old, died yesterday [October 11, 1782], of smallpox; buried October 12, in the chapel graveyard.

Burchart, William, lawful son of Martin Burchart, born April 5, died of small pox; buried November 14, 1782, in the chapel graveyard.

Norbeck, ———, infant child of John Norbeck; buried February —, 1783.

Noel, Catharine, twice widowed, wife first of NN. Kraft, then of Ignatius Noel, seventy-five years of age; buried March 22, 1783.

Dunckel, Jacob, over eighty years of age; buried March 28, 1783, in the chapel graveyard.

Walker, ———, a little daughter, two years old, of Daniel Walker; buried April —, [1783].

Braun, John, son of Andrew Braun, six years old; buried May 3, 1783.

Marx, Thomas, an old man, died July 15, 1783, after a short illness, after having received in due season all the sacraments of the Church; buried July 17, in the chapel graveyard.

Keffer, Elizabeth, daughter of Peter Keffer, two years old; buried October ———.

Kuhn, Eva, wife of Peter Wurf, about twenty-five years of age, died December 1, 1783, after having received in due season the Holy Viaticum; buried December 3, in our graveyard here.

Mild, Catharine, wife of Charles Mild, died May 2, 1784, of ulcerated thighs, after having been fortified in due season with all the sacraments of holy Roman Church ; buried May 4, in the same place.

Keffer, ———, an infant child, seven months old, of Peter Keffer, buried June 7, 1784.

Hartman, Margaret, wife of Michael Hartman, born Hammerstein, died of dysentery, contracted in child-birth seven months ago ; buried August 30, 1784, in the same place.

Isinger, Margaret, a widow, sixty-six years of age, died September 10, 1784, in Magunshi ; buried September 11, in the same place, [that is, "in our graveyard here"].

Heitz, Eva, widow, by her second marriage, of Michael Heitz, formerly Wagner, died December 23, 1784 ; buried December 25, in the graveyard.

Sigfried, John Michael, fifty-seven years of age, died in the Oli [Oley] hills, leaving a widow, the mother of his fifteen children, ten still being alive ; buried Feb. 2, 1785, in the same place.

Butz, Charles, son of William Butz, four months old ; buried February 16, 1785, in the same place.

Dietrichs, Maria, infant child, two days old, of John Dietrichs ; buried March 9, 1785, in the same place.

Litzinger, Anna Maria, born Schmitt, died May 16, [1785] ; buried May 18, in the graveyard.

Reppert, Stephen, an old man, died November 3, 1785 ; buried Novem- 4, in the graveyard.

[With this entry, on page 276, closes apparently the list of deaths and burials, all having been recorded in Father Ritter's hand-writing.

On the page that follows, namely, page 277, the same Father Ritter has left a memorandum of something or other that I am unable to interpret. It begins with a line at the top of the page, as follows, " 29 June, near Cedar creek [*prope torrentem cedron*] 1767 " ; this is followed by a list of names, written one under the other, namely, "Anna M. Holstein, Henry Luther, Geor. [ge] Ad. [am] Ruffner, Sim. [on] Ruffner, Anna M. Luther, Barbara Hornberger," and leaving a space for a line or two in blank, it ends with " Phl. [query Philip ?] Miller and brother," [here follows what looks like a " 2 sacro," 19 July, 1768."]

[The number of deaths and burials is one hundred and twelve.]

121

GOSHENHOPPEN REGISTERS.

OF

Baptisms, Marriages, Confirmations, Deaths, Etc.

(Third Series.) [†]

1787–1800.

TRANSLATED AND ANNOTATED BY REV. THOMAS C.
MIDDLETON, D.D., O.S.A.

In former volumes of these RECORDS were published the
registers from 1741 to 1785, belonging to the interesting
old mission church of St. Paul's, (now since 1837 known
as the church of the Blessed Sacrament,) at Goshenhoppen,
(now Bally,) in Berks County, Pa.

During that period this mission being in charge of
the Jesuit Fathers Theodore Schneider and John Baptist
Ritter, or De Ritter, were recorded 1,126 baptisms, 16
conversions, 178 marriages and 115 deaths and burials.

Fr. Ritter was in residence at Goshenhoppen up to his
death, in the early part of 1787. But the registers kept
by him during the last two years of his life—from 1785 to
1787—are missing.

In this—the second—volume of the registers belonging
to Goshenhoppen church, which we are treating of in this
present paper, are contained the sacramental records of
that mission for the 32 years from 1787 down to 1819. In
it are recorded the baptisms (in number 934) down to 1807;

[†]*Unless indicated otherwise, page references in the text refer to pages
in the original Goshenhoppen registers, not to this volume.*

marriages (in number 270) down to 1819 ; and deaths and burials (in number 114) down to 1818.

In this Third Series are transcribed the registrations belonging to the last century alone, ending with the year 1800. The entries therein relating to the years subsequent to this date it is not the purpose of this SOCIETY to publish at present.**

This second volume here translated, is a book bound in boards of 172 pages,* measuring 8 inches in length and 6½ in width, in very fair state of preservation, as a rule carefully and neatly filled up, and no parts of it apparently wanting. (At the end of the volume six leaves have been cut out close to the sewing of the book. But they did not contain, it is likely, any church records.) On the inside of the front cover of it the Register bears the following inscription (in Latin) † in Fr. Helbron's hand, of which the following is a translation.

TITLE OF VOLUME II OF GOSHENHOPPEN REGISTERS.

" Book of Baptisms, Marriages and Deaths of the Church of ' Goschenhoppen, Herfordt Daunschipp Bergs Kaunti ' ; begun under Peter Helbronn, Third Missionary, delegated thereto on November 22, 1787, by the Superior of the Mission, the Right Reverend D. [*Dominus*] Carroll [*here these words*—' à Missionaribus Electo ' *have been crossed out* by Fr. Helbron], confirmed by Pius VI Supreme Pontiff, and in 1790 consecrated Bishop of the Church of Baltimore at Lullworth [*sic,*Lulworth] castle in England."

Underneath this inscription (also in Fr. Helbron's hand) is a Note (in Latin) calling attention to the fact that at

---

* The paging employed throughout this description of it has been made by a modern hand ; the old missionaries themselves having used it without any paging,

† It should be observed that in these records following what was a common custom among missionaries in the last century and even in the early part of the present one, all registrations, with one exception (to be noted further on,) are in the Latin language. Though the reader will occasionally meet here and there a word or so in English, or German.

**See pp. 186-262, this volume.

the end of the book is a statement of the repairs and improvements made (at Goshenhoppen) in the church building, house, and farm—"*plantatione*," which, (he says,) had all gone to ruin—"*ubique devastata.*"

Not unlike in this respect to other old mission registers of the period, Fr. Helbron has made his one book a repository of all church memoranda. In the beginning of it he has opened his Baptismal Register; towards the centre of it his records of marriages; then further on he gives the list of deaths and burials; while at the very end of the book, (as we have seen from the title page,) is an account of the temporalities of St. Paul's mission.

In this Series have been set down the various registrations in the Goshenhoppen Book with few exceptions just as they stand in the original. These, very few however in number, are certain entries in the baptismal and marriage records wherein has been noted by the missionaries the fact that the subjects baptized or married had been born out of wedlock. (Moreover in the Marriage Register in two entries Fr. Helbron has employed a singular phrase,—the writer has never met it before,—to signify, it seems, a not common, and perhaps,—though this interpretation of it is stated with some misgivings as to the correctness of it, a not wholly honorable position of one of the parties to marriage. The wording of these entries referred to includes in one case these terms—"married so and so *cum cortâ sua*"; and in the other * * * * * "*cum sua cortâ acatholicâ*". In the translation of the two entries these words have been omitted.)

The names of such unfortunates and of all related to them—parents and witnesses—have been left out of this translation, that the records may be to no one needlessly a shame, but to all concerned therein a source of honor and pride.

In 1787, on the death of Fr. Ritter, the second missionary, and until some time in the present century, the last Jesuit, in charge of Goshenhoppen, succeeded Rev. Peter

Helbron, or Helbronn, for this clergyman wrote his name in more than one way, who held charge of it for four years. Fr. Helbron came to Goshenhoppen in 1787, and remained there in residence until 1791, when, on his being transferred to Philadelphia, his place was given to Rev. N. [*Nicholas ?*] Delvaux, the fourth. missionary in charge, who held it for two years up to 1793; his successor being Rev. Paul Erntzen, the missionary in care of St. Paul's for 25 years until his death in 1818.

Fr. Helbron's first entry in the Register—a baptism—is dated November 13, 1787 ; his first marriage February 3, the same year ; * his last baptism August 19, 1791; and his last official entry—a marriage—on the following day, August 20, of the same year. †

Yet in subsequent years (as we learn from the registers) on his occasional visits to Goshenhoppen he was called upon to administer the sacraments by Fr. Erntzen. Thus during the latter's rectorship Fr. Helbron married a couple on November 29, 1798 ; and again on September 8, the year after ; while on June 10 and 16 of the same year— 1799, he has recorded two baptisms.

During the rectorship of Fr. Helbron, he was assisted in his charge (though only for a short while at the outset of his term in 1787) by his brother—Rev. John Baptist Charles Helbron, whose name appears only three times, all

---

* Here in this marriage entry is an open conflict of dates, which I am utterly unable to reconcile. From the *Title-page* of the *Register* (given ahead), where Fr. Helbron has set down the date of his appointment to Goshenhoppen as " November 22, 1787 "; and from the List of *Memoranda* at the end of the *Register*, where in unmistakable terms he says that he entered into the Mission on " November 22, 1787 ",— from these two clearly written entries, no other date can be fixed for his having taken charge of St. Paul's, than just what he has himself recorded.

And yet following the marriage-entry given in the text for " February 1787 ", are others for the subsequent months for that same year yet all earlier than the recorded date of his arrival. But contenting ourselves with the observation that most likely the year—" 1787 "—at the head of the marriage entries is an error for 1788 we leave other ways of solving this mystery to our readers.

† In all sketches of Rev. Peter Helbron, as far as the writer is acquainted with them, the date of his closing his missionary career at Goshenhoppen is set for " August 19, 1791 "—the date of his last entry in the *Baptismal Register ;* (p. 31.) But he himself has recorded a marriage—Anthony Zweyer's with Mary Zweyer, on the day after— " August 20." (See p. 81 of the *Marriage Register.*)

on the first page of the Baptismal Register. There in recording the first baptism administered by his brother Fr. Helbron writes—"*Baptizante Joanne Baptista Carolo Helbron Germano fratre et petri in Missione Socio.*"

At Goshenhoppen Fr. Peter made various improvements in the church buildings and mission;—among them he built a tower, or steeple—"*turris,*" and put in it a bell, weighing, Dr. Shea says, 112 pounds.*

On his removal from Goshenhoppen Fr. Peter was stationed at Holy Trinity church, in Philadelphia, where his brother Fr. John, had been in care since 1789. Here on July 4, 1791, Fr. Peter was chosen by the trustees of that church their assistant rector, and with his brother as chief, who remained with him up to the latter part of the year, took charge of the faithful until August 18, 1799.†

In this year he was appointed to the care of the Catholics in the central part of the State in Westmoreland county, in place of the Rev. Francis Fromm, not long deceased, with his residence at the old mission centre known as Sportman's Hall.

Fr. Peter reached his new field of labor on November 17, 1799. His first official entry recorded there—the baptism of Judith Gyrven—is dated the day after his arrival—November 18th ; and his last entry—the marriage of Charles Flennigen and Catharine Kuhn on September 12, 1815.

Rev. Peter Helbron died in Carlisle, Pa., of throat ulcer, on his way homeward from Philadelphia, whither he

---

* See his *History of the Catholic Church*, ii, p. 202.

† From the records at Holy Trinity church, copied for the writer by the rector Rev. E. O. Hiltermann, May 18, 1897.

The original at Holy Trinity reads thus—"*Rev. Petrus Helbron, 1787 moratur in oppido Goschenhoppen usque ad 19—Aug. 1791. Aeditui Ecclesiae ad SS. Trinitatem proprio marte eum constituerunt assistentem proximi superioris die 4. Julii 1791 usque 18 —Aug. 1799. Ab autumno 1799 designatus est Pastor fidelium in Comitatu Westmoreland. Postremo ulcere in gula divexatus, obiit in Dño in oppido Carlisle ; ubi redux Philadelphia in itinere morari coactus est.*"

126

he had gone for medical treatment, sometime in 1815, or the early part of 1816.*

The Rev. John Baptist Charles Helbron, whom we have seen at Goshenhoppen in the latter part of 1787, took up his residence at St. Mary's, Philadelphia, from the November of that year. On the completion of Holy Trinity church in 1789, he was chosen by the trustees rector of it —a position he held up to November 13, 1791, when he sailed for Spain to collect alms for his church to pay off the debts on it.†

His brother Peter remained now in charge of that mission. Of John nothing positively was ever learned beyond the bare facts of his departure for Europe. There were reports that he had been drowned at sea on his Atlantic voyage to Spain ; and again that he had fallen victim for his Faith to the revolutionists in France.

To these few memoranda on Rev. John Helbron, we may add that from the old *Baptismal Register* belonging to St. Mary's church, Lancaster, Pa., it appears that he was the immediate successor there of Rev. J. B. Causse. In it he has written these words—" *Continuatio Neo-renatorum per me J. Carolum Heilbron* [sic], *qua successorem immediatum. J. B. Causse, A. D. 1789.*" ‡

Fr. Delvaux, the immediate successor of Fr. Peter Helbron at Goshenhoppen, who opens his registrations with a baptism on September 8, 1791, and a marriage on the 18th

---

* The above data relating to this Westmoreland county missionary have been communicated to the writer by Rev. Vincent Huber, O.S.B., president of St. Vincent's College in the said county.

Much of interest relating to the old mission of Sportsman's Hall may be found in a Paper by the same clergyman in these RECORDS, iii, pp. 142-73.

† The following is an extract from the records of Holy Trinity church, Philadelphia :—

" Rev. Joannes Carolus Helbron vixit apud St. Mariam Philadelphiae, a Novb. 1787. Postea finitā Ecclesiā Germanorum ab anno 1789 curam habuit pastoralem Ecclesiae SS. Trinitatis usque ad 18. Nov. 1791, quo die navim adscendit, ut in Hispauiam secederet pro Eccl. SS. Trinitatis collecturus, unde debita ejus solveret." (Copied for the writer by the rector of Holy Trinity—Rev. E. O. Hiltermann, May 18, 1897.)

‡ From *Letter* to the writer, Feb. 11, 1887, from Mr. S. M. Sener, of Lancaster, who adds that Fr. John's name, appears in the registers there at St. Mary's from February 25 to Oct. 3, 1789.

of the following November, signed his name variously as
" *N. Delvaux Missirio*"—the latter word an abbreviation
for missionary ; " *R. D. Delvaux*"—"*Delvaux Parochus*" ,
" *Parous* "—parish-priest, or simply as " *Delvaux.*"

His last entries are a baptism of a child born on March
16, 1793, (—he has not put the date of the baptism,) and a
marriage on April 18th, in the same year.*

Three days after Fr. Delvaux's last registration at Goshenhoppen first appears Fr. Erntzen's,—a baptism on
April 21, 1793, signed " *à R. D. Paulo Erntzen successore
R. Dñi Delvaux* "; his first marriage being witnessed two
days subsequently ; while his last baptism (in this volume)
is dated March 29, 1807 ; and his last marriage April 12,
1818.†

Besides the names of these three clergymen—Helbron,
Delvaux and Erntzen, who all were in residence at Goshenhoppen, with care of the out-lying missions dependent
on it, for thirty-one years, we here and there in the registers encounter other missionaries—visitors, who occasionally were called upon to perform the rites of the Church.

Thus on November 2, 1818, a marriage was witnessed
(see p. 117) by the congregation and Rev. Maximilian
Rantzau, who assists at a like ceremony on the 12th of the
same month.

On February 7, 1819, Rev. Louis de Barth, a priest of
noble birth, who however, (through humility, it is said,)
wrote his name (as was his fashion) simply as " L. Barth",
records the marriage by him of two parties in Philadelphia,
which was witnessed among others by a clergyman, whose
name is given as " Rev. John Roselly ". (See p. 117.)
Why this Philadelphia marriage—a public ceremony—

---

* The name of Rev. N. Delvaux is not in the *Indexes* to Dr. Shea's *History;* nor so
far as the writer is aware does it appear elsewhere than in Goshenhoppen Registers.
Nothing more absolutely is known of this missionary.

† By some writers Fr. Erntzen has been given a middle name—" *Dominic*". In the
present registers he never signed but " *P.*," or " *Paulus, Erntzen* "

Mr. Sener, (in his *Letter* quoted ahead,) states that Fr. Erntzen's name appears at
times in St. Mary's registers at Lancaster from 1789 to 1795.

should be recorded at a country church in Berks County is utterly a mystery to the writer. Nor can he throw any light on the personality of the priest-witness named. Fr. "Roselly" appears but this once in church records, as far as known to the writer, and then disappears from them. On May 31, of the preceding year—1818, (see p. 116,) Fr. de Barth had assisted at another marriage. On May 2, 1819, there is an entry—a marriage, (see p. 117,) written by a strange hand.

As far as concerns the character of these Goshenhoppen missionaries certain glimpses of their peculiarities have been taken from the registers themselves. From the singular fashion employed by Fr. Helbron in writing the names of persons and places, I take it that he was but indifferently, if at all, versed in English, as little in fact as it seems Fr. Delvaux knew Latin. Thus for township. Fr. Helbron writes "*Daunschipp*", "*dauschipp*" and "*Daunship*"; for county, "*Kaunti*" and "*caunty*"; and for Berks, "*Bercks*" and "*Bergs*".

Still his records though showing signs at times of having been hastily written, are very easily read ; there are no abbrevations in them. Where in their marriage entries Frs. Delvaux and Erntzen invariably have employed but one term to signify the fact for instance of a marriage, as "*juncti sunt*" = they were joined, (so writes Fr. Delvaux,) and "*matrimonium iniere*", (Fr. Erntzen's way of putting it,) Fr. Helbron varies his terms; he had a rather copious and sometimes a not unpoetical vocabulary. In his marriage entries for instance he used indifferently such phrases as—"*inierunt*", "*iniere*", "*juncti sunt*", "*intronizati sunt*", *nupta fuit*", "*ingressus est matrimonium*". While in his baptismal entries he not unfrequently uses the phrase "*baptismatis unda renatus*", or "*renata*".

Another peculiarity of Fr. Helbron's, that one observes in his records (of baptisms,) was his almost invariable fashion of giving the godmother's name first place when the subject of the sacrament was female; but when male then the godfather's preceded.

Usually he signed his name " *Petrus Helbron* "; once (as at bottom of page 31) writing his family name with a double " *n* " = Helbronn; and once (see page 12) he adds to his name (in contracted style) his official title thus "*p. t. pastore* ".

Different from Fr. Helbron was Fr. Delvaux, who so far as can be judged from his hand-writing, while not exactly slovenly, was what one might style rather careless in making his entries. Usually he has omitted to register the date of baptism. Moreover his entries are often spread out over the page to a sad loss of space in it; four of them commonly, though sometimes yet rarely five, fill a page of his baptismal records.

As regards Fr. Erntzen I should judge from his writing that he was a pains-taking man of methodical ways; his records are all very plain and precise in form; his letters neatly and well shaped, and (though heavy looking) are written carefully and all of them in invariably the same way. Then Fr. Erntzen was a time-saver; his entries, though it is easy enough to make out the sense in them when one finds the key, are full of abbreviations and space-sparing expedients. His register,—I am here referring to his baptismal records, is the only one I am acquainted with wherein to save time and space by writing over and over again on a page the same words so necessary in baptismal records as *born* and *baptized*, this missionary has set them down once at the top of each page; and then underneath them in columnar fashion the respective dates of birth and baptism.

Where Fr. Helbron enters only eight baptisms on a page, Fr. Erntzen records usually fifteen. Fr. Helbron wrote from 21 to 24 lines to a page; Fr. Delvaux from 16 to 18; and Fr. Erntzen from 26 to 28.

From this Goshenhoppen Register we draw the evidence of a visit once paid to it by the Right Rev. John Carroll, bishop of Baltimore, and his having administered there the sacrament of confirmation.

Though it seems rather hard to suppose that the bishop should have confirmed but one person on his visit to this large mission, yet in the Register itself is recorded the name of only one recipient of that sacrament. In fact this record (so far at least as known to the writer) is the only proof of positive and explicit character that Bishop Carroll ever visited Berks County.*

Here is the entry of the confirmation, which Fr. Erntzen has put (at page 83) among the records of marriages.

"April 19, 1793, being confessed and having made his First Communion this same day Anthony Reichard, son of William Reichard and his wife Elizabeth Redert, was confirmed by the Right Reverend John Carroll, bishop of Baltimore".

The following excerpts from the Registers are given as the names therein recorded may be of some interest to the lover of genealogy.

(1) " Blanche jeanne Marie Louise fille legitime de Mr Aimé Jean Gerbier de Vologé et de Madame Claudine françoise Chaussée. elle est née le 15 juin 1793 et baptisée [by Fr. Erntzen] 1 Mars 1794. Parrain M^r jean Keating. Marraine Mad^e Marie Louise Julienne Baronne de Montullé." (From p. 52.)

[The preceding is the only entry in the book wholly in the French language.]

(2) Joseph Elizabeth Julius Chaudron, son of John Simon Chaudron and John [a mistake for Jane] Genevieve Stollawerk, both Catholics; he was born January 13, 1799; and baptized September 24 following by Fr. Erntzen; his godparents were Joseph E. G. M. de la Grange and Elizabeth Regina Laurence. (From p. 140.)

---

* In his *History*, ii, pp. 273-74, Dr. Shea refers to the purpose of Father Carroll, in 1785, to visit the country missions around Philadelphia. At this time, though not yet bishop, he was Superior of the missions.

(3) Regina Frances Genevieve Charlotte Gaschet de Lisle, born June 11, 1799, of Joseph Louis Gaschet de Lisle and Elizabeth Regina Laurence, both Catholics; she was baptized by Fr. Erntzen September 24 following; and her godparents were Charles Nicholas Donatus Gervais and Jane Genevieve Stollawerk. (From p. 140.)

(4) Francis Duval, unmarried, a native of Calais [*in France*,] died at Pottsgrove June 30, 1808; and was buried near the church at Goshenhoppen on July 1. (From p. 131.)

With reference to the family names one encounters in these registers, the writer has thought it well especially for the sake of the student to set them down just as they were written by the missionaries themselves, although at times, as is very clear, they have been mis-spelled, or may be,—the conjecture is not wholly unwarrantable, they afford evidence that the language itself was in a transition-stage. Non-English proper names were being Anglicized gradually by a kind of orthographical evolution. Thus one reads—" *Flauer* " and " *Flower* "; " *Schwittmann*", " *Swuitman*" and " *Sweetman* "; " *Schwarz* " and " *Shwarz*"; " *Schmidt* ", " *Shmid* ", " *Schmit* ", and " *Shmidt* "; " *Welcher* " and " *Welker* "; " *Braun*", " *Brawn* " and "*Brown* "; " *Eckenrodt*", " *Eccorod*", "*Eckorod*", "*Eckerod* " and "*Eckerott*"; " *Kaiffer*", "*Kaeffer*", and " *Keffer* "; " *Ashburner*", " *Ashburn* " and "*Ashborn* "; "*Schneider* " and "*Shneider* "; and so on with other family-names of non-English origin.

Among the names set down in the Registers of Goshenhoppen mission one will meet frequently with the family named " *M'Carty*", who were residents in Berks county from the early part of the XVIIIth century.

In this present Register this name will be observed under several singular and odd-looking forms, for the reason, (though this is merely a surmise of the translator,) that the ear of the non-English speaking missionaries had not been trained to catch the Gaelic, or Celtic, sound of *c*, *t* and *th*.

Thus we find the name M'Carty,—the old and perhaps the only proper way of spelling it,—written "*Megaddy*", "*McGaddy*", "*Gaddy*", "*MeCardy*", "*Mecarty*" and "*Mécarty*".

With regard to his translation of the Christian names of parties encountered in these Registers, which (as usual) were recorded in the Latin form of spelling them, the writer unable to determine with certainty the precise way of turning them in the vernacular, left to his own devices has chosen to render "*Aloitina*" Louisa; "*Jacobus*" James; "*Joanna*" Jane; "*Ludovicus*" Louis. Fr. Erntzen has turned Nancy into "*Nancia*"; Peggy he has written "*Peggé*", while Polly in his registers assumes the Latin form of "*Polli*".

As regards the various localities referred to in these registers besides the home residence of the missionaries at Goshenhoppen* mention is made of several other places,

---

* In the registers this name has been set down in various forms, as "*Goschenhoppen*"; (for which see the *Title-page* given ahead ;) then abbreviated to " Gosh ", " Goshenh." —a fancy employed by Fr. Erntzen.

As a kind of archæological curiosity I subjoin here a list of variants of the name of Goshenhoppen, set in chronological order. The authorities for these various spellings are the *Colonial Records of Penna.* (First Series ;) Hazard's *Pennsylvania Archives ;* and the *Mission Registers* of Goshenhoppen church published by this SOCIETY in its RECORDS. They are quoted below as *Col. Rec.; Archives;* and *Records.*

LIST OF VARIANTS OF GOSHENHOPPEN.

NAME	EMPLOYED IN THE YEAR	AUTHORITIES
1 Cosshehoppa	1735	*Col. Rec.*, iii, 619
2 Quesohopen	1735	*id.*, iii, 590
3 New Cosshehoppa	1735	*id.*, iii, 617
4 New Quessohopen	1735-36	*id.*, iii, 617
5 Cushenhopen	1743	*Records*, ii. 319
6 Cussahoppen	1755	*Col. Rec.*, vi, 503
7 Old Coshehoppe	1755	*Archives*, ii, 251
8 Old Goshehoppe	1755	*ibid.*
9 Old Cowshoppen	1755	*ibid.*
10 Goshenhopen	*ante* 1764	*Records*, ii, 332
11 Goshenhoppen	1764	*id.*, ii. 328
12 Couissahopen	1764-65	*id.*, ii, 328 ; iii. 303 4
13 Gosshenhopen	1766	*id.*, iii, 306
14 Gosscheuhopen	1766	*id.*, ii, 306, 379
15 Gosshehopen	1766	*id.*, iii. 379
16 Gossenhoppen	1773	*id.*, iii, 382
17 Goschenhoppen	1787	this present *Paper.*

While in the *Baptismal Registers* of Goshenhoppen for 1817-20, not yet published, are—

18 Goshenhopen	20 Coseheopen	22 Cosehenhopen
19 Kosehehopen	21 Koshenhopen	

—some of them visited by the clergymen in the course of their priestly ministrations, others,—the residence of the parties concerned.

These places are: Bucks county, sometimes written "*Bocks*"; Berks written "*Bergs*"; Conewago, as "*Conewago*", in Adams county; "*Crenners*" township; "*Crimitz*" county; "*Dollpenhacken*" apparently meant for Tulpehocken; "*Hegau*" in Bucks county; "*Herfordt*" = Hereford in Berks county; "*Kutschenstatell*" and "*Kutsenstattall*"; "*Kutsdam*"; "*Libanon*", that is, Lebanon, township; "*Langenschwam*" = Long Swamp; "*Manthobb*"; "*Monte acuto*" = "Sharp Mountain; "*Obersobfort*" township in "*Mont Commery*", i. e. Montgomery, county; "*Quitopahill*", a place where on November 15, 1795, Fr. Erntzen married a couple in the presence of the whole congregation; Reading, at times written "*raiding*"; "*Reeking*" township; and "*Veidhom*" township.

At the back of the Register, as Fr. Helbron has noted in his Title of it, will be read the following memoranda relating to the mission of Goshenhoppen, which here have been turned from Latin into English.

MEMORANDA.

"22 November 1787. I entered the Mission of "*Goschenhoppen*" and the next year for the solace of souls I had erected in the graveyard a Mission Cross made by Zimmermartin and Kemp, the donors of it.

"1788. The field next the house and barn I had fenced —"*circumsepiri*"—for seven pounds and ten shillings. The same year I had built a kitchen* with a bed-room and granary for thirty-six pounds and fifteen shillings.

"1789. For the church and as a matter of fact by alms-gathering I got banners to be carried in processions.

---

* The word—"*caulinam*", though by itself I take it to mean a sheepfold, here because of its connection with a sleeping room—"*cubiculo*" I think means what I have written.

134

The same year with the aid of the parishioners and bene-
factors I built a steeple—"*turris*"—and put a bell in it
for the glory of God and the honor of the place purchased
for this purpose from a certain Mennonist [*in the text*
"a quodam Mennisto,"] by Rev. Father Schneider, that
thereby it may be honored the more by all and be the
better preserved.

"1790. For the safe-keeping of the chalice, vestments
and other sacred things needed for the altar and Mass I had
set up back of the altar two little closets, and this for the
glory of God and the convenience of the priest.

"1791. The room of the man-servant—"*famuli*", that
needed repairs inside and out I had fitted up together with
a little stable for five pounds and eight shillings.

[*Then subjoined to the foregoing is a memorandum in
Fr. Delvaux's hand, which reads as follows:*]

"25 May 1792. For the ornament of the Church I got
six white cassocks [in the text "*vestes*"] item six red
ones for the acolytes item the same year I got 12 large
candelabra item for the communion-rail a red cloth item a
canopy, [*so at least I make out the words, which are part
in Latin and part in German*—'coelum oder Himmel',]
to be borne in solemn procession [*of the Blessed Sacrament.*]" And this ends the list of memoranda relating to
St. Paul's church at Goshenhoppen.

To these observations on the old registers of the church
of St. Paul we may add as conclusion that the mission
records that follow this paper comprise six hundred and
fifty-four (654) baptisms, among them six (6) sets of twins
and eight (8) illegitimates; ninety-seven (97) marriages;
one (1) confirmation; and forty-eight (48) deaths and
burials.

So that by adding these figures to the numbers given in
the two preceding Series, we find that at Goshenhoppen in
the last century from 1741–1800,* were recorded seventeen

---

* The registrations for the years 1785–1787, it is to be remembered, are wanting.

hundred and eighty (1780) baptisms ; sixteen (16) conversions ; two hundred and seventy-five (275) marriages ; one (1) confirmation and one hundred and sixty-three (163) deaths and burials.

In the following table of registrations the annotations, which the translator has thought well to interweave in the text, have all been set in square brackets.

Villanova College, Pa.,

    May 4, 1897.

            Fr. Thomas C. Middleton, O.S.A.

BAPTISMS FOR THE YEAR 1787.

Arens, Elizabeth, born October 10, 1787, of James Arens and his wife Margaret ; sponsors, John Gaucker and his wife Marina ; baptized November 13,* by Peter Helbron, missionary.

Webel, ———, daughter of Frederick Webel and his wife Elizabeth Egen, born October 25 ; baptized November 18, by John Baptist Charles Helbron, brother german of Peter and his companion in the Mission ; sponsors, John Matheis, of Reeking [sic] township, and Anna Maria Egg.

Kun, Teresa, born September 25, of Henry Kun and Anna Margaret Weider, of Veidhom township ; baptized by John Baptist Charles Helbron ; sponsors, Catharine Kuns and John Kuns, of Herford township.

Matheis, ———, daughter of John Matheis and his wife Mary Egg ; born October 26 ; baptized by the above ; sponsors, Eva Egg and Peter Eck, of [name illegible.]

Flemenn [?], Mary, born December 1, of Jerome Flemenn and his wife Rosina ; baptized by Peter Helbron, missionary † sponsors, John Kanner [?] and Mary Kobele.

Küns, Anna Mary Juliana, born November 11, of George Küns and his wife Marina Maria, of Herford township ; baptized December 23 ; sponsors, Joseph Röhr and his wife Juliana.

Andres, Peter, born September [?] 30, of Christian Andres and his wife Mary ; baptized December 18 ; sponsors, Peter Kees [?] and his wife Margaret.

Schmidt, Michael, born ——— 10, of Joseph Schmidt and his wife Catharine ; baptized when two months old ; sponsors, Michael Schmidt, youth, and Mary Ruffner.

Muthardt, John George, born ——— 25, of Frederick Muthardt, non-Catholic, and his wife Barbara, Catholic ; baptized when two months old ; sponsors, John George Michael Keffer and wife.

[The number of baptisms from November 13 is nine.]

BAPTISMS FOR THE YEAR 1788.

Hammerstein, Elizabeth, born September 24, of Andrew Hammerstein and his wife Barbara ; baptized February 24 ; sponsors, Elizabeth Gaddy and her husband Nicholas Megaddy [sic,] McCarty.

---

* Fr. Helbron in two places in this *Register* has set down the date of his arrival at Goshenhoppen on " November 22, 1787." (See the *Note* in the *Preface*.) And yet the first entry made by this missionary in his *Baptismal Register* is dated " November 13, 1787," which, unless explainable in some way not known to the writer, implies a manifest conflict of dates. It is barely possible,—so peculiar a way had Fr. Helbron of making his figure one (1) that it often looks like a two (2)—that the date " November 22 " in the title page should in reality be *November 12*. Thus the entry in the *Baptismal Register* would present no further difficulty. Or,—was the figure " 22 " a blunder ?

† From this date, unless otherwise noted, all the baptisms were administered by Rev. Peter Helbron, missionary in charge of Goshenhoppen. He rarely signs his entries.

137

Ilein, Daniel, born January 9, of Francis Ilein and his wife Marina ; baptized March 2 ; sponsors, Daniel Eck and his wife Eva.

Braun, Joseph, born March 2, of Andrew Braun and his wife Regina ; baptized March 16 ; sponsors, Joseph Ilein and his wife Magdalen.

Kaeffer [?], Anthony, born February 14, of Martin Kaeffer and his wife Anna Maria ; baptized March 16 ; sponsors, Leonard Bock and Margaret Gibson [*written* " Gibsen."]

Gaucker, John George, born March 13, of John Gaucker and his wife Anna Barbara ; baptized March 24 ; sponsors, John Jacob Arens and his wife Margaret.

Schnabell, Elizabeth, born March 7, of Joseph Schnabell and his wife Mary Busch ; baptized March 28 ; sponsor, Elizabeth Eck.

Ruhl, Salome Elizabeth, born February 6, of Frederick Ruhl and his wife Anna Maria Schorb ; baptized March 28 ; sponsor, Salome Elizabeth Scorb.

Fischwasser, Rosina, thirty-five years old, of the Quaker sect, deserted by her husband ; before her baptism on April 3, I ratified her marriage with another by name Schimmplemmer [?], which she had contracted on learning of the death of her former husband. [*Signed*] " Petrus Helbron."

Cred, Susan, October 3, [1787 ?], of Nicholas Cred and his wife Susan ; baptized March 30 ; sponsors, Mary Susan Cred and Andrew.

Eccorod, Mary Elizabeth, born February 27, of Henry Eccorod and his wife Mary Elizabeth ; baptized March 30 [?] ; sponsors, Mary Elizabeth Schinmfassel and Philip Strunck.

Geisweiler, Henry, born May 29, [1787 ?], of Philip Geisweiler and his wife Catharine ; baptized March 30 ; sponsors, Henry and Elizabeth Eccorod.

Domm, Michael, born December 26, [1787 ?], of Jacob Domm and his wife Elizabeth ; baptized March 30 ; sponsors, Michael Schnabel and Rosina Domm.

Gans, William, born October 10, [1787 ?], of John Gans and his wife Catharine ; baptized March 30 ; sponsors, Jacob and Dorothy Lambert.

Wans, Abraham, born October 10, [1787 ?], of George Wans and his wife Mary ; baptized March 30 ; sponsors, John Flauer and his wife Catharine.

Zweier, Mary Ann, born December 24, [1787], of Adam Zweier and his wife Barbara ; baptized March 31 ; sponsors, Mary Huber and Peter Rauch.

Zweier, Mary Elizabeth, born December 25, [1787], of Anthony Zweier and his wife Mary ; baptized March 31 ; sponsors, Elizabeth and Balthasar Zweier.

Laurentii, [*Lorenz*], Mary, born September 8, [1787 ?], of Moritz Laurentii and his wife Mary Apollonia ; baptized April 6 ; sponsors, Joseph Schlosser and his wife Mary.

Henrich, Eva Catharine, born January 2, of Philip Henrich and his wife Elizabeth ; baptized April 6 ; sponsors, Adam Reich and his wife Eva Catharine.

Reintz, Rosina, born August 1, [1787], of Valentine Reintz and his wife Anna Maria ; baptized April 6 ; sponsors, Rosina Domm and Henry Bever.

Weibel, Anna Maria, born January 19, of Joseph Weibel and his wife Margaret ; baptized April 6 ; sponsors, Anna Maria Weibel and Maurice Laurers [*Lorenz.*]

Schmidt, Andrew, born November 16, [1787], of Joseph Schmidt and his wife Regina ; baptized April 6 ; sponsors, Andrew Cred and his wife Magdalen.

Megaddy [*M'Carty*], Nicholas, born February 10, of Nicholas Megaddy and his wife Elizabeth ; baptized April 28 ; sponsors, Nicholas Mygaddy [*sic*]and his wife Albertina.

Strautenbach, Antony, born December 13, [1787], of John Strautenbach and his wife Barbara, now abandoned by her husband ; baptized April 28 ; sponsors, Antony Lamberg and Catharine Mullen.

Eccorod, James, born June 23, of George Eccorod and his wife Maria Weuer [*or* Neuer] ; baptized May 25 ; sponsors, James Frederich Aitz and Elizabeth Eccorod.

Hartmann, John Joseph, born May 19, of Jacob Hartmann and his wife Catharine Kemp ; baptized June 29 ; sponsors, John Jacob Kemper and his wife Anna Bender.

Hartmann Elizabeth, born May 9, of Francis Hartmann and his wife Angela Herb ; baptized June 29 ; sponsors, Peter Keffer and Elizabeth Brick.

Walker, Mary Ann, born January 8, 1788, of Jacob Walker and his wife Catharine Dollingers, of Crenners township; baptized July 6 ; sponsors, Bartholomew Koble and his wife Mary Ann.

Adam, Elizabeth, born June 20, 1788, of Simon Adam and his wife Catharine Eck ; baptized July 6 ; sponsors, John Schwittman and Elizabeth Eck, maiden.

Delkamm, Mary Eve, born April 17, of Henry Delkamm and his wife Susan Weismüller ; baptized July 14 ; sponsors, William Strunck and Elizabeth Weismüller.

Zweier, Anna, born April 24, of Thomas Zweier and his wife Mary ; baptized July 14 ; sponsors, Michael Schedler and Anna Maria Fischer.

Weber, Caspar, born May 28, of Matthias Weber and his wife Mary Magdalen ; baptized August 15 ; sponsors, Caspar Shoenebruck and his wife Margaret.

Canner, John, seven years old, son of Paul Canner and his wife Margaret Eber ; baptized August 15 ; sponsors, John Michael Kun and Mary Kaner.

Canner, Mary, eight years old, daughter of the above ; baptized with the above ; sponsors, John Canner and Catharine Els, maiden.

Schmid, John, eight weeks old, son of John Schmid and his wife Mary Hartranfer ; baptized August 16 ; sponsors, John Eck and his wife Dorothy.

Laurentii [*Lorenz*], Anna Maria, born June 26, of Joseph Laurentii and his wife Catharine Brettes ; baptized August 31 ; sponsors, Jacob Lawrenz and Anna Maria Margaret Schlosser.

Rebbert [*Reppert*], Joseph, two months old, son of Stephen Rebbert and his wife Magdalen ; baptized September 28 ; sponsors, Joseph Kasser and Barbara Rebbert, maiden.

Cred, Catharine, one month old, daughter of Andrew Cred and his wife Mary ; baptized October 5 ; sponsors, John Cred, youth, and Catharine Bock, maiden.

Brück, Anna Margaret, two months old, daughter of Matthias Brück and his wife Catharine ; baptized October 12 ; sponsors, Carl and Anna Margaret Kees, wife of John Kees.

Kesner, Henry Adam, half-year old, son of John Kesner and his wife Catharine ; baptized October 19 ; sponsors, John Henry Hoenig, youth, and Mary Ruppel, maiden.

Waehtwein, Matthias Joseph, eight days old, son of John Waehtwein and his wife Mary ; baptized October 29 ; sponsors, Matthias Röhr and his wife Margaret.

Stalter, Anna Maria, four weeks old, daughter of Henry Stalter and his wife Apollonia ; baptized November 1 ; sponsors, Anna Maria and George Kins.

Kuhns, Joanna, four weeks old, daughter of John Kuhns and his wife Catharine ; baptized November 16 ; sponsors, Joanna Cremers, maiden, and John Kuhns, youth.

Cred, Nicholas Andrew, seven weeks old, son of Andrew Cred and his wife Elizabeth ; baptized November 23 ; sponsors, Nicholas Andrew Cred and his wife Anna dewald.

Schmid, Mary Catharine, three months old, daughter of George Schmid and his wife Barbara ; baptized December 6 ; sponsors, Peter Kass, youth, and Mary Catharine Schmid, maiden.

Röhr, John Charles, one month old, son of Joseph Röhr and his wife Catharine ; baptized December 8 ; sponsors, John Charles Schwitman, youth, and Elizabeth Röhrs, maiden.

Rottmann, Elizabeth, two months old, daughter of Bernard Rottmann and his wife Catharine ; baptized December 14 ; sponsors, Elizabeth Bock and her husband Joseph Leonard Bock.

Reichert, John William, two months old, son of Stephen Reichert and his wife Mary ; baptized December 21 ; sponsors, John William Kemp and his wife Anna.

Welcker, Henry Stephen, four weeks old, son of John Jacob Welcker and his wife Magdalen ; baptized December 26 ; sponsors, Henry John Els and his wife Anna Elizabeth.

[The number of baptisms for the year is forty-eight.]

BAPTISMS FOR THE YEAR 1789.

Hartmann, Jacob Frederick, two months old, son of John Hartmann and his wife Susan ; baptized January 6 ; sponsors, John Jacob Els, youth, and Anna Barbara, maiden.

Reichert, John Augustine, ten days old, son of John Reichert and his wife Catharine ; baptized January 6 ; sponsors, John Augustus Koble, youth, and Anna Eva Koble, maiden.

Eck, Elizabeth, two weeks old, daughter of Theodore Eck and his wife Mary Elizabeth ; baptized January 6 ; sponsors, Elizabeth Eck, maiden, and John Gaucker, youth.

Lambert, John, three months old, son of Jacob Lambert and his wife Dorothy ; baptized January 11 ; sponsors, Sebastian Algeyer and his wife Catharine.

Rittner, John, four months old, son of Peter Rittner and his wife Barbara ; baptized January 11 ; sponsors, John Joseph Rittner and his wife Eva.

Algeyer, Elizabeth, five months old, daughter of Sebastian Algeyer and his wife Catharine ; baptized January 11 ; sponsors, William Strunck and his wife Elizabeth.

Schmids, Juliana Seraphina, born November 7, 1788, of Cosmas Schmids and his wife Anna ; baptized January 18 ; sponsors, Juliana Margaret Stand, wife, and Seraphinus Lambert.

Foelix, Regina, fourteen days old, daughter of Nicholas Foelix and his wife Anna Maria ; baptized March 8 ; sponsors, William Strunck and his wife Elizabeth.

Schimfassel, Anthony, four weeks old, son of Andrew Schimfassel and his wife Margaret ; baptized March 8 ; sponsors, Anthony Fricker and his wife Eva.

Flauer, Anna Maria, four months old, daughter of John Flauer and his wife Catharine ; baptized March 15 ; sponsors, George Wantz and his wife Maria.

Zweyer, Balthasar, six weeks old, son of Joseph Zweyer and his wife Catharine ; baptized March 15 ; sponsors, Balthasar Zweyer, youth, and Magdalen Huck, maiden.

Els, Mary Juliana, four weeks old, daughter of John Els and his wife Anna Elizabeth ; baptized March 20 ; sponsors, Mary Juliana Koble and her husband Daniel.

Cred, Susanna Barbara, four weeks old, daughter of Michael Cred and his wife Catharine ; baptized March 20 ; sponsors, Barbara Gaucker and her husband John Gaucker.

Ilein, Catharine Regina, four weeks old, daughter of Joseph Ilein and his wife Margaret ; baptized March 20 ; sponsors, Regina Braun and her husband Andrew.

Schmids, Juliana Seraphina, three months old, daughter of John Schmids and his wife Margaret ; baptized March 22 ; sponsors, Juliana Margaret, wife of John Standt, of Kutsenstattall, and Seraphinus Lamberton, living with Standt.

Eckorod, Christian, two months old, son of Christian Eckorod and his wife Mary ; baptized March 22 ; sponsors, Christian Henrich and Anna Magdalen Eckerod, maiden.

Flauer, Joseph, three months old, son of Christopher Flauer and his wife Magdalen ; baptized March 22 ; sponsors, Joseph Schlosser, youth, and Elizabeth Henrichs, maiden.

Burgie, John, two months old, son of Joseph Burgie and his wife Anna Maria ; baptized March 22 ; sponsors, John Weibel and his wife Margaret.

Domm, Mary Elizabeth, two months old, daughter of Thomas Domm and his wife Elizabeth ; baptized March 22 ; sponsors, Eva Grünenwald, maiden, and Joseph Domm, youth.

Reichert, Rosina, one month old, daughter of Adam Reichert and his wife Eva ; baptized March 22 ; sponsors, Rosina Domm, maiden, and John Schlosser, youth.

Koch, Catharine, five months old, daughter of John Henry Koch and his wife Dorothy ; baptized March 27 ; sponsors Catharine Röhr and her husband Matthias.

Schoenebruck, Margaret, three months old, daughter of Caspar Schoenebruck and his wife Margaret ; baptized March 29 ; sponsors, Anna Margaret Bock and her husband Joseph.

Kuhn, Mary Magdalen, three months old, daughter of Henry Kuhn and his wife Margaret ; baptized March 29 ; sponsors, Eva Mary Schmid, maiden, and Peter Kass [or Kay], youth.

Andres, Jacob, three months old, son of Christian Andres and his wife Mary ; baptized March 29 ; sponsors, Jacob Kass [or Kay] and his wife Barbara.

Schorb, Joseph, born January 27, of John Schorb and his wife Elizabeth ; baptized April 5 ; sponsors, Joseph Schorb, youth, and Magdalen Schnaebels, maiden.

Bock, Mary Magdalen, seven weeks old, daughter of Leonard Bock and his wife Elizabeth ; baptized April 12 ; sponsors, Magdalen Eck, maiden, and Nicholas Bock, youth.

Frickert, George, born February [?] 24, of Joseph Frickert and his wife Catharine ; baptized April 19 ; sponsors, George Gaddy and Barbara Dabre, both unmarried.

Kohl, John Anthony, born March 5, of George Kohl and his wife Catharine ; baptized April 19 ; sponsors, John Anthony Lambing, youth, and Elizabeth Gaddy [M'Carty], maiden.

Embs, John Paul, born December 28 [?], 1788, of Valentine Embs and his wife Juliana ; baptized April 24 ; sponsors, Balthasar Zweyer, youth, and Joanna Hock, maiden.

[*This entry has been recorded at the end of May, and is here put in its proper order.*]

Eccorod, Mary Catharine, two months old, daughter of Henry Eccorod and his wife Elizabeth ; baptized May 10 ; sponsors, Ludovic Schimfassel and his wife Catharine.

Buker, Jacob, born April 12, of John Buker and his wife Mary ; baptized May 17 ; sponsors, Jacob Schnabell, youth, and Magdalen Ratschar, maiden.

Henrich, John George Conrad, born March 29, of John Henrich and his wife Mary Barbara ; baptized May 24 ; sponsors, Conrad Spring, youth, and Elizabeth Henrichs, maiden.

Eccorod, Elizabeth, two months old, daughter of Adam Eccorod and his wife Barbara ; baptized May 24 ; sponsors, Frederick Lütz and his wife Elizabeth.

Zweyer, Magdalen, born May 11, of Anthony Zweyer and his wife Mary ; baptized June 7 ; sponsors, Balthasar Zweyer, youth, and Elizabeth Magdalen [?] Zweyer, maiden.

Geven, Rosina, born June 7, of Peter Geven and his wife Catharine ; baptized July 5 ; sponsors, Rosina Domm, maiden, and Jacob Els, youth. [*This entry has been recorded at the end of November.*]

Gery, Elizabeth, born February 23, of Philip Gery and his wife Sara ; baptized July 7 ; sponsors, Elizabeth Schmid and her husband Caspar.

Semigoter, Catharine, fourteen years old, daughter of Peter Semigoter and his wife Catharine, non-Catholics ; baptized July 8 ; sponsors, Catharine Reichert, married, and John Koble, youth.

Hammerstein, Philip, four months old, son of Andrew Hammerstein and his wife Barbara ; baptized August 16 ; sponsors, George Philip Kohl and his wife Catharine.

Sigfrid, Philip Charles, fourteen days old, son of John Sigfrid and his wife Mary ; baptized September 6 ; sponsors, Philip Charles Strunek, youth, and Catharine Sigfrid, maiden.

Grünewald, Rosina, three weeks old, daughter of Peter Grünewald and his wife Susan Mariana ; baptized September 6 ; sponsors, Rosina, maiden, and Jacob Grünewald, youth.

Eck, John, ten days old, son of Joseph Eck and his wife Catharine ; baptized September 14 ; sponsors, John Kemper, youth, and Juliana Eck.

Schmid, Jacob Peter, born September 22, of Joseph Schmid and his wife Catharine ; baptized October 11 ; sponsors, Jacob Peter Kass, married, and Ursula Schmid, widow.

Röhr [*but written* " Rhör "], Eva Margaret, born September 22, of Nicholas Rhör and his wife Mary ; baptized November 8 ; sponsors, Eva Margaret Strung, maiden, and Leonard Foelix, youth.

Mackel, Christopher, fourteen days old, son of Adam Mackel and his wife Elizabeth ; baptized November 18 ; sponsors, Joseph Mackel, widower, and Elizabeth, wife of Thomas Mackel.

Mackel, Thomas, born last year, son of the above ; baptized with the above ; sponsors Thomas Mackel and his wife.

Mackel [*but written* " Magel "], Maria, three weeks old, daughter of Thomas Magel and his wife Elizabeth ; baptized with the above ; sponsors, Adam Mackel and his wife.

Bock, John Caspar, born November 7, of Joseph Bock and his wife Elizabeth ; baptized December 13 ; sponsors, John Caspar Schoenebruck and his wife Margaret.

Matheis, Mary Magdalen, born 7th inst., of John Matheis and his wife Maria ; baptized December 25 ; sponsors, Magdalen Eck, maiden, and George Zweyer, youth.

[The number of baptisms for the year is forty-eight.]

BAPTISMS FOR THE YEAR 1790.

Ilein, Jacob John, born 5th ult., of Francis Ilein and his wife Catharine ; baptized January 1 ; sponsors, John Ilein, youth, and Elizabeth Eck.

Gaucker, Michael, born 19th ult., of John Gaucker and his wife Barbara ; baptized January 1 ; sponsors, Michael Cred and his wife Catharine.

Hartmann, Catharine, born November 22, of Jacob Hartmann and his wife Catharine ; baptized January 3 ; sponsors, Catharine Bock, maiden, and John Kemper, youth.

Schwittmann, Joseph Richard, [" Reichardus " *in the text*], born January 9, of John Schwittmann and his wife Margaret ; baptized February 2 ; sponsors, Joseph Röhr and his wife Juliana.

Rittner, Peter, born March 4, of Peter Rittner and his wife Barbara ; baptized March 14 ; sponsors, Joseph Peter Rittner and his wife Eva.

Eysenmann, Jacob, born January 7, of Christian Eysenmann and his wife Susan ; baptized March 14 ; sponsors, Jacob Lambert and his wife Dorothy.

Koble, Jacob, born 11th inst., of Bartholomew Koble and his wife Anna Maria ; baptized March 14 ; sponsors, Jacob Els and Eva Koble, youths.

Seyvert, Philip, fourteen days old, son of Joseph Seyvert and his wife Catharine ; baptized March 15, at Tulpohocken ["Dollpenhacken" *in the text*] ; sponsor, Philip Schmid, youth.

Schommo, Andrew, three weeks old, son of Anthony Schommo and his wife Elizabeth ; baptized March 16, at " Dollpenhacken "; sponsors, Joseph Seyvert and his wife.

Cred, Joseph, four weeks ago, son of John Cred and his wife Elizabeth; baptized March 16 ; sponsors, Philip Joseph Schmidt and his wife.

Röhr, Margaret, born March 6, of Matthias Röhr and his wife Catharine ; baptized March 19 ; sponsors, John Schwittman and his wife Margaret.

Moltzbeger, Joseph, born January 16, of Jacob Moltzbeger and his wife Catharine ; baptized March 28 ; sponsors, Joseph Gibsen, youth, and Catharine Mintzers [?], maiden.

Rebbert [*Reppert*], Catharine Elizabeth, born March 5, of Stephen Rebbert and his wife Magdalen ; baptized March 28 ; sponsors, Catharine Reichert and her husband John Reichert.

Mutthart, Mary Magdalen, four weeks old, daughter of Frederick Mutthart, non-Catholic, and his wife Magdalen, Catholic ; baptized March 30 ; sponsors, Anna Mary Allsman, maiden, and John George Hopp.

Röhr, Mary Ann, born March 29, of Joseph Röhr and his wife Juliana; baptized May 2 ; sponsors, Anna Mary Koble and her husband Daniel.

Ilein, Jacob Isidore, born April 4, of Francis Louis Ilein and his wife Juliana ; baptized May 2 ; sponsors, Jacob Els, youth, and Anna Maria Allsman, maiden.

Gersweiler, Andrew, born March 29, of Philip Gersweiler and his wife Catharine ; baptized May 9 ; sponsors, Andrew Schimpfassel and his wife Mary.

Zweyer, John Anthony, born April 17, of Stephen Zweyer and his wife Anna Maria ; baptized May 12 ; sponsors, John Kemp and his wife Anna.

Schmid, Elizabeth, born September 5, [1789,]of Joseph Schmid and his wife Regina ; baptized May 16 ; sponsors, Thomas Domm and his wife Elizabeth.

Schott, John William, born January 27, of Peter Schott and his wife Sophia ; baptized May 13 ; sponsors, John Schwittmann and his wife Margaret.

Klee, Henry, born December 16, [1789], of Ernest Klee and his wife Christina ; baptized May 13 ; sponsors, Henry Gibsen and his wife Catharine.

Schnabell, John, born April 23, of Joseph Schnabell and his wife Mary ; baptized May 13 ; sponsors, John Ilein, youth, and Magdalen Schnabell, maiden.

Kuns, John Jacob, born April 9, of John Kuns and his wife Catharine; baptized May 13 ; sponsors, John Kemp, youth, and Rosina Scnabells, maiden.

Schmid, Jacob Caspar, born November 30, [1789], of John Schmid and his wife Mary ; baptized May 23 ; sponsors, Caspar Schmidt and his wife Elizabeth.

Bernen, John, twenty-three years old, son of Peter Bernen and his wife Maria, of no religion ; baptized and made profession of the Roman Catholic faith, June 6, in the presence of me and witnesses. [Signed] " Petrus Helbron."

Kremer, George, born April 23, of Matthias Kremer and his wife Mary ; baptized June 20 ; sponsors, Joseph Fricker and his wife Catharine.

Reisner, Benjamin Jacob, born March 29, of John Reisner and his wife Catharine ; baptized June 20 ; sponsors, Jacob Ruppel, youth, and Catharine Bock, maiden.

Schorb, Margaret, born June 26, of John Schorb and his wife Elizabeth ; baptized July 4 ; sponsors, Margaret Geogen [?], maiden, and George Hopp, youth.

Dellecan, Mary Charlotte [written " Scharlotta "], born April 8, of Henry Dellecan and his wife Susan ; baptized July 11 ; sponsors, Mary Elizabeth Strunck and her husband William.

Schmids, Mary Ann Barbara, born 4th inst., of Cosmas Schmids and his wife Anna ; baptized July 24 ; sponsors, John Stand, married, and Barbara Gallejar, maiden.

Reichert, Joseph, born July 2, of John Reichert and his wife Catharine; baptized August 1 ; sponsors, Joseph Kaeffer, youth, and Catharine Els, maiden.

Reichert, Mary, born June 6, of Stephen Reichert and his wife Mary ; baptized August 1 ; sponsors, Martin Gery and his wife Mary.

Hoenig, Catharine, two months old, daughter of Michael Hoenig and his wife Helen ; baptized August 15 ; sponsors, Catharine Hoenig, maiden, and John Megaddy [McCarty], youth.

Stalter, John, five weeks old, son of Henry Stalter and his wife Apollonia ; baptized September 5 ; sponsors, Martin Matheis and his wife Catharine.

Arenz, Margaret, born 4th inst., of Jacob Arenz and his wife Margaret; baptized September 11 ; sponsors, Margaret Gibsen, maiden, and George Hopp, youth.

Eckerott, Louis, born 1st inst., of Henry Eckerott and his wife Elizabeth ; baptized September 12 ; sponsors, Louis Schimpfasel and his wife Catharine.

Domm, Philip, born last of July, son of Thomas Domm and his wife Elizabeth ; baptized September 12 ; sponsors, Philip Schmid, youth, and Mary Eve Strunck, maiden.

Wantz, John, born July 3, of George Wantz and his wife Mary ; baptized September 12 ; sponsors, John Flauer and his wife Catharine.

Müller, Peter, born September 13, 1788, of Christian Müller and his wife Mary ; baptized September 12 ; sponsors, Peter Pott and his wife Catharine.

Müller, Peter, born February 30 [sic], 1790, of Christian Müller and his wife Catharine ; baptized September 21 ; sponsors, Peter Arrold, youth, and Catharine, married sister of the mother.

Weber, John Henry, born August 30, of Matthias Weber and his wife Mary Magdalen ; baptized September 29 ; sponsors, Adam Karpf and his wife Margaret.

Gery, John, four weeks old, son of Martin Gery and his wife Mary ; baptized October 3 ; sponsors, Stephen Reichert and his wife Mary.

Bock, Mary Apollonia, born August 15, of Leonard Bock and his wife Elizabeth ; baptized October 17 ; sponsors, Matthias Kremer and his wife Mary Apollonia.

Gling, William, born 4th inst., of Peter Gling and his wife Mary ; baptized October 17 ; sponsors, John William Megaddy [McCarty], youth, and Margaret Megaddy.

Mackel, Elizabeth, born April 10, of George Mackel and his wife Magdalen ; baptized October 17 ; sponsors, Joseph Mackel, youth, and Susan, maiden.

Hartmann, Joseph, born August 27, of Francis Hartmann and his wife Mary ; baptized October 24 ; sponsors, Joseph Bock and his wife Elizabeth.

Reinzel, Catharine, born ——— 13, 1789, of Felten Reinzel and his wife Anna Maria ; baptized November 1 ; sponsors, Catharine Scheven and her husband Peter.

Brück, Catharine, born October 9, of Matthew Brück and his wife Mary ; baptized November 1 ; sponsors, Eva Catharine Schmid, maiden, and John Kay [or Kass], youth.

Schimfassel, Mary Barbara, born October 23, of Andrew Schimfassel and his wife Margaret ; baptized November 14 ; sponsors, William Strunck and his wife Mary Elizabeth.

Hopp, Margaret, born 2d inst., of Andrew Hopp and his wife Magdalen ; baptized December 8 ; sponsors, Elizabeth Margaret Hopp and her husband George.

[The number of baptisms for the year, including two illegitimates, is fifty-three.]

BAPTISMS FOR THE YEAR 1791.

Dennes, Catharine, sixteen years old, daughter of John Dennes, Catholic, and his wife Catharine Elizabeth, Lutheran ; made profession of faith and baptized January 6 ; sponsors and witnesses, John Kemp and his wife Elizabeth.

Grünewalt, Andrew Jacob, born 2d inst., of Jacob Grünewalt and his wife Susan ; baptized January 9 ; sponsors, Andrew Jacob Schimfassel and his wife Margaret.

Buregy, Jacob Joseph, born October 24, of Joseph Buregy and his wife Anna Maria ; born January 23 ; sponsors, Joseph Henrich, youth, and Catharine Zing, maiden.

Cred, John, born 6th inst., of Andrew Cred and his wife Barbara ; baptized January 25 ; sponsors, John Henrich and his wife Barbara.

Cred, Barbara, born October 5, 1790, of Nicholas Cred and his wife Susan, non-Catholic ; baptized January 25 ; sponsors, Christian Henrich and his wife Elizabeth.

Baumann, Elizabeth, born August 5, 1790, of John Baumann and his wife Magdalen ; baptized January 25 ; sponsors, John Standt, married, of Kutsdam, and Magdalen, wife of Cred.

Eck, Peter, born 13th inst., of Theodore Eck and his wife Barbara ; baptized January 27 ; sponsor and substitute, Simon Adam.

Schmidt, Elizabeth, eight days old, daughter of John Schmidt and his wife Elizabeth ; baptized January 28 ; sponsors, Elizabeth Schmid, maiden, and John Schmidt, youth.

MeCardy [McCarty], Catharine, born January 2, of John MeCardy and his wife Elizabeth ; baptized February 28 ; sponsors, Catharine Helen Hoenigs and her husband Michael.

Hartmann, Mary Magdalen, born December 18, of John Hartmann and his wife Susan ; baptized March 4 ; sponsors, Magdalen Repperts and her husband Stephen.

Siegfrid, Joseph, born February 6, of Joseph Siegfrid and his wife Barbara ; baptized March 13 ; sponsors, Joseph Röhr, married, and Barbara Siegfrid, maiden.

Eisenmann, Susan, born February 6, of Christian Eisenmann and his wife Susan ; baptized March 13 ; sponsors, Dorothy Lambert and her husband Jacob Lambert.

Hoop, Andrew Francis, born this month, of George Hoop and his wife Margaret ; baptized March 25 ; sponsors, Andrew Hopp and his wife Catharine.

Braun, Mary Ann, born 2d inst., of Andrew Braun and his wife Regina ; baptized April 17 ; sponsors, George Gibsen, youth, and Mary Koble, maiden.

Kaeffer, Regina Catharine, eight days old, daughter of Martin Kaeffer and his wife Anna Maria ; baptized April 25 ; sponsors, Regina Candel, widow, and Simon Adam.

Grünewald, Philip Joseph, six months old, son of Joseph Grünewald and his wife Mary Ann ; baptized May 8 ; before the baptism of her offspring, the mother made profession of faith in public and was sacramentally refreshed ; sponsors, Philip Schmidt and his wife Elizabeth.

Flauer, Catharine, born March 28, of John Flauer and his wife Catharine ; baptized May 8 ; sponsors, George Wans and his wife Mary.

Poth, Mary Eve, two months old, daughter of Adam Poth and his wife Catharine ; baptized May 9 ; sponsors, Mary Eve Frickerts and John Buker, married.

Bock, Nicholas John, born April 26, of Jacob Bock and his wife Susan ; baptized May 11 [?] ; sponsors, Nicholas Bock and his wife Magdalen.

Ilein, Mary Magdalen, born April 29, of Francis Ilein and his wife Catharine ; baptized May 15 ; sponsors, Magdalen Eck, maiden, and John Kemp, youth.

Eckenrot, Catharine Elizabeth, born March 26, of George Eckenrot and his wife Mary ; baptized May 22 ; sponsors, Henry Beven, youth, and Catherine Stal, maiden.

Reichert, Catharine Christine, born April 15, of Adam Reichert and his wife Eve ; baptized May 23 ; sponsors, Peter Scheven and his wife Catharine.

Brestal, Joseph, born January 30, of Charles Brestal and his wife Mary Ann ; baptized May 23 ; sponsors, Joseph Seywert and his wife Catharine.

Seywert, John Benjamin, born March 30, of Joseph Seywert and his wife Catharine ; baptized May 23 ; sponsors, John Cred and his wife Mary Elizabeth.

Ems, Anna Maria, born March 12, of Valentine Ems and his wife Juliana ; baptized June 5 ; sponsors, John Benner and his wife Anna.

Welcker, Anna Maria Helen, born June 14, of Jacob Welcker and his wife Magdalen ; baptized June 26 ; sponsors, Daniel Koble and his wife Mary Ann Helen.

Kaeffer, Joseph, born 24th inst., of Jacob Kaeffer and his wife Magdalen ; baptized June 27 ; sponsors, Joseph Kaeffer, youth, and Margaret Kemp, maiden.

Hartmann, Anthony Michael, born 16th inst., of Jacob Hartmann and his wife Catharine ; baptized June 29 ; sponsors, Michael Cred, youth, and Margaret Kemp, maiden.

Zweyer, John Balthasar, born 14th ult., of Thomas Zweyer and his wife Mary ; baptized July 3 ; sponsors, Balthasar and Mary Zweyer, unmarried.

Buker, John Thomas, born 15th ult., of John Buker and his wife Mary ; baptized July 3 ; sponsors, Thomas Zweyer, married, and Eve Frickert, wife.

Lambert, William, born May 1, of Jacob Lambert and his wife Dorothy ; baptized July 10 ; sponsors, John William Gans and his wife Catharine.

Gans, Catharine, born January 6, of John Gans and his wife Catharine ; baptized July 10 ; sponsors, [*Jacob*] Lambert and his wife Dorothy. othy.

Zenner, Mary Elizabeth, born June 12, of David Zenner and his wife Elizabeth ; baptized July 24 ; sponsors, Anna Maria Elizabeth Henrichs and her husband Christian.

Bottman, Mary Magdalen, born May 29, of Bernard Bottman and his wife Catharine ; baptized July 31 ; sponsors, Mary Magdalen Bock and her husband Nicholas.

Meyer, Clara, eighteen years old, born of Jewish father ; baptized August 19 ; assistant and sponsor, Eva Frickert, wife of Anthony Frickert, in Reading.

[*The foregoing entry is the last one made by Rev. Peter Helbron in the Baptismal Register. The following down to April, 1793, were made by Rev. N. Delvaux, successor of Helbron in the Mission of Goshenhoppen.*

In the register the page is headed —" August.— Beginning of the mission of N. Delvaux."

His first entry is signed " a me N. Delvaux missirio " (i.e., his abbreviation for the word missionary) ; *three others bear the signature,* "Delvaux," " Delvaux parous " (i.e., parochus or parish priest), *and* " Delvaux parochus," *while the rest are unsigned.*]

Great, Jacob, born August 17, of Michael Great and his wife Catharine ; baptized, September 8, 1791 ; sponsors, Jacob Kaiffer and Magdalen Keiffer.

Kuntz, Theresa, born June 24, of John Kuntz and his wife Catharine ; baptized September 8 ; sponsors, Theresa Röhr [*though written* " Rhor "] and Michael Schnab.

Henrich [*written* " Hennrich "] Conrad, born September 13, of John Henrich and his wife Barbara ; baptized September 26 ; sponsors, Conrad and Barbara Haffner.

Givin [*or* Geven], Catharine, born July 13, of Peter Given and his wife Catharine ; baptized September 26 ; sponsors, Andrew and Catharine Werner.

Poth [*written* " Both "], Elizabeth, born September 20, of Jacob Both and his wife Catharine ; baptized October 2 ; sponsors, George and Elizabeth Bauer.

Schmidt [*written* " Schmith "], Henry, born December 22, 1790, of Joseph Schmith and his wife Catharine ; baptized October 9 ; sponsors, Henry Gibson and Eva Schmidd. [*To this entry is appended the significant word* "solvit," *i. e., something was given as an honorarium.*]

Els, Henry, born September 27, of John Els and his wife Elizabeth ; baptized October 16 ; sponsors, John and Catharine Reicherd [*Reichert.*]

Alexander, Catharine, daughter of Solomon Alexander and his wife Margaret ; baptized October 16 ; sponsor, Bernard Steward.

Gaucker, George, born October 15 ; of John Gaucker and his wife Barbara Weibel ; baptized November 2 ; sponsors, George and Margaret Hopp [*written* " Hop "].

Ilein [*written* "Ilain"], Matthias, born October 25, of Louis Ilain and his wife Juliana Kremer ; baptized November 20 ; sponsors, Matthias Kemp and his wife.

Schwartz, Anna Maria, born October 18, of Philip Schwartz and his wife Margaret ; baptized November 27 ; sponsors, Joseph and Anna Maria Schlösser.

[The number of baptisms for the year, including one illegitimate, is forty-seven.]

BAPTISMS FOR THE YEAR 1792.

Reichert [*written* "Richert"], Mary, born December 12, of John Richert and his wife Catharine Butz ; baptized January 1, 1.ˌ2 ; sponsors, Jacob Els and Margaret Koble [*written* Koblets."]

Hopp [*written* " Hop "], George, born December 11, 1791, of Andrew Hop and his wife Magdalen Kirchenman ; baptized January 6 ; sponsors, Joseph Gibson and Christina Hop.

Zweyer, Elizabeth, born October 7, 1791, of Adam Zweyer and his wife Barbara Siegfried ; baptized January 9 ; sponsors, Balthasar Zweyer and Mary Siegfried.

Zweyer, Catharine, born October 6, of Anthony Zweyer and his wife Mary Dresen ; baptized January 9 ; sponsors, Joseph Siegfried and Catharine Müller.

Eck, Abraham, born November 2, of John Eck and his wife Charlotte Knauer [?] ; baptized February 9 ; sponsors, Joseph Eck and his wife Agatha.

Eck, John, born November 3 [?], of Joseph Eck and his wife Mary Agatha Riffels ; sponsors, John Eck and his wife Charlotte.

Bock, Joseph, born December 5, of Joseph Bock and his wife Elizabeth Meikle ; sponsors, John Kemp and Catharine Els.

Müller, Margaret, born December 2, of Frederick Müller, non-Catholic, and his wife Elizabeth Breier ; suonsors, Erardus and Margaret Stott.

Melcker, John, about ten weeks old, son of Michael Melcker and his wife Magdalen Hoenig ; baptized February 26 ; sponsors, John Hoenig and Elizabeth Mecarty [*McCarty*].

Müller, Magdalen, born February 19, 1792, of Jacob Müller and his wife Mary Eve Burkhard ; sponsors, Andrew and Regina Braun [*written* " Brawn "].

150

Schoenebruck, Catharine, born February 26, 1792, of Caspar Schoenebruck and his wife Margaret Meckel; sponsors, Jacob Kaes and his
wife Barbara.

Swuitman, Bridget, born March 11, 1792, of John Swuitman and his
wife Margaret Röhr ; baptized April 9 ; sponsors, John and Elizabeth Els.

Clemer, Christian, non-Catholic, son of Christian Clemer and his wife
Catharine Zatip ; baptized April 10.

Hammerstein, ———, born February 12, 1792, daughter of Andrew
Hammerstein and his wife Barbara ; baptized April 22 ; sponsors,
Joseph Fricker and his wife.

Gerstweiler, Susan, born January 21, 1792, 𝑜𝑓 Philip Gerstweiler and
his wife, Catharine Schimpfessel ; sponsors, Philip Strunck and
Mary Siegfried. [*Appended to this entry is the word* " Gratis."]

Reppert, Barbara, born March 15, of Stephen Reppert and his wife
Magdalen Kaiffer ; sponsors, George Kemp and Barbara Kaiffer.

Müller, Margaret, eleven months old, daughter of Christian Müller
and his wife Eva ; baptized April 27 ; sponsors, Sebastian Allgayer and Catharine Poth.

Allgayer, Anthony, born March 11, 1792, of Sebastian Allgayer and
his wife Catharine.

Walker, John, born April 8, of Daniel Walker and his wife Gertrude
Schmith ; sponsors, John Kemp and Catharine Gibson.

Schmit, Catharine, born November 9, 1791, of Joseph Schmit and his
wife Regina Kemmel ; sponsors, Andrew Great and his wife.

Pannen, Joseph, born November 20, 1791, of John Pannen and his wife
Anna Huck ; sponsor, Juliana Ems.

Reichert [*written* " Richerd "], Elizabeth, born October 5, 1792 [*sic*,
1791 ?], of Stephen Richerd, non-Catholic, and his wife Mary
Gery ; sponsor, Martin Gery.

Canner, Mark, born May 17, 1792, of John Canner and his wife Anna
Carr ; sponsors, Louis Gincken and Mary Canner.

Böhr, Elizabeth, born June 6, 1792, of Joseph Böhr and his wife
Juliana Siegfried ; sponsors, Jacob Arens and Eva Coblet.

Gluin, Thomas, born June 20, 1792, of Patrick Gluin and his wife
Mary Thomasen [*Thompson* ?] ; sponsors, Thomas and Salome
Mécarty.

Röhr, Nancy [*in the Latin*, " Nancia "], born May 27, 1792, of Matthias
Röhr and his wife Catharine Siegfried ; sponsors, Daniel Coblet
and his wife Mary.

Rittner [*written* " Rittener "], Jacob, born July 6, 1792, of Peter
Rittener and his wife Barbara Berlis ; baptized July 16 ; sponsors,
Sebastian Allgayer and his wife Catharine.

Flauer, Anna Maria, born September 4, 1792, of Christopher Flauer
and his wife Magdalen ; sponsors, Philip and Margaret Swartz.

Burke, Philip, born June 23, 1792, of Joseph Burke and his wife Anna
Maria ; sponsors, John Henrich and his wife Barbara.

Kaes, John, born September 1, 1792, of Peter Kaes and his wife Magdalen ; sponsors, John Eck and his wife Margaret.

Marty, Jacob, born September 4, 1792, of John Marty and his wife Margaret ; sponsors, Peter Kaes and his wife Magdalen.

Grunewald, John, born September 20, of Joseph Grunewald and his wife Anna Maria ; sponsors, John Arens and Mary Siegfried.

Adam, John, born September 6, 1792, of Simon Adam and his wife Catharine Eck ; sponsors, John Eck and his wife Dorothy.

Ilein, [written " Ylain "], Elizabeth, born September 29, 1792, of Joseph Ylain and his wife Magdalen Swoab ; sponsors, John and Elizabeth Ylain.

Dum, Jacob, born in 1792 ; on October 31 he was ten weeks old, son of Jacob Dum and his wife Elizabeth ; sponsors, Jacob Arens and Christina Hop [Hopp].

Carens, John, born ten weeks before Christmas Day, 1792, of John Carens and his wife Christina ; sponsors, John and Elizabeth Mécarty [McCarty].

Eck, Peter, born October 21, 1792, of Peter Eck and his wife Magdalen Kaes ; sponsors, John and Eva Eck.

Bock, Catharine, born November 11, 1792, of Leonard Bock and his wife Elizabeth Cremer ; sponsors, John Frickert and his wife Catharine.

Kuntz, Andrew, born November 31 [?], 1792, of John Kuntz and his wife Catharine Eysehuden ; sponsors, Caspar Schmith and Magdalen Schnabel.

[The number of baptisms for the year, including one illegitimate. is forty.]

BAPTISMS FOR THE YEAR 1793.

Guery, George, born March 16, 1793, of Philip Guery and his wife ——— ; sponsors, George Kemp and Catharine Kuns.

Clemer, Mary, born February 15, 1793, of Christian Clemer and his wife Catharine Bock ; sponsors, Nicholas and Magdalen Bock.

Guery, George, born October 31, 1792, of Martin Guery and his wife Margaret Mottin [or Mollin] ; sponsors, George Bauer and his wife Elizabeth.

Hartman, Polly [written " Polli "], born September 11, 1793 [sic, 1792 ?], of Franz Hartman and his wife Engel Herb ; sponsors, John Kemp and Barbara Kaiffer.

Hartman, George, born January 30, 1793, of John Hartman and his wife Susan Marlip ; sponsors, George Kemp and Catharine Kaiffer.

Hop, Catharine, born March 21, 1792, of George Hop and his wife Mary ; sponsors, John Arens and Catharine Gibson.

[With this entry is closed the Baptismal Register of Rev. N. Delvaux. Those that follow were made by Rev. Paul Erntzen, who records the fact in his first certificate that he was the successor of Father Delvaux.]

Shurp, Anthony, born April 2, 1793, of John Shurp and his wife Elizabeth ; baptized April 21 ; sponsors, Joseph and Juliana Röhr.

Gret, Michael, born October 10, 1792, of John Gret and his wife Mary Elizabeth ; baptized April 9 ; sponsors, Nicholas Gret and his wife Susan.

Gret, Anna, born September 1, 1792, of Nicholas Gret and his wife Susan ; baptized April 9 ; sponsors, Philip Sanneffert and his wife Mary Barbara.

Illein, John Peter, born March 19, 1793, of Francis Illein and his wife Catharine Eck ; baptized May 5 ; sponsors, Peter Eck and his wife Magdalen.

Keffer, Susan, born March 29, 1793, of Jacob Keffer and his wife Magdalen Kemp ; baptized May 9 ; sponsors, Susan Kemp and John Keffer.

Keffer, John, born May 3, of Joseph Keffer and his wife Christina Rohrbach ; baptized May 13 ; sponsors, John Kemp and Barbara Keffer, sister of Joseph Keffer.

Hartman, John David, born April 7, 1793, of Jacob Hartman and his wife Hartman ; baptized May 19 ; sponsors, John Gaucker and his wife Barbara.

Shnabel, Mary Theresa, born March 6, 1793, of Joseph Shnabel and his wife Mary Bush ; baptized May 28 ; sponsors, Andrew Shnabel and his wife Eva.

Gibson, Joseph, born May 22, 1793, of Joseph Gibson and his wife Christina Hopp ; baptized June 11, in Henry Gibson's house ; sponsors, Joseph Arens and Magdalen Hopp.

Kohler, Nicholas, born May 16, 1793, of Jacob Kohler and his wife Elizabeth ; baptized June 23 ; sponsors, Nicholas Bock and his wife Magdalen.

Hönig, Margaret, born April 24, 1793, of Simon Hönig and, his wife Anna Maria ; baptized June 23 ; sponsors, John M'Carty and his wife Elizabeth.

Hönig, Mary, born April 1, 1792, of John and Helen Hönig ; baptized June 23, in Nicholas M'Carty's house ; sponsors, Simon and Anna Mary Hönig.

Magel, David, born December 3, 1790, of Daniel Magel and his wife Mary ; baptized June 24, in Christopher Magel's house ; sponsor, Adam Magel.

Magel, Jacob, born January 31, 1791, of Adam Magel and his wife Elizabeth ; baptized with the above ; sponsor, Christopher Magel.

Magel, Peter, born March 17, 1792, of George Magel and his wife Magdalen ; baptized with the above ; sponsor Christopher Magel.

Eck, John Joseph, born May 27, 1793, of Theodore Eck and his wife Mary Elizabeth Wider ; baptized July 7 ; sponsors, John and Barbara Gaucker.

Sauffert, Magdalen, born March 21, 1793, of Joseph Sauffert and his wife Catharine ; baptized July 14 ; sponsors, Joseph Gret and Catharine Shmidt.

Shurp, John William, born July 10, of Joseph Shurp and his wife Mary Elizabeth ; baptized July 15 ; sponsors, John William and Mary Elizabeth Strunk.

Shudder, Mary, born January 26, 1793, of Peter Shudder and his wife Sophia Wenzel ; baptized August 4 ; sponsors, William Gayde and Catharine Gibson.

Brown, Magdalen, born August 18, 1793, of Andrew Brown and his wife Regina ; baptized September 1 ; sponsors, John Jacob Welker and his wife Magdalen.

Ashburner, William, about 24 years old, son of Jacob Ashburner and his wife Sara, Quaker ; baptized September 2 ; sponsor, Joseph Gaucker.

Gret, Christian, born August 27, 1793, of Andrew Gret and his wife Elizabeth Henrich ; baptized September 24 ; sponsors, Christian Henrich and his wife Mary Margaret.

Oeckkenrodt, John Louis, born August 15, 1793, of Henry Oeckkenrodt and his wife Elizabeth ; baptized September 8 ; sponsors, Louis Gerstweiler and Gertrude Strunk.

O'Donnel, Edward, born May 22, 1792, of Neal O'Donnel and his wife Elizabeth ; baptized September 8 ; sponsors, Adam Poth and Eva Franzel.

O'Donnel, John, born December 20, 1790, of the above ; baptized with the above ; sponsor, Sebastian Algeier.

Shevein, Mary Elizabeth, born September 19, 1793, of Peter Shevein and his wife Catharine Dum ; baptized September 21 ; sponsors, Caspar Dum and his wife Mary.

Hofman, John Henry, born July 31, 1793, of Michael Hofman and his wife Catharine ; baptized October 6 ; sponsors, John and Barbara Gaucker.

Becker, Elizabeth, born September 5, 1793, of John Becker and his wife Mary ; baptized September 29 ; sponsors George Bauer and his wife Elizabeth.

Kemp, Anna Barbara, born September 21, 1793, of Margaret Kemp and ——— ; baptized September 30 ; sponsors, Peter Keffer and his wife Barbara.

Melchior, Catharine, born October 11, 1793, of Michael Melchior and his wife Mary ; baptized October 27 ; sponsors, John M'Carty and Eva Hoenig.

Bauer, Agidius Michael, born September 7, 1793, of Peter Bauer, non-Catholic, and his wife Rosina Shnabel, Catholic ; baptized November 23, in Andrew Shnabel's house ; sponsor, Michael Shnabel ; witness, Margaret Hansel.

Müller, Daniel, born October 10, 1793, of Nicholas Müller and his wife Anna ; baptized November 24, in Christian Henrich's house, near *Mons Acutus* [Sharp Mountain] ; sponsors, Jacob Spring and his wife Catharine.

Shwarz, John, born October 26, 1793, of Philip Shwarz and his wife Margaret ; baptized November 24 ; near *Mons Acutus* [Sharp Mountain] ; sponsors, John Schlosser and Magdalen Henrich.

Flower, Peter, born October 15, 1793, of John Flower and his wife
Catharine ; baptized November 27, in Andrew Gret's house ;
sponsors, Peter Putta and his wife Catharine.

Shmid, Elizabeth, born September 13, 1793, of George Shmid and his
wife Barbara Nagel; baptized October 13 ; sponsors, Joseph Buck
and his wife Elizabeth.

Kaes, Peter, born ———, of John Kaes and his wife Catharine ; baptized October 13 ; sponsors, Peter Kaes and his wife Margaret.

Greenwald, John, born ———, of Jacob Greenwald and his wife Susan;
baptized September 29 ; sponsor, John Greenwald.

Miller, Mary Barbara, born November 29, 1793, of Frederick Miller
and his wife Elizabeth ; baptized December 15 ; sponsor, Laurence Gubernator.

Botmann, Mary Ann, born December 2, 1793, of Bernard Botmann and
his wife Catharine ; baptized December 22, in N. M'Carty's house;
sponsors, Joseph Buck and Salome M'Carty.

Reichard, Elizabeth, born November —, 1793, of Adam Reichard and
his wife Mary Eve ; baptized December 29 ; sponsors, ———
Arens and ——— Dom.

[The number of baptisms for the year, including one illegitimate,
is forty-seven.]

BAPTISMS FOR THE YEAR 1794.

Kemp, Mary Catharine, born November 2, 1793, of Matthias Kemp
and his wife Catharine ; baptized January 12, at Reading ; sponsor, Mary Greenwald.

Berton, Esther, born October 8, 1793, of Thomas Berton, non-Catholic,
and [his wife] Elizabeth, Catholic ; baptized January 12, at Reading ; sponsors, Sebastian and Catharine Allgeier.

Reichard, Anna Elizabeth, born January 11, 1794, of John Reichard
and his wife Catharine Butz ; baptized February 9 ; sponsors,
John and Anna Elizabeth Els.

Both, Elizabeth Ann, born February 14, 1794, of Jacob Both and his
wife Catharine ; baptized February 21 ; sponsors, George Bauer
and his wife Elizabeth.

de Vologé, Blanche Jeanne Marie Louise. [*For this Baptism see the
Preface. This entry, belonging to the year 1794, has been recorded at the end of the Baptisms, for 1793*].

Eck, Catharine, born March 9, 1794, of Peter Eck and his wife Magdalen Käss ; baptized March 22 ; sponsors, John Eck and his wife
Eva.

Reppert, Mary, born March 16, 1794, of Stephen Reppert and his wife
Magdalen Keffer ; baptized March 24 ; sponsors, John Reppert
and Catharine Keffer.

Röhr, Daniel, born February 23, 1794, of Nicholas Röhr and his wife
Mary ; baptized March 8 ; sponsors, Anthony Twicker and his
wife Eva.

Röhr, Salome, born February 15, 1794, of Joseph Röhr and his wife
Juliana ; baptized March 27 ; sponsors, Bartholomew and Mary
Ann Coblet.

Zweyer, Mary Juliana, born January 31, 1794, of Thomas Zweyer and his wife Mary Ann ; baptized March 30 ; sponsors, Balthasar and Mary Juliana Zweyer.

Jones, John Amos, born December 9, 1767 [?], of Amos Jones and his wife Magdalen Tenes, non-Catholic ; baptized April 3 ; sponsor, Jacob Malzberger.

Röhr, Catharine, born February 5, 1794, of Matthias Röhr and his wife Catharine ; baptized April 20 ; sponsors, George Sigfrid and Catharine Gibson.

Kuns, Salome, born March 29, 1794, of John Kuns and his wife Catharine ; baptized April 21 ; sponsors, John Gauger and his wife Barbara.

Henrich, Francis Joseph, born February 5, 1794, of John Henrich and his wife Barbara ; baptized March 23 ; sponsors, Nicholas Miller and his wife Catharine.

Ursenbach, Mary Elizabeth, born February 14, 1794, of John Ursenbach and his wife Catharine ; baptized March 23 ; sponsors, Joseph Henrich and Mary Elizabeth Stahler.

Uhlein, Laurence Agnellus, born December 22, 1793, of Francis Louis Uhlein and his wife Juliana ; baptized at home by his father in case of necessity ; ceremonies supplied March 25 ; sponsors, Laurence Gubernator and wife.

M'Carty, Francis, born December 29, 1793, of John M'Carty and his wife Elizabeth ; baptized April 27 ; sponsors, Nicholas and Aloi-
· tina [Louisa ?] M'Carty.

M'Carty, Edward, born December 3, 1793, of Nicholas M'Carty and his wife Elizabeth ; baptized April 28 ; sponsors, Joseph Eck and Catharine Adam.

Gubernator, John Laurence, born March 30, 1794, of Lawrence Gubernator and his wife Joanna ; baptized May 2 ; sponsors, John and Margaret Sweetman.

Saüvert, Susan, born February 27, 1794, of Philip Saüvert and his wife Mary Barbara ; baptized May 4 ; sponsors, Nicholas Gret and his wife Susan.

Flower, Anna, born April 11, 1794, of Christopher Flower and his wife Magdalen ; baptized May 4 ; sponsors, John Adam Gret and Sophia Gellhoff.

Opold, Elizabeth, born January 19, 1794, of Joseph Opold and his wife Margaret ; baptized May 13 ; sponsors, Philip and Elizabeth Shmidt.

Orendorff, Mary, born April 24, 1794, of Christian Orendorff and his wife Eva ; baptized May 13 ; sponsors, Matthias and Christina Orendorff.

Dorret, Mary, born April 12, 1794, of Neal Dorret and his wife Guess M'Cu ; baptized May 13 ; sponsors, Charles Dever and Mary Dugan.

Shmidt, Catharine, born April 14, 1794, of Caspar Shmidt and his wife Susan ; baptized May 18 ; sponsors, John Coblet and Catharine Gibson.

Hönig, Susan, born April 7, 1794, of Michael Hönig and his wife Helen ; baptized June 22 ; sponsors, Anthony and Rachel Greeser:

Buck, John Nicholas, born May 13, 1794, of Nicholas Buck and his wife Magdalen ; baptized June 22 ; sponsors, John and Dorothy Egg.

Eckenrodt, Margaret, born April 19, 1793, of Christian Eckenrodt and his wife Magdalen ; baptized May 25 ; sponsors, Philip Michael and Margaret Shwarz.

Welker, John Jacob, born May 17, 1794, of John Jacob Welker and his wife Magdalen ; baptized July 6 ; sponsors, Jacob Els and Catharine Brown.

Reichert, John Henry, born June 8, 1794, of Anthony Reichert and his wife Catharine ; baptized July 6 ; sponsors, John Els and his wife Elizabeth.

Els, Mary Magdalen, born April 30, 1794, of John Els and his wife Elizabeth ; baptized May 9 ; sponsors, John Jacob Welker and his wife Magdalen.

Shere, George, born July 4, of Daniel Shere and his wife Anna ; baptized July 20 ; sponsors, George and Anna Maria Pfeffer.

Conner, Mary, born June 16, 1794, of John Conner and his wife Anna ; baptized August 3 ; sponsors, Hugh O'Neal and Mary Conner.

Egg, John Laurence, born April 12, 1794, of John Egg and his wife Charlotte ; baptized August 17 ; sponsors, Lawrence and Joanna Gubernator.

Zweyer, Joseph, born August 30, 1794, of Adam Zweyer and his wife Barbara Sigfrid ; baptized August 31 ; sponsors, Joseph and Agatha Sigfrid.

[*After their names Father Erntzen has written the word "fratres," to mean, I suppose, that they were brother and sister of the child's mother.*]

Egg, John George, born September 5, 1794, of Joseph Egg and his wife Mary Agatha ; baptized October 5 ; sponsors, Peter and Magdalen Egg.

Käss, Elizabeth, born September 23, 1794, of John Käss and his wife Catharine Kuns ; baptized October 12 ; sponsors, Matthias Käss and Elizabeth Kuns.

Lorentz, Anna Barbara, born March 17, 1794, of Joseph Lorentz and his wife Catharine ; baptized September 28 ; sponsors, Jacob Spring and his wife Catharine.

Shnabel, Joseph, born September 21, 1794, of Joseph Shnabel and his wife Mary ; baptized December 25 ; sponsors, Jacob Snabel and Barbara Keffer.

Gery, Elizabeth Eva, born November 1, 1794, of Martin Gery and his wife Mary ; baptized December 26 ; sponsors, George and Elizabeth Bouer.

Buck, Jacob, born October 10, 1794, of Jacob Buck and his wife Susan Hering ; baptized December 29 ; sponsors, Leonard and Elizabeth Buck.

Buck, Susan, born December 22, 1794, of Leonard Buck and his wife Elizabeth Krämer ; baptized December 29 ; sponsors, Jacob and Susan Buck.

Leitig, Mary Magdalen, born September 6, 1794, of John Leitig and his wife Christina ; baptized December 28 ; sponsors, Matthias and Magdalen Krämer.

[The number of baptisms for the year is forty-three.]

BAPTISMS FOR THE YEAR 1795.

Illain, Magdalen, born January 24, 1795, of Joseph Illain and his wife Margaret Shorb ; baptized February 2 ; sponsors, Joseph Coblet and Catharine Braun.

Käss, Elizabeth, born February 16, 1795, of Peter Käss and his wife Magdalen ; baptized March 8 ; sponsors, John Illain and his wife Elizabeth.

Gauger, Peter and Mary, twins, born February 18, 1795, of John Gauger and his wife Elizabeth Kemp ; baptized March 13 ; sponsors, for Peter, Peter Gauger and Magdalen Gret, and for Mary, Mary Gauger and Michael Gret.

Mattes, Mary, born January 19, 1795, of John Mattes and his wife Mary Egg ; baptized March 15 ; sponsors, Peter Egg and his wife Magdalen.

Bauer, John, born November 26, 1794, of Peter Bauer and his wife Rosina Shnabel ; baptized March 21 ; sponsors, John Shnabel and Susan Kieffer, non-Catholic.

Eckenrodt, Daniel, born November 13, 1794, of George Eckenrodt and his wife Mary, non-Catholic ; baptized March 22 ; sponsors, Philip and Magdalen Burkhard.

Burkhard, John George, born December 12, 1794, of Philip and Magdalen Burkhard ; baptized March 22 ; sponsors, George and Mary Eckenrodt.

Burgy, Christina, born January 21, 1795, of Joseph Burgy and his wife Anna Maria ; baptized March 22 ; sponsors, Andrew and Elizabeth Gret.

Clemmer, Elizabeth, born March 1, 1795, of Christian Clemmer and [his wife] Catharine ; baptized March 1,; sponsors, Joseph Buck and Sabina Egg.

Brück, George, born March 4, 1795, of Matthias Brück and his wife Mary ; baptized April 12 ; sponsors, George Shmidt and his wife Barbara.

Käss, Mary Barbara, born March 7, 1795, of Jacob Käss and his wife Mary Barbara ; baptized April 12 ; sponsors, Caspar Shönebruck and his wife Margaret.

Gibson, Catharine, born March 26, 1795, of Joseph Gibson and his wife Christina Hopp ; baptized April 20 ; sponsor, Catharine Hopp.

Kemp, Mary Magdalen, born March 29, 1795, of John Kemp and his wife Barbara Buck ; baptized April 21 ; sponsors, John and Anna Christina Kemp.

Greenvald, Jacob, born February 24, 1795, of Joseph Greenvald and his wife Mary Ann ; baptized April 19 ; sponsors, Jacob and Margaret Arens.

Gret, John, born August 13, 1795 [*sic*, 1794 ?], of Nicholas Gret and his wife Susan ; baptized April 19 ; sponsors, John and Mary Elizabeth Gret.

Henrich, Philip Adam, born March 6, 1794, of Philip Henrich and his wife Elizabeth ; baptized April 19 ; sponsors, Adam and Eva Reichert.

Baumann, John, born July 6, 1794, of John Baumann and his wife Anna Magdalen ; baptized April 19 ; sponsors, Nicholas and Magdalen Gret.

Shnabel, Mary, born April 15, 1795, of Michael Shnabel and his wife Margaret Hentzing ; baptized May 2 ; sponsors, Jacob and Barbara Shnabel.

Strack, William, born January 20, 1795, of Henry Strack and his wife Catharine Hofman ; baptized April 26 ; sponsors, Nicholas and Albertina M'Carty.

Hundsmann, Louis, born June 25, 1794, of William Hundsmann and Mary Oberholser ; baptized April 28 ; sponsors, Anthony and Sara Honig.

Keffer, Elizabeth, born February 2, 1795, of Joseph Keffer and his wife Christina ; baptized May 10 ; sponsors, Peter and Barbara Keffer.

Shorp, Elizabeth, born April 9, 1795, of Joseph Shorp and his wife Mary Strunk ; baptized May 10 ; sponsors, Jacob Lambert and Gertrude Strunk.

Sigfrid, Magdalen, born ———, of Jacob Sigfrid and his wife Susan ; baptized May 10 ; sponsors, ———.

Rittner, Joseph and Simon, twins, born February 13, 1795, of Peter Rittner and his wife Barbara, non-Catholic ; baptized May 10 ; sponsor for Joseph, Catharine Allgeier, and for Simon, Philip and Agatha Strunk.

Opold, John, born April 29, 1795, of Joseph Opold and his wife Mary Margaret ; baptized May 12 ; sponsors, Anthony and Elizabeth Chaudmont.

Illain, George, born April 23, 1795, of Francis Louis Illain and his wife Catharine ; baptized May 21 ; sponsors, Peter and Magdalen Käss.

Bond, Samuel, aged 21 years, son of John Bond and his wife Charte, non-Catholics ; baptized solemnly *in facie Ecclesiæ*, on the II. feria after Pentecost ; sponsor, Joseph Illain.

Shmidt, John Adam, born April 5, 1795, of Joseph Shmidt and his wife Catharine ; baptized June 14 ; sponsors, George and Ursula Shmidt.

Rupple, William, born May 27, 1795, of Jacob Rupple and his wife Peggé [*Peggy*] ; baptized June 28 ; sponsors, William Shäfer and Eliz. Kohl.

Rupple, John, born February 10, 1795, of Joseph Rupple and his wife Barbara ; baptized June 28 ; sponsors, John and Sally M'Carty.

Rupple, Anna Maria, born December 18, 1793, of George Rupple and his wife Elizabeth ; baptized June 28 ; sponsors, John Shäfer and Barbara Rupple.

Miller, Anna Maria, born May 7, 1795, of Nicholas Miller and his wife Anna ; baptized June 27, by the father in case of necessity ; ceremonies supplied July 26 ; sponsors, George Miller and Anna Maria Spring.

Osenbacher, Eva Mary, born May 22, 1795, of Catharine Stahler, Catholic, and her husband John Osenbacher, non-Catholic ; baptized [*in case of necessity*] July 5 ; ceremonies supplied July 26 ; sponsors, Adam and Eva Mary Stahler.

Egg, Magdalen, born July 9, 1795, of Peter Egg and his wife Magdalen Käss ; baptized July 28 ; sponsors, Peter and Magdalen Käss.

Magel, George, born January 16, 1794, of George Magel and his wife Magdalen ; baptized August 25 ; sponsor, Daniel Magel.

Magel, William, born February 15, 1795, of Daniel Magel and his wife Mary ; baptized August 25 ; sponsor, George Magel.

M'Carty, Sara, born September 1, 1795, of John M'Carty and his wife Elizabeth Hönig ; baptized September 6 ; sponsors, John Buck and Salome M'Carty.

M'Carty, Unity Juliana, born September 5, 1795, of Mary M'Carty and ———— ; baptized September 6 ; sponsors, Thomas and Mary M'Carty.

Shmidt, Elizabeth, born September 5, 1795, of Caspar Shmidt and his wife Susan ; baptized October 4 ; sponsors, George and Elizabeth Bauer.

Shmidt, John, born September 20, 1795, of George Shmidt and his wife Barbara ; baptized October 12 ; sponsors, Caspar and Margaret Shönebruck.

————, Elizabeth, born October 15, of ———— and Mary ———— ; baptized October 18 ; sponsors, George and Elizabeth Bauer.

Shorp, Simon Lazarus, born September 24, 1795, of John Shorp and his wife Elizabeth ; baptized November 1 ; sponsors, Simon Adam and his wife Catharine.

Egg, Jacob, born October 4, 1795, of Theodore Egg and his wife Mary Elizabeth ; baptized November 1 ; sponsors, Jacob Els and Sabina Egg.

Reninger, John, born October 25, 1795, of Frederick Reninger and his wife Catharine ; baptized December 6 ; sponsors, John and Peggé Sweetman.

Hartmann, Magdalen, born October 12, 1795, of Jacob Hartmann and his wife Catharine ; sponsors, Frederick Kemp and Magdalen Gret.

Shwarz, Francis Philip, born October 27, 1795, of Philip Shwarz and his wife Margaret ; baptized November 29 ; sponsors, Francis and Catharine Hopp.

Shreer, Adam Daniel, born March 13, 1795, of John George Shreer and his wife Catharine ; baptized November 29 ; sponsors, Adam and Eva Reichert.

M'Farthy, Catharine, born October 14, 1795, of Eva M'Farthy and her husband John ; baptized December 9 ; sponsors, Daniel and Mary Ann Coblet.

Shönebruck, Joseph, born December 5, 1795, of Caspar Shönebruck and his wife Margaret ; baptized December 14 ; sponsors Joseph Buck and his wife Rosina.

Röhr, Joseph, born November 16, 1795, of Joseph Röhr and his wife Juliana ; baptized December 27 ; sponsors, John Coblet and Eva Sigfrid.

Hartman, Charles, born November 2, 1795, of John Hartman and his wife Susan ; baptized December 27 ; sponsors, John and Anna Conner.

[The number of baptisms for the year is fifty-three.]

BAPTISMS FOR THE YEAR 1796.

Reichert, Catharine, born December 18, 1795, of John Reichert and his wife Catharine ; baptized January 6 ; sponsors, Michael and Eva Kuhn.

Reichert, John Jacob, born January 12, 1796, of Anthony Reichert and his wife Catharine ; baptized February 2 ; sponsors, Jacob Els and Barbara Gauger.

Reichert, Adam, born January 11, 1796, of Adam Reichert and his wife Eva ; baptized January 31 ; sponsors, John Adam Gret and Magdalen Henrich.

Gret, Samuel, born December 19, [sic, 1795 ?], of Andrew Gret and his wife Elizabeth ; baptized January 31 ; sponsors, Francis Eichhorn and Barbara Henrich.

Hönig, Michael, born November 15, 1795, of Simon Hönig and his wife Anna Maria ; baptized February 28 ; sponsors Michael Hönig and his wife Helen.

Melchior, Susan, born November 6, 1795, of Michael Melchior and his wife Magdalen ; baptized February 28 ; sponsors, Simon Hönig and his wife Anna Mary.

Fricker, George, born February 29, 1796, of Barbara Sigfrid and George Fricker ; baptized March 14 ; sponsors, Philip and Agatha Strunk.

Brown, John, born February 20, 1796, of Andrew Brown and his wife Regina ; baptized March 20 ; sponsors, John and Anna Elizabeth Els.

Bott, William, born February 27, 1796, of Jacob Bott and his wife Catharine ; baptized March 20 ; sponsors, Laurence Gubernator and Mary Coblet.

Eckenrodt, John Henry, born November 20, 1795, of Henry Eckenrodt and [his wife] Elizabeth ; baptized April 3 ; sponsors, John Gerstweiler and Barbara Felix.

Buck, Jacob, born April 4, 1796, of Joseph Buck and his wife Rosina ; baptized April 10 ; sponsors, Andrew Shönebruck and Elizabeth Dum.

Illain, Catharine, born January 9, 1796, of·Francis Illain and his wife Juliana ; baptized April 6 ; sponsors, John and Catharine Kuns.

Käss, Jacob, born April 1, 1796, of John Käss and his wife Catharine ; baptized April 11 ; sponsors, Jacob and Mary Margaret Käss.

Kuns, Paul, born March 23, 1796, of John Kuns and his wife Catharine; baptized April 15 ; sponsors, [Rev.] Paul Erntzen and Anna Mary Zweyer.

Hopp, Magdalen, born January 9, 1796, of George Hopp and his wife Margaret ; baptized April 17 ; sponsors, John Shlosser and Magdalen Hopp.

Saüvert, Solomon, born February 12, 1796, of Philip Saüvert and his wife Barbara ; baptized April 17 ; sponsors, John and Mary Elizabeth Gret.

Shmidt, John, born February 19, 1796, of Joseph Shmidt and his wife Regina ; baptized April 17 ; sponsors, John Arens and Elizabeth Dum.

Chevain, Valentine Peter, born January 30, 1796, of Peter Chevain and his wife Catharine ; baptized April 17 ; sponsors, Valentine Dum and Magdalen Henrich.

Reppert, Anna, born March 16, 1796, of Stephen Reppert and his wife Magdalen ; baptized May 1 ; sponsors, Matthias Reichert and Magdalen Gret.

Rupple, Catharine, born February 23, 1796, of George Rupple and his wife Elizabeth ; baptized April 26 ; sponsors, John Rupple and Anna Mary Miller.

Shäfer, Eleonor, born March 17, 1795 [or 1796], of John Shäfer and his wife Mary ; baptized April 26 ; sponsors, William and Susan Shäver.

Hönig, Catharine, born April 22, 1796, of Michael Hönig and his wife Helen ; baptized April 27 ; sponsors, Joseph Hönig and Eva Willheim.

Röhr, Theresa, born January 16, 1796, of Matthias Röhr and his wife Catharine ; baptized July 3 ; sponsors, Peter and Theresa Herbst.

Shnabel, John, born May 22, 1796 of Jacob Shnabel and his wife Barbara ; baptized July 3 ; sponsors, John and Magdalen Gret.

Dotendorf, Jacob, born April 14, 1796, of John Andrew Dotendorf and his wife Mary Theresa ; baptized June 27 ; sponsors, Joseph and C.[atharine] Fricker.

Käss, Anna Margaret, born July 19, 1796, of John Käss and his wife Elizabeth ; baptized August 14 ; sponsors, Peter and Margaret Käss.

Buck, Elizabeth, born August 1, 1796, of John Buck and his wife Salome ; baptized August 28 ; sponsors, Nicholas and Louisa [Aloitina] M'Carty.

Boatman, John, born August 9, 1796, of Bernard Boatman and his wife Catharine ; baptized August 28 ; sponsors, Joseph and Catharine Fricker.

Greenewald, Barbara, born August 11, 1796, of Joseph Greenewald and his wife Mary Ann ; baptized September 25 ; sponsors, John and Barbara Henrich.

Flower, Samuel, born September 27, 1796, of Christopher Flower and his wife Magdalen ; baptized October 30 ; sponsors, Jacob Arens and Magdalen Gret.

Shlosser, Anna Mary, born October 17, 1796, of John Shlosser and his wife Magdalen ; baptized October 30 ; sponsors, Joseph and Mary Shlosser.

[*The three baptisms that follow were recorded by Father Erntzen among the baptisms for February, 1797.*]

Obold, Philip, born November 10, 1796, of Joseph Obold and his wife Margaret ; baptized November 14 ; sponsors Philip and Elizabeth Shmidt.

Gret, George, born October 1, 1796, of Joseph Gret and his wife Christina ; baptized November 13 ; sponsors, George Repplier and Margaret Lambert.

Kiesling, Elizabeth, born September 22, 1796, of Sebastian Kiesling and his wife Catharine ; baptized November 14 ; sponsors, Philip and Elizabeth Shmidt.

Shäfer, William, born October 17, 1796, of John Shäfer and his wife Mary ; baptized December 5 ; sponsors, William Shäfer and Mary Barbara Rupple.

Ashburn; Elizabeth, born August 28, 1796, of William Ashburn and his wife Catharine ; baptized December 6 ; sponsor, Elizabeth Miller.

Buck, Elizabeth, born November 16, 1796, of Jacob Buck and his wife Susan ; baptized December 6 ; sponsors Jacob and Elizabeth Kohl.

Langbe, Mary, born September 28, 1796, of Mary Barbara Langbe and ——— ; baptized December 6 ; sponsors, Christopher Langbe and Margaret Kohl.

M'Gullery, James, born October 9, 1796, of James M'Gullery and his wife Mary ; baptized December 6 ; sponsors, James and Elizabeth Kohl.

[The number of baptisms for the year is thirty-nine.]

BAPTISMS FOR THE YEAR 1797.

Flower, William, born October 8, 1796, of John Flower and his wife Catharine ; baptized January 8 ; sponsors James Lambert and his wife Dorothy.

Hartman, John Peter, born October 21, 1796, of Francis Hartman and his wife Mary ; baptized January 8 ; sponsors, Peter Keffer and his wife Barbara.

Keffer, George, born January 6, 1797, of Joseph Keffer and his wife Christina ; baptized January 8 ; sponsors, John Gans and his wife.

Reninger, Catharine, born December 14, 1796, of Frederick Reninger and his wife Catharine ; baptized January 15 ; sponsors, John Coblet and Gertrude Gibson.

Arens, John, born December 23, 1796, of John Arens and his wife Elizabeth ; baptized January 29 ; sponsors, Caspar and Eva Dum.

Egg, Benjamin, born October 2, 1796, of John Egg and his wife Charlotte ; baptized February 5th ; sponsors, Francis and Catharine Illain.

Buck, Rosina, born December 10, 1796, of Leonard Buck and his wife Elizabeth ; baptized February 26 ; sponsors, Joseph and Rosina Buck.

M'Carty, Joseph, born January 27, 1797, of John M'Carty and his wife Elizabeth ; baptized February 26 ; sponsors, Joseph Hönig and [his wife ?] Elizabeth Griser.

Adam, Paul, born February 5, 1797, of Simon Adam and his wife Catharine ; baptized February 28 ; sponsors, [Rev.] Paul Erntzen and Veronica Egg.

Clerk, John, born January 29, 1797, of William Clerk and his wife Mary Eve ; baptized March 5 ; sponsors, Martin and Gertrude Burkhard.

Gery, Joseph, born December 27, 1797 [1796 ?], of Martin Gery and his wife Mary ; baptized March 5 ; sponsors, Christian and Catharine Clemmer.

Miller, Jacob, born December 4, 1796, of Nicholas Miller and his wife Anna ; baptized March 26 ; sponsors, George and Susan Catharine Spring.

Burkhard, Catharine Margaret, born October 19, 1796, of Philip Burkhard and his wife Magdalen ; baptized March 26 ; sponsors, John Adam Henrich and Margaret Spring.

Kemp, Jacob, born March 5, 1797, of John Kemp and his wife Barbara ; baptized March 25 ; sponsors, Christian and Catharine Clemmer.

Egg, Joseph, born March 4, 1797, of Joseph Egg and his wife Mary Agatha ; sponsors, Joseph Gret and Mary Adam.

Melchior, Jacob, born February 15, 1797, of Michael Melchior and his wife Mary ; baptized April 23 ; sponsors, Jacob and Elizabeth Kohl.

Buck, Salome, born March 13, 1797, of Nicholas Buck and his wife Mary ; baptized April 23 ; sponsors, John and Salome Buck.

Bauer, Catharine, born February 11, 1797, of Rosina Bauer and her husband Peter ; baptized April 30 ; sponsors, Thomas Dum and his wife Elizabeth.

Sweetman, Clara, born April 1, 1797, of John Sweetman and his wife Margaret ; baptized May 7 ; sponsors, John and Catharine Reichert.

Kolb, John, born October 7, 1764, of Peter Kolb and his wife Magdalen; [after their names follows, as far as I can make it out, the word "Anabaptists"] ; baptized May 8 ; sponsors, John and Elizabeth Gret.

Marks, Thomas Anthony, born March 5, 1797, of Anthony Marks and his wife Charlotte ; baptized May 14 ; sponsors, Michael Anthony Bré and Eva Rittner.

Röhr, Nicholas, born January 28, 1797, of Nicholas Röhr and his wife Mary ; baptized May 14 ; sponsors, George Sigfrid and Eva Fricker, widow.

Zweyer, Joseph, born January 12, 1797, of Thomas Zweyer and his wife Mary ; baptized May 14 ; sponsors, Joseph and Catharine Zweyer.

Hopp, Elizabeth, born May 10, 1797, of Joseph Hopp and his wife Christina ; baptized May 21 ; sponsors, Henry Gibson and Catharine Hopp.

Conner, Catharine, born February 3, 1797, of John Conner and his wife Anna ; baptized April 17 ; sponsors, George Kemp and Catharine Coblet.

Burgy, Mary Barbara, born May 25, 1797, of Joseph Burgy and his wife Mary ; baptized May 28 ; sponsors, Christopher and Anna Margaret Eckenrodt.

Shmidt, Mary, born May 15, 1797, of Caspar Shmidt and his wife Susan ; baptized June 4 ; sponsors, Michael Shmidt and Mary Kuns.

Kemp, John, born June 10, 1797, of Jacob Kemp and his wife Susan ; baptized June 12 ; sponsors, John and ———.

Allgeier, Anna Mary, born May 23, 1797, of Sebastian Allgeier and his wife Catharine ; baptized June 11 ; sponsors, Peter Rittner and Anna Mary Chaudmont.

Shmidt, Christina, born February 24, 1797, of Joseph Shmidt and his wife Catharine ; baptized June 18 ; sponsors, Joseph and Rosina Buck.

Shmidt, Margaret, born April 5, 1797, of George Shmidt and his wife Barbara ; baptized June 18 ; sponsors, Michael Shmidt and Elizabeth Shönebruck.

Weber, Andrew, born March 19, 1797, of Matthias Weber and his wife Magdalen ; baptized June 18 ; sponsors, Andrew Shönebruck and Anna Mary Shuppert.

Coblet, John, born June 2, 1797, of Catharine Coblet and ——— ; baptized July 2 ; sponsors, John Els and his wife Ann Elizabeth.

Reitmeyer, Margaret, born December 23, 1797, of Mary Reitmeyer and ——— ; baptized July 2 ; sponsors, John Gret and Mary Coblet.

Shnabel, Barbara, born June 18, 1797, of Michael Shnabel and his wife Margaret ; baptized July 16 ; sponsors, John Shnabel and Magdalen Gret.

Hartman, Margaret, born May 31, 1797, of Jacob Hartman and his wife Catharine ; baptized July 9 ; sponsors, Michael Hartman and his wife Mary.

Rittner, Elizabeth, born August 5, 1797, of Peter Rittner and his wife Barbara ; baptized August 14 ; sponsors, George Sigfrid and Barbara Felix.

Kerlin, Bridget, born April 5, 1797, of Edward Kerlin and his wife Eleonor ; baptized September 10 ; sponsor, William Daren [or Dwen].

Gauger, Anna Christina, born September 15, 1797, of John Gauger and his wife Elizabeth; baptized October 10; sponsors, John and Anna Christina Kemp.

Brück, Magdalen Margaret, born October 11, 1797, of Matthias Brück and his wife Mary ; baptized October 15 ; sponsors, Joseph and Rosina Buck.

Buck, Nicholas, born August 29, 1797, of John Buck and his wife Salome ; baptized October 23 ; sponsors, Nicholas and Magdalen Buck.

Rupple, Anna, born August 22, 1797, of Jacob Rupple and his wife Margaret ; baptized October 23 ; sponsors, Thomas and Margaret M'Carty.

Hopp, Mary, born August 18, 1797, of George Hopp and his wife Margaret ; baptized October 29 ; sponsors, Joseph Arens and Catharine Hopp.

Shröer, Mary, born May 2, 1797, of John George Shröer and his wife Catharine ; baptized October 29 ; sponsors, Joseph Henrich and Mary Reichert.

Illain, Anna Mary, born August 10, 1797, of Joseph Illain and his wife Margaret ; baptized November 1 ; sponsors Michael and Catharine Gret.

Reichert, Mary Magdalen, born October 9, 1797, of John Reichert and his wife Catharine ; baptized November 1 ; sponsors, Jacob and Mary Magdalen Welker.

Matthes, John, born September 17, of John Matthes and his wife Anna Mary ; baptized November 1 ; sponsors, John Gret and Catharine Egg.

Tenneser, John Frederick and Veronica, twins, born June 17, 1797, of John Henry Tenneser and his wife Elizabeth ; baptized November 1 ; sponsors John Gret and Veronica Egg and John Adam and Catharine Gret.

Buck, Joseph, born November 16, 1797, of Joseph Buck and his wife Rosina ; baptized December 17 ; sponsors, Caspar and Margaret Shönebruck.

Brück, Henry, born October 31, 1797, of Henry Brück and his wife Elizabeth ; baptized December 17 ; sponsors, Matthias Brück and his wife Mary.

Shnabel, Anna Margaret, born October 24, 1797, of Joseph Shnabel and [his wife] Mary ; baptized December 25 ; sponsors, George Kemp and Margaret Egg.

Egg, Mary, born December 28, 1797, of Peter Egg and his wife Magdalen ; baptized December 30 ; sponsors, John and Elizabeth Illain.

Gret, Eva Margaret, born December 9, 1797, of Nicholas Gret and his wife Susan ; baptized December 31 ; sponsors, Jacob and Margaret Arens.

Krell, William, aged 5 years and 10 months ; Jacob and Anna, twins, aged 4 years and 3 months; children of John and Sara Krell; baptized in 1797 ; sponsors of William, Adam and Eva Reichert ; of Jacob, Joseph and Regina Shmidt; and of Anna, Andrew and Mary Magdalen Gret. [*This baptism has been recorded among the baptisms of 1798.*]
[The number of baptisms for the year is fifty-six.]

BAPTISMS FOR THE YEAR 1798.

Shnabel, Catharine, born January 17, 1798, of Jacob Shnabel and his wife Barbara ; baptized February 7 ; sponsers, Andrew Shnabel and Catharine Mutard.

Illain, David, born December 30, 1797, of Francis Illain and his wife Catharine ; baptized March 4 ; sponsors, John and Elizabeth Illain.

Gibson, Susan, born February 27, 1798, of Henry Gibson and his wife Elizabeth ; baptized April 1 ; sponsors, Caspar and Susan Shmidt.

Clemmer, John, born February 23, 1798, of Christian Clemmer and his wife Catharine ; baptized April 8 ; sponsors, John and Barbara Kemp.

Miller, Anna Catharine, born March 25, 1798, of Frederick Miller and his wife Elizabeth ; baptized April 9 ; sponsors, John and Catharine Reichert.

Röhr, Richard James, born March 3, 1798, of Joseph Röhr and his wife Juliana ; baptized April 9 ; sponsors, Charles Fortmann and Barbara Gret.

Opold, Catharine, born January 20, 1798, of Joseph Opold and his wife Margaret ; baptized April 15 ; sponsors, Sebastian and Catharine Kiesling.

Sigfrid, Joseph, born March 12, 1798, of Jacob Sigfrid and his wife Susan ; baptized April 17 ; sponsors, Joseph Sigfrid and his mother, Justina Albrecht.

Gording, Theresa, 21 years old, daughter of John Golding and his wife Sara, non-Catholics ; baptized April 22 ; sponsors Jacob and Elizabeth Kohl.

Hönig, John, born December 20, 1797, of Jacob Hönig and his wife Theresa Gording ; baptized April 22 ; sponsors, Anthony and Rachel Griser.

Käss, Henry, born February 20, 1798, of Jacob Käss and his wife Barbara ; baptized April 27 ; sponsors, Henry Käss and Elizabeth Shönebruck.

Käss, John, born February 9, 1798, of John Käss and his wife Catharine ; baptized April 27 ; sponsors, John Kuns and Mary Käss.

———, Jacob and Elizabeth, twins, born January 23, 1798 ; baptized April 29 ; sponsors of Jacob, Jacob and Mary Arens, and of Elizabeth, John and Elizabeth Arens.

Greenwald, Magdalen, born January 4, 1798, of Joseph Greenwald and his wife Anna Mary ; baptized April 29 ; sponsors, Joseph and Magdalen Henrich.

Egg, Paul, born April 4, 1798, of Theodore Egg and his wife Mary Elizabeth ; baptized May 19 ; sponsors, Rev. Paul Erntzen and Mary Adam.

Dotendorff, Theodore, born February 27, 1798, of John Andrew Dotendorff and his wife Theresa ; baptized May 21 ; sponsors, Caspar and Margaret Shönebruck.

Käss, Mary, born May 6, 1798, of Peter Käss and his wife Magdalen ; baptized May 27 ; sponsors, Peter and Magdalen Egg.

Bauer, Peter, born February 23, 1798, of Peter Bauer and his wife Rosina ; baptized June 4 ; sponsors, Thomas and Elizabeth Shmidt.

Saüvert, Joseph, born April 13, 1798, of Joseph Saüvert and his wife Catharine ; baptized June 11 ; sponsors, Joseph and Margaret Opold.

Orth, Anna Margaret and Philip, twins, born May 15, 1798, Anna at 7 o'clock in the morning, Philip at 5 in the afternoon, of Peter Orth and his wife Anna Catharine ; baptized June 12 ; sponsors for Anna, Anna Margaret Ely, and for Philip, Philip Strunk and Eva Sigfrid.

Käss, Catharine, born May 25, 1798, of Matthias Käss and his wife Elizabeth ; baptized July 15 ; sponsors, John and Catharine Kuns.

Gret, Solomon, born July 7, 1798, of Andrew Gret and his wife Elizabeth ; baptized July 29 ; sponsors, Jacob and Margaret Arens.

Reichert, Magdalen, born June 10, 1798, of Adam Reichert and his wife Eva ; baptized July 29 ; sponsors, Valentine Dum and Magdalen Arens.

Saüvert, Mary Magdalen, born April 15, 1798, of Philip Saüvert and his wife Barbara ; baptized July 29 ; sponsors, Andrew and Magdalen Gret.

Chevain, Magdalen, born April 5, 1798, of Peter Chevain and his wife Catharine ; baptized July 30 ; sponsors, Thomas and Elizabeth Dum.

Reninger, Joseph, born June 30, 1798, of Frederick Reninger and his wife Catharine ; baptized July 5 ; sponsors, Joseph and Christina Gibson.

Shurp, John, born June 7, 1798, of John Shurp and his wife Elizabeth ; baptized July 5 ; sponsors, John Adam and Catharine Gret.

Eckenrodt, Margaret, born June 23, 1798, of Henry Eckenrodt and his wife Elizabeth ; baptized August 12 ; sponsors, Michael and Margaret Hartman.

M'Carty, Peter, born December 15, 1796, of Nicholas M'Carty and Sara Reiss ; baptized August 26 ; sponsors, Nicholas and Louisa M'Carty.

Wenamer, Elizabeth, born July 25, 1773, of Bernard Wenamer and his wife Elizabeth ; baptized August 26 ; sponsors, Nicholas and Louisa M'Carty.

M'Carty, Unity, born July 23, 1798, of John M'Carty and his wife Elizabeth ; baptized August 26 ; sponsors, Nicholas and Mary M'Carty.

Shneider, Jacob, born May 28, 1798, of Daniel Shneider and his wife Catharine ; baptized August 26 ; sponsors, John and Eleonor Hönig.

Carass, Salome, born April 12, 1798, of John Carass and his wife Christina ; baptized August 27 ; sponsors, Nicholas and Mary Buck.

Sutten, William, born February 19, 1795, of Martin Sutten and his wife Sara ; baptized August 28 ; sponsor, [Rev.] Paul Erntzen.

Bennen, Paul, born May 20, 1798, of John Bennen and his wife Anna ; baptized October 7 ; sponsors, Valentine Emms and his wife Juliana.

Emms, Joseph, born February 18, 1798, of Valentine Emms and his wife Juliana ; baptized October 7 ; sponsors, John and Anna Bennen.

Welker, Joseph, born February 18, 1798, of Jacob Welker and his wife Magdalen ; baptized October 21 ; sponsors, Jacob and Mary Els.

M'Carty, John, born September 17, 1798, of Nicholas M'Carty and his wife Elizabeth ; baptized October 28 ; sponsors, John Buck and his wife Salome.

Reichert, Thomas, born October 20, 1798, of John Reichert and his wife Barbara ; baptized October 28 ; sponsors, Nicholas and Louisa M'Carty.

Krippel, Matthew, born September 17, 1798, of Matthew Krippel, and his wife Mary ; baptized October 28 ; sponsors, Henry and Joannetta Gergel.

Buck, Salome, born October 11, 1798, of Leonard Buck and his wife Elizabeth ; baptized October 28 ; sponsors, John Buck and his wife Salome.

Molzberger, John, born Octobef 11, 1798, of Jacob Molzberger and his wife Mary ; baptized November 1 ; sponsors, John and Susan Shnieringer.

Shmidt, John, born October 8, 1798, of Michael Shmidt and his wife Mary ; baptized November 4 ; sponsors, John Gret and Barbara Kuns.

Brück, John, born October 7, 1798, of Matthias Brück and his wife Mary ; baptized November 18 ; sponsors, Michael and Mary Shmidt.

Els, Margaret, born November 1, 1798, of Jacob Els and his wife Mary ; baptized December 25 ; sponsors, John Coblet and Sophia Els.

Eckenrod, Mary Barbara, born November 5, 1798, of George Eckenrod and his wife Mary ; baptized December 15 ; sponsors, Peter Eckenrod and his wife Mary.

Neuer, Eva Mary, born August 5, 1798, of John Neuer and his wife Mary ; baptized September 30 ; sponsors, Caspar and Mary Eva Dum.

Hopp, Anthony, born November 1, 1798, of George Hopp and his wife Margaret ; baptized December 29 ; sponsors, Francis and Catharine Hopp.

Arens, Jacob, born October 19, 1798, of John Arens and his wife Elizabeth ; baptized December 29 ; sponsors, Jacob and Margaret Arens.

Shlosser, Catharine, born November 24, 1798, of John Shlosser and his wife Magdalen ; baptized December 29 ; sponsors, Joseph Shlosser and Catharine Hopp.

Flower, Magdalen, born December 17, 1798, of Christopher Flower and his wife Magdalen ; baptized December 29 ; sponsors, Joseph and Anna Mary Shlosser.

[The number of baptisms for the year is fifty-four.]

BAPTISMS FOR THE YEAR 1799.

Rohrbach, Elizabeth, born December 26, 1798, of Jacob Rohrbach and his wife Susan ; baptized February 2 ; sponsors, George Kemp and Elizabeth Buck.

Reppert, Margaret, born December 6, 1798, of Stephen Reppert and his wife Magdalen ; baptized February 2 ; sponsors, Frederick and Catharine Reninger.

Ashborn, Jesse, born October 14, 1798, of George Ashborn and his wife Catharine ; baptized February 24 ; sponsors, George and Catharine Kohl.

Botman, Margaret, born January 5, 1799, of Bernard Botman and his wife Catharine ; baptized February 24 ; sponsors, Thomas M'Carty and Anna Mary Overbeck.

Buck, Jacob, born January 26, 1799, of John Buck and his wife Salome; baptized February 24 ; sponsors, Jacob and Susan Buck.

Shmidt, Susan, born February 13, 1799, of Caspar Shmidt and his wife Susan ; baptized March 25 ; sponsors, Joseph and Christina Gibson.

Bott, Catharine, born March 1, 1799, of Jacob Bott and his wife Catharine ; baptized March 29 ; sponsors, John Welker and Catharine Coblet.

Felix, Samuel, born March 1, 1799, of Michael Felix and his wife Elizabeth ; baptized April 1 ; sponsors, Joseph Arens and Mary Gret.

Buck, Christian, born February 25, 1799, of Joseph Buck and his wife Rosina ; baptized April 7 ; sponsors, Christian and Catharine Clemmer.

[*In the Register immediately following the preceding baptism (which is on page 72), come the marriages from 1787 to 1819; then the deaths and burials for the same period; and (on page 137) re-begins the Baptismal Register for 1799 as follows :*]

Keffer, Magdalen, born January 6, 1799, of Jacob Keffer and his wife Magdalen ; baptized April 14 ; sponsors, Joseph Allgeyer and Magdalen Hartman.

Hartman, Henry, born February 3, 1799, of Jacob Hartman and his wife Catharine ; baptized April 14 ; sponsors, Francis Hartman and Eve Fricker.

Lambert, Jonathan, born September 14, 1798, of James Lambert and his wife Mary ; sponsors, Sebastian and Catharine Allgeyer.

Conner, Margaret, born February 21, 1799, of John Conner and his wife Anna ; baptized May 2 ; sponsors, John Coblet and Margaret Brown.

Opold, Margaret, born April 4, 1799, of Joseph Opold and his wife Margaret ; baptized May 6 ; sponsor, Elizabeth Shmidt.

Shnabel, Mary, born March 23, 1799, of Jacob Shnabel and his wife Barbara ; baptized May 12 ; sponsors, George Kemp and Catharine Reppert.

Gery, Elizabeth, born March 13, 1799, of Martin Gery and his wife Mary ; baptized May 12 ; sponsors, John and Barbara Kemp.

Rupple, Sarah, born December 21, 1798, of Joseph Rupple and his wife Barbara ; baptized May 18 ; sponsor, Elizabeth Miller.

Buck, Mary Magdalen, born March 14, 1799, of Nicholas Buck and his wife Magdalen ; baptized May 18 ; sponsors, Jacob Kohl and Magdalen Buck.

Buck, Joseph, born March 10, 1799, of Jacob Buck and his wife Susan ; baptized May 18 ; sponsors, John and Salome Buck.

Ruffner, Anthony, born January 17, 1799, of Philip Ruffner and his wife Margaret ; baptized May 18 ; sponsors, Nicholas and Magdalen Buck.

Hönig, Michael, born October 10, 1798, of Michael Hönig and his wife Helen ; baptized May 18 ; sponsors, Jacob and Elizabeth Kohl.

Strack, Henry, born February 28, 1799, of Henry Strack and his wife Catharine ; baptized May 18 ; sponsors, Benjamin and Catharine Botman.

Hönig, Anna, born March 15, 1799, of Joseph Hönig and his wife Mary ; baptized May 18 ; sponsors, John and Elizabeth M'Carty.

Melchior, Sara, born December 31, 1798, of Michael Melchior and his wife Magdalen ; baptized May 18 ; sponsors, John and Petronella Hönig.

Streebe, Mary, born February 13, 1799, of George Streebe and his wife Elizabeth ; baptized May 20 ; sponsors, Nicholas and Louisa M'Carty.

M'Carty, Abner Paul, born March 21, 1799, of Nicholas M'Carty and his wife Elizabeth ; baptized May 20 ; sponsors, Nicholas and Elizabeth M'Carty.

Gibson, Mary, born May 12, 1799, of Joseph Gibson and his wife Christina ; baptized June 2 ; sponsors, John Gret and Gertrude Gibson.

Kemp, Salome Elizabeth, born June 8, 1799, of John Kemp and his wife Barbara ; baptized by Rev. P. Helbron, June 10 ; sponsors, Elizabeth Buck and Frederic Kemp.

Shönebruck, Rosina, born April 29, 1799, of John Shönebruck and his wife Eve Rodt ; baptized June 2 ; sponsors, Joseph and Rosina Buck.

Shmidt, George, born April 10, 1799, of Joseph Shmidt and his wife Regina ; baptized July 1 ; sponsors, George Arens and Magdalen Gret.

Keffer, John George, born May 7, 1799, of Joseph Keffer and his wife Christina ; baptized by Rev. P. Helbron, June 16 ; sponsors, John and Catharine Gans.

Geyde, George, born March 27, 1799, of William Geyde and his wife
Sophia ; baptized June 16 ; sponsors, Peter Lambert and Elizabeth Shindler.

Reichert, Anthony, born May 16, 1799, of Anthony Reichert and his
wife Catharine ; baptized July 7 ; sponsors, John Coblet and Mary
Els.

Egg, George, born June 30, 1799, of Joseph Egg and his wife Agatha ;
baptized August 15 ; sponsors, George Kemp and Catharine Gret.

Shäfer, Susan, born October 10, 1798, of John Shäfer and his wife
Mary ; baptized August 25 ; sponsors, Michael and Helen Hönig.

Shäfer, William, born November 11, 1797, of William Shäfer and his
wife Mary ; baptized August 25 ; sponsors, William and Susan
Shäfer.

M'Canny, William, born April 10, 1798, of Matthias M'Canny and his
wife Mary ; baptized August 25 ; sponsors, Nicholas and Louisa
M'Carty.

Egg, John, born August 25, 1799, of John Egg and his wife Louisa ;
baptized August 27 ; sponsors, John and Dorothy Egg.

Röhr, Joseph, born August 16, 1799, of Matthias Röhr and his wife
Catharine ; baptized September 1 ; sponsors, Joseph and Juliana
Röhr.

Egg, Sabina, born July 31, 1799, of Peter Egg and his wife Magdalen ;
baptized September 1 ; sponsors, Francis and Catharine Illain.

[*Here follows what seems to be in part a record of the baptism of
John Georgius Haffer, or Hasser, born May 7th, 1799.*]

Wummer, John, born May 6, 1799, of Adam Wummer and his wife
Magdalen ; baptized September 9 ; sponsors, Philip and Elizabeth
Shmidt.

Kiesel, Catharine, born July 21, 1799, of Sebastian Kiesel and his wife
Catharine ; baptized September 9 ; sponsors, Joseph and Catharine Saüvert.

Rittner, George, born August 27, 1799, of Peter Rittner and his wife
Barbara ; baptized September 11 ; sponsors, Joseph Allgeyer and
Eve Sigfrid.

Sigfrid, John, born August 17, 1799, of George Sigfrid and his wife
Barbara ; baptized September 11 ; sponsors, Nicholas and Anna
Mary Felix.

Leop, [*Leopold ?*] Charles Bernard, born August 30, 1799, of Charles
Leop. [*old?*] and his wife Margaret Fortman ; baptized by his
father in case of need, September 13 ; ceremonies supplied on the
17th ; sponsors, P. and Ther. Herbst.

Reichert, Henry, born March 28, 1797, of Anthony Reichert and his
wife Catharine ; baptized —— ; sponsors, John and Catharine
Reichert.

Reichert, Margaret, born September 13, 1799, of John Reichert and
his wife Catharine ; baptized October 6 ; sponsors, Charles Leopold and Margaret Fortman.

Hauss, Jacob, born September 22, 1777, 22 years old ; son of Abraham
Hauss and his wife Veronica ; baptized November 3 ; sponsor,
John Conner.

Fine, Anna, 21 years old ; daughter of John Fine and his wife Elizabeth ; baptized in church along with Jacob.

Shnabel, Catharine, born November 7, 1799, of Michael Shnabel and his wife Margaret ; baptized November 26 ; sponsors, Andrew and Catharine Shnabel.

Greenwald, Peter, born August 27, 1799, of Philip Joseph Greenwald and [*his wife*] Mary Ann; baptized September 30 ; sponsors, Peter Arens and Barbara Henrich.

Hopp, Margaret, born September 30, 1799, of Andrew Hopp and his wife Magdalen ; baptized December 29 ; sponsors, George and Margaret Hopp.

Neuer, Catharine, born December 11, 1799, of John Neuer and his wife Mary ; baptized December 30 ; sponsors, Adam and Mary Eve Reichert.

Chaudron, Joseph Elizabeth Julius. [*For this baptism see the Preface.*]

Gaschet de Lisle, Regina Frances Genevieve Charlotte. [*For this baptism see the Preface.*]

[The number of baptisms for the year, including two illegitimates, is fifty-eight.]

BAPTISMS FOR THE YEAR 1800.

Reninger, Henry, born November 25, 1799, of Frederic Renninger and his wife Catharine ; baptized January 5 ; sponsors, Michael Gret and Gertrude Gibson. [*This record has been entered on p.* 139 ; *the following midway on p.* 140.]

Käss, Catharine, born November 28, 1799, of John Käss and his wife Catharine ; baptized February 19 ; sponsors, Joseph Käss and Margaret Kuns.

M'Carty, Nicholas, born December 23, 1799, of John M'Carty and his wife Elizabeth ; baptized February 23 ; sponsors, Thomas M'Carty and Catharine Kohl.

Metz, Mary, born January 1, 1800, of John Metz and his wife Mary Elizabeth ; baptized February 23 ; sponsors, John Kohl and Mary M'Carty.

Dennis, Catharine, born December 30, 1799, of John Dennis and his wife Elizabeth ; baptized January 27 ; sponsors, John and Catharine Henrich.

Egg, Esther, born October 21, 1799, of John Egg and his wife Charlotte ; baptized March 5 ; sponsors, Francis and Catharine Illain.

Mattes, George, born January 7, 1800, of John Mattes and his wife Mary ; baptized March 5 ; sponsors, Francis and Catharine Illain.

Dum, Jacob, born March 12, 1800, of Valentine Dum and his wife Magdalen ; baptized March 30 ; sponsors, Jacob and Margaret Arens.

Eckenrodt, Peter, born November 27, 1799, of Peter Eckenrodt and his wife Mary ; baptized April 1 ; sponsors, Christopher and Margaret Eckenrodt.

Shmidt, John Frederick, born January 20, 1800, of Frederick Shmidt and his wife Catharine ; baptized April 20 ; sponsors, George Leaf and Mary Jones.

Röhr, George, born April 7, 1800, of Nicholas Röhr and his wife Mary ; baptized April 22 ; sponsors, George and Barbara Sigfrid.

Crämer, Mary Magdalen, born April 8, 1800, of Joseph Crämer and his wife Veronica ; baptized April 27 ; sponsors, Nicholas and Mary Buck.

Hönig, Mary, born September 8, 1799, of Jacob Hönig and his wife Theresa ; baptized April 28 ; sponsors, Jacob and Susan Buck.

Rupple, Rebecca, born October 27, 1799, of Jacob Rupple and his wife Mary ; baptized April 27 ; sponsors, John Rupple and Mary M'Carty.

Brown, John, born December 25, 1799, of William Brown and his wife Margaret ; baptized April 20 ; sponsors, John Gerstweiler and Eve Fricker.

Brück, Peter, born March 3, 1800, of Henry Brück and his wife Elizabeth ; baptized May 4 ; sponsors, Peter Brück and Barbara Shönebruck.

Shmidt, George, born March 8, 1800, of Michael Shmidt and his wife Mary ; baptized May 4 ; sponsors, George and Barbara Shmidt.

Käss, Henry, born March 4, 1800, of Matthias Käss and his wife Elizabeth ; baptized May 6 ; sponsors, Henry Käss and Mary Brück.

Clemmer, Joseph, born April 26, 1800, of Christian Clemmer and his wife Catharine ; baptized May 8 ; sponsors, John Kuns and Elizabeth Buck.

Shmidt, Charles, born August 20, 1799, of John Shmidt and his wife Catharine ; baptized May 11 ; sponsors, Francis Huver and Eve Fricker.

Saüvert, William, born October 29, 1799, of John Saüvert and his wife Magdalen ; baptized May 12 ; sponsors, Joseph and Catharine Saüvert.

Miller, Jacob, born May 25, 1800, of Frederick Miller and his wife Elizabeth; baptized June 12 ; sponsors, Jacob Els and his wife Magdalen.

Shott, Peter, born September 13, 1799, of Anthony Shott and his wife Catharine ; baptized June 22 ; sponsors, Nicholas and Louisa M'Carty.

Shott, Philip James, born December 4, 1797, of John George Shott and his wife Mary ; baptized June 22 ; sponsors, Philip James and Catharine Shott.

Shott, Joseph, born June 5, 1797, of Anthony Shott and his wife Catharine ; baptized June 22 ; sponsors, Michael M'Canna and Anna Elizabeth Marien [?]

M'Canna, Martha, born January 31, 1800, of Michael M'Canna and his wife Mary ; baptized June 22 ; sponsors, Thomas and Mary M'Carty, brother and sister—" Fratres."

174

Bachmann, Clara, born March 28, 1798, of Henry Bachmann and his wife Anna Elizabeth ; baptized June 22 ; sponsors, John Thorn and Catharine Shott.

Shneider, Peter, born ———, of Daniel Shneider and his wife Catharine ; baptized June 22 ; sponsors, Simon Hönig and Magdalen Melchior.

Dotendorff, Dorothy, born May 3, 1800, of John Dotendorff and his wife Theresa ; baptized June 23 ; sponsors, George Shmidt and Wilhelmina Dorothy Mattes.

Gibson, Margaret Elizabeth, born April 3, 1800, of Henry Gibson and his wife Elizabeth ; baptized April 14 ; sponsors, John Coblè and Margaret Brown.

Allgeyer, George, born June 13, 1800, of Sebastian Allgeyer and his wife Catharine ; baptized July 13 ; sponsors, George Repplier and Eve Sigfrid.

Illain, William, born July 21, 1800, of Francis Illain and his wife Catharine ; baptized August 15 ; sponsors, Peter and Magdalen Egg.

Shönebruck, John, born June 12, 1800, of Andrew Shönebruck and his wife Mary ; baptized July 20 ; sponsors, James and Barbara Käss.

Shnabel, Andrew, born July 12, 1800, of John Shnabel and his wife Anna ; baptized July 28 ; sponsors, Andrew and Mary Eve Shnabel.

Walter, Henry, born April 5, 1795, of Henry Walter and his wife Margaret ; baptized August 24 ; sponsors, Simon and Anna Mary Hönig.

Strack, Elizabeth, born April 5, 1800, of Daniel Strack and his wife Elizabeth ; baptized August 24 ; sponsors, Henry and Catharine Strack.

Walter, Joseph, born May 21, 1796, of Jacob Walter and his wife Catharine ; baptized August 24 ; sponsors, John and Elizabeth M'Carty.

Walter, George, born July 30, 1799, of [the above] ; baptized [with the above] ; sponsors, Nicholas and Mary M'Carty.

Korb, Anna Christina, born ———, of Adam Korb and his wife Margaret ; baptized September 7 ; sponsors, John and Anna Christina Kemp.

Eckenrodt, Peter, born June 28, 1800, of Henry Eckenrodt and his wife Elizabeth ; baptized September 14 ; sponsors, Peter and Barbara Keffer.

Shnabel, Elizabeth, born July 8, 1800, of Jacob and Barbara Shnabel ; baptized September 14 ; sponsors, Francis and Elizabeth Hartman.

Ganss, John, born April 17, 1800, of George Ganss and his wife Magdalen ; baptized September 14 ; sponsors, Nicholas and Anna Mary Felix.

Felix, Eve, born December 1, 1790, of Martin Felix and his wife Barbara ; baptized September 14 ; sponsors, Peter Rittner and Eve Fricker.

Felix, Jacob, born June 28, 1793, of [the same ;] baptized September 14 ; sponsors, Nicholas and Anna Mary Felix.

Felix, Anna, born March 7, 1798, of [*the same;*] baptized September 14 ; sponsors, George and Barbara Sigfrid.

Shnabel, Mary, born August 12, 1800, of Andrew Shnabel and his wife Catharine ; baptized September 29 ; sponsors, Michael and Margaret Shnabel.

Bachman, John, born September 20, 1800, of Henry Bachman and his wife Elizabeth ; baptized October 26 ; sponsors, Andrew Shindler and Anna Bachman.

———, Christina, born ———, of ——— and Christina ——— ; baptized October 26 ; sponsors, Leonard and Elizabeth Buck.

———, Elizabeth, born ———, of ———, and Anna ——— ; baptized October 26 ; sponsors, Thomas and Catharine M'Carty.

Hönig, John, born October 9, 1800, of Michael Hönig and his wife Helen ; baptized October 27 ; sponsors, John and Eleonor Hönig.

Huver, Anna, born April 27, 1800, of Adam Huver and his wife Susan ; baptized November 9 ; sponsors, Henry Norbeck and Eve Fricker.

Flower, Andrew, born November 10, 1800, of Christopher Flower and his wife Magdalen ; baptized November 30 ; sponsors, Andrew and Magdalen Hopp.

Arens, Joseph, born October 15, 1800, of John Arens and his wife Elizabeth ; baptized November 30 ; sponsors, Adam and Eve Reichert.

Chevin, Catharine, born April 10, 1800, of Peter Chevin and his wife Catharine ; baptized November 30 ; sponsors Adam and Eve Reichert.

Els, John Henry, born October 19, 1800, of Jacob Els and his wife Mary ; baptized December 7 ; sponsors, John and Elizabeth Els.

Ruffner, Philip, born November 19, 1800, of Philip Ruffner and his wife Margaret ; baptized December 28 ; sponsors, John Adam and Catharine Hammerstein.

Buck, Rebecca, born November 22, 1800, of John Buck and his wife Salome ; baptized December 28 ; sponsors, Thomas M'Carty and Elizabeth Griser.

M'Carty, Mary, born December 23, 1800, of Nicholas M'Carty and his wife Elizabeth ; baptized December 28 ; sponsors, Nicholas and Louisa M'Carty.

[The number of baptisms for the year, including one illegitimate, is fifty-nine.]

MARRIAGES. *

1787—1800.

Oboltz—Moltzberger : February 3, 1787, the banns having been called, Anthony Obolt, youth, of Conewago, and Catharine Moltzberger, maiden, of *Herford* township, in Berks county.

Megaddy [*M'Carty*]—Hoenig : February 23, 1787, John Megaddy and Elizabeth Hoenig, Catholics, having previously been married before a preacher (" *coram prædicantio* " [*sic*]), renew their consent.

Hoenig—Peyl : February 23, 1787, Simon Hoenig, Catholic, and Anna Peyl, non-Catholic, having married before a Lutheran minister, renew their consent.

Stalter—Matheis : April 15, 1787, Henry Stalter, youth, of Manthobb, and Apollonia Matheis, maiden, of *Herford* township in Berks county.

Laurenz—Ebrers : April 16, 1787, Joseph Laurenz and Catharine Ebrers.

Bock—Kremer : June 2, 1787, banns having been called, Leonard Bock, youth, and Elizabeth Kremer, maiden, of Bucks (*in the record* " Bocks ") county.

Burgarth—Eccorod : June 3, 1787, the usual banns having been called, Philip Burgarth, youth, and Magdalen Eccorod, maiden. [*In the Baptismal Register (p. 6), whence this marriage there recorded by mistake has been transferred, Philip Burgarth is put down as resident of Herford township, and Magdalen of " crimitz " county.*]

Bock—Meccle : December 2, 1787, the usual banns having been called, Joseph Bock, youth, and Elizabeth Meccle, maiden.

Melchior—Hoenigs : February 1, 1788, Michael Melchior and Mary Magdalen Hoenigs, both resident in Hegau in Bucks county. On the day of his marriage, the bridegroom, having received the sacraments of Penance and Eucharist, made public profession of Faith before the altar.

Siegfried—Kobel : February 3, 1788, the banns having been called, Joseph Siegfried, youth, and Barbara Koble, maiden, of Berks county.

Eysenmann—Schos : February 17, 1788, the banns having been called, Christian Eysenmann and Susan Schos of —— township, in Berks county.

---

* The page, whereon opens the *Marriage Register*, is headed "*Nomina Copulatorum 1787.*" Underneath are recorded marriages for February of that year and the months preceding November, when, as Father Helbron has stated in two places in his *Register*, he took charge of Goshenhoppen Mission. (But see the *Note* on this conflict in dates in the *Preface*.)

Hoenig—Schöffer : the usual banns having been called, Michael Hoenig, youth, and Mary Magdalen Schöffer.

Schwittmann—Rohr : May 28, 1788, the usual banns having been called, John Schwittmann, youth, and Margaret Rohr, maiden.

Gery—Schall : July 7, 1789, after having been married before a lay judge, Philip Gery and Sara Schall renew their consent according to the prescribed rite.

Ilein—Kremers : July 7, 1789, the banns having been called, Francis Ilein, widower, and Juliana Kremers, maiden.

Müller—Dossert : October 11, 1789, Isaias Müller and Susanna Dossert, non-Catholic.

Orendorff—Eck : November 30, 1789, the three banns having been called as decreed by Trent, Christian Orendorff, youth, of Lebanon township —— county, and Mary Eva Eck, maiden, of Langenschwam township in Berks county.

Kemp — —— : February 2, 1790, John Kemp and ——, non-Catholic, having previously been married by a Calvinist minister, are re-married by me, his wife first making a profession of Faith and being admitted to the Sacraments.

Bauer—Kuhn : April 6, 1790, the usual banns having been called, John Bauer, widower, and Elizabeth Kuhn, maiden.

Ilein—Eck : June 22 1790, John Anthony Ilein, youth, and Elizabeth Eck, single.

Berner—Hock : September 6, 1790, after the usual banns of the Church, and the bridegroom, previously of no religion, having made profession of Faith and received the sacraments of Baptism, Penance and Eucharist, John Berner and Anna Hock.

Ems—Hock : September 6, 1790, having previously been married by the Calvinist pastor, and the bridegroom first making his profession of Faith and having received the sacraments, Valentine Ems and Juliana Hock, Catholic ?

Hopp—Gibsen : September 29, 1790, after the usual banns of the Church, at Mass, George Hopp and Mary Gibsen.

Bock—Eck : October 19, 1790, after the usual banns of the Church, at John Eck's house, in Obersobfort township in Montgomery county, Nicholas Bock and Magdalen Eck.

Guttmann—Strunck : March 2, 1791, having first been instructed in the Faith, which he now has professed, at Mass, John Guttmann, youth and formerly a Calvinist, and Eva Strunck, maiden ; both from Reading ("raiding" in the text) Berks county.

Grünewald— —— : May 8, 1791, having first been married by a Calvinist minister, and the wife before the baptism of their offspring, having being duly instructed in the Faith, received the sacraments and made a profession of Faith, John Grünewald and his wife Mary Ann, formerly Calvinist.

Huver—Geth : May 8, 1791, the banns having been called as prescribed by Trent and as usual in the Church, Francis Huver and Anna Mary Geth.

Müller—Breyer : July 5, 1791, after the usual banns, Frederick Müller and Elizabeth Breyer.

Kanner—Carr : July 7, 1791, after the usual banns, at Mass, John Kanner and Anna Carr.

Kaes—Bies ? : August 7 1791, the usual banns having been called, after Mass, John Kaes and Mary Bies ?

Zweyer—Zweyer : August 20, 1791, the bride having been duly instructed, absolved from the Calvinist heresy, and having made her profession of Faith before Mass in her own home (" *in domo propria*"), Mary Zweyer and Anthony Zweyer, Catholic.

[*All the foregoing marriages were solemnized in the presence of Rev. Peter Helbron, who attached his signature to the several entries. The following were celebrated before Rev. N. Delvaux.*]

Kaes—Eck : November 18, 1791, Peter Kaes, lawful son of Peter Kaes and Margaret Kun, and Magdalen Eck, lawful daughter of John Eck and Eva Staal.

Eck—Kaes : December 26 1791, the usual banns having been called, Peter Eck, lawful son of John and Eva Eck, and Magdalen Kaes, lawful daughter of Peter and Margaret Kaes.

Clemer—Bock : April 10, 1792, having first been baptized, Christian Clemer and Katharine Bock.

Kaiffer—Rohrbach : December 26, 1792, the banns having first been called, Joseph Kaiffer, lawful son of Peter Kaiffer and Barbara Hartman, and Christina Rohrbach, lawful daughter of George Rohrbach.

Strunck—Siegfried : December 26, 1792, the banns having been called. Philip Strunck, lawful son of William Strunck and Elizabeth Weismiller, and Mary Agatha Siegfried, lawful daughter of Andrew Siegfried and Agatha Zweyer.

Scharp—Strunck : February 12, 1793, in church, Joseph Scharp, lawful son of Andrew and Mary Scharp, and Anna Maria Strunck, lawful daughter of Philip and Elizabeth Strunck.

Johns—Minsen : April 18, 1793, Emaus Johns, widower, and —— Minsen, widow of the deceased John Minsen.

[*With the foregoing end the marriages solemnized in the presence of Rev. N. Delvaux.*]

Reichard—Els : [*For the confirmation of Anthony Reichard see the Preface.*]

On the 23rd inst., the usual three banns having been called, the said Anthony Reichard was married according to the rite of Holy Church to Catharine Els, daughter of John Els and his wife Anna Elizabeth Welken.

Arnold—Smidt : May 20, 1793, after the usual banns, before Mass, in the presence of a large congregation, John Arnold, son of John Arnold and his wife Elizabeth, and Eva Smidt, daughter of Philip and Ursula Smidt.

Smidt—Trolling : June 3, 1793, Caspar Smidt, widower, and Susan Trolling, his servant—a respectable woman.

Ashburner—Miller : September 2, 1793, after being baptized, William Ashburner and Catharine Miller.

Kaes—Kuns : October 13, 1793, at Caspar Shoenebruck's house, having previously been married before a lay judge, John Kaes and Catharine Kuns.

Gibson—Zweyer : January-14, 1794, the three banns having been called, before Mass, George Gibson, son of Henry Gibson and his wife Catharine, Catholic, and Elizabeth Zweyer, daughter of Stephen Zweyer and his wife Mary.

Zweyer—Sigfrid : April 1, 1794, with dispensation, and without banns, Balthasar Zweyer, son of George Zweyer and his wife Juliana, and Mary, daughter of Michael Sigfrid and his wife Justina ; witnesses John Gauger and Elizabeth Kemp.

Rupple—Greenwald : June 22, 1794, in Edward M'Carty's house, having previously been married by a lay judge, Joseph Rupple and Barbara Greenwald.

Strack—Hoffmann : June 24, 1794, in Edward M'Carty's house, Henry Strack and Catharine Hoffmann.

Gauger—Kemp : August 19, 1794, in church after Mass, John Gauger, son of John Gauger and his wife Barbara, and Elizabeth Kemp, daughter of John Kemp and his wife Catharine.

Reppert—Keffer : October 5, 1794, having previously been married by a lay judge, John Reppert and Catharine Keffer.

Sigfrid—Minder : October 7, 1794, the banns having been called, Jacob Sigfrid, son of Michael and Justina Sigfrid, and Susan Minder, daughter of Frederick and Catharine Minder ; witnesses Joseph Sigfrid and Burchard Minder.

Shmidt—Shnabel : October 7, 1794, the banns having been called once, Thomas, son of Christian Shmidt and his wife Mary Magdalen, non-Catholic, and Elizabeth, daughter of Andrew Shnabel and his wife Mary Eve, Catholic ; witnesses Michael Shnabel and George Bauer.

Shnabel—Henziger : October 28, 1794, the banns having been called, Michael Shnabel, son of Andrew Shnabel and his wife Mary Eve, Catholics, and Margaret, daughter of Jacob Henziger, Catholic, and his wife Barbara, non-Catholic ; witnesses Magdalen Taubetsen and Jacob Shnabel.

Shnabel—Keffer : December 30, 1794, the banns having been called, Jacob, son of Andrew Shnabel and his wife Mary Eve, and Barbara, daughter of Peter Keffer and his wife Barbara ; witnesses Andrew Shnabel and John Keffer.

Kemp—Buck : February 10, 1795, the banns having been called, John Kemp, son of John Kemp and his wife Anna, Catholics, and Barbara Buck, daughter of Nicholas Buck and his wife Elizabeth ; witnesses Jacob Keffer and Frederick Kemp.

Reninger—Gibson : April 14, 1795, the banns having been called, Frederick Reninger, son of Frederick and Anna Mary Reninger, Catholics, and Catharine Gibson, daughter of Henry and Catharine Gibson, Catholics ; witnesses Caspar Shmidt and George Bauer.

Buck—Dum : April 20, 1795, the banns having been called, Joseph Buck, son of Nicholas and Apollonia Buck, and Rosina Dum, daughter of Caspar and Eva Dum.

Orendorff—Aloine : July 12, 1795, the banns having been called once, in the presence of the congregation at Reading, John Orendorff and Magdalen Aloine.

Keisling—Shmidt : November 8, 1795, banns having been called once, in the presence of the congregation at Reading, Sebastian Kiesling, non-Catholic, and Catharine Shmidt, daughter of Philip Shmidt.

Zweyer—Arnold : November 15, 1795, the banns having been called once, in the presence of the congregation at Quitopahill on Sunday, George Zweyer, son of Stephen and Mary Zweyer, and Christina, daughter of John and Elizabeth Arnold.

Käss—Kuns : December 26, 1795, before Mass, Mathias Käss, son of Peter and Margaret Käss, and Elizabeth, daughter of John and Catharine Kuns.

Striby—M'Carty : January 26, 1796, George Striby and Elizabeth M'Carty ; witnesses John M'Carty and John Buck.

Els—Engel : April 5, 1796, the banns having been called, Jacob Els, son of John and Elizabeth Els, and Mary, daughter of Henry and Catharine Engel, Catholics.

Shlosser—Hopp : April 18, 1796, at Caspar Dum's house, John Shlosser, son of Joseph and Mary Shlosser, Catholics, and Magdalen, daughter of Francis and Catharine Hopp, Catholics.

Arens—Dum : the same day, John Arens, son of Jacob and Margaret Arens, Catholics, and Elizabeth Dum, daughter of Caspar and Eva Dum, Catholics.

Buck—M'Carty : April 28, 1796, in N. [Nicholas] M'Carty's house, in the presence of the congregation, John Buck and Sally M'Carty.

Rohrbach—Kemp : October 18, 1796, the three banns having been called, Jacob Rohrbach, son of George and Eliz. Rohrbach, and Susan, daughter of John and Anna Kemp, Catholics.

Arens—Richer : November 31 [sic], 1796, in Caspar Dum's house, the banns having been called once, [it seems at Mass,] Jacob Arens, son of Jacob and Margaret Arens, and Mary Richer, daughter of Martin Richer and Susan Gret, Catholics.

Kolb—Buck : May 8, 1797, John Kolb, widower, and Elizabeth Buck, widow.

Shmidt—Kuns : January 7, 1798, the banns having been called three times, Michael, son of Philip and Ursula Shmidt, and Mary, daughter of John and Catharine Kuns, Catholics.

Ruffner—Hammerstein : April 8, 1798, Philip, son of Philip and Eva Ruffner, Catholics, and Margaret Hammerstein, daughter of [the names omitted.]

Hönig—Gording : April 22, 1798, in Nicholas M'Carty's house, Jacob, son of Jacob and Catharine Hönig, and Theresa Gording ; witnesses Anthony Griser and Anthony Hönig.

M'Carty—Emmery : April 24, 1798, in the same house, Nicholas, son of Nicholas and Louisa M'Carty, and Elizabeth, daughter of Andrew Emmery.

Egg—Hammerstein : July 10, 1798, John, son of John and Magdalen Egg, Catholics, and Louisa, daughter of Andrew and Barbara Hammerstein, Catholics ; witness Dorothy Egg.

Neuer—Reichert : July 29, 1798, in Adam Reichert's house, John Neuer and Mary Reichert; witnesses Thomas and Valentine Dum.

Rupple—Wenarmer : August 26, 1798, in Nicholas M'Carty's house, George Rupple, widower, and Elizabeth, daughter of Bernard and Elizabeth Wenarmer ; witness Mother Rupple.

Hönig—Weaver : August 27, 1798, in the same house, Joseph, son of Jacob and Catharine Hönig, and Catharine, daughter of Jacob and Anna Weaver ; witnesses Jacob Hönig and — Weaver, the bride's brother.

Shnabel—Mutard : September 15, 1798, Andrew, son of Andrew and Eva Shnabel, and Catharine, daughter of Frederick and Magdalen Mutard, Catholics ; witnesses Jacob Shnabel and Christian Shmidt.

Bryan—Gerstweiler : October 14, 1798, at Reading, Cherry Bryan, after having received Baptism, and Elizabeth Gerstweiler.

Saüvert—Berger : October 15, 1798, John Saüvert and Magdalen Berger ; [witnesses ?] Adam Bomer and Magdalen Shmidt.

Sigfrid—Felix : October 21, 1798, at Goshenhoppen, before Mass, George, son of Michael and Justina Sigfrid, and Barbara, daughter of Nicholas and —— Felix, Catholics.

Kelly—ONeal : September 6, 1798, at Gosh [enhoppen], John Kelly and Anna O Neal.

Fortman—Sweetman : November 29, 1798, Charles Leopold Fortman and Margaret, widow of John Sweetman ; witnesses Joseph Röhr and Rev. Mr. Peter Helbron.

Eckenrod—Egg : November 26, 1798, in Stephen Eckenrod's house near the Blue Mountains, Peter, son of Christopher and Anna Margaret Eckenrod, and Maria —.

Shönebruck—Rodt : February 5, 1799, in Goshenhoppen church before Mass, John Shönebruck and Eva, daughter of John and Eva Rodt ; witnesses Elizabeth Shönebruck and the bride's brother.

Dum—Arens : April 2, 1799, at Adam Reichert's house, Valentine, son of Caspar and Eva Dum, and Magdalen, daughter of Jacob and Margaret Arens; witnesses Thomas Dum and Joseph Arens.

Hess—Hopp: April 15, 1799, at Reading, John, son of Jeremiah and Margaret Hess, non-Catholic, and Catharine, daughter of Francis and Catharine Hopp; witnesses Andrew and George Hopp.

Huver—Pantan: August 11, 1799, at Reading, Adam, son of Francis and Mary Ann Huver, Catholics, and Susan, daughter of Jonathan and Nelly Pantan, Catholics; witnesses Thomas Zweyer and John Huver.

Burkopp—Uhlein: September 8, 1799, by Rev. P. Helbron, John Burkopp and Juliana, widow of Francis Uhlein.

Krämer—Egg: November 5, 1799, Joseph, son of Mathias and ——
Krämer, Catholic, and Veronica, daughter of John and Magdalen
Egg, Catholics; witnesses Nicholas and Jacob Buck.

Shnabel—Fine: on the same day, John, son of Andrew and Eva Shnabel, Catholics, and Anna, daughter of John and Elizabeth Fine,
Catholics; witnesses Andrew and Michael Shnabel.

Hauss—Els: January 19, 1800, Jacob, a convert to the Catholic Religion, son of Abraham and Veronica Hauss, non-Catholics, and
Mary, daughter of John and Anna Elizabeth Els, Catholics ; witnesses Jacob Els and Jacob Rankings.

Gret—Egg: January 28, 1800, John, son of John and Elizabeth Gret,
Catholics, and Catharine, daughter of Joseph and Agatha Egg,
Catholics; witnesses George Kemp and Philip Gret.

Henrich—Shönebruck: May 5, 1800, at Caspar Shönebruck's house,
the banns having been called three times, Joseph, son of Philip
and Elizabeth Henrich, Catholics, and Elizabeth, daughter of Caspar and Margaret Shönebruck, Catholics.

Shönebruck—Hill: the same day, the marriage consent renewed between Andrew Shönebruck and Mary Hill, non-Catholic, before
Mathias Brück.

Hartman—Lutz [?]: May 14, 1800, in the church at Reading, Francis
Hartman, widower, and Widow Lutz [?]; witnesses Sebastian
Allgeyer and Eva Fricker.

Miller—Gibson: July 1, 1800, Jacob, son of William and Barbara
Miller, Catholics, and Gertrude, daughter of Henry and Catharine
Gibson, Catholics; witnesses Jacob Hauss and his wife.

Queen—Coblet: August 19, 1800, the banns having been called three
times, Thomas, son of Thomas and Catharine Queen, and Mary,
daughter of Daniel and Mary Coblet; witnesses John and John
Coblet, kinsmen, [in the text " cognati ".]

The number of marriages from 1787 to 1800 is ninety-seven.

DEATHS AND BURIALS.*

1787-1800.

No deaths during 1787.

Fischwasser, Rosine, married, for thirty-five a Quakeress, having been
instructed by me [Rev. Peter Helbron], and baptized and strengthened with all the sacraments of Holy Church ; died in the Lord
April 12, 1788.

Winek, Caspar, ninety-five years old, the only one of his family hold-
ing fast to the Roman Catholic Religion, to whom after some
visits I administered once the sacraments of Penance and of the
Eucharist. When near his dying day, and in the presence of his
son, he begged me at his funeral to give a discourse on death to
his non-Catholic children, and his other relatives present. And
this was done. He died unexpectedly near Kutschenstattel on
October 5, 1788; buried on the 7th; [place not named.]

---

*Unless otherwise indicated all the burials were made in the graveyard at Goshenhoppen.

No deaths during the year 1789.

Schwob [?], Anna Elizabeth, married, strengthened with all the sacraments; died in the Lord January 25, 1790.

Koble, James, lawful son of Bartholomew Koble, three weeks old; died January 23, 1790.

Welcker, Henry Stephen, son of James Welcker and his wife Magdalen, one year and seven months old; buried July 3, 1790.

Arens, Elizabeth, widow, strengthened early with all the sacraments of the Church; died in the Lord October 19, 1790; buried during my absence from home.

Depre, James, widower, strengthened with the sacraments of the dying; buried with the usual rites of the Church, October 23, 1790.

Muthards, Magdalen, for 40 years Catholic, wife of Frederick Muthard, non-Catholic; buried February 18, 1791, a large assembly of the people hearkening to the funeral sermon.

Arens, Margaret, one half-year old, daughter of James Arens and his wife Margaret; buried on March 8, 1791.

Hopp, Elizabeth Margaret, three months old, daughter of Andrew Hopp and his wife Magdalen; buried on March 10, 1791.

Gaijner, Edward, died suddenly; buried solemnly on December 6, 1791 [place not named.]

Schmitt, Catharine, wife of Caspar Schmitt, on account of the alms given by her to the church was solemnly buried therein on Friday before Pentecost, 1792.

Sibert, John Felix, a noble ("nobilis vir"); buried after solemn Mass, July 13, 1793.

Egg, Elizabeth, daughter of John and Dorothy Egg.

Sigfrid, Joseph, son of Andrew and Agatha Sigfrid; buried in Reading graveyard.

Gret, Susan Barbara, daughter of Michael and Catharine Grett, aged 5 years, 4 months and 2 days ; died April 21, 1794 ; buried on the 23rd.

Gibson, Margaret, widow, seventy years and upwards of age; died June 18, 1794; buried on the 19th.

Rittner, Joseph, aged 74; died July 19, 1794; buried on the 21st at Reading.

Burk, Mary Elizabeth, wife of Joseph Burk; about 35 years old; died August 24, 1794; buried on the 26th.

Käss, John, son of Peter and Magdalen Käss; two and a half years old; died March 6, 1795; buried on the 8th.

Röhr, Joseph, son of Matthias and Catharine Röhr ; about 9 years old ; died July 17, 1795 ; buried on the 19th.

Röhr, John, son of the same ; about 6 years old ; died July 20, 1795 : buried on the 21st.

Henrich, Mary Margaret, wife of Christian Henrich ; aged about 71 years and 10 weeks ; died May 14, 1795 ; buried on the 16th near Sharp Mountain.

Henrich, George, son of John and Barbara Henrich ; six and a half years old ; died May 2, 1795 ; buried at Sharp Mountain on the 4th.

Gery, Philip, aged 29 years ; died September 21, 1795.; buried on the 23rd.

Diderich, John ; aged 37 years ; out of his mind about 7 years ; died September 27, 1795 ; buried on the 29th.

Welker, Mary Magdalen, wife of Gottlib Welker ; aged 70 years ; died December 3, 1795 ; buried on the 5th.

Gauger, Peter, son of John and Elizabeth Gauger ; aged 1 year and 7 months ; died September 16, 1796 ; buried on the 18th.

Fricker, Anthony, of Reading ; aged 65 years ; died November 27, 1796 ; buried on the 28th.

Gaas, Salome, at Reading ; aged 16 years ; died December 4, 1796 : buried on the 5th.

Burk, James, son of Joseph and Rosina Burk ; nine months and 12 days old ; died January 17, 1797.; buried on the 18th.

Buck, Joseph, son of Joseph and Elizabeth Buck ; aged 5 years, 6 weeks and 6 days ; died January 21, 1797 ; buried on the 23rd.

Burkhard, Peter, son of Martin and Dorothy Burkhard ; aged 18 years ; died February 7, 1797 ; buried on the 8th.

Shurp, Joseph, son of John and Elizabeth Shurp ; aged 8 years and 8 months ; died on August 8, 1797 ; buried on the 10th.

Shurp, Simon Lazarus, son of the same ; one year and 11 months old ; died August 10, 1797 ; buried on the 11th.

Weegllain [?], Daniel ; died September 1, 1797 ; buried on the 3rd.

Walter, James ; aged 67 years ; [dates of death and burial not entered.]

Sweetman, John, aged 35 years ; died January 22, 1798 ; buried on the 25th.

Kuhn, Eve, aged 68 years ; died February 1, 1798 ; buried on the 3rd.

Illain, Francis, aged 75 years ; died July 8, 1798 ; buried on the 10th.

Hartman, Magdalen, aged 84 years ; died July 30, 1798 ; buried August 1.

Henrich, Christian, aged 83 years ; died December 12, 1798 ; buried on the 14th near Sharp Mountain.

Brück, John, son of Matthias and Mary Brück, aged 4 months and 3 days ; died January 30, 1799 ; buried February 1.

Illain, David, son of Francis and Catharine Illain; died February 8, 1799; buried the 10th.

Meckel, Elizabeth, aged 74 years; married 52; died June 30, 1799; buried July 2.

Reichert, William, son of John and Catharine Reichert; aged 13 years and 5 months; drowned in a well August 29, 1799; buried on the 31st; [place not named.]

Mattes, George, son of John and Mary Mattes; two months old; died March 18, 1800 ; buried on the 20th ; [place not named.]

Bennen, Anna, wife of John Bennen; aged 30 years and 5 weeks; died March 18, 1800; buried on the 20th; [place not named.]

The number of deaths and burials from 1787 to 1800 is forty-eight.

GOSHENHOPPEN REGISTERS

OF

BAPTISMS (1801-1807); MARRIAGES (1801-1819); AND DEATHS (1801-1818).†

(Fourth Series.)

Translated and Annotated by Rev. Thomas C. Middleton,
D. D., O. S. A.

In a former paper were published the sacramental entries belonging to the old mission-church of St. Paul at Goshenhoppen, in Pennsylvania, down to the close of the last century,—the end of December, 1800. They were contained in volume two of the church registers kept by the missionaries of the above-named place ; and with this fourth series end the registrations contained in that volume. *

In earlier papers too reference was made to certain singularities to be met with in these old-time memoranda, as variants in spelling Christian and family names, as well as of places : fashions besides (not wholly local however) as giving each subject in baptism the Christian name of godparent—of godfather, or godmother,—according to sex. Here the reader will encounter the same peculiarities in orthography and ritual, though not perhaps in such marked degree of discrepancy.

But a charm he will miss, if he remember how often such memoranda were met in the old registers, was the fashion the missionaries had of making their church register, (—they only had one book,—) a kind of local cyclopædia, wherein was jotted down by them any point of interest (to their mission). It was gazetteer besides and dictionary in one. This mass of

---

†Unless indicated otherwise, page references in the text refer to pages in the original Goshenhoppen registers, not to this volume.

*A fifth and final series of church registers was published in Vol. LXI of RECORDS. See pp. 221-262, this volume.

odds and ends of information about persons, places and things that the student was sure to glean from their register-pages, we miss sadly.

Our more modern church-books, kept as they are now-a-days by rule on a species of machine-made plan, giving the merest statements of fact in the meagerest form of official terminology, while thereby wholly in accord with statute are yet of far less interest to read through this very lack of old-time gossipy and half-encyclopædical character. (But we must take our records as we find them.)

As will be observed the final dates in this volume (No. II) vary greatly, according as the clerk got to the end of the pages assigned him for the registration of given matter.

The baptisms (in this Series) close with the year 1807 ; while deaths and burials are recorded as far down as 1818; and marriage-entries run along one year at least later, if not two.

The reader will notice that in our translation of the Latin of the Christian names *Jacobus, Anna, Maria*, these (according as we thought would be their equivalents in English) have been rendered variously Jacob and James, Anna and Ann, Maria and Mary.

Among the death-notices is the record of a black child,— the only person of color in this Series,—named '' Frederick Green,'' who died aged three years on September 15, 1813.

The baptisms, running from 1801 to 1807, all administered by Rev. Paul Erntzen, number three hundred and twenty-seven (327), including two (2) pairs of twins, and seven (7) illegitimates, whose names, (we refer only to the latter—the only unfortunates at birth) as well as any trace even the faintest that might lead to their identification,—these we have carefully kept from our pages for reasons the reader will not be slow to recognize as meet and just.

The deaths and burials (down to 1818) number ninety-seven (97) ; the marriages (to 1819, or, maybe 1820, for the last entry in the volume is not clear as to the year,) one hundred and seventy-nine (179.)

With this paper (on Goshenhoppen mission-records) extending for sixty years and upwards from the year 1741, when the church records in this volume open, to the dates in this series, we have now published in all two thousand one hundred and twenty-three (2123) baptisms, including 16 marked in earlier transcripts as "Conversions"; four hundred and fifty-four (454) marriages; one (1) confirmation; and two hundred and sixty (260) deaths and burials.

FR. THOMAS C. MIDDLETON, O. S. A.

VILLANOVA COLLEGE, PA., June 4, 1899.

BAPTISMS FOR THE YEAR 1801.

[NOTE.—The following Baptisms were administered by Rev. Paul Erntzen, who made the several entries thereof.

Unless otherwise noted, the birth-year corresponds with the year of Baptism.

To the translator are due the various notes, set in square brackets, to be encountered in this paper.]

Felix, Anthony, born Dec. 7, 1800, of Martin Felix and his wife Barbara; bapt. Jan. 11; spon. Anthony Felix and Eve Sigfrid.

Gererd, Catharine, born ——, of John Gererd and his wife Margaret; bapt. Jan. 11, aged one year, seven months; spon. Joseph Allgeier and Barbara Sigfrid.

Sigfrid, Catharine, born Dec. 21, 1800, of George Sigfrid and his wife Barbara; bapt. Jan. 11; spon. George Repplier and Catharine Allgeier.

Queen, John, born Dec. 10, 1800, of Thomas Queen and his wife Mary; bapt. Jan. 11; spon. Daniel and Mary Coblet.

Reichert, Mary, born Dec. 14, 1800, of Anthony Reichert and his wife Catharine; bapt. Jan. 13; spon. John and Elizabeth Els.

Shmidt, John, born Dec. 15, 1800, of Caspar Shmidt and his wife Susan; bapt. Jan. 18; spon. John and Elizabeth Grett.

Bauer, Anna, born Sept. 18, 1799, of Peter Bauer and his wife Rosine; bapt. Jan. 28; spon. George Kemp and Mary Adam.

Bauer, David, born Jan. 10; of Peter Bauer and his wife Rosine; bapt. Jan. 28; spon. Peter and Magdalen Egg.

Käss, Daniel, born Jan. 11, of Peter Käss and his wife Magdalen; bapt. Jan. 28; spon. Peter and Magdalen Egg.

Shnabel, Mary Catharine, born Nov. 15, 1800, of Joseph Shnabel and his wife A. Maria; bapt. Feb. 2; spon. John and Catharine Grett.

Engel, William, born July —, 1800, of Henry Engel and his wife Catharine; bapt. Feb. 21; spon. John and Elizabeth Grett.

Strack, Elizabeth, born Jan. 7, of Henry Strack and his wife Catharine; bapt. Feb. 22; spon. Nicholas and Elizabeth M'Carty.

Botman, Catharine, born Jan. 11, of Bernard Botman and his wife Catharine; bapt. Feb. 22; spon. Jacob and Elizabeth Kohl.

Buck, Elizabeth, born Jan. 7, of Leonard Buck and his wife Elizabeth ; bapt. Feb. 22 ; spon. Jacob and Catharine Kohl, *cognati*, [cousins].

Sweikert, Susan, born Nov. 23, 1800, of David Sweikert and his wife Magdalen ; bapt. March 8 ; spon. John Zweyer and Eve Stricker.

Lemons, John, born Feb. 24, of Henry Lemons and his wife Catharine ; bapt. Mar. 8 ; spon. Martin and Barbara Felix.

Rohrbach, Susan, born Feb. 19, of Jacob Rohrback and his wife Susan ; bapt. Mar. 10; spon. John and Barbara Kemp.

Egg, Anthony, born Nov. 30, 1800, of Theodore Egg and his wife Mary Elizabeth ; bapt. Mar. 15; spon. Christian and Catharine Clemmer.

Shmidt, George, born Feb. 21, of George Shmidt and his wife Barbara ; bapt. Mar. 25; spon. George Kemp and Mary Humm.

Felix, Daniel, born [*date wanting*,] of Michael Felix and his wife Elizabeth ; bapt. Mar. 30; spon. Andrew and Elizabeth Gret.

Burkopp, Frederick, born Feb. 1, of John Burkopp and his wife Juliana ; bapt. Apr. 11 ; spon. Frederick Kemp and Elizabeth Buck.

Lambert, Benjamin, born Mar. 4, of Jacob Lambert and his wife Mary ; bapt. Apr. 12 ; spon. Philip and Elizabeth Shmidt.

Shindler, Jacob, born Oct. 18, 1800, of Andrew Shindler and his wife Sara ; bapt. Apr. 12 ; spon. Thomas Zweyer and Mary Shindler.

Henrich, John, born Feb. 27, of Joseph Henrich and his wife Elizabeth ; bapt. Apr. 19 ; spon. Caspar and Margaret Shönebrück.

Buck, Henry, born Mar. 30, of Joseph Buck and his wife Rosine ; bapt. Apr. 19; spon. Henry Käss and Barbara Shönebrück.

Hönig, Joseph, born Apr. 6, of Jacob Hönig and his wife Theresa ; bapt. Apr. 26 ; spon. Jacob Kohl and Mary Buck.

Melchior, Mary Ann, born Mar. 18, of Michael Melchior and his wife Magdalen ; bapt. Apr. 26; spon. Michael and Helen Hönig.

Shneider, Margaret, born Feb. 24, of Daniel Shneider and his wife Catharine ; bapt. Apr. 26; spon. Joseph and Magdalen Hönig.

Buck, Jacob, born Apr. 21, of Nicholas Buck and his wife Magdalen ; bapt. Apr. 26; spon. Jacob and Susan Buck.

Buck, Nicholas, born Mar. 4, of Jacob Buck and his wife Susan ; bapt. Apr. 26 ; spon. Jacob Kohl and Mary Buck.

Ashburn, Joseph, born Dec. 19, 1800, of William Ashburn and his wife Catharine ; bapt. Apr. 27 ; spon. Christopher and Anna Mary Langby.

Shurp, Solomon, born Feb. 26 [*or* 28,] of John Shurp and his wife Elizabeth ; bapt. May 3 ; spon. Theodore and Elizabeth Egg.

Clee, John, born June 24, 1800, of Ernest Clee and his wife Christine ; bapt. May 10; spon. Anthony Felix and Eve Sigfrid.

Conner, Anna Maria, born Mar. 18, of John Conner and his wife Anna ; bapt. May 14 ; spon. Jacob Wanghan and Catharine Brown.

Hauss, Frances, born May 4, of Jacob Hauss and his wife Mary; bapt. May 24 ; spon. Jacob and Mary Els.

Malzberger, Ernest, born May 15, of Jacob Malzberger and his wife Mary ; bapt. May 28 ; spon. Jacob and Catharine Malzberger.

Hopp, Francis, born Apr. 2, of George Hopp and his wife Margaret ; bapt. May 31 ; spon. Andrew and Magdalen Hopp.

Gret, David, born May 15, of John Gret and his wife Catharine ; bapt. June 7 ; spon. Joseph and Agatha Egg.

Reppert, Stephen, born May 1, of John Reppert and his wife Catharine ; bapt. June 13 ; spon. Stephen and Anna Barbara Reppert.

Wummer, George, born Dec. 14, 1800, of Adam Wummer and his wife Magdalen ; bapt. June 14 ; spon. Sebastian and Catharine Kiesel.

Röhr, Sophia, born June 11, of Joseph Röhr and his wife Juliana ; bapt. July 5 ; spon. John and Elis. Els.

Käss, Daniel, born June 17, of Nicholas Käss and his wife Margaret ; bapt. July 5 ; spon. Matthias Röhr and Christine Kuns.

Shmidt, Jacob, born Jan. 31, of John Shmidt and his wife Catharine, non-Catholic ; bapt. July 12 , spon. Philip and Elizabeth Shmidt.

Gibson, Francis, born July 3, of Joseph Gibson and his wife Christine ; bapt. July 30 ; spon. Francis and Catharine Hopp.

Reichert, Frances, born June 30, of John Reichert and his wife Catharine ; bapt. Aug. 2 ; spon. John Reichert and Frances Röhr.

Shlosser, Charles Francis, born July 30, of John Shlosser and his wife Magdalen ; bapt. the same day ; spon. Francis and Catharine Hopp.

Sauevert, [but elsewhere " Säuvert"], Sara, born Oct. 13, 1800, of Joseph Sauevert and his wife Catharine ; bapt. Aug. 9 ; spon. Philip and Elizabeth Shmidt.

Gret, Catharine, born June 6, of Joseph Gret and his wife Christine ; bapt. Aug. 9 ; spon. Sebastian and Catharine Allgeyer.

Reppert, John and Peter, twins, born July 17, of Stephen Reppert and his wife Magdalen ; bapt. Aug. 15 ; spon. for John, John and A. Xt· [Anna Christine ?] Kemp ; for Peter, Peter and Barbara Keffer.

Bush, Margaret, born Apr. 26, of Henry Bush and his wife Magdalen ; bapt. Aug. 30 ; spon. John Adam Gret and Elizabeth Richert, [sic, a misspelling perhaps for Reichert.]

Reichert, Margaret, born Aug. 30, of Adam Reichert and his wife Eve; bapt. Aug. 31 ; spon. Jacob and Margaret Arens.

Bryan, Mary Catharine, born June 26, of John Bryan and his wife Elizabeth ; bapt. Sept. 12 ; spon. Henry and Elizabeth Eckenrodt.

Kemp, Catharine. born Sept. 14, of John Kemp and his wife Barbara ; bapt. Sept. 28 ; spon. Jacob Kemp and Mary Buck.

Gede, Margaret, born June 25, of William Gede and his wife Sophia ; bapt. Oct. 11 ; spon. Joseph Allgeyer and Margaret Lambert.

Keffer, Jacob, born Aug. 31, of Jacob Keffer and his wife Magdalen ; bapt. Oct. 11 ; spon. Jacob and Barbara Shnabel.

Hartmann, Mary Elizabeth, born Sept. 5, of Jacob Hartmann and his wife Catharine ; bapt. Oct. 11 ; spon. Francis and Elizabeth Hartmann.

Käss, Anna Maria, born Sept. 6, of John Käss and his wife Catharine ; bapt. Nov. 1 ; spon. John and Catharine Kuns.

Egg, Paul, born Nov. 1, of John Egg and his wife Louisa [*Aloitina*] ; bapt. Nov. 10; spon. [*Rev.*] Paul Erntzen and Barbara Hammerstein.

Dollhager, [*though may be* Dollhagen,] Elizabeth, born Oct. 17, of Henry Dollhager [*?*] and his wife M[*ary*] Barbara ; bapt. Nov. 11 ; spon, Bartholomew Coblet and Elizabeth Wineyard.

Merkel, Benjamin, born Nov. 14, of John Merkel and his wife Barbara ; bapt. Nov. 22 ; spon. John and Barbara Henrich.

Neuer, Elizabeth, born Nov. 4, of John Neuer and his wife Mary ; bapt. Nov. 30; spon. Michael Reichert and Elizabeth Henrich.

Beringer, Mary Elizabeth, born Oct. 12, of Mathias Beringer and his wife Magdalen ; bapt. Dec. 25 ; spon. George Kemp and Elizabeth Welker.

Gery, Jacob, born Sept. 8, of Martin Gery and his wife Mary ; bapt. Dec. 26 ; spon. Jacob Kemp and Salome Reichert.

[*Number of Baptisms sixty-four.*]

BAPTISMS FOR THE YEAR 1802.

Kemp, Magdalen, born Jan. 12, of George Kemp and his wife Elizabeth ; bapt. Jan. 30; spon. Jacob and Susan Röhrbach.

Dum, Joseph, born Jan. 3, of Valentine Dum and his wife Magdalen ; bapt. Jan. 31 ; spon. Peter Arens and Elizabeth Dum.

Gret, John, born Dec. 29, 1801, of Michael Gret and his wife Esther; bapt. Jan. 31 ; spon. Michael and Catharine Gret.

Kiesel, John, born Nov. 14, of Sebastian Kiesel and his wife Catharine ; bapt. Feb. 15 ; spon. Joseph and Margaret Opold.

Opold, George, born Jan. 1, of Joseph Opold and his wife Margaret ; bapt. Feb. 15 ; spon. Philip and Magdalen Shmidt.

Adam, Catharine, born Feb. 5, of John Adam and his wife Catharine ; bapt. Feb. 18 ; spon. Simon and Catharine Adam.

Shnabel, Margaret, born Jan. 30, of John Shnabel and his wife Anna ; bapt. Mar. 6; spon. Michael and Margaret Shnabel.

Egg, Anna, born Feb. 21, of Peter Egg and his wife Magdalen ; bapt. Mar. 6; spon. John and Eva Egg.

Mattes, John Elias, born Feb. 24, of John Mattes and his wife Anna Maria ; bapt. Mar. 6; spon. John and Elizabeth Illain.

Vögely, Mary, born Feb. 6. of George Vögely and his wife Catharine ; bapt. Mar. 7 ; spon. John and Catharine Coblet.

Gruver, Mary, born Jan. 31, of Philip Gruver and his wife Barbara ; bapt. Mar. 7 ; spon. John Welker and Philippina Coblet.

Plank, John, born Dec. 29, 1801, of Jacob Plank and his wife Elizabeth ; bapt. Mar. 14 ; spon. John Ganss and Magdalen Hartmann.

Ganss, Sara, born Dec. 17, 1801, of George Ganss and his wife Magdalen (*formerly* Heller) ; bapt. Mar. 14 ; spon. George and Barbara Sigfrid.

Shmidt, George, born Mar. 10, of Frederick Shmidt and his wife Catharine (*formerly* Leaf); bapt. Mar. 14; spon. George Leaf.

Egg, Mary Elizabeth, born Feb. 13, of Joseph Egg and his wife Agatha; bapt. Mar. 21; spon. John and Elizabeth Gret.

Eckenrodt, Mary Elizabeth, born Jan. 8, of Peter Eckenrodt and his wife Mary; ceremonies supplied March 28; spon. John Eckenrodt and Elizabeth Burgy.

Keffer, Catharine, born Feb. 21, of Joseph Keffer and his wife Christine; bapt. Apr. 4; spon. Michael and Catharine Gret.

Kohl, Mary Magdalen, born Feb. 9, of Jacob Kohl and his wife Elizabeth; bapt. Apr. 25; spon. Nicholas and Magdalen Buck.

M'Carty, Mary, born Feb. 1, of John M'Carty and his wife Elizabeth; bapt. Apr. 25; spon. Charles M'Entire and Mary M'Carty.

Strack, John, born Dec. 10, 1801, of Daniel Strack and his wife Elizabeth; bapt. Apr. 25; spon. John and Salome Buck.

Rittner, Anna Maria, born Apr. 28, of Peter Rittner and his wife Barbara; bapt. May 9; spon. George and Catharine Repplier.

Käss, Mathias, born Apr. 9, of Mathias Käss and his wife Elizabeth; bapt. May 17; spon. John and Mary Käss, cousins, [*cognati.*]

Shnabel, John, born Apr. 9, of Michael Shnabel and his wife Margaret; bapt. May 25; spon. John and Anna Shnabel.

Dienes, Mary Barbara, born Apr. 4, of John Dienes and his wife Elizabeth; bapt. May 28; spon. Elizabeth Wingart.

Bauer, Rosine, born Apr. 29, of Peter Bauer and his wife Rosine; bapt. June 1; spon. Joseph and Anna Maria Shnabel.

Egg, Peter, born Mar. 29, of John Egg and his wife Charlotte; bapt. June 6; spon. Peter and Magdalen Käss.

Zweyer, Adam, born Aug. 4, of Adam Zweyer and his wife Barbara; bapt. June 12; spon. Joseph and Catharine.

Shnabel, Barbara, born Apr. 23, of Jacob Shnabel and his wife Barbara; bapt. June 13; spon. John Keffer and Magdalen Hartmann.

Queen, Catharine Philippina, born May 8, of Thomas Queen and his wife Mary; bapt. June 6; spon. Joseph Wingart and Philippina Coblet.

Huver, Thomas, born May 1, of Adam Huver and his wife Susan; bapt. July 11; spon. John Huver and Eve Sigfrid.

Käss, Peter, born May 22, of Jacob Käss and his wife Barbara; bapt. July 18; spon. Henry Käss and Mary Ann Shönebruck.

Shnabel, Aegidius Andrew, born July 11, of Andrew Shnabel and his wife Catharine; bapt. July 25: spon. Andrew and Mary Eve Shnabel.

Hughes, Catharine, born Aug. 6, of John Hughes and his wife Ann; bapt. Aug. 8; spon. Thomas Zweyer and Eve Sigfrid.

Orth, Sebastian Peter, born Dec. 20, 1801, of Peter Orth and his wife Catharine; bapt. Aug. 9; spon. Sebastian and Catharine Allgeier.

Miller, Elizabeth, born June 22, of Frederick Miller and his wife Elizabeth; bapt. Aug. 15; spon. Jacob and Gertrude Miller.

Hopp, Elizabeth, born July 1, of George Hopp and his wife Margaret ; bapt. Aug. 29; spon. Henry Gibson and Elizabeth Arens.

Repplier, Mary Sophia, born Aug. 13, of George Repplier and his wife Catharine ; bapt. Sept. 12; spon. Sebastian and Catharine Allgeyer.

Ems, John, born Nov. 15, 1801, of Valentine Ems and his wife Juliana ; bapt. Sept. 13; spon. Joseph Zweyer and Mary Jones.

Sigfrid, Elizabeth, born Sept. 14, of George Sigfrid and his wife Barbara; bapt. Oct. 10; spon. Anthony and Elizabeth Felix, cousins, [*cognati.*]

Watter, John, born Aug. 26, of John Watter and his wife Mary ; bapt. Oct. 11 ; spon. Denis M'Cue and Phenenna Remstone.

Clemmer, Samuel, born Sept. 6, of Christian Clemmer and his wife Catharine ; bapt. Oct. 24 ; spon. Thomas M'Carty and Magdalen Buck.

Els, Catharine, born Sept. 16, of Jacob Els and his wife Mary Magdalen ; bapt. Nov. 1 ; spon. Bartholomew Coblet and Catharine Engel.

Hauss, Jacob, born Sept. 21, of Jacob Hauss and his wife Mary ; bapt. Nov. 1 ; spon. Jacob Hauss and Sophia Els.

Hopp, Susan, born Sept. 22, of Andrew Hopp and his wife Magdalen ; bapt. Oct. 31 ; spon. Francis and Catharine Hopp.

Shlosser, Francis Joseph, born [*date wanting,*] of George Shlosser and his wife Elizabeth ; bapt. Oct. 31 ; spon. Joseph and Anna Maria Shlosser.

Reichert, Elizabeth, born Aug. 13, of Anthony Reichert and his wife Catharine ; bapt. Aug. 21 ; spon. Martin and Gertrude Burkard.

Felix, Elizabeth, born Sept. 30, of Michael Felix and his wife Elizabeth ; bapt. Nov. 14 ; spon. Joseph Sigfrid and Elizabeth Felix.

Henrich, Jacob, born Aug. 18, of Joseph Henrich and his wife Elizabeth ; bapt. Nov. 21 ; spon. Jacob Shönebruck and Mary Henrich.

Eckenrodt, Charles, born Oct. 3, of George Eckenrodt and his wife Mary ; bapt. Nov. 28; spon. Philip and Elizabeth Henrich.

Stahler, Christian, born Sept. 23, of Christian Stahler and his wife Margaret; bapt. Nov. 28 ; spon. J. Spring and —— Stahler.

Eisemann, Frances, born Sept. 28, of Christian Eisemann and his wife Susan ; bapt. Dec. 12 ; spon. John Allgeyer and Mary Lambert.

Rohrbach, Jacob, born Dec. 6, of Jacob Rohrback and his wife Susan ; bapt. Dec. 14 ; spon. Jacob Kemp and Mary Buck.

Shmidt, Mary, born Nov. 16, of Caspar Shmidt and his wife Susan ; bapt. Dec. 25 ; spon. Stephen and Mary Reichert.

[*Number of Baptisms fifty-four, including one illegitimate.*]

BAPTISMS FOR THE YEAR 1803.

Burkop, Mary, born Nov. 16, 1802, of John Burkop and his wife Juliana ; bapt. Jan. 8 ; spon. J. H. E. Martin and his wife Catharine.

Shmidt, Mary, born Dec. 3, 1802, of George Shmidt and his wife Barbara; bapt. Jan. 15; spon. [*Rev.*] Paul Erntzen and Catharine Shmidt.

Engel, Elias, born Oct. 22, 1802, of Henry Engel and his wife Catharine; bapt. Jan. 30; spon. Nicholas and Susan Gret.

Reninger, Elizabeth, born Jan. 15, of Frederick Reninger and his wife Catharine; bapt. Mar. 6; spon. Wendel and Hethe Reninger non-Catholic.

Shots, John, born Feb. 27, of Anthony Shots and his wife Catharine; bapt. April 10; spon. John and Catharine Martin.

Gret, Daniel, born Mar. 12, of John Gret and his wife Catharine; bapt. Apr. 10; spon. Daniel Gret and Margaret Egg.

M'Canna, Charles, born Oct. 8, 1802, of Michael M'Canna and his wife Mary; bapt. Apr. 10; spon. Theodore and Elizabeth Egg.

Vögely, Elizabeth, born Mar. 27, of George Vögely and his wife Catharine; bapt. Apr. 11; spon. Daniel Coblet and wife.

Buck, George, born Jan. 25, of Joseph Buck and his wife Rosine; bapt. Mar. 20; spon. George and Barbara Shmidt.

Gauss, George, born Jan. 1, of John Gauss and his wife Ann; bapt. March 14; spon. George and Magdalen Gauss.

Gording, Catharine, born Dec. 31, 1802, of John Gording and his wife Catharine; bapt. Feb. 28; spon. Jacob and Catharine Kohl.

Lehmon, Anna Maria, born Apr. 3, of Henry Lehmon and his wife Catharine; bapt. Apr. 17; spon. George and Barbara Sigfrid.

Eckenrodt, Jacob, born Feb. 5, of Henry Eckenrodt and his wife Elizabeth; bapt. Apr. 19; spon. Jacob and Magdalen Keffer.

Odere, Patrick, born Sept. 16, 1802, of John Odere and his wife Debora; bapt. April 19; spon. John and Susan Keffer.

Chevain, Elizabeth, born Feb. 26, of Peter Chevain and his wife Catharine; bapt. May 22; spon. George Arens and Elizabeth Dum.

Wummer, Elizabeth, born Oct. 23, 1803, [*sic, but* 1802?] of Adam Wummer and his wife Magdalen; bapt. May 22; spon. Elizabeth Shmidt.

Reichert, Catharine Lydia, [*in the text* "lidia,"] born Apr. 17, of John Reichert and his wife Catharine; bapt. May 29; spon. John and Catharine Gassawer.

Gibson, Margaret, born May 22, of Joseph Gibson and his wife Christine; bapt. June 12; spon. George and Margaret Hopp.

Lambert, Elias, born Feb. 2, of Jacob Lambert and his wife Mary; bapt. June 12; spon. Henry and Rosine Norbeck.

Röhr, David, born June 23, of Joseph Röhr and his wife Juliana; bapt. July 3; spon. Daniel Focht and Sophia Els.

Burkard, John, born June 4, of Joseph Burkard and his wife Catharine; bapt. June 29; spon. John and Elizabeth Coblet.

Keffer, Samuel, born July 20, of John Keffer and his wife Susan; bapt. Aug. 14; spon. Samuel Hartmann and Magdalen Keppert.

Wineyard, Joseph, born Aug. 4, of John Wineyard and his wife Philippina ; bapt. Aug. 21 ; spon. Daniel Coblet and Elizabeth Wineyard.

Fortmann, Charles Joseph, born Aug. 25, of Charles Leopold Fortmann and his wife Margaret ; bapt. Sept. 4 ; spon. Bartholomew Coblet and Sophia Els.

Greenewald, Catharine, born May 24, of Jacob Greenewald and his wife Susan ; bapt. Sept. 11 ; spon. John M'Gurgan and Catharine Gerstweiler.

Shnabel, Jacob, born Aug. 2, of Jacob Shnabel and his wife Barbara ; bapt. Sept. 11 ; spon. Jacob and Magdalen Keffer.

Handly, Margaret, born Mar. 31, 1801, of Thomas Handly and his wife Margaret ; bapt. Sept. 12 ; spon. Henry Eckenrodt.

Handly, Thomas, born May 24, of [the above; bapt. the same day and with the same godfather as " Margaret "]

Clark, John, born Feb. 28, 1796, of Henry Clark and his wife Rachel ; bapt. Sept. 13 ; spon. John M'Gurgan.

Clark, James, born April 14, 1798, of [the above; bapt. with "John ";] spon. Henry Eckenrodt.

Clark, Patrick, born Mar. 19, 1800, of [the above; bapt. with "John ";] spon. Philip Gerstweiler.

Clark, Anna, born July 12, 1802, of [the above; bapt. with " John ";] spon. John M'Gurgan.

Shnabel, Elizabeth, born Sept. 26, of John Shnabel and his wife Ann ; bapt. Sept. 29 ; spon. Thomas and Elizabeth Shmidt.

Shmidt, John, born Dec. 23, 1802, of John Shmidt and his wife Catharine ; bapt. Oct. 9 ; spon. Sebastian and Catharine Allgeyer.

Gret, Sara, born Aug. 13, of Joseph Gret and his wife Christine ; bapt. Oct. 9 ; spon. Jacob and Dorothy Lambert.

Kemp, Anna Catharine, born Oct. 9, of George Kemp and his wife Elizabeth ; bapt. Oct. 11 ; spon. John and Anna Christine Kemp.

Shurp, Philip, born Oct. 8, of John Shurp and his wife Elizabeth ; bapt. Oct. 16 ; spon. Philip and Elizabeth Gret.

Neuer, Philip, born Aug. 8, of John Neuer and his wife Mary ; bapt. Oct. 30 ; spon. Philip Reichert and Susan Gret.

Bryan, John, born July 3, of John Bryan and his wife Elizabeth ; bapt. Nov. 13 ; spon. John Gerstweiler and Magdalen Hartmann.

Zweyer, Anna Maria, born Oct. 17, of Mathias Zweyer and [his wife] Elizabeth ; bapt. Nov. 13 ; spon. Anna Maria Zweyer.

Shönebruck, Solomon, born Sept. 8, of Andrew Shönebruck and his wife Magdalen ; bapt. Nov. 20 ; spon. Joseph and Rosine Buck.

Stahler, Susan, born Oct. 4, of Christian Stahler and his wife Margaret ; bapt. Nov. 27 ; spon. Jacob and Susan Catharine Spring.

Coblet, Daniel, born Nov. 4, of John Coblet and his wife Elizabeth ; bapt. Dec. 4 ; spon. Daniel and Mary Ann Coblet.

Queen, Henry Daniel, born Nov. 7, of Thomas Queen and his wife Mary ; bapt. Dec. 4 ; spon. Henry and Catharine Coblet.

Reichert, Mary Catharine, born Oct. 15, of Anthony Reichert and his wife Catharine ; bapt. Nov. 1 ; spon. Jacob and Mary Els.

Keffer, Daniel, born Nov. 6, of Joseph Keffer and his wife Christine ; bapt. Dec. 11 ; spon. Anthony Felix and Barbara Gret.

Norbeck, Elizabeth, born Dec. 11, of Henry Norbeck and his wife Rosine ; bapt. Dec. 12 ; spon. Nicholas and Mary Röhr.

[*Number of Baptisms forty-seven.*]

BAPTISMS FOR THE YEAR 1804.

Shmidt, Elizabeth, born Nov. 27, 1803, of Michael Shmidt and his wife Mary ; bapt. Jan. 15 ; spon. John Kuns and Mary Barbara Shönebruck.

Gehry, Mary Catharine, born Jan. 19, of Martin Gehry and his wife Mary ; bapt. Jan. 19 ; spon. John and Elizabeth Gret.

Eckenrodt, Margaret, born Jan. 27, of Peter Eckenrodt and his wife Mary ; bapt. Jan. 29; spon. John Burgy and Elizabeth Eckenrodt.

Kemp, John, born Dec. 23, 1803, of John Kemp and his wife Barbara ; bapt. Jan. 31 ; spon. Martin and Mary Gehry.

Egg, Andrew, born Dec. 26, 1803, of John Egg and his wife Louisa ["*Aloitina*"] ; bapt. Feb. 2 ; spon. Philip and Anna Margaret Ruffner, Denis, Mary, born Oct. 10, 1803, of John Denis and his wife Elizabeth ; bapt. Feb. 5 ; spon. Daniel Gret and Catharine Coblet.

Malzberger, George, born Dec. 10, 1803, of Jacob Malzberger and his wife Mary ; bapt. Feb. 7; spon. Joseph Malzberger and his sister Elizabeth.

Benton, Mary, born Mar. 11, 1784, of Jonathan Benton and his wife Nelly, non-Catholic ; bapt. Feb. 12 ; spon. Adam and Susan Huver.

Huver, Jonathan, born Dec. 11, 1803, of Adam Huver and his wife Susan ; bapt. Feb. 12 ; spon. John Huver and Mary Benton.

Grill, Eve, born Dec. 22, 1803, of John Grill and his wife Sara ; bapt. Feb. 12 ; spon. H. [?] Thomas Dum and Eve Fricker, widow.

Shmidt, Henry William, born Jan. 4, of Frederic Shmidt and his wife Catharine ; bapt. Feb. 12 ; spon. William Münzer.

Dum, Thomas, born Dec. 1, 1803, of Valentine Dum and his wife Magdalen ; bapt. Feb. 19 ; spon. Thomas Dum and Elizabeth Arens.

——, Susan, born Sept. 16, 1803, of Michael —— and his wife Esther ; bapt. Feb. 19 ; spon. Nicholas and Susan Gret.

Egg, Jacob, born Jan. 11, of Peter Egg and his wife Magdalen ; bapt. Feb. 18 ; spon. Peter and Magdalen Käss.

Gret, Charles, born Mar. 2, of Philip Gret and his wife Elizabeth ; bapt. Mar. 6 ; spon. John and Elizabeth Shurp.

Allgeyer, Catharine, born Mar. 10, of Joseph Allgeyer and his wife Margaret; bapt. Mar. 11 ; spon. Sebastian and Catharine Allgeyer.

Shnabel, Elizabeth, born Feb. 9, of Andrew Shnabel and his wife Catharine ; bapt. Mar. 18 ; spon. Joseph and Elizabeth Henrich.

Käss, Henry, born Mar. 9, of Nicholas Käss and his wife Margaret ; bapt. Mar. 29 ; spon. Henry Käss and Magdalen Kuns.

Shnabel, Paul Andrew, born Feb. 3, of Joseph Shnabel and [*his wife*] M. ; bapt. Apr. 1 ; spon. John and Elizabeth Illain.

Dollhauer, Mary Philippina, born Mar. 12, of Henry Dollhauer and his wife Barbara ; bapt. Apr. 2 ; spon. John and Philippina Vingart.

Hartmann, John Peter, born Jan. 18, of Jacob Hartmann and his wife Catharine ; bapt. Apr. 8 ; spon. Peter and Barbara Keffer.

Lehmon, Mary Elizabeth, born Mar. 24, of Henry Lehmon and his wife Catharine ; bapt. Apr. 8 ; spon. Francis and Elizabeth Hartmann.

Shmidt, Elizabeth, born Mar. 26, of Philip Shmidt and his wife [*Magdalen ?*] ; bapt. Apr. 10 ; spon. Philip and Elizabeth Shmidt.

Kiesel, Magdalen, born Mar. 1, of Sebastian Kiesel and his wife Catharine ; bapt. Apr. 10 ; spon. Daniel Gret and Elizabeth Shmidt.

Saüvert, Daniel, born Nov. 21, 1803, of John Saüvert and his wife Magdalen ; bapt. Apr. 10 ; spon. Daniel Saüvert.

Saüvert, John, born May. 29, 1803, of Jonathan Saüvert and his wife Magdalen ; bapt. Apr. 10 ; spon. Philip and Magdalen Shmidt.

Keffer John, born Mar. 26, of Jacob Keffer and his wife Magdalen ; bapt. May 13 ; spon. John Hartmann and Magdalen Reppert

Käss, Elizabeth, born Mar. 7, of Mathias Käss and his wife Elizabeth ; bapt. May 20 ; spon. Nicholas and Margaret Käss.

Kiesy, Catharine, born Dec. 18, 1803, of George Kiesy and his wife Anna ; bapt. June 10 ; spon. Jacob and his sister Catharine Weisenburg, [*in the MS.,* " *Fratres.*"]

Shnabel, Margaret, born May 26, of Michael Shnabel and his wife Margaret ; bapt. July 5 ; spon. Peter and Rosine Bauer.

Eichorn, Mary Ann, born June 17, of Francis Eichorn and his wife Eve ; bapt. July 8 ; spon. Andrew and Agatha Sigfrid.

Gauss, William, born June 14, of George Gauss and his wife Magdalen ; bapt. Aug. 12 ; spon. John and Anna Gauss.

Eisenmann, Salome, born Apr. 10, of Christian Eisenmann and his wife Susan ; bapt. Aug. 12 ; spon. Joseph and Margaret Lambert.

Gruver, Elizabeth, born Aug. 1, of Philip Gruver and his wife Barbara ; bapt. Sept. 2 ; spon. John and Elizabeth Coblet.

Vögely, Sara, born Aug. 13, of George Vögely and his wife Catharine ; bapt. Sept. 2 ; spon. Henry Coblet and Sophia Els.

Gibson, Joseph, born Aug. 21, of Henry Gibson and his wife Catharine ; bapt. Sept. 30 ; spon. Joseph and Mary Burgy.

Wummer, Margaret, born July 28, of Adam Wummer and his wife Magdalen ; bapt. Sept. 30 ; spon. George and Margaret Hopp.

Reppert, Sara, born Aug. 31, of Stephen Ruppert and his wife Magdalen ; bapt. Oct. 7 ; spon. John and Barbara Kemp.

Keffer, Anna Maria Barbara, born Aug. 5, of John Keffer and his wife Susan ; bapt. Oct. 14 ; spon. Peter and Barbara Keffer.

Sigfrid, Anna Maria, born Sept. 21, of George Sigfrid and his wife Barbara ; bapt. Oct. 14 ; spon. Anthony Felix and Agatha Sigfrid.

Adam, Simon, born Sept. 21, of John Adam and his wife Catharine ; bapt. Nov. 1 ; spon. Michael Reichert and Mary Adam.

Beringer, Mary Magdalen, born Oct. 2, of Mathias Beringer and his wife Mary M.; bapt. Nov. 1 ; spon. Michael Kuhn and Elizabeth Wingart.

Els, Anthony Jacob, born Sept. 21, of Jacob Els and his wife M. Magdalen ; bapt. Nov. 1 ; spon. Anthony and Catharine Reichert.

Shlosser, Charles, born Sept. 10, of George Shlosser and [his wife] Elizabeth ; bapt. Dec. 9 ; spon. John and Magdalen Shlosser.

Ganss, Catharine, born Sept. 30, of John Ganss and his wife Anna ; bapt. Dec. 9 ; spon. Magdalen Ganss. [Appended to this last entry for the year—1804 is the prayerful exclamation of Father Erntzen " Laus; Deo Soli."]

[Number of Baptisms forty-seven, including two illegitimates.]

Baptisms for the Year 1805.

Reuinger, George, born Nov. 28, 1804, of Frederick Reninger and his wife Catharine ; bapt. Jan. 24 ; spon. George and Margaret Hopp.

Bauer, Samuel M., born Dec. 24, 1804, of Peter Bauer and his wife Rosine ; bapt. Jan. 29 ; spon. John and Anna Shnabel.

Shnabel, Anna, born Dec. 31, 1804, of John Shnabel and his wife Anna ; bapt. Jan. 29 ; spon. Peter and Rosine Bauer.

Käss, Mary Margaret, born Oct. 7, 1804, of John Käss and his wife Catharine ; bapt. Feb. 16 ; spon. John and Mary Käss, [cognati], cousins.

Buck, Susan, born Nov. 19, 1804, of Joseph Buck and his wife Rosine ; bapt. Feb. 17 ; spon. Henry and Susan Käss.

Henrick, Joseph, born Dec. 4, 1804, of Joseph Henrick and his wife Elizabeth ; bapt. Feb. 17 ; spon. Caspar Shönebruck, Jr., and Elizabeth Henrich.

Conner, Paul, born Feb. 23, of John Conner and his wife Anna ; bapt. Feb. 26 ; spon. [Rev.] Paul Erntzen and Mary Conner.

Reichert, David, born Jan. 14, of John Reichert and his wife Catharine ; bapt. Mar. 3 ; spon. Joseph and Juliana Röhr.

Wingart, [though written " Vingart,"] Mary Elizabeth, born Feb. 13, of John Wingart and his wife Philippina ; bapt. Mar. 3 ; spon. Henry Coblet and Juliana Els.

M'Farthing, Andrew, born Dec. 27, 1797, of John M'Farthing and his wife Eve ; bapt. by a Pr[otestant] minister [sic ;] spon. John and Catharine Coblet.

M'Farthing, Daniel, born Aug. 14, 1799, of [the above] ; bapt. Mar. 3 ; spon. Daniel and M. Anna Coblet.

M'Farthing, Catharine, born Jan. 28, 1802, of [the above ;] bapt. with Daniel ; spon. George and Catharine Vögely.

198

Engel, Sara, born Jan. 30, of Henry Engel and his wife Catharine; bapt. Mar. 12; spon. Michael Hartmann and wife.

Miller, John Frederick, born Sept. 28, 1804, of Frederick Miller and his wife Elizabeth; bapt. Mar. 25; spon. Jacob Waghon and Catharine Adam, widow.

Arents, Elizabeth, born Mar. 6, of George Arents and his wife Margaret; bapt. Mar. 31; spon. Daniel Grett and Elizabeth Arents.

Hopp, John George, born Mar. 23 of George Hopp and his wife Margaret; bapt. Apr. 1; spon. Francis Anthony and Catharine Hopp.

Stahler, Salome, born Nov. 28, 1804, of Christian Stahler and his wife Margaret; bapt. Apr. 4; spon. Joseph and Susan Spring.

Henrich, John Adam, born Jan. 19, of John Adam Henrich and [*his wife*] Barbara; bapt. Apr. 4; spon. Christopher and Margaret Eckenrodt, [*though written* " Eckenrod."]

Spring, Charles, born Apr. 3, of Joseph Spring and his wife Susan; bapt. Apr. 4; spon. Christian and Margaret Stahler.

Dom, [*sic*, Dum?], Joseph, born May 2, 1804, of John Dom and his wife Anna Elizabeth; bapt. Apr. 14; spon. Joseph Coblet and Catharine Martin.

Eckenrodt, Michael, born Nov. 14, 1804, of Henry Eckenrodt and his wife Elizabeth; bapt. Apr. 21; spon. Michael Gerstweiler and Magdalen Reppert.

Shmidt, Anna Margaret, born Apr. 17, of George Shmidt and his wife Barbara; bapt. May 5; spon. Caspar and Margaret Shönebruck.

Zweyer, Elizabeth, born Mar. 10, of Mathias Zweyer and his wife Elizabeth; bapt. May 12; spon. Joseph and his sister Frances Zweyer, [*in the text* " Fratres."]

Bott, Anna Maria, born Mar. 4, of Jacob Bott and his wife Catharine; bapt. May 12; spon. Anthony Felix and Barbara Sigfrid.

Lambert, Eleanor, born Jan. 7, of Peter Lambert and his wife Susan; bapt. May 13; spon. Jacob and Dorothy Lambert.

Lambert, Anna Maria, born Mar. 21, of Jacob Lambert and his wife Anna M.; bapt. May 13; spon. John his sister Mary Lambert; [*in the Text* " Fratres."]

Egg, Paul, born May 14. of John Egg and his wife Charlotte; bapt. May 16; spon. [*Rev.*] Paul Erntzen.

Kuns, Magdalen, born Apr. 16, of John Kuns and his wife Barbara; bapt. May 19; spon. Jacob Shönebruck and Magdalen Kuns.

Hunsberger, John, born Apr. 29, of Peter Hunsberger and his wife Catharine; bapt. May 19; spon. John and Elizabeth Grett.

Burkopp, Elizabeth, both Mar. 29, of John Burkopp and his wife Juliana; bapt. May 23; spon. John and Barbara Kemp.

Reichert, Salome, born Apr. 30, of Anthony Reichert and his wife Catharine; bapt. June 2; spon. John Els and Mary Röhr.

Röhr, John, born June 3, of Joseph Röhr and his wife Juliana; bapt. June 13; spon. John and Catharine Reichert.

199

Gibson, Anna, born Apr. 27, of Joseph Gibson and his wife Christine; bapt. June 30 ; spon. Andrew Hopp and wife.

M'Farthing, John, born May 27, of John M'Farthing and his wife Eve ; bapt. July 7 ; spon. John Els and Elizabeth Coblet.

Kich, [or Kich,] Rose, born Nov. 27, 1804, of Michael Kich and his wife Elizabeth ; bapt. July 14 ; spon. John Huver and Mary Shindler.

Rohrbach, George, born July 2, of Jacob Rohrbach and his wife Susan; bapt. July 16 ; spon. George and Elizabeth Kemp.

Eckenrod, Margaret, born July 13, of John Eckenrod and his wife Catharine ; bapt. July 28 ; spon. John Henrich and Elizabeth Eckenrod.

Coblet, Henry, born July 5, of John Coblet and his wife Elizabeth ; bapt. Aug. 4 ; spon. Henry and Catharine Coblet.

Grett, Jonathan, born June 5, of John Grett and his wife Catharine ; bapt. Aug. 4 ; spon. Daniel Grett and Mary Arenz, [sic, though elsewhere Arens]

Shnabel, Andrew, born May 20, of Jacob Shnabel and his wife Barbara ; bapt. Aug. 11 ; spon. Joseph Shmidt and Magdalen Reppert.

Watter, Mary, born Dec. 10, 1804, of John Watter and his wife Mary ; bapt. Aug. 11 ; spon. Mary Weissemburg.

Flower, Thomas Christopher, born July 18, of Christopher Flower and his wife Magdalen ; bapt. Aug. 11 ; spon. Joseph and Mary Allgeyer.

Strack, Catharine, born Feb. 28, of Daniel Strack and his wife Elizabeth ; bapt. Aug. 18; spon. Jacob and Mary Els.

Kemp, George, born July 26, of Jacob Kemp and his wife Magdalen ; bapt. Oct. 15 ; spon. George and Catharine Mayer.

Shlosser, George Stephen, born June 23, of John Shlosser and his wife Magdalen; bapt. Oct. 20; spon. George and Magdalen Hopp.

Grett, Henry, born June 24, of Michael Grett and his wife Esther; bapt. Oct. 20 ; spon. Philip and Susan Reichert.

Hopp, Litta, born Aug. 8, of Andrew Hopp and his wife Magdalen ; bapt. Oct. 20; spon. Joseph and Christine Gibson.

Reichert, Elizabeth, born Sept. 2, of Philip Reichert and his wife Susan ; bapt. Oct. 20; spon. Michael Reichert and Elizabeth Dum.

Meck, George, born May 12, of George Meck and his wife Catharine ; bapt. Oct. 20 ; spon. John Reichert and Elizabeth Dum.

Dauny, Thomas, born June 28, of John Dauny and his wife Margaret ; bapt. Dec. 8 ; spon. Sebastian and Catharine Allgeyer.

——, Joseph, born Dec. 3, of Joseph —— and Catharine ; bapt. Dec. 26 ; spon. Joseph Wingart and Catharine Coblet.

Dum, George, born Nov. 17, of Valentine Dum and his wife Magdalen ; bapt. Dec. 30; spon. George and Margaret Arens.

[Number of Baptisms fifty-five, including three illegitimates.]

Neuer, Magdalen, born Nov. 14, 1805, of John Neuer and his wife Mary ; bapt. Jan. 1 ; spon. Michael Reichert and Elizabeth Burgy.

Shönebruck, Margaret, born Dec. 11, 1805, of Jacob Shönebruck and his wife Susan ; bapt. Jan. 6 ; spon. Margaret Shönebruck.

Shönebruck, Jacob, born Dec. 27, 1805, of Andrew Shönebruck and his wife Magdalen ; bapt. Jan. 7 ; spon. Caspar and Margaret Shönebruck.

Egg, Lia, born Feb. 9, of Joseph Egg and his wife Agatha ; bapt. Feb. 11 ; spon. Peter and Magdalen Käss.

Bauer, Solomon Jacob, born Mar. 13, of Peter Bauer and his wife Rosine ; bapt. Mar. 22 ; spon. John and Anna Maria Mattes.

Eckenrodt, Benjamin, born Feb. 1, of Peter Eckenrodt and his wife Mary ; bapt. Mar. 23 ; spon. Philip and Elizabeth Henrich.

Gibson, Henry, born Jan. 14, of Henry Gibson and his wife Catharine ; bapt. Mar. 23 ; spon. John Gibson and Elizabeth Burgy.

Grett, Anna Maria, born Jan. 1, of John Adam Grett and his wife Mary ; bapt. Mar. 23 ; spon. Jacob and Catharine Spring.

Shmidt, John, born Feb. 7, of Caspar Shmidt and his wife Susan ; bapt. Mar. 25 ; spon. Joseph and Juliana Röhr.

Erb, John, born Mar. 24, of Peter Erb and his wife Christine ; bapt. Mar. 27 ; spon. John and Catharine Kuns.

Zweyer, Daniel, born Apr. 26, of Thomas Zweyer and his wife Mary ; bapt. Mar. 30 ; spon. Adam and Magdalen Wummer.

Wummer, Mary, born Mar. 17, of Adam Wummer and his wife Magdalen ; bapt. Mar. 30 ; spon. Joseph and Mary Zweyer.

Egg, Mary Barbara, born ·Mar. 25, of John Egg and his wife Louisa, [Aloitina;] bapt. Apr. 4 ; spon. Joseph Kohl and Barbara Hammerstein.

Egg, Elizabeth, born Mar. 3, of Daniel Egg and his wife M.[ary] Magdalen ; bapt. Apr. 6 ; spon. John and Charlotte Egg.

Kemp, Mary, born Mar. 15, of John Kemp and his wife Barbara ; bapt. Apr. 6 ; spon. Joseph Kemp and Mary [commonly known]—" Vulgo "— as Illain

Shmidt, Angela, born Feb. 16, of Frederick Shmidt and his wife Catharine ; bapt. Apr. 12 ; spon. William and Ann Minzen.

Eichorn, Eve Helen, born Mar. 5, of Francis Eichorn and his wife Eve ; bapt. Apr. 13 ; spon. [Rev.] Paul Erntzen and Barbara Sigfrid.

Keffer, Francis Joseph, born [date wanting], of Joseph Keffer and his wife Christine ; bapt. Apr. 13 ; spon. Francis and Elizabeth Hartmann.

Gehry, Mary, born Mar. 12, of Martin Gehry and his wife Mary ; bapt. Apr. 20 ; spon. John and Barbara Kemp.

Connolly, Catharine, born Dec. 2, 1805, of John Connolly and his wife Mary ; bapt. Apr. 30 ; spon. Bernard Connolly and Elizabeth Buck.

Shutt, Jacob, born Feb. 14, of Anthony Shutt and his wife Catharine ; bapt. May 4 ; spon. William Röhr and Elizabeth Wingart.

Saüvert, Joseph, born Feb. 6, of John Saüvert and his wife [*Magdalen*] ; bapt. May 11 ; spon. Samuel Saüvert.

Keffer, Catharine, born Mar. 2, of John Keffer and his wife Susan ; bapt. May 11 ; spon. Joseph Grett and Catharine Hartman, [*commonly in the text* "Hartmann."]

Strack, Susan, born Apr. 5, 1803, of Daniel Strack and his wife Elizabeth ; bapt. May 13 ; spon. John and Christine Kemp.

Dollhauer, Catharine, born Apr. 22, of Henry Dollhauer and his wife M. [*ary*] Barbara ; bapt. May 4 ; spon. John and Barbara Kuns.

Käss, Paul, born May [?] 8, of Peter Käss and his wife Magdalen ; bapt. May 16 ; spon. John Illain and Susan Mattes.

Käss, John Peter, born Mar. 8, of Mathias Käss and his wife Elizabeth ; bapt. May 18 ; spon. Michael and Mary Shmidt.

Grett, Salome, born May 9, of Philip Grett and his wife Elizabeth ; bapt. June 1 ; spon. John and Elizabeth Grett.

Grett, Daniel, born May 26, of Daniel Grett and his wife Elizabeth ; bapt. June 29 ; spon. Andrew and Elizabeth Grett.

Dapper, Jacob, born June 13, of Jacob Dapper and his wife Mary ; bapt. July 6 ; spon. Daniel Grett and Catharine Adam.

Huver, Francis, born Dec. 10, 1805, of Adam Huver and his wife Susan ; bapt. July 13 ; spon. John Allgeyer and Sara Benden.

Kiesy, William, born Dec. 14, 1805, of George Kiesy and his wife Anna ; bapt. July 13 ; spon. Jacob and Margaret Bernheiser.

Shmidt, Thomas, born July 2, of Michael Shmidt and his wife Mary ; bapt. July 20 ; spon. Caspar Shönebruck and Mary Shmidt.

Henrich, Catharine, born June 28, of Joseph Henrich and his wife Elizabeth ; bapt. July 20 ; spon. Jacob Käss and Margaret Shönebruck.

Egg, David and John, twins, born July 15, of Peter Egg and his wife Magdalen ; bapt. July 22 ; spon. for David, John and Mary Mattes ; for John, John Ihlein, [*elsewhere* "Illain,"] and Susan Mattes.

Arnold, Mary Elizabeth, born May 2, of John Arnold and his wife Eve ; bapt. Aug. 10 ; spon. Jacob and Mary Arens.

Allgeyer, Margaret, born July 27, of Joseph Allgeyer and his wife Margaret ; bapt. Aug. 10 ; spon. Jacob and Dorothy Lambert.

Repplier, Mary, born July 23, of George Repplier and his wife Catharine ; bapt. Aug. 10 ; spon. Sebastian and Catharine Allgeyer.

Orth, Mary Catharine, born Aug. 9, of Peter Orth and his wife Mary Catharine ; bapt. Aug. 10 ; spon. George and Catharine Repplier.

Stahler, Rebecca, born Apr. 22, of Christian Stahler and his wife Margaret ; bapt. Aug. 31 ; spon. Thomas Dum and Catharine Spring.

Eierson, Thomas, born Apr. 10, 1804, of John Eierson and his wife Anna ; bapt. Sept. 15 ; spon. Joseph Watters and Frances Remstone.

Malzberger, Catharine, born Sept. 14, of Jacob Malzberger and his wife Mary ; bapt. Sept. 15 ; spon. Catharine Malzberger.

Good, John, born Feb. 10, of Jacob Good and his wife Catharine ; bapt. Sept. 19 ; spon. Andrew Grett and Catharine Diederich.

Shurp, Lazarus, born Sept. 14, of John Shurp and his wife Elizabeth; bapt. Oct. 5; spon. Bartholomew and Elizabeth Coblet.

Wagener, Israel, born Sept. 9, of —— Wagener and his wife Mary; bapt. Oct. 5; spon. Daniel Grett and —— Shurp.

Sterling, John, twenty-three years old, son of John Sterling and his wife ——, non-Catholic, husband of Elizabeth Wingart; bapt. conditionately Oct. 5; spon. John and Ph. [*ilippina*] Wingart.

Wingart, John, born Sept. 3, of John Wingart and his wife Philippina; bapt. Oct. 5; spon. John and Elizabeth Sterling.

Kiesel, Jacob, born Aug. 26, of Sebastian Kiesel and his wife Catharine; bapt. Nov. 9; spon. Philip and Susan Reichert.

Shmidt, Catherine, born Oct. 5, of Philip Shmidt and his wife Magdalen; bapt. Nov. 9; spon. Joseph and Margaret Obold.

Käss, Susan, born Oct. 29, of Nicholas Käss and his wife Margaret; bapt. Nov. 23; spon. Andrew Grett and Susan Kuns.

Arens, George, born Sept. 21, of George Arens and his wife Margaret; bapt. Nov. 30; spon. Thomas Dum and Susan Grett.

Burgy, Margaret, born Aug. 21, of Joseph Burgy and his wife Anna M.; bapt. Dec. 1; spon. Andrew Grett and Anna Maria Henrich.

Reninger, Mary, bapt. Oct. 25, of Frederick Reninger and his wife Catharine; bapt. Dec. 1; spon. Francis and Catharine Hopp.

——, Joseph, [*rest wanting*]; spon. Joseph and Catharine Burkard.

[*Number of Baptisms fifty-six, including one illegitimate.*]

BAPTISMS FOR THE YEAR 1807.

Reichert, Anna Juliana, born Nov. 2, of Anthony Reichert and his wife Catharine; bapt. Jan. 4; spon. Jacob Bauss and Juliana Els.

Kuns, John, born Feb. 2, of John Kuns and his wife Barbara; bapt. Mar. 23; spon. Caspar and Margaret Shönebruck.

Reppert, Anna, born Jan. 22, of Stephen Reppert and his wife Magdalen; bapt. Mar. 26; spon. John and Anna Conner.

Hauss, Anna Elizabeth, born Aug. 31, 1806, of Jacob Hauss and his wife Mary; bapt. Mar. 29; spon. John and Elizabeth Els.

[*Number of Baptisms four. Total from 1801 (included) three hundred and twenty-seven.*]

GOSHENHOPPEN REGISTERS

OF

MARRIAGES (1801-1819).

(FOURTH SERIES. Continued.)

TRANSLATED AND ANNOTATED BY REV. THOMAS C. MIDDLETON,
D.D., O. S. A.

MARRIAGES, 1801–1819.

Vögely—Coblet: April 6, 1801, George, son of John and Catharine Vögely, and Catharine, dau. of Daniel and Mary Coblet; witnesses Thomas Queen and Barbara Gruver.

Adam—Hammerstein: April 21, 1801, John, son of Simon and Catharine Adam, and Catharine, dau. of Andrew and Barbara Hammerstein; witnesses John Egg and Philip Ruffner.

Kohl—Buck: April 28, 1801, Jacob, son of Joseph and Margaret Kohl, and Elizabeth, dau. of Nicholas and Elizabeth Buck; witnesses Jacob Buck and Nicholas M'Carty.

Repplier—Allgeyer: May 10, 1801, at Sebastian Allgeyer's house, George Repplier and Catharine Allgeyer; witnesses Francis Eichorn and Eve Sigfrid.

Merkel—Henrich: May 17, 1801, John Merkel, non-Catholic, and Barbara Henrich.

Gret—Reisinger: May 25, 1801, Philip Gret and Elizabeth Reisinger; witnesses John and Elizabeth Gret.

Stahler—Spring: December 16, 1801, Christian, son of Adam and Mary Stahler, Catholics, and Margaret, dau. of Jacob and Catharine Spring.

Kemp—Mayer: January 30, 1802, George, son of John and Anna Christina Kemp, and Elizabeth, dau. of George and Catharine Mayer, non-Catholics; witnesses Jacob Rohrbach and Elizabeth Weller.

Wingart—Coblet: June 17, 1802, John, son of Joseph and Elizabeth Wingart, and Philippina, dau. of Daniel and Mary Anne Coblet; witnesses Bartholomew Coblet and George Vögely.

204

Burkhard—Refshneider: September 5, 1802, Joseph, son of Martin and Gertrude Burkhard, and Catharine, dau. of Henry and Sophia Refshneider.

Coblet—Refshneider: January 11, 1803, John, son of Daniel and Mary Anne Coblet, and Elizabeth, dau. of Henry and Sophia Refshneider; [witnesses] Henry Refshneider and George Vögely.

Henrich—Meyer: March 28, 1803, Philip, son of Christian and Magdalen Henrich, and Mary Elizabeth, dau. of Simon and Elizabeth Meyer, non-Catholics; witnesses George and Christopher Eckenrodt.

Keffer—Spang: April 19, 1803, John Keffer, Catholic, and Susan Spang, Lutheran ; witnesses Joseph Keffer and James Shnabel.

Allgeier—Lambert: May 9, 1803, Joseph, son of Sebastian and Catharine Allgeier, and Margaret, dau. of James and Dorothy Lambert ; witnesses the father of the groom and the mother of the bride.

Fricker—Malzberger: May 29, 1803, Nicholas, son of Joseph and Catharine Fricker, and Margaret, dau. of James and —— Malzberger ; witnesses James and Joseph Malzberger, brothers of the bride.

Eichhorn—Sigfrid : June 12, 1803, at Reading, Francis Eichhorn and Eve Sigfrid ; witnesses Sebastian Allgeyer and John Cunius.

Lambert—Weiss: the same dáy, Peter Lambert and Susan Weiss ; witnesses Joseph Grett and George Miller.

Riegel—Künstler : July 17, 1803, having previously been married before a Protestant minister, Daniel Riegel, non-Catholic, and Margaret Künstler, Catholic, renew their consent ; witnesses Caspar Shönebruck, Jr., and Elizabeth Henrich.

Gibson—Burgy : October 30, 1803, Henry Gibson and Catharine Burgy ; [witnesses] A. Reichert and C. Shönebr. [sic, Caspar Shönebruck.]

Arens—Egg : December 8, 1803, Peter Arens and Mary Egg ; witnesses Peter Egg and John Grett.

Spring—Gret: April 16, 1804, Joseph, son of James and Catharine Spring, and Susan, dau. of Andrew and Elizabeth Gret; also

Gret—Spring : same day, John Adam, son of Andrew and Elizabeth Gret, and Anna Mary, dau. of James and Catharine Spring ; witnesses George Spring and Susan Baumann.

Kuns—Shönebruck: May 1, 1804, John, son of John and Catharine Kuns, and Mary Barbara, dau. of Caspar and Margaret Shönebruck ; witnesses Bartholomew Coblet and John Gret.

Dum—Hoff : July 8, 1804, Thomas Dum and Mary Hoff; witnesses Mary Rogert and her daughter.

Eckenrodt—Reppert: September 24, 1804, John, son of Christopher and Margaret Eckenrodt, and Catharine, dau. of Stephen and Magdalen Reppert ; witnesses Peter and Mary Eckenrodt.

Hunsberger—Gret : October 11, 1804, Peter, son of Peter and Catharine Hunsberger, and Catharine, dau. of John and Elizabeth Gret ; witnesses [not named.]

Glassmeier—Egg: January 1, 1805, John, son of Peter and Catharine Glassmeier, non-Catholics, and Theresa, dau. of John and Charlotte Egg; witnesses Daniel Egg and Catharine Korb.

Arens—Egg: January 22, 1805, George Arens and Margaret Egg; witnesses Adam Reichert and Elizabeth Arens.

Reichert—Shmidt: April 23, 1805, Philip, son of Adam and Eva Reichert, and Susan, dau. of Philip and Elizabeth Shmidt; witnesses Philip Shmidt, Jr., and John Reichert.

Coblet—Vingart: May 21, 1805, Bartholomew Coblet, widower, and Elizabeth Vingart, widow; witnesses John Grett and Christina Kuns.

Egg—Käss: May 23, 1805, Daniel, son of John and Charlotte Egg, and Mary Margaret, dau. of Peter and Anna Margaret Käss; witnesses Peter Egg and Magdalen Käss.

Shönebruck—Mensch: June 13, 1805, James, son of Caspar and Margaret Shönebruck, Catholics, and Susan, dau. of Adam and Margaret Mensch, Catholic; witnesses John Grett and John Kuns.

Kemp—Mayer: July 7, 1805, James Kemp and Magdalen Mayer; witnesses [illegible] Kemp and James Waghon.

Beaver—Beyer: July 14, 1805, Christopher Beaver and Susan Beyer; witnesses Michael Hartmann and his wife.

Erb—Kunz: December 1, 1805, Peter Erb, non-Catholic, and Christina, dau. of John and Catharine Kunz; witnesses John Grett, Sr., and Philip Grett, Jr.

Sigfrid—Felix: February 16, 1806, Joseph Sigfrid and Elizabeth Felix; witnesses John Grett and Bartholomew Coblet.

Zweyer—Klein: April 13, 1806, at Reading church, James, son of Thomas and Mary Zweyer, and Elizabeth, dau. of Philip Klein, non-Catholic.

Sauvert—Dum: At the same time, Daniel, son of Joseph and Catharine Sauvert, and Elizabeth, dau. of Thomas and Elizabeth Dum; witnesses Adam Reichert and George Hopp.

Reichert—Sauvert: May 11, 1806, before the congregation at Reading, Michael, son of Adam and Eve Reichert, and Elizabeth, dau. of Joseph and Catharine Sauvert.

Sterling—Wingart: May 27, 1806, John Sterling and Elizabeth Wingart; witnesses John and Joseph Wingart.

Gibson—[blank]: June 8, 1806, before the congregation at Reading, John Gibson and Christine [blank], non-Catholic.

Beaver—Grett: December 1, 1806, John, son of Conrad and Margaret Beaver, and Barbara, dau. of Nicholas and Susan Grett; witnesses Daniel Grett and Joseph Burgy.

Reichert—Uhlein: December 9, 1806, John, son of Adam and Eva Reichert, and Mary, dau. of John and Elizabeth Uhlein; witnesses John Egg, Sr., and Thomas Dum, Jr.

Els—Plock : January 6, 1807, John Els, son of John and Elizabeth Els, Catholic, and Susan Plock, non-Catholic ; witnesses George Rohrbach and Sophy Els.

Shweyer—Burgy : January 27, 1807, John Nicholas Shweyer and Elizabeth Burgy ; witnesses Henry Gibson and John Burgy.

Fenstermacher—Mattes : February 10, 1807, George Fenstermacher and Susan Mattes ; witnesses Peter Käss and Peter Egg.

Wingart—McFarthing : June 9, 1807, Joseph Wingart and Eve M'Farthing, widow ; witnesses Joseph Martin and James Waghon.

Felix—Martin : July 5, 1807, Anthony Felix and Catharine Martin ; witnesses John Kunz, Sr., and James Els.

Käss—Henrich : July 12, 1807, John, son of James and Barbara Käss, and Mary, dau. of Philip and —— Henrich, Catholic ; witnesses the brother and sister of the bride.

Aloin—Miller : October 11, 1807, at Reading, in widow Fricker's house, John Aloin, Sr., and Magdalen Miller ; in the presence of me, Paul Erntzen, *parochus* of the place.

Adam—Groskop : on the same day, James, son of Simon and Catharine Adam, and Mary, dau. of Paul and —— Groskop ; witnesses James Allgeyer and Margaret Fortmann.

Weirich—Aloin : December 13, 1807, at Reading, James, son of James and Magdalen Weirich, non-Catholic, and Elizabeth, dau. of Conrad and Catharine Aloin, Catholic ; witnesses Sebastian Allgayer and John Franz.

Kohl—Bock : December 26, 1807, at Goshenhoppen, Nicholas, son of Joseph and Margaret Kohl, and Mary, dau. of Nicholas and Elizabeth Bock ; witnesses Nicholas Bock and Thomas M'Carty.

Gilbert—Shnabel : December 27, 1807, James, son of Nicholas and Mary Gilbert, non-Catholic, and Elizabeth, dau. of Joseph and Mary Shnabel ; witnesses John Grett, Jr., and Daniel Shnabel.

Shnabel—Adam : January 19, 1808, Andrew, son of Andrew and Eve Shnabel, widower, and Mary, dau. of Simon and Catharine Adam ; witnesses Michael Shnabel and James Adam.

Käss—Rodt : April 18, 1808, John Käss, widower, and the widow of Christian Rodt ; witnesses John and Catharine Kuns.

Shimfessel—Arens ; May 8, 1808, at Reading, Peter, son of Andrew and Mary Shimfessel, and Elizabeth, dau. of James and M. Arens ; witnesses Adam Reichert and Thomas Dum, J. [*Junior ?*]

Klee—Hartman : May 26, 1808, in church, Ernest, son of Ernest and Christina Klee, Catholic, and Magdalen, dau. of Michael and Margaret Hartman, Catholic ; witnesses John Adam and his wife, Catharine.

Röhr—Els : on the same day, William, son of Joseph and Juliana Röhr, Catholic, and Sophia, dau. of John and Elizabeth Els, Catholic ; witnesses James Els and Henry Covely.

Henrich—Eckenrodt : July 31, 1808, Christian Henrich, widower, and Mary Eckenrodt, widow, having been married before a non-

Catholic minister, renew their consent ; witnesses Andrew Grett and his wife Elizabeth.

O'Boil—Hoff : September 4, 1808, Neal O'Boil and Susan Hoff ; witnesses Thomas Dum and John Grett.

Covely—Röhr : November 24, 1808, John, son of Bartholomew and ——— Covely, Catholic, and Mary, dau. of Joseph and Agatha Röhr, Catholic ; witnesses Bartholomew Covely and Joseph Röhr.

Covely—Covely : February 2, 1809, Henry, son of Daniel and M. An. Covely, and Elizabeth, dau. of John and Catharine Covely, second cousins ; [*the Register has it* " Cons. 3 Gr."]; witnesses Bartholomew and Daniel Covely.

Lutz—Hartmann : February 10, 1809, James, son of Frederick and Mary Elizabeth Lutz, and Catharine, dau. of Francis and Angela Hartmann ; witnesses Daniel Lutz and D. Hartmann.

Dum—Grett : March 21, 1809, Thomas, son of Thomas and Elizabeth Dum, and Anna, dau. of Nicholas and Susan Grett ; witnesses Ad. Reichert, Val. [*entine*] Dum and Peter Shimpfessel.

Sebold—Diederich : April 3, 1809, Peter, son of Nicholas and Anna Sebold, and Catharine, dau. of John and Elizabeth Diederich ; witnesses James Els and Michael Grett.

Hartman—Liess : April 10, 1809, Michael Hartman and Susan Liess, non-Catholic, renew their consent.

Kapus—Shäfer : May 14, 1809, at Reading, Lothaire Kapus and Christina Shäfer in the presence of the congregation.

Gerstweiler—Ramstone : May 15, 1809, at Reading, John Gerstweiler and Frances Ramstone ; [*witnesses*] Michael and Elizabeth Gerstweiler.

Saüvert—Ziegler : July 16, 1809, Joseph Saüvert, non-Catholic and Magdalen Ziegler ; witnesses Joseph Reichert and M. Grett.

Egg—Ettinger : August 8, 1809, Solomon, son of John and Charlotte Egg, and Anna, dau. of Frederick and Catharine Ettinger, witnesses Andrew Ettinger and M. Grett.

Angst—Zweyer : August 22, 1809, Daniel, son of Daniel and Elizabeth Angst, and Mary, dau. of Joseph and Catharine Zweyer ; witnesses Daniel Stewart and Catharine Zweier, [*better* Zweyer ?]

Härzel—Shönebruck : October 1, 1809, Henry, son of Henry and Eve Härzel, and Margaret, dau. of Caspar and Margaret Shönebruck ; witnesses Peter and Christine Erb.

Mohr—Eckenrod : November 14, 1809, Joseph, son of Albert and Catharine Mohr, Catholic, and Mary Catharine, dau. of Henry and Elizabeth Eckenrod, Catholic ; witnesses John and Mary Gerstweiler, and Joseph and Frances Wolter.

Grett—Egg : December 26, 1809, Daniel, son of John and Elizabeth Grett, and Salome, dau. of Joseph and Agatha Egg ; witnesses Peter Egg and John Grett.

Reichert—Röhr : February 27, 1810, Augustine, son of John and Catharine Reichert, Catholic, and Anna, dau. of Joseph and Jul. [iana] Röhr, Catholic ; witnesses John B. Covely and William Röhr.

Huver—Benton : May 13, 1810, John, son of Francis and M. Ann Huver, Catholic, and Elizabeth, dau. of Jonathan and Helen Benton ; witnesses Th. and J. Benton, and James Lambert.

Trout—Zweyer : July 2, 1810, William, son of George and Eve Trout, and Catharine, dau. of Adam and Barbara Zweyer ; witnesses James Sigfrid and Mary Zweyer.

Shell—Kunz : August 16, 1810, John, son of James and Catharine Shell, Catholic, and Susan, dau. of John and Catharine Kunz ; witnesses John Grett and his daughter Theresa.

Röhr—Clemmer : October 25, 1810, Charles, son of John and Juliana Röhr, Catholic, and Elizabeth, dau. of Christian and Catharine Clemmer; witnesses John Kunz and Daniel Grett.

Egg—Bernt : November 4, 1810, John, son of Joseph and Agatha Egg, Catholic, and Mary, dau. of Frederick and Margaret Bernt, non-Catholic ; witnesses John Grett and his wife Catharine.

Shönebruck—Back : November 20, 1810, Caspar, son of Caspar and Margaret Shönebruck, and Apollonia, dau. of Leonard and Elizabeth Back ; witnesses John Kunz and Elizabeth Henrich.

Rittner—Felix : December 10, 1810, John, son of Peter and ——— Rittner, Catholic, and Elizabeth, dau. of Martin and ——— Felix, Catholic ; witnesses James Felix and Catharine Hartman.

Kunz—Hinderleiter : January 29, 1811, Joseph, son of John and Catharine Kunz, and Elizabeth, dau. of Mathias and Catharine Hinderleiter, non-Catholic; witnesses James Waghen and Theresa Grett.

Kunss—Meister : March 17, 1811, Andrew, son of John and Catharine Kunss, Catholic, and Elizabeth, dau. of Balthasar and Magdalen Meister, Catholic ; witnesses John and Daniel Grett.

Zweyer—Hopp : May 13; 1811, Thomas, son of Joseph and Catharine Zweyer, Catholic, and Catharine, dau. of Andrew and Magdalen Hopp, Catholic ; witnesses William Fricker and Daniel Steward.

Sigfrid—Wingart : June 2, 1811, at Goshenhoppen in presence of the congregation, Charles, son of John and Barbara Sigfrid, and Helen, dau. of Joseph and Elizabeth Wingart.

Burgy—Shreer : June 30, 1811, John, son of Joseph and Mary Burgy, Catholic, and Catharine, dau. of George and Catharine Shreer, Catholic ; witnesses Adam Reichert and Valentine Dum.

Martin—Felix : August 15, 1811, Anthony, son of John and Catharine Martin, and Eve, dau. of Martin and ——— Felix ; witnesses John Kunss and Magdalen Reichert.

Bachman—Covely : September 16, 1811, Joseph Bachman and Mary Covely renew their consent before John Kunss and H. Covely.

Eckrodt—Hartmann: October 13, 1811, at Reading before the congregation, Christian, son of Henry and Elizabeth Eckrodt, and Elizabeth, dau. of Francis and ——— Hartmann.

Hartman—Clee: October 14, 1811, Michael, son of James and Catharine Hartman, and Elizabeth, dau. of Ernest and ——— Clee.

Budde—Shorp: November 17, 1811, Maurice, son of Fr. Anthony Budde, and Catharine, dau. of John and Rebecca Shorp; witnesses John Kunz and Richard Röhr.

Wack—Bock: November 24, 1811, having been before a lay judge Martin, son of Frederick and Elizabeth Wack, and Catharine, dau. of Leonard and Elizabeth Bock, renew their consent; witnesses C. Shönebruck and J. Käss.

Dum—Zweyer: January 12, 1812, James, son of Thomas and Elizabeth Dum, and Juliana, dau. of Thomas and ——— Zweyer; witnesses George Arentz and B. M'Bright.

Kunss—Shmidt: February 2, 1812, in the presence of the congregation, George, son of John and Catharine Kunss, and Elizabeth, dau. of Caspar and Susan Shmidt.

M'Gill—Walter: March 8, 1812, in the presence of the congregation, at Reading, James, son of James and Mary M'Gill, and Frances, dau. of John and Mary Walter.

Minzer—Minzer: March 9, 1812, William and Sara Minzer renew their consent, before Anna Minzer and Mary Jones.

Reichert—Reichert: March 30, 1812, Joseph and ——— Reichert renew their consent before John Kunss and Henry Covely.

Dapper—Adam: April 16, 1812, George, son of Andrew and Margaret Dapper, and Sabina, dau. of Simon and Catharine Adam; witnesses Andrew Shuabel and Catharine Adam.

Flower—Mayer: May 31, 1812, Joseph Flower and Rebecca Mayer, dau. of Henry and Dinah Mayer, non-Catholics, a convert, renew their consent, before George and Margaret Hopp.

Seifert—Henrich: June 14, 1812, at midday before the congregation at Reading, Philip, son of Joseph and Catharine Seifert, and Elizabeth, dau. of Philip and Elizabeth Henrich.

Binder—Lora: June 14, 1812, in the afternoon, George, son of George and Theresa Binder, and Catharine, dau. of Henry and Christine Lora; witnesses Sebastian Allgayer and Peter Rittner.

Oberdorf—Gibson: August 10, 1812, in the presence of the congregation at Reading, Abraham, son of John and Christine Oberdorf, and Elizabeth, dau. of Joseph and Christine Gibson.

Samson—Miller: September 6, 1812, in presence of the congregation at Goshenhoppen, Peter, son of Paul and "Gené" [Jenny ?] Samson and Mary, dau. of Frederick and Elizabeth Miller.

Rüttner—Scott: October 11, 1812, Peter, son of Peter and Barbara Rüttner, and Sara Scott; witnesses John and Catharine Hahn.

Reppert—Sherf: February 21, 1813, in the presence of the congregation at Goshenhoppen, Joseph, son of Stephen and Magdalen Reppert, and Eve, dau. of James and —— Sherf.

Walker—Käss: April 19, 1813, John, son of Daniel and Gertrude Walker, and Elizabeth, dau. of John and Catharine Käss.

Käss—Ilain : the same day, in the presence of the congregation, [*Goshenhoppen*?] James, son of James and Mary Barbara Käss, and Mary Magdalen, dau. of Fr. Louis and Catharine Ilain.

Lehr—Ebert: July 12, 1813, William Lehr, widower, Catholic, and Elizabeth Ebert, widow, non-Catholic; witnesses Andrew and Margaret Shimfessel.

Grett—Aloine: July 11, 1813, at Reading, John, son of Andrew and Elizabeth Grett, and Theresa, dau. of Conrad and Catharine Aloine; witnesses Magdalen Shmidt and John Sigfrid.

Becker—Becker: August 8, 1813, James and Elizabeth Becker, renew their consent, having been married before a Protestant [*minister.*]

Lonberg—Röhr: August 15, 1813, Michael, son of Michael and Mary Lonberg, and Elizabeth, dau. of Joseph and Jul. Röhr, renew their consent, having been married before a Protestant [*minister;*] witnesses Henry Covely and Joseph Röhr, Sr.

Eyan—Eckenrod: October 10, 1813, George, son of John and Anna Eyan, and Barbara, dau. of Henry and Elizabeth Eckenrod, having been married before a lay judge, renew their consent, before John Allgayer and Elizabeth Rittner.

Shorp—Shmidt: February 6, 1814, before the congregation Anthony, son of John and Elizabeth Shorp, and Catharine, dau. of Caspar and Susan Shmidt.

Rodger—Felix : March 14, 1814, James, son of Michael and Sara Rodger, and Mary, dau. of Nicholas and Mary Felix, renew their consent; witnesses Sebastian Allgaier and John Sigfrid.

Henrich—Egg: April 11, 1814, the second feria of Easter, in the presence of the congregation, John, son of Philip and Elizabeth Henrich, and Catharine, dau. of Peter and Magdalen Egg.

Ilein—Käss: May 29, 1814, in presence of the congregation, James, son of Fr. and Catharine Ilein, and Margaret, dau. of James and M. Barbara Käss.

Shnabel—Miller : May 30, 1814, in the presence of the congregation, John, son of Joseph and Mary Shnabel, and Margaret, dau. of Frederick and Elizabeth Miller.

Shnabel—Adam : August 7, 1814, in presence of the congregation, Daniel, son of Joseph and Mary Shnabel, and Catharine, dau. of Simon and Catharine Adam.

Grosskopp—Shnabel: September 4, 1814, Jonathan Grosskopp and Mary Shnabel renew their consent, in presence of Joseph Röhr and John Kuhnss.

Zerly—Shnabel: October 5, 1814, at the house of Michael Shnabel, James, son of Louis and Eve Zerly, and Barbara, dau. of Michael and Margaret Shnabel; witnesses Jonathan and Margaret Grosskopp.

Gilgert—Grett: January 31, 1815, Jonas, son of Adam and Elizabeth Gilgert, non-Catholic, and Eve, dau. of Nicholas and Susan Grett; witnesses John Grett and Sara Kemp.

Grett—Kiesel: April 9, 1815, at Reading before the congregation, Christian, son of Andrew and Elizabeth Grett, and Elizabeth, dau. of Sebastian and Catharine Kiesel.

Burgy—Reninger: the same day, Philip, son of Joseph and Mary Burgy, Catholic, and Catharine, dau. of Frederick and Catharine Reninger.

Burkop—Will: April 18, 1815, at Goshenhoppen, John Burkop, widower, and Margaret Will, widow; witnesses John Kunss and Barbara Kemp.

Hoffman—M'Farthring: May 15, 1815, Abraham, son of Michael and Christine Hoffman, and Mary, dau. of John and Eve M'Farthring; witnesses Daniel and Mary Coblet.

Zettelmayer—Kunz: June 18, 1815, at Goshenhoppen before the congregation, Jonathan Zettelmayer, widower, and Theresa, dau. of John and Catharine Kunz.

M'Carr—Kall: July 23, 1815, Henry, son of Francis and Bridget M'Carr, and Elizabeth, widow of Dennis Kall; witnesses Bernard Ferry and Michael Sires.

Egg—Shmidt: September 3, 1815, at Goshenhoppen before the congregation, Peter, son of Peter and Magdalen Egg, and Susan, dau. of Caspar and Sus. Shmidt.

Clee—Harvey: September 10, 1815, Charles, son of Ernest and Christine Clee, and Sara, dau. of Job and Anna Harvey; witnesses James and John Hartmann.

Röhr—Febinger: December 24, 1815, in the presence of the congregation, Joseph, son of Joseph and Juliana Röhr, and Margaret, dau. of Frederick and Catharine Febinger, non-Catholic.

Egg—Bauer: January 9, 1816, Joseph, son of Joseph and Agatha Egg, and Mary, dau. of Peter and Rosine Bauer; witnesses John Grett and John Bauer.

Felix—Reese: January 12, 1816, James, son of Martin and Barbara Felix, and Barbara, dau. of John and Barbara Reese, non-Catholic.

Waters—Felix: at the same time, Anthony, son of Anthony and Margaret Waters, non-Catholic, and Anna, dau. of Martin and Barbara Felix; witnesses John Kemp and Bartholomew Covely.

Felix—Shmidt: January 16, 1816, James, son of Nicholas and Mary Felix, and Elizabeth, dau. of Joseph and Regina Shmidt; witnesses George Shmidt and Mary Shlosser.

Melchior—Buck : February 4, 1816, John, son of ——— Melchior, and Sara, dau. of Leonard and Elizabeth Buck ; witnesses Christian Clemmer and John Kemp, Jr.

Windbiegler—Hartmann : February 20, 1816, Philip Windbiegler, widower, non-Catholic, and Catharine, dau. of James and Catharine Hartmann ; witnesses John and Sara Kemp.

Hartmann—Kemp: February 25, 1816, Michael, son of Michael and Margaret Hartmann, and Mary Magdalen, dau. of John and Barbara Kemp; witnesses John Hartmann and John Kemp.

Grett—Fink : March 31, 1816, John, son of Nicholas and Susan Grett, and Magdalen, dau. of John and Catharine Fink; witnesses Henry Fink and Susan Grett.

Grett—Arnold : April 21, 1816, at Reading in presence of the congregation, Samuel, son of Andrew and Elizabeth Grett, and Christine, dau. of John and Eve Arnold.

Umbenhauer—Obold : Samuel Umbenhauer and Catharine, dau. of Joseph and Margaret Obold.

Shed—Seifert: John Shed, non-Catholic, and Magdalen, dau. of Joseph and ——— Seifert.

Arnold—Arentz : June 9, 1816, at Reading, before the congregation, Peter, son of Herman and Catharine Arnold, and Margaret, dau. of James and Mary Arentz.

Hartmann—Bauer : John, son of James and Catharine Hartmann, and Elizabeth, dau. of Joseph and Christine Bauer.

Aloin—Eckenrod : August 11, 1816, at Reading, John, son of Conrad and Catharine Aloin, widower, and Magdalen, dau. of Henry Eckenrod; witnesses John Arnold and Ph. Aloin.

Shnabel—Miller: August 18, 1816, at Goshenhoppen, Joseph, son of Joseph and Mary Shnabel, and Juliana, dau. of Frederick and Elizabeth Miller; witnesses Richard Röhr and John Egg.

Connor—Bock : September 1, 1816, before the congregation at Goshenhoppen, Peter, son of Peter and Rose Connor, and Mery, dau. of Nicholas and Magdalen Bock.

Egg—Denis : October 6, 1816, John Laurence Egg and Anna Denis renew their consent; witnesses John and Charlotte Egg.

Arnold—Wolf : October 13, 1816, before the congregation at Reading, James, son of John and Eve Arnold, and Catharine, dau. of Abraham and Elizabeth Wolf.

Grett—Shæfer: November 10, 1816, at Reading, Solomon, son of Andrew and Elizabeth Grett, and Catharine, dau. of Henry Shæfer.

Shmidt—Moon : November 11, 1816, Andrew, son of Joseph and Regina Shmidt, Catholic, and Philippina, dau. of Josue and Sara Moon, non-Catholic ; witnesses James and Elizabeth Felix.

Grett—Obold : November 14, 1816, Andrew, son of Andrew and Elizabeth Grett, Catholic, and Margaret, dau. of Joseph and Margaret Obold, Catholic; witnesses Philip Obold and Elizabeth Grett.

Bergleit—Friderer: December 3, 1816, at Lebanon, [*in the text* Libanon,*] Joseph, son of Joseph Bergleit and Anna Mary Varendorf, and Catharine, dau. of Stephen and Catharine Friderer; witnesses Christian Miller and wife.

Rohrback—Röhr: January 23, 1817, John, son of James and Susan Rohrbach, and Sara, dau. of Joseph and Juliana Röhr; witnesses Charles M'Entire and wife.

Reichert—Egg: February 23, 1817, before the congregation at Goshenhoppen, Adam, son of Adam and Eve Reichert, Catholic, and Mary, dau. of Peter and Magdalen Egg, Catholic.

Eyerson—Eckenrodt: April 13, 1817, before the congregation at Reading, Joseph, son of John and Anna Eyerson, Catholic, and Mary, dau. of Henry and Elizabeth Eckenrodt.

Dillon—Hopp: July 2, 1817, in Fr. Hopp's house, Daniel, son of Johnson and Sara Dillon, non-Catholic, and Elizabeth, dau. of George and Margaret Hopp, Catholic ; witnesses John Shmidt and Francis Hopp.

Reimel—Reicher: August 17, 1817, John, son of John and Magdalen Reimel, Catholic, and Magdalen, dau. of Adam and Eve Reicher ; witnesses the congregation, Adam Reichert and Peter Egg.

Ilain—.——? : September 8, 1817, before the congregation, Laurence, son of Francis and Juliana Ilain, and Margaret, dau. of [*parents' names left out.*]

Covely—Bachman : September 22, 1817, John Covely and Mary Bachman ; witnesses Joseph Röhr and Henry Dollhauer.

Felix—Leckis: November 9, 1817, at Reading, Solomon, son of Martin and Barbara Felix, and Mary, dau. of John and Mary Leckis ; witnesses Anthony Merten and Barbara Sigfrid.

Bauer—Kunss : December 25, 1817, at Goshenhoppen, John, son of Peter and Rosina Bauer, and Juliana, dau. of John and Catharine Kunss ; witnesses John Röhr and James Clemmer.

Eckenrod—Hartmann : January 12, 1818, John, son of Henry and Elizabeth Eckenrod, and Mary, dau. of Francis and —— Hartmann ; witnesses John Allgaier and Christian Eckenrodt.

Bauer—Egg : January 19, 1818, Egidius, son of Peter and Rosine Bauer, and Magdalen, dau. of Peter and Magdalen Egg; witnesses Joseph Röhr and John B. Covely.

Kohl—M'Carty : February 1, 1818, Joseph, son of Joseph and Margaret Kohl, and Mary, dau. of John and Elizabeth M'Carty ; witnesses Nicholas Bock and Peter McCarty.

Eckenrodt—Burkard : February 8, 1818, having first obtained a dispensation from the second degree of affinity, Christian, widower, son of Henry and Elizabeth Eckenrodt, and Esther, widow, dau. of Christian and Esther Burkard ; witnesses Fr. and Elis. Hartmann, and John and Mary Eckenrodt.

Kunz—Heurich: March 3, 1818, John, widower, son of John and Catharine Kunz, and Catharine, daughter of Philip and Elizabeth Henrich; witnesses Joseph and George Kunz, and John Henrich.

Henrich—Kiesel: March 15, 1818, before the congregation at Reading, Philip, son of Philip and Elizabeth Henrich, and Catharine, dau. of Sebastian and Catharine Kiesel.

Weber—Shreer: March 29, 1818, Mathias Weber, widower, and Catharine Shreer, widow, renew their consent; witnesses Adam Reichert, Peter Egg, Sr., and Nicholas Grett.

Miller—Burgy: March 30, 1818, Daniel, son of Nicholas and Anna Miller, Catholic, and Magdalen, dau. of Joseph and Mary Burgy, Catholic.

Miller—Burgy: on the same day, John, son of George and Margaret Miller, non-Catholic, and Christine, dau. of Joseph and Mary Burgy, Catholic; witnesses Nicholas Grett, Adam Reichert and Andrew Grett.

Spengler—Lambert: April 12, 1818, before the congregation at Reading, Adam, son of Christ. and Elizabeth Spengler, non-Catholic, and Sara, dau. of James and Mary Lambert; witnesses Anthony Felix and William Röhr.

Kuntz—Bauer: May 31, 1818, by Rev. L. Barth, Paul Kuntz and Catharine Bauer; witnesses George Kuntz and John Bauer.

Redener—Richard: November 2, 1818, before the congregation and me [*Rev.*] Maximilian Rautzau, James Redener and Catharine Richard.

Adams—Hudel [?]: November 12, 1818, Paul Adams and Magdalen Hudel [?]; witnesses Simon Adams and Joseph Huoben.

Love—Reichard: May 2, 1819, Louis Love and Elizabeth Reichard; witnesses Charles McIntire and John Kiler.

Beyler—Mathews: May 16, 1819, Balthasar Beyler and Mary Mathews; witness ——— Bechtel. [*This entry with the following—the last record in the Marriage Register—is in Father Barth's hand. No year-date is given in the latter registration, so possibly it may belong to 1820.*]

Algayer—Ellz: February 7, [*1820 ?*] at Philadelphia, by Rev. L. Barth, Jacob Algayer and Margaret Ellz; witnesses Rev. John Rosetty and John Victor.

Total Marriages from 1801 to 1819, or 1820,=179.

GOSHENHOPPEN REGISTERS

OF

DEATHS AND BURIALS (1801-1818).

(FOURTH SERIES. Continued.)

TRANSLATED AND ANNOTATED BY REV. THOMAS C. MIDDLETON,
D.D., O. S. A.

DEATHS AND BURIALS, 1801-1818.

Egg, James, son of Theodore and Mary Elizabeth, aged 5 y., 5 m., 12 d.; drowned March 16, 1801 ; buried on the 18th ; [*place not named.*]

Shmidt, George, son of George and Barbara ; died May 25, 1801 ; buried on the 27th.

Hopp, Francis Anthony, son of George and Margaret ; aged 2 y., 9 m.; died July 26, 1801 ; buried on the 28th near Massillum.

Hopp, Magdalen, dau. of the above ; aged 5 y., 6 m., 19 d.; died July 28, 1801 ; buried on the 30th near Massillum.

Adam, Simon, died March 27, 1803.

Frydenberg, Eve, aged 20 y.; died April 29, 1804.

Clark, William, aged 25 y.; died October 1, 1801. [*sic,* but apparently an error for 1804. Then among the burials for 1806, comes the following :]

Gibson, Henry, died February 22, 1804 ; buried on the 24th.

Shnabel, Catharine, wife of Andrew, died August 18, 1805.

Gehry, Eve, aged 80 y.; died January 15, 1806.

Grett, Magdalen, aged 86 y.; died February 4, 1806.

Käss, Daniel, son of Nicholas and Margaret ; aged 5 y. ; died March 7, 1806 ; buried on the 8th.

Egg, Lia, dau. of Joseph and Agatha ; one m., one d. old ; died March 10, 1806 ; buried on the 12th.

Kohl, Michael, died April 3, 1806 ; buried on the 6th in the graveyard near Haycock.

NOTE.—The abbreviations, *y., m., w., d.,* stand for years, months, weeks and days.

Burkard, Martin, died April 11, 1806; buried on the 13th near the church.

Erb, John, son of Peter and Christine, died April 23, 1806; buried on the 24th.

Egg, David, died July 25, 1806, and his twin brother John on the 26th; sons of Peter and Magdalen; buried on the 27th; [*place not named.*]

Welker, Theophilus, aged 89 y.; died August 24, 1806; buried on the 26th.

Obold, John, aged 11 y., 4 m., 2 d.; died August 31, 1806; buried September 1.

Shutt, James, son of Anthony and Catharine; died November 27, 1806; buried on the 28th.

Burkard, Gertrude, aged 66 y.; died December 29, 1806; buried on the 31st.

Arenz, Jacob, aged 69 y., 2m., 1 w.; died January 21, 1807; buried on the 23d.

Martin, John, aged 53 y.; died January 31, 1807; buried at Reading, February 1.

Stoll, Erhard, died [*rest wanting.*]

Stoll, Eve Margaret, wife of above, aged 75 y.; died March 20, 1807; on the 22d, buried in the graveyard near the church.

Walker, Gertrude, aged 51 y.; died May 20, 1807; buried on the 22d.

Queen, Henry, son of Thomas and his wife Mary; aged 3 y.; died June 2, 1807; buried on the 4th.

Reichert, Michael, son of Adam and Eve, aged 25 y.; died September 23, 1807; buried on the 25th.

Shmidt, Philip, aged 61 y.; died March 6, 1808; buried on the 8th.

Grett, John Adam, aged 29 y., 4 ws., 5 d.; died April 3, 1808; buried on the 5th.

Huver, Jonathan, son of Adam and his wife Susanna; aged 4 y., 5½ m.; died May 31, 1808; buried June 2.

Repplier, Anna Catharine, dau. of George and his wife Catharine; aged 7 m., 11 d.; died June 11, 1808; buried on the 12th.

Duval, Francis, single, born at Calais [*France*]; died June 30, 1808, at Pottsgrove; buried July 1 near the church.

Wummer, Jacob, son of Adam and his wife Magdalen; aged 10 m., 4 d.; died July 25, 1808; buried on the 27th.

Beaver, Samuel, son of Christopher and his wife Susanna; aged 6 m.; died in the month of August, 1808.

Egg, Paul, son of John and his wife Louisa [*Aloilina*]; aged 6 y., 9 m., 2 w.; died September 11, 1808; buried on the 13th.

Diederich, Elizabeth, died October 26, 1808; buried on the 28th.

Hopp, Elitta, died December 18, 1808; and Margaret on the 20th, daughters of Andrew and his wife Margaret; buried on the 21st in the same grave.

Kemp, John, aged 76 y., 9 m.; died November 21, 1808; buried in the cemetery on the 23d.

Egg, John, Sr., aged 89 y., 4 m.; died June 9, 1809; buried on the 12th.

Arenz, formerly Egg, Margaret, wife of G. [*eorge*]; died June 26, 1809; buried on the 28th.

Shnabel, Mary Eve, widow of Andrew, aged 78 y., 5 m.; died August 26, 1809; buried on the 29th.

Burkop, Juliana, wife of John, aged 45 y.; died suddenly December 21, 1809; buried on the 24th.

Gobele, Magdalen, dau. of John and Mary, aged 7 m., 3 w., 3 d.; died April 4, 1810; buried on the 6th.

Sigfrid, Andrew, aged 78 y., 5 m., 4 d.; died June 29, 1810; buried in the graveyard at Reading July 1.

Sebold, John Jacob, son of Peter and his wife Catharine; aged 1 m., 1 w., 1 d.; died July 23, 1810; buried on the 24th.

Grett, Andrew, aged 90 y., 1 w., 3 d.; died January 5, 1811; buried on the 8th.

Arens, Margaret, widow of Jacob, aged 68 y.; died July 6, 1811; buried on the 8th.

Huck, Juliana, widow of Paul; aged 71 y.; died July 9, 1811; buried on the 10th.

Shnabel, Jacob, son of Michael and Margaret, aged 11 m.; died July 10, 1811; buried on the 11th.

Keffer, Barbara, wife of Peter, aged 71 y., 8 m.; died June 20, 1811; buried on the 22d.

Hoff, Magdalen, aged 73 y.; died August 9, 1811; buried on the 11th,

Grett, Andrew, aged 56 y., 2 mo., 15 d.; died October 2, 1811; buried on the 4th.

Mintzer, Joseph, son of Engelbert and Mary, aged 30 y., 10 m., 6 d.; died March 10, 1812; buried on the 12th.

Mattes, Mary, wife of John, aged 49 y.; died April 13, 1812; buried on the 15th.

Kunss, Mary Barbara, wife of John, aged 29 y.; died June 8, 1812; buried on the 10th.

Ilain, Francis Louis, aged 65 y., 1 month less 3 d.; died December 4, 1812; buried on the 6th.

Sweetman, Joseph Richard, son of John and Margaret, aged 23 y., 2 m.; died March 9 [?], 1813; buried on the 12th.

Hauss, John Jacob, son of Jacob and his wife Mary, aged 1 y., 7 m., 3 w., 4 d.; died April 28, 1813; buried on the 30th.

Dollhauer, Mary Barbara, wife of Henry, aged 44 y.; died May 14, 1813; buried on the 16th.

Felix, Nicholas, aged 82 y.; died May 22, 1813; buried at Reading on the 23d.

Becker, Elizabeth, dau. of Jacob and his wife Elizabeth, aged 1 y., 2 m.; died July 7, 1813; buried on the 9th.

Kunz, Mary Barbara, dau. of John and M. [ary] B. [arbara], deceased, aged 1 y., 2 m., 2 w., 6 d.; died August 3, 1813; buried on the 5th.

Budde, Henrietta, dau. of Maurice and his wife Catharine, aged 11 m., 2 w., 1 d.; died September 4, 1813; buried on the 5th.

Dollhauer, Henry, aged 54 y.; died September 6, 1813; buried on the 8th.

Green, Frederick, black or mulatto [*Aethiops, vel mulato (sic)*], son of Abraham and Mary; aged 3 y.; died September 15, 1813; buried on the 17th.

Jones, Anna Maria, aged 60 y., 5 m., 21 d.; died at Pottsgrove November 13, 1813; buried on the 15th.

Kemp, Elizabeth, dau. of John and Barbara, aged 3 m., 17 d.; died December 28, 1813; buried on the 30th. [*Ahead of this in the Register is the following entry:—*]

Keffer, Peter, aged 73 y.; died January 20, 1814; buried at Reading on the 22d.

Egg, Eva, wife of John Egg, Sr.; aged 84 y.; died February 13, 1814; buried on the 15th.

Egg, Anna, dau. of Daniel and his wife M. Margaret; aged 1 y., 1 m., 13 d.; died February 13, 1814; buried on the 15th.

Keffer, Jacob, son of Jacob and Magdalen; aged 13 y.; died March 12, 1814; buried on the 14th.

Keffer, Jacob, Sr., aged 50 y.; died March 16, 1814; buried on the 18th.

Obold, Elizabeth, widow of Joseph Obold and Phil. Shmidt; aged 70 y.; died March 20, 1814; buried on the 22d.

Engel, Catharine, died August 24, 1814; buried at Reading on the 26th.

Herbst, Richard, aged 23 [?] y.; died September 5, 1814; buried at Reading on the 6th.

Shmidt, Philip, aged 45 y.; died October 21, 1814; buried on the 23d.

Cassely, Michael, aged 50 y.; died November 13, 1814; buried on the 15th.

Fortmann, Margaret, wife of C.; died January 31, 1815; buried February 3.

Martin, Catharine, widow of John Henry, aged 66 y.; died April 8, 1815; buried at Reading on the 10th.

Gayner, Elizabeth, widow, aged 91 y., 5 m.; died May 7, 1815; buried at Gohenshoppen on the 9th.

Els. Mary, dau. of Jacob and Mary M., aged 13 y., less 2 w.; died September 2, 1815; buried on the 4th.

Budde, Antoninus, son of M. and Catharine; died September 8, 1815 [*burial date not given.*]

Käss, David, son of Jacob and Magdalen ; [*death date not given ;*] buried November 20.

Mattes, John, [*died, or buried*] February 13, 1816.

Grett, Michael, [*died, or buried*] March 6, 1816.

Covely, John, aged 36 y., 1 m., 29 d. ; died April 22, 1816.

Walker, Elizabeth, wife of John, aged 21 y., 10 m., less 4 d. ; died July 19, 1816 ; buried on the 21st.

Covely, Elizabeth, wife of Henry, died in child-bed January 18, 1817 ; buried on the 19th.

Covely, Mary Ann, wife of Daniel, aged 75 y. ; died September 22, 1817 ; buried on the 24th.

Egg, Samuel, son of Peter and Susan ; aged 9 m., 3 w. ; died December 25, 1817 ; buried on the 27th.

Shorp, Catharine, dau. of Caspar and Susan Shmid and wife of Anthony Shorp, aged 23 y., 10 m. ; died February 14, 1818 ; buried on the 16th.

Gernand, Mary Magdalen, aged 21 y., 6 m., 14 d. ; died February 19, 1818 ; buried on the 22d.

Reichert, John, son of Anthony and Catharine, aged 23 y., 6 m., 3 w., 3 d. ; died February 24, 1818 ; buried on the 26th.

Dens [?], Conrad, of Baaden, aged 39 y. ; died March 2, 1818 ; buried on the 4th.

Total Deaths from 1801 to 1818 = 97.

Document

The Goshenhoppen Registers: Fifth Series

Baptisms, 1807-1818

Translated and annotated by John R. Dunne, O.S.A., Villanova, Pa.

In previous issues of its RECORDS the Society has published the church registers of the old Pennsylvania mission at Goshenhoppen (nowadays Bally) from its foundation in 1741 by Father Theodore Schneider. The last section of these registers, containing the records of baptisms from 1807 to 1818 are here published Thus the Society completes the publication of all of the records of old Goshenhoppen which are in its custody.

The present register was entrusted to the Society by Father Alois Misteli, the pastor at Bally, in February, 1894. It was received for the Society by the Reverend Thomas C. Middleton, O.S.A., at the time Chairman of the Historical Research Committee. Father Middleton, it seems, intended publication of the records and prepared an introduction to them. But, for some reason now unknown, the register was misplaced in the historical collections of the Society and was never published. It was rediscovered in late 1948 by the Reverend Bartholomew F. Fair among the manuscripts in the Society's Archives.

All of the extant records of the Bally parish for the years from 1741 to 1818 are in the custody of the Society. They are contained in two bound volumes with some loose supplementary pages. It is on these additional pages that the present records are contained. The second volume of sacramental registers, begun by Father Peter Helbron in 1787, contains the record of baptisms from 1787 to 1808, and the records of marriages, and deaths and burials from 1787 to 1818. Since the space in this second volume was exhausted, Father Paul Erntzen evidently continued the baptismal registers on these additional pages, while completing his marriage register and record of death and burial in the old book which he had received from Father Nicholas Delvaux, his predecessor.

There are ten large sheets in the present register, folded in half to give leaves measuring each about twelve and a half by seven and three quarter inches. It seems that the register was preserved folded, for all of the leaves are broken badly across the center. The manuscript is of heavy paper, and is still in fair condition. The first and last two leaves, however, are in poor condition: the margins are much broken and many dates are now indecipherable. The missionary priests used both sides of each leaf, so that there are in all forty pages, each containing about seventeen entries.

Almost all of the records published here were made by Father Paul

Erntzen, pastor at Bally from 1793 to 1818. He had a clear and easily read hand. At the top of each page he wrote the following heading:

Dies Gener.	Dies Regener.	Nomina Baptizatorum Anno Domini . . . .

In the first column he entered the date of birth *(dies generationis);* in the second column, the date of baptism *(dies regenerationis);* in the third the name of the child, of its parents, and of the sponsors.

The last two pages of the register contain entries written in divers hands. These entries are written across the page, and contain a complete statement without the columnar arrangement used by Father Erntzen.

The translation of the registers, written of course in Latin, is here made exactly from the original. The following points need especially to be mentioned: 1) All of the illegitimate births have been omitted, in accord with the Society's custom. 2) Family names have been retained in the exact orthography of the original. In many cases there are obvious misspellings, but it has been thought better to transcribe them exactly, since the interpretation is thus made easier. 3) A few Christian names also give difficulty. *Magdalena* has been translated throughout Madeline. *Jacobus* is always translated James, even though it is perhaps more likely that Jacob would be correct, particularly where the surname is of German origin. The use of a German dialect is still quite common among the people of Bally. 4) The translation follows throughout the order of the original. In some cases the missionary did not enter the record until some time after the ceremony.

Analysis of the Contents of the Goshenhoppen Registers (1807-1819) by the Reverend Thomas C. Middleton, O.S.A.

The priests registering the Baptisms are as follows:

1. Paul Erntzen   from 1807, Jan. 11 to 1818, April 7
2. an unknown   from 1818, May 30 to July 12
   (who may be the following:)
3. Maximilian Rantzau   from 1818, Sept 13 to Nov. 3
4. an unknown   from 1819, Mch. 7 to May 5
5. D. Schoenfelder   from 1819, Mch. 10 to Aug. 27
6. Thomas Praniewitz   from 1819, Sept. 12 to Oct. 17
7. P. Paul Kohlman   from 1819, Oct. 13 to 1820, Feb.
8. an unknown

N.B. 1.   Father Rantzau baptizes in Reading, 1818, Sept. 13;
          in Goshenhoppen, Sept. 19;
          in Haycock, Sept. 27;
          in Reading, October 11;
          in Orwigsburg, October 12;
          "Ad Missilum fluvium," October 18;
          in Goshenhoppen, November 1.

N.B. 2. Father Praniewitz baptizes in Goshenhoppen;
in Folgner Schwam;
in Winzer Schwam;
in Herford Taunschip;
in Happor Taunschip;
in Massilum Taunschip.

N.B. 3. In 1817, October 2, Fathern Erntzen baptizes in the house of Peter Maison, near Philadelphia, the three daughters of the same, viz., Catharine, born May 26, 1813; Christine Anna, born June 12, 1815; Josephine Angela Theresa, born May 26, 1817. John Alphonse Maison, brother of Peter, was sponsor for all three. Peter Maison is mentioned earlier in the Goshenhoppen Registers (RECORDS, III, 358) as living in 1781 at Haycock. *

---

*Page 81, this volume.

Date of Birth	Date of Baptism	Names of those baptized
2 December 1806	11 January 1807	John, son of Joseph and Mary Ritshy[1] Sponsors: John Allgayer and Mary Anna Lambert
28 October 1806	11 January 1807	John Peter, son of James and Barbara Shnabel Sponsors: John Peter and Barbara Keffer
4 December 1806	11 January 1807	Joseph, son of Peter and Barbara Rittner Sponsors: Joseph and Margaret Allgayer
21 December 1806	11 January 1807	Anna Madeline, daughter of James and Madeline Keffer Sponsors: Anthony Merten and Catherine Hartman
9 November 1806	12 January 1807	James, son of Michael and Elisabeth Keetch Sponsors: James and Mary Huver
14 September 1804	12 January 1807	Anna Mary, daughter of Henry and Mary Madeline [?] Sponsors: Francis and Mary Anna Huver
14 November 1806	23 January 1807	George, son of James and Elisabeth Zweyer Sponsors: George and Margaret Hopp
7 January 1807	1 March 1807	Elias, son of Peter and Catherine Hunsberger Sponsors: John and Catherine Reichert
[10?] September 1806	9 March 1807	William Solomon, son of George and Elisabeth [?] Sponsors: Joseph and Catherine Schlosser
	22 March 1807	Anna Philippina, daughter of Philip and Barbara G[?] Sponsors: John and Philippina Wingart
31 January 1807	30 March 1807	Mary Juliana, daughter of John and Elisabeth Denis Sponsors: James Adam and Juliana Els
10 April 1807	3 May 1807	Elisabeth, daughter of John and Catherine Adam Sponsors: Augustine Reichert and Catherine Adam
1 January 1807	12 April 1807	Joseph, son of Michael and Esther Grett Sponsors: Samuel Hartman and Barbara Grett
8 August 1806	12 April 1807	Mary, daughter of John and Anna Ganss Sponsors: Charles Klee and Catherine Ganss
11 December 1806	14 April 1807	James, son of John and Anna Mary Flower Sponsors: James and Dorothy Lambert
24 August 1806	12 April 1807	George, son of Henry and Elisabeth Eckenrodt Sponsors: Francis and Elisabeth Hartman
[1?] February 1807	18 April 1807	Samuel, son of John and Barbara Beaver Sponsors: Nicholas and Susan Grett
12 March 1807	19 April 1807	Christine, daughter of Joseph and Christine Gibson Sponsors: William Gallacher and Catherine Hopp

1 The abbreviation C standing for *conjugum*, spouses, is written after the names of the parents. It has been omitted throughout the translation.

Date of Birth	Date of Baptism	Names of those baptized
[15?] March [1807?]	19 April 1807	Elisabeth, daughter of Henry and Catherine [?] Sponsors: [Carolus?] [?]
[?]	19 April 1807	F. Joseph, son of Joseph and Susan Stahler Sponsors: James and Susan Catherine Spring
[?]	15 October 1805	Mary, daughter of John and Catherine Shmidt[2] Sponsors: Sebastian and Catherine Allgayer
[?]	10 May 1807	Catherine, daughter of John and Catherine Shmidt Sponsors: John Keffer and Madeline Hart- man
[?] 1807	12 May 1807	Mary Anna, daughter of Peter and Theresa Herbst Sponsors: Eva Fricker, widow
[?] 1806	13 May 1807	Catherine, daughter of Michael and Yeomy Mitchel, non-Catholic I, Paul Erntzen, godfather
[? March] [?]	24 May 1807	Catherine, daughter of George and Barbara Shmidt Sponsors: James Kass and Catherine Shone- bruek
[?]	24 May 1807	Thomas, son of Andrew and Madeline Shone- bruek Sponsors: Caspar Schonebruek and Margaret Shand
[?]	24 May 1807	John, son of James and Susan Shonebruek Sponsors: John and Eva Shonebruek
[?]	25 May 1807	Henry, son of John and Catherine Kass Sponsors: Mathias and Elisabeth Kass
[?] 1807	31 May 1807	John Adam, son of Joseph and Mary Nener Sponsors: Adam and Eva Reichert
[?] May 1807	31 May 1807	Catherine, daughter of Philip and Susan Reichert Sponsors: Adam and Eva Reichert

At Oxford Furnace in New Jersey

17 January 1807	30 June 1807	Anna, daughter of John and Anna Elisabeth Dum Sponsors: James Harken and Mary Coblet
	30 June 1807	Charles, son of Bartholomew and Helen Coblet Sponsors: Joseph Coblet and Catherine Bach- mann
	30 June 1807	William, son of Bartholomew and Helen Coblet Sponsors: William Cammel and Mary Coblet
	30 June 1807	William, son of William and Anna Coblet Sponsors: James Harkens and Mary Covely

2 Under Dies Regen. the date 15 October, 1805 is to be found, and the Dies Gener. is blank. This may mean that the date 15 October, 1805 is the date of birth for what may be a set of twins, for the marginal piece of the page for the Dies Gener. of the following is missing. The other possibility is that the 15 October, 1805 is the birthday of Mary, sister of Catherine Schmidt, one or two years older than her sister.

Date of Birth	Date of Baptism	Names of those baptized
	30 June 1807	Martin, son of William and Anna Coblet Sponsors: Martin and Barbara Bachman
	30 June 1807	John, son of Ferdinand and Anna Bachman Sponsors: John and Anna Elisabeth Dum
	[?] 1807	John Shippen, aged 20 Sponsors: [?] and Helen Coblet
[?] December 1806	12 July 1807	Mechtilde, daughter of Peter and Susan Lambert Sponsors: John Lambert and Madeline Hartman
[?] May 1807	12 July 1807	Anna Mary, daughter of Joseph and Elisabeth Sigfrid Sponsors: Anthony Felix and Mary Leckis
[?] February 1807	2 August 1807	Mary, daughter of John and Elisabeth Covely Sponsors: John Covely and Sophia Els
[7?] March 1807	2 August 1807	Mary Susan, daughter of Joseph and Anna M. Shnabel Sponsors: Caspar and Susan Shmidt
[?] June 1807	2 August 1807	Susan, daughter of Frederick and Elisabeth Miller Sponsors: John and Catherine Kunss
[?] April [?]	5 August 1807	John, son of George and Elisabeth Kemp Sponsors: Joseph Kemp and Madeline Report
[?]	5 August 1807	Leah, daughter of Peter and Madeline Egg Sponsors: Henry and Susan Kass
[?]	[?] August 1807	Daniel, son of Daniel and Elisabeth Strack Sponsors: James and Madeline Kemp
[?] 1807	9 August 1807	Margaret, daughter of James and Catherine Bott Sponsors: James and Margaret Bernheiser
[?] July 1807	9 August 1807	Margaret, daughter of George and Barbara Sigfrid Sponsors: Nicholas and Margaret Felix
[?] October 1807	9 August 1807	Philip, son of Hugh and Mary M'Cormick Sponsors: Philip and Catherine Gerstweiler
[11?] July 1807	15 August 1807	John, son of John and Catherine Grett Sponsors: John Egg and Theresa Grett
26 July 1807	16 August 1807	George, son of Peter and Christine Erb Sponsors: George Kunss and Mary Rohr
12 June 1807	30 August 1807	Charles, son of Christian and Margaret Stahler Sponsors: James and Susan Catherine Spring
14 July 1807	31 August 1807	Leah, daughter of Michael and Margaret Shnabel Sponsors: Joseph and Anna M. Shnabel
15 August 1807	6 September 1807	Robert, son of Joseph and Aloitina Egg Sponsors: Joseph and Catherine Kunss
[?]	[?] 1807	Elisabeth, [?] [?] [Henry?] Covely and Sophia Els

Date of Birth [?]	Date of Baptism [?]	Names of those baptized [?] [?] and [Sarah?] Shindler, spouses. [?]
16 August 1807	22 September 1807	Daniel, son of Daniel and Elisabeth Sauvert Sponsors: Thomas and Madeline Dum
21 September 1807	25 September 1807	James, son of Adam and Madeline Wummer Sponsors: Philip and Susan Reichert
17 August 1807	4 September 1807	Margaret, daughter of Daniel and M. Margaret Egg Sponsors: Nicholas and Margaret Kass
15 April 1807	1 November 1807	Litta, daughter of James and Elisabeth Feels Sponsors: Joseph and Eva Wingart
19 October 1807	15 November 1807	Catherine, daughter of John and Mary Wagner Sponsors: John and Elisabeth Grett
[27?] October 1807	22 November 1807	William, son of John and Elisabeth M'Gorgan Sponsors: Dominick and Margaret Cornyn
11 November 1807	28 November 1807	Mary Sarah, daughter of John and Mary Mattes Sponsors: Peter and Salome Egg
[?] November 1807	28 November 1807	Anna, daughter of George and Susan Ferstermacher Sponsors: Peter and Madeline Egg
[?]	29 November 1807	Anna Mary, daughter of John Nicholas and Elisabeth Sweyer Sponsors: Joseph and Mary Burgy
[?] September 1807	13 December 1807	Mary, daughter of Joseph and Christine Grett Sponsors: Joseph and Margaret Allgayer
11 October 1807	13 December 1807	Anna Catherine, daughter of George and Catherine Repplier Sponsors: Sebastian and Catherine Allgayer
18 November 1807	14 December 1807	Ernest and Catherine, twins of William and Mary Ganss Sponsors: For Ernest: Ernest and Mary [C?] and for Catherine, the Godmother was Catherine Ganss, widow
24 November 1807	25 December 1807	James, son of Thomas and Mary Queen Sponsors: Henry Covely and Anna Dollhauer
16 October 1807	25 December 1807	Mary, daughter of John and Anna Shnabel Sponsors: Andrew Shnabel and Mary Adam

Document

The Goshenhoppen Registers: Fifth Series

Baptisms, 1808-1811

Date of Birth	Date of Baptism	Names of those baptized
21 July 1807	5 January 1808	Anna Elisabeth, daughter of John and Susan Els Sponsors: John and Anna Elisabeth Els
11 December 1807	17 January 1808	Litta, daughter of Joseph and Juliana Rohr Sponsors: John and Anna Elisabeth Els
26 December 1807	31 January 1808	Joseph, son of George and Margaret Hopp Sponsors: Joseph and Christine Gibson
[?] February 1808	8 March 1808	Samuel, son of Daniel and Elisabeth Grett Sponsors: Andrew Grett and Elisabeth Reich [ert?]
6 January 1808	9 March 1808	Madeline, daughter of John and Madeline Seifert Sponsor: Widow Elisabeth Reichert
23 December 1807	13 March 1808	Joseph, son of James and Barbara Shnabel Sponsors: Thomas Dum and Mary Lecky
[?] December 1807	13 March 1808	John James, son of John and Susan Keffer Sponsors: James and Madeline Keffer
[?] March 1808	13 March 1808	William, son of Joseph and Margaret Allgayer Sponsors: Sebastian and Catherine Allgayer
18 February 1808	15 March 1808	Margaret, daughter of James and Mary Kemp Sponsors: John and Anna Christine Kemp, [Senior?]
13 January 1808	15 March 1808	Frederick, son of James and Susan Rohrbach Sponsors: John and Philippina Wingart
21 February 1808	7 April 1808	Madeline Elisabeth, daughter of Peter and Rosine Bauer Sponsors: Mathias and Madeline Beringer
10 March 1808	18 April 1808	Elisabeth, daughter of John and Philippine Wingart Sponsors: Joseph and Eva Wingart
[?] February [?]	18 April 1808	George, son of Anthony and Catherine [Reichert?] Sponsors: John Reichert and Sophia Els
1 May 1807	20 April 1808	Catherine, daughter of John and Catherine Ettinger Sponsors: John and Anna Christine Kemp
22 May 1807	8 May 1808	Philip, son of John and Elisabeth Bryan Sponsors: Philip and Catherine Gerstweiler
1 March 1808	8 May 1808	Susan, daughter of Henry and Elisabeth Eckenrodt Sponsors: James and Barbara Shnabel

228

Date of Birth	Date of Baptism	Names of those baptized
10 December 1807	8 May 1808	Susan, daughter of Henry and Madeline Aggy Sponsors: Adam and Susan Huver
12 April 1808	8 May 1808	John, son of Adam and Susan Huver Sponsors: John Huver and Mary Zweyer
2 May 1808	26 May 1808	Daniel, son of Philip and Elisabeth Grett Sponsors: Daniel Bohm and Theresa Grett
	19 May 1808	George, Negro Sponsor: Anna Milty
17 April 1808	29 May 1808	John, son of Valentine and Madeline Dum Sponsors: Thomas Dum and Margaret Arenz
28 April 1808	30 May 1808	Philip, son of John and Mary Kass Sponsors: Philip and Elisabeth Henrich
8 April 1808	30 May 1808	Charles, posthumous son of J. Adam and M. Grett Sponsors: John Grett and Elisabeth Henrich
4 May 1808	5 June 1808	Catherine Sophia, daughter of Joseph and Catherine Burkard Sponsors: John and Catherine Reichert
30 April 1808	5 June 1808	Madeline, daughter of Mathias and Elisabeth Kass Sponsors: Peter and Christine Erb
19 March 1808	12 June 1808	Elisabeth, daughter of John and Anna Ganss Sponsors: Catherine Ganss, widow
20 May 1808	12 June 1808	Joseph, son of James and Susan Shlosser Sponsors: Joseph Flower and Susan Dillinger
31 July 1807	12 June 1808	Elisabeth, daughter of George and Anna Kiesig Sponsors: James and Margaret Weissenburg
[?] April 1808	12 June 1808	Christine, daughter of Frederick and Catherine Reninger Sponsor: Elisabeth Shmidt
[?] May 1808	12 June 1808	Madeline, daughter of John and Madeline Shlosser Sponsors: Andrew and Madeline Hopp
9 July 1808	24 July 1808	Mary Anna, daughter of Michael and Mary Shm[idt?] Sponsors: George Kunz and Elisabeth Shmidt
[?] July 1808	16 August 1808	Henry, son of Anthony and Catherine Shutt Sponsors: Henry and Susan Kass
6 September 1807	19 August 1808	Bartholomew, son of John and Elisabeth Sterling Sponsors: Bartholomew and Elisabeth Covely
30 June 1808	14 August 1808	Catherine, daughter of Joseph and Margaret Ritshi Sponsors: Sebastian and Catherine Allgayer
	14 August 1808	Henry, son of Henry and Catherine Lehmon Sponsors: Anthony and Catherine Felix
26 June 1808	11 September 1808	Juliana, daughter of George and Elisabeth Hoffmeister Sponsors: John Hartmann and Barbara Grett

Date of Birth	Date of Baptism	Names of those baptized
21 August 1808	11 September 1808	Anna Mary, daughter of Anthony and Catherine Felix Sponsors: Nicholas and Anna Mary Felix
14 April 1808	11 September 1808	Mary Margaret, daughter of John and Madeline Aloin Sponsors: Joseph and Margaret Obold
30 August 1808	11 September 1808	John Francis, son of J. F. and Eva Eichorn Sponsors: George and Catherine Repplier
[?] August [?]	19 October 1808	John, son of John and Mary Shaefer Sponsors: [Paul?] Erntzen and Susan Shaefer, widow
[?] 180[?]	[?] 1808	John, son of Nicholas and Margaret Kass Sponsors: John Jhlein and Juliana Kunz
23 [?] 1807	2 October 1808	Elias Jonas, son of Andrew and Sarah Shindler Sponsors: Henry Covely and Elizabeth Bachmann
1 September 1808	5 October 1808	Margaret, daughter of George and Margaret Arentz Sponsor: Margaret Arentz
22 September 1808	9 October 1808	Mary Catherine, daughter of Frederick and Catherine Shmidt Sponsors: William and Anna Minzen
7 September 1805	18 October 1808	Margaret, daughter of Charles and Mary Philipps Sponsors: John and Margaret Rupell
11 September 1807	18 October 1808	Anna, daughter of Charles and Mary Philips Sponsors: William and Elisabeth Rupel
16 June 1790	18 October 1808	Catherine, wife of Anthony Stroback. On the same day I married them.
13 July 1805	18 October 1808	Anna and Catherine, twins of Richard and Elisabeth Walsh Sponsors: Thomas M'Carty and Margaret Rupel; M. Honig and Elisabeth Rupel
[?] March 1808	18 October 1808	Elisabeth, daughter of Richard and Elisabeth Walsh Sponsors: James M'Donnel and Catherine Honig
[?] [1805?]	18 October 1808	Joseph, son of George and Elisabeth Rupel Sponsors: James and Margaret Ruple
[?] October [?]	1808	Anna Louise, 30 years of age Sponsors: Michael Honig and S. Shaefer
[?] January 1807	19 October 1808	Margaret, daughter of John and Mary Shaefer Sponsors: Michael Honig and Margaret Shaefer
8 September 1808	30 October 1808	Madeline, daughter of Andrew and Madeline Hopp Sponsors: Joseph Flower and Catherine Hopp
[?] August 1808	30 October 1808	Augustine, son of John and Barbara Beaver Sponsors: Andrew and Anna Grett, cousins

Date of birth	Date of baptism	Names of those baptized
24 September 1808	30 October 1808	Thomas, son of James and Elisabeth Zweyer Sponsors: Thomas and Mary Zweyer
25 October 1808	21 November 1808	Joseph, son of John and Barbara Kemp Sponsors: James and Catherine Hartmann
28 October 1808	4 November 1808	Litta, daughter of Peter and Catherine Hunsberger Sponsors: John Reichert and Theresa Grett
[?5] October 1808	4 November 1808	Catherine, daughter of John and Barbara Kunz Sponsors: John and Catherine Kunz
[23?] November 1808	23 December 1808	Abraham, son of James and Mary Adam Sponsors: Abraham Groskop and Sabina Adam
29 December 1808	26 January 1809	Elias Paul, son of Peter and Elisabeth [?] Sponsors: P. Erntzen and widow, Margaret Arenz
22 January 1809	26 January 1809	Salome, daughter of Joseph and Christine Gibson Sponsors: George and Margaret Hopp
	29 January 1809	Joseph, son of John Nicholas and Elisabeth Shweyer Sponsors: Henry and Catherine Gibson
	29 January 1809	Catherine, daughter of Henry and Catherine Gibson Sponsors: Philip and Elisabeth Henrich
	29 January 1809	Mary, daughter of Christian and Margaret Stahler Sponsors: John Grett and Elisabeth Henrich
11 March 1809	21 March 1809	Paul James, son of Philip and Susan Reichert Sponsors: Paul Erntzen and Widow Shmidt
8 February 1809	26 March 1809	Elisabeth, daughter of Joseph and Eva Wingart Sponsors: Bartholomew and Elisabeth Coble
6 February 1809	2 April 1809	Catherine, daughter of Daniel and M. Margaret Egg Sponsors: Francis and Catherine Jlain
[?6] November 1808	[2?] April 1809	John, son of Abraham Mundan and M. Margaret [?] Sponsors: John and Charlotte Egg
15 February 1809	3 April 1809	Litta, daughter of Stephen and Madeline Reppert Sponsors: Augustine Reichert and Anna Rohr
1 March 1809	3 April 1809	Litta, daughter of Henry and Barbara Dollhauer Sponsors: John and Elisabeth Grett
3 November 1808	3 April 1809	Jesse James,[3] son of Lazarus and Madeline Weidener Sponsors: Maurice [?] and Catherine Adam

---

[3] Note the names Jesse and James used as a double Christian name. Later the full name of an infamous bandit of the west. In most instances where German family names follow after *Jacobus* in Latin, Jacob rather than James probably was used among these people.

Date of Birth	Date of Baptism	Names of those baptized
3 March 1809	3 April 1809	Theresa, daughter of Peter and Christine Erb Sponsors: John Reichert and Theresa Kunz
11 December 1808	9 April 1809	Andrew, son of Joseph and [?] Shindler Sponsors: Joseph Walter and Mary Shindler
7 November 1808	10 April 1809	George, son of George and Madeline Ganss Sponsors: James and Catherine Hartmann
18 February 1809	16 April 1809	George, son of Christian and Catherine Clem [er?] Sponsors: George Kunz and Margaret Shonebruck
12 February 1809	16 April 1809	Elisabeth, daughter of John and Elisabeth Shurp Sponsors: Andrew and Sybil Reeser
2 April 1809	30 April 1809	Catherine, daughter of Christopher and Madeline [?] Sponsors: Michael Becker and Catherine [?]
9 April 1809	2 May 1809	Catherine, daughter of John and Mary Kass Sponsors: Andrew Grett and Catherine Henrich
6 May 1809	8 May 1809	Salome, daughter of Peter and Madeline Egg Sponsors: John and Mary Mattes
12 August 1808	15 May 1809	Mary, daughter of Michael and Elisabeth Gerstweiler Sponsors: John and Frances Gerstweiler
6 December 1808	28 May 1809	Solomon, son of John and Susan Kass Sponsors: John and Eva Shonebruck
27 January 1809	28 May 1809	Philip, son of James and Mary Wagener Sponsors: Joseph and Elisabeth Henrich
12 May 1809	28 May 1809	Sarah, daughter of George and Barbara Shmidt Sponsors: Michael and Mary Shmidt
26 February 1809	11 June 1809	Samuel, son of Peter and Susan Lambert Sponsors: Anthony and Catherine Felix
3 June 1809	11 June 1809	Eva Louise, daughter of George and Catherine Repplier Sponsors: Francis and Eva Eichhorn
8 May 1809	2 July 1809	John, son of John and Juliana Burkop Sponsors: Francis and Catherine Jlain
[?] May 1809	11 June 1809	Christine, daughter of Anthony and M. Madeline Shaefer Sponsors: Lothar and Christine Kapus
20 June 1809	16 July 1809	Mary, daughter of William and Sophia Rohr Sponsors: Joseph Malzberger and Juliana Els
26 July 1809	31 July 1809	Samuel, son of Adam and Madeline Wummer Sponsors: Paul Erntzen and Widow Margaret Arenz
11 June 1809	6 August 1809	James, son of John and Catherine Adam Sponsors: James and Mary Adam
29 June 1809	9 August 1809	Joseph, son of John and Catherine Grett Sponsors: Joseph Kunz and Salome Egg

Date of Birth	Date of Baptism	Names of those baptized
28 July 1809	9 August 1809	Henry, son of Peter and Rosine Bauer Sponsors: Henry and Susan Kass
10 July 1809	13 August 1809	John, son of Philip and Barbara Gruber Sponsors: Sebastian and Catherine Allgayer
28 March 1809	13 August 1809	Mary, daughter of Sebastian and Catherine Kiesel Sponsors: Philip and Susan Reichert
7 July 1809	20 August 1809	Joseph, son of James and Mary Malzberger Sponsors: Joseph Malzberger and Anna Minzen
28 August 1809	10 September 1809	George, son of James and Madeline Keffer Sponsors: George and Catherine Repplier
13 February 1809	10 September 1809	Mary, daughter of George and Anna Keesy Sponsors: Joseph and Frances Walter
18 June 1809	10 September 1809	Madeline Eva, daughter of Philip and Madeline Shmidt Sponsors: Francis and Eva Eichhorn
11 August 1809	17 September 1809	Madeline, daughter of John and Mary Cobele Sponsors: Joseph and Juliana Rohr
18 May 1809	17 September 1809	Margaret, daughter of Patrick and Rachel Hagaty Sponsors: Henry and Elisabeth Coble
2 September 1809	24 September 1809	William, son of James and Susan Shonebruck Sponsors: James Kunz and Margaret Shaut
19 September 1809	24 September 1809	Reuben, son of Andrew and Madeline Shonebruck Sponsors: Henry Harzel and Margaret Shonebruck
30 September 1809	8 October 1809	Daniel, son of George and Barbara Sigfrid Sponsors: Anthony and Catherine Felix
8 September 1808	12 November 1809	Margaret, daughter of John and Catherine Shmidt Sponsors: Henry and Elisabeth Eckenrod
24 October 1809	12 November 1809	Andrew George, son of Francis and Eva Eichhorn Sponsors: Joseph and Margaret Allgayer
27 September 1809	15 November 1809	John, son of Joseph and Christine Lambert Sponsors: John Allgayer and Mary Lambert
15 October 1809	24 December 1809	Joseph, son of John and Elisabeth Coble Sponsors: Joseph Reichert and Anna Dollhauer
26 July 1809	24 December 1809	John, son of John and Susan Els Sponsors: John Bernt and Anna Rohr
12 September 1809	29 October 1809	John, son of Neal and Susan Boyle Sponsors: Thomas and Madeline Dum
4 November 1809	1 January 1810	Elias, son of James and Elisabeth Grett Sponsors: Andrew and Elisabeth Grett

Date of Birth	Date of Baptism	Names of those baptized
5 December 1809	7 January 1810	Henrietta, daughter of Henry and Elisabeth Coblet Sponsors: John and Catherine Coblet
16 October 1809	21 January 1810	Judith, daughter of John and Anna Shnabel Sponsors: Daniel Shnabel and Theresa Grett
22 January 1810	18 February 1810	William, son of John and Philippina Wingart Sponsors: John Reichert and Helen Wingert
25 January 1810	18 February 1810	Mary Rose, daughter of James and Mary Hauss Sponsors: William and Sophia Rohr
16 January 1810	25 February 1810	Anna Mary, daughter of George and Susan Fenstermacher Sponsors: John and Mary Mattes
16 November 1809	26 February 1810	Salome, daughter of James and Madeline Kemp Sponsors: John and Barbara Kemp
	18 March 1810	Henrietta, daughter of John and Elisabeth Sterling Sponsors: Joseph Reichert and [?] Focht
19 January 1810	18 March 1810	Barbara, daughter of Joseph and Mary Shnabel Sponsors: John Egg and Elisabeth Shmidt
2 December 1809	18 March 1810	Daniel, son of James and Elisabeth Gilbert Sponsors: Daniel Shnabel and Catherine Spring
6 January 1806	Baptized the year in which they were born.	John, son of Christopher and Susan Beaver Sponsors:
18 February 1808		Samuel, son of Christopher, as above Sponsors:
18 August 1809		Mary, daughter, as above Sponsors:
29 January 1810	8 April 1810	Anna Margaret, daughter of Joseph and Margaret Ritshi Sponsors: Joseph and Margaret Allgayer
31 December 1809	8 April 1810	Henry, son of James and Barbara Shnabel Sponsors: Christian Eckenrod and Barbara Grett
27 August 1808	October 1808	Margaret, daughter of Ernest and Madeline Klee Sponsors: Michael and Margaret Hartmann
18 September 1809	8 April 1810	Anna Elisabeth, daughter of Ernest and Madeline Klee Sponsors: Michael and Catherine Hartman, cousins
9 April 1810	9 April 1810	Sarah, daughter of Anthony and Catherine Felix Sponsors: Martin and Barbara Felix
11 March 1810	10 April 1810	Catherine, daughter of Joseph and Elisabeth Sigfrid Sponsors: Thomas and Catherine Sigfrid

Date of Birth	Date of Baptism	Names of those baptized
6 January 1810	22 April 1810	Daniel, son of Thomas and Mary Queen Sponsors: Daniel and Mary Anna Coble
[?] March 1810	22 April 1810	Esther, daughter of John and Aloitine Egg Sponsors: John and Catherine Adam
3 January 1810	22 April 1810	Esther, daughter of Anthony and Catherine Reichert Sponsors: John and Barbara Kemp
28 February 1810	22 April 1810	Catherine, daughter of Solomon and Anna Egg Sponsors: John and Charlotte Egg
26 October 1809	23 April 1810	Juliana, daughter of John and Frances Windeler Sponsors: Joseph and Juliana Rohr
1 January 1810	29 April 1810	John, son of George and Margaret Hopp Sponsors: John and Madeline Shlosser
12 February 1810	29 April 1810	James, son of Frederick and Catherine Reninger Sponsors: Andrew and Madeline Hopp
17 February 1810	29 April 1810	Susan, daughter of John and Mary Neuer Sponsors: Philip and Susan Reichert
2 February 1810	29 April 1810	Benjamin, son of James and Elisabeth Zweyer Sponsors: Thomas and Madeline Dum
26 February 1810	6 May 1810	Esther, daughter of Andrew and Sarah Shindler Sponsors: Daniel Shnabel and Susan Kunz
28 March 1810	13 May 1810	Mary, daughter of Michael and Esther Grett Sponsors: James Grett and Mary Felix
22 November 1809	13 May 1810	John, son of John and Madeline Sauvert Sponsor: Philip Sauvert
27 February 1810	13 May 1810	Helen, daughter of Adam and Susan Huver Sponsors: James and Dorothy Lambert
17 April 1791	13 May 1810	Elisabeth, daughter of Jonathan and Helen Benton, non-Catholics Sponsors: Adam and Susan Huver
	13 May 1810	Elisabeth, daughter of Daniel and Elisabeth Grett Sponsor: Catherine Kiesel
9 December 1809	14 May 1810	William Adam, son of Bernard and Elisabeth Hart Sponsors: Adam and Barbara Zweyer
15 February 1810	14 May 1810	Mary Casa, daughter of Daniel and Mary Angst Sponsors: David and Juliana Stewart
9 May 1810	10 June 1810	Joseph, son of John and Barbara Kunz Sponsors: Joseph Kunz and Appollonia Bock
15 June 1810	15 July 1810	John James, son of Peter and Catherine Sebold Sponsors: James and Mary Els
22 July 1810	5 August 1810	Mary Madeline, daughter of Daniel and Salome Grett Sponsors: John and Elisabeth Grett

Date of Birth	Date of Baptism	Names of those baptized
29 June 1810	12 August 1810	Margaret, daughter of John and Anna Ganss Sponsors: Peter and Barbara Katzenmeyer
3 August 1810	12 August 1810	Louise, daughter of Joseph and Margaret All-gayer Sponsors: George and Catherine Repplier
12 June 1810	14 August 1810	Reuben, son of David and Juliana Stewart Sponsor: Joseph Zweyer
4 August 1810	19 August 1810	Margaret, daughter of Valentine and Madeline Dum Sponsors: Adam and Eva Reichert
2 June 1810	19 August 1810	David, son of Nicholas and Elisabeth Shweyer Sponsors: John Henrich and Madeline Burgy
5 July 1810	19 August 1810	Peter, son of Peter and Elisabeth Shimpfessel Sponsors: John Grett and Elisabeth Reichert
11 August 1810	23 August 1810	James, son of Michael and Margaret Shnabel Sponsors: Peter and Madeline Egg
9 June 1810	2 September 1810	Anna, daughter of James and Susan Rohrbach Sponsors: James Jlain and Mary Kemp
1 May 1810	9 September 1810	Juliana, daughter of John and Catherine Shmidt Sponsors: James and Dorothy Lambert
16 August 1810	9 September 1810	Elisabeth, daughter of John and Susan Bott Sponsor: Elisabeth Gibson
17 March 1810	9 September 1810	James, son of John and Susan Wennerich, non-Catholics Sponsors: James and Catherine Bott
13 September 1810	30 September 1810	Madeline, daughter of Adam and Madeline Wummer Sponsors: George Arens and Anna M. Lambert
20 August 1810	30 September 1810	Anna, daughter of John and Barbara Beaver Sponsors: John Henrich and Susan Grett
10 August 1810	7 October 1810	Elisabeth, daughter of Joseph and Catherine Burkard Sponsors: Henry and Elisabeth Covely
28 September 1810	8 October 1810	Joseph, son of Nicholas and Margaret Kass Sponsors: Joseph Kunz and Mary Kass
10 September 1810	1 November 1810	Thomas, son of Martin and Mary Gery Sponsors: John and Barbara Kemp
16 October 1810	18 November 1810	Litta, daughter of Caspar and Susan Shmidt Sponsors: Christian and Catherine Clemmer
17 September 1810	25 November 1810	John George, son of John and Susan Kass Sponsors: George Kunz and Margaret Kass
17 October 1810	25 November 1810	James, son of Michael and Mary Shmidt Sponsors: James and Margaret Hagenbuch
2 November 1810	9 December 1810	Joseph, son of Anthony and M. Madeline Shaefer Sponsors: Joseph Rochol and Eva Felix

236

Date of Birth	Date of Baptism	Names of those baptized
12 October 1810	9 December 1810	Samuel, son of George and Madeline Ganss Sponsors: Anthony and M. Madeline Shaefer
28 October 1810	9 December 1810	Michael, son of John and Susan Keffer Sponsors: Michael Hartman and Susan Keffer
1 November 1810	9 December 1810	Frederica, daughter of Frederick and Catherine Shmidt Sponsors: William and Anna Minzen
26 October 1810	9 December 1810	Anthony, son of James and Madeline Keffer Sponsors: Anthony and Catherine Felix
6 December 1810	22 December 1810	Reuben, son of Peter and Rosine Bauer Sponsors: Peter Egg and Margaret Shnabel
14 November 1810	26 December 1810	Esther, daughter of Philip and Elisabeth Grett Sponsors: Peter and Catherine Hunsberger
14 December 1810	30 December	John, son of Henry and Catherine Gibson Sponsors: John and Mary Kass
24 November	30 December 1810	Susan, daughter of John and Mary Kass Sponsors: Joseph and Mary Burgy
	18 January 1811	Rachel, daughter of William and Catherine Traut Sponsors: Adam and Barbara Zweyer
23 December 1810	20 January 1811	Angela, daughter of William and Sophia Rohr Sponsors: John and Elisabeth Els
22 December 1810	20 January 1811	Mechtilde, daughter of Peter and Christine Erb Sponsors: Michael Grett and Salome Kunz
2 December 1810	3 February 1811	Reuben, son of Augustine and Anna Reichert Sponsors: Joseph and Juliana Rohr
30 January 1811	22 February 1811	Salome, daughter of John and Mary Egg Sponsors: Daniel and Salome Grett
26 February 1811	6 March 1811	James, son of Peter and Catherine Hunsberger Sponsors: James Vaughen and Theresa Grett
4 January 1811	11 March 1811	David James, son of Joseph and Christine Gibson Sponsors: James Vaughen and Catherine Gibson
	17 March 1811	Elizabeth, 21 years old, daughter of Balthasar and Madeline Meister, non-Catholics Sponsors: John and Catherine Kunss
21 March 1811	24 [March] [1811]	Philip, son of Joseph and Elisabeth Henrich Sponsors: Philip and Elisabeth Henrich
21 February 1811	31 March 1811	Anna Mary, daughter of Philip and Susan Reichert Sponsor: Anna Mary Lambert
15 February 1811	3 April 1811	Salome, daughter of Daniel and M. Margaret Egg Sponsors: Henry and Susan Kass
25 January 1811	14 April 1811	Charles, son of Matthias and Elisabeth Kass Sponsors: John and Barbara Kunss

Date of Birth	Date of Baptism	Names of those baptized
28 February 1811	15 April 1811	Judith, daughter of Joseph and Elisabeth Kunss Sponsors: John and Barbara Kunss
3 January 1811	15 April 1811	Helen, daughter of Henry and Barbara Doll-hauer Sponsors: Michael Grett and Barbara Reppert
18 February 1811	21 April 1811	William, son of Ernest and Madeline Clee Sponsors: Charles Clee and Eva Felix
2 March 1811	21 April 1811	Mary, daughter of Michael and Elisabeth Felix Sponsors: John Henrich and Mary Felix
13 April 1811	21 April 1811	Theresa Margaret, daughter of George and Catherine Repplier Sponsors: Joseph and Margaret Allgayer
20 April 1811	24 April 1811	Rachel, daughter of Peter and Madeline Egg Sponsors: Aegidius Bauer and Mary Kass
30 March 1811	12 May 1811	Anna Elisabeth, daughter of Henry and Elisabeth Eckenrod Sponsors: Francis and Elisabeth Eckenrod
3 February 1811	16 May 1811	Anna, daughter of James and Agatha Eisenhauer Sponsors: John and Justine Albrecht
12 May 1811	2 June 1811	Sarah, daughter of Christian and Catherine Clemmer Sponsors: John Adam and his wife, Catherine
28 April 1811	2 June 1811	Martha, daughter of John and Barbara Kemp Sponsors: John Hartman and Madeline Jlain
8 May 1811	30 June 1811	Anna, daughter of John and Madeline Shlosser Sponsors: Joseph and Christina Gibson
3 June 1811	30 June 1811	James,, son of Neal and Susan Boyle Sponsors: John Grett and Mary Dum
14 April 1811	7 July 1811	Sophia, daughter of Frederick and Elisabeth Muller Sponsors: John and Elisaoeth Grett
9 June 1811	14 July 1811	Sarah, daughter of John and Elisabeth Ruttner Sponsors: Anthony Merten and Eva Felix
29 May 1811	16 July 1811	Twins, children of James and Madeline Kemp, conditionally baptized Sponsors: for John: George and Elizabeth Kemp for James: James and Susan Rohrbach
9 June 1811	21 July 1811	Francis, son of Patrick and Rachel Hagety Sponsors: Andrew Shindler and Catherine Covely
12 May 1811	28 July 1811	Mary, daughter of Bernard and Catherine M'Manus Sponsors: Michael and Barbara Shmidt
10 July 1811	15 August 1811	Aaron, son of John and Mary Covely Sponsors: Bartholomew and Elisabeth Covely
19 October 1810	8 September 1811	John, son of Henry and Catherine Lehmon Sponsors: Anthony and Eva Martin

Date of Birth	Date of Baptism	Names of those baptized
17 March	8 September 1811	Francis, son of John and Elisabeth Huver Sponsors: Adam and Susan Huver
17 July 1811	9 September 1811	John Paul, son of Daniel and Elisabeth Grett Sponsors: P. Erntzen and Widow Elisabeth Shmidt
11 April 1811	9 September 1811	Catherine, daughter of Benjamin Hanss and Elisabeth Obold Sponsors: Joseph and Margaret Obold
11 August 1811	15 September 1811	James, son of James and Mary Els Sponsors: James Jlain and Elisabeth Reichert
9 August 1811	15 September 1811	Louis, son of Joseph and Mary Bachman Sponsors: John and Philippina Wingart
21 August 1811	15 September 1811	Litta, daughter of Andrew and Elisabeth Kunss Sponsors: Simon Adam and Elisabeth Shmidt
3 September 1811	15 September 1811	John James, son of James and Mary Hanss Sponsors: John and Barbara Kunss
9 August 1811	6 October 1811	Mary Anna, daughter of John and Catherine Grett Sponsors: John and Elisabeth Grett
1 October 1811	14 October 1811	Mary, daughter of Joseph and Elisabeth Sigfrid Sponsors: Nicholas and Anna Mary Felix
8 September 1811	1 November 1811	Mary, daughter of Andrew and Sarah Shindler Sponsors: James Vaughen and Theresa Grett
14 September 1811	1 November 1811	Catherine, daughter of John and Susan Shell Sponsors: John and Catherine Kunss
31 October 1811	8 November 1811	Salome, daughter of George and Elisabeth Kemp Sponsors: John and Barbara Kemp
10 August 1811	9 November 1811	John, son of Bernard and Elisabeth Hart Sponsors: James and Agatha Eisenhauer
3 October 1811	10 November 1811	Margaret, daughter of James and Barbara Shnabel Sponsors: Charles Clee and Barbara Reppert
1 April 1811	10 November 1811	Elisabeth, daughter of William and Mary Ganss Sponsors: Michael and Elisabeth Hartman
22 September 1811	11 November 1811	William, son of Peter and Susan Lambert Sponsors: James and Dorothy Lambert
19 September 1811	17 November 1811	Twins, children of Joseph and Christina Lambert Sponsors: for Anna: James and Dorothy Lambert for Elisabeth: Peter and Susan Lambert
21 September 1811	17 November 1811	John, son of John and Catherine Reppert Sponsors: Stephen and Madeline Reppert
10 November 1811	9 December 1811	Michael, son of Michael and Esther Grett Sponsors: Michael and Catherine Grett
29 July 1811	11 August 1811	Catherine, daughter of Joseph and Margaret Sigfrid Sponsors: John Allgayer and Catherine Sigfrid

Document

The Goshenhoppen Registers, Fifth Series

Baptisms, 1812-1814

Date of Birth	Date of Baptism	Names of Those Baptized
19 December 1811	12 January 1812	John Anthony Nicholas, son of Anthony and Catherine Felix Sponsors: Anthony and Eva Martin
1 November 1811	2 February 1812	Ferdinand, son of William and Anna Covely Sponsors: Andrew and Sarah Shindler
7 January 1809	2 February 1812	Mary, daughter of William and Anna Covely Sponsors: Joseph and Mary Bachmann
31 December 1811	16 February 1812	Mary Catherine, daughter of Henry and Elisabeth Covely Sponsors: Daniel and Mary Anna Covely
14 December 1811	12 January 1812	Anna Elisabeth, daughter of Joseph and Margaret Rutshi Sponsor: Anna Shaffner
9 years old	9 March 1812	Mary, daughter of John and Mary Mintz, Non-Catholic Sponsor: Anna Minzer
1 October 1810	9 March 1812	Englebert, son of William and Sarah Minzer Sponsors: George Leaf and Mary Jones
13 February 1812	22 March 1812	Juliana, daughter of John and Philippina Wingart Sponsors: John and Elisabeth Covely
14 February 1812	29 March 1812	Sophia, daughter of Anthony and Catherine Reichert Sponsors: Joseph and Mary Kemp
6 March 1812	29 March 1812	John, son of John and Elisabeth Sterling Sponsors: John and Mary Covely
23 December 1811	5 April 1812	Anna Mary, daughter of John and Catherine Burgy Sponsors: Joseph and Anna Mary Burgy
4 October 1811	5 April 1812	Salome, daughter of Andrew and Salome Byrner Sponsors: John and Mary Kass
30 December 1811	5 April 1812	Solomon, son of James and Elisabeth Zweyer Sponsors: James and Juliana Dum
22 December 1811	7 April 1812	Salome, daughter of Frederick and Catherine Reninger Sponsors: Thomas and Anna Dum
28 December 1811	9 April 1812	Litta, daughter of David and Juliana Stewart Sponsor: Elisabeth Hart
6 March 1812	10 April 1812	John, son of Philip and Madeline Shmidt Sponsors: Paul Erntzen and Elisabeth Shmid, widow

Date of Birth	Date of Baptism	Names of Those Baptized
2 February 1812	10 April 1812	Sarah, daughter of Sebastian and Catherine Kiesel Sponsors: P. Erntzen and Anna Mary Lambert
5 April 1812	13 April 1812	Catherine, daughter of Anthony and Eva Martin Sponsors: James Felix and Anna Felix (cousins)
28 March 1812	13 April 1812	Louise, daughter of John and Francis Windeler Sponsors: John Allgayer and Salome Rohr
8 March 1812	3 May 1812	Joseph, son of Joseph and Eva Wingart Sponsors: Joseph and Catherine Burkard
23 February 1812	7 May 1812	Ruben, son of Henry and Margaret Harzel Sponsors: Caspar and Margaret Shonebruck
11 March 1812	10 May 1812	Eleanor, daughter of John and Susan Keffer Sponsors: James and Catherine Hartmann
6 December 1811	31 May 1812	Judith, daughter of Christian and Margaret Stahler Sponsors: Adam Reichert and Catherine Spring
14 April 1812	31 May 1812	John, son of John and Mary Neuer Sponsors: John Shnabel and Rosina Reichert
26 April 1812	31 May 1812	Madeline, daughter of Valentine and Madeline Dum Sponsors: Andrew and Madeline Hopp
20 September 1811	31 May 1812	Catherine, daughter of Daniel and Mary Angst Sponsors: Thomas and Catherine Zweyer
3 April 1812	31 May 1812	Louis, son of Joseph and Rebecca Flower Sponsors: George and Margaret Hopp
18 May 1812	31 May 1812	Anthony, son of George and Margaret Hopp Sponsors: Adam and Madeline Wummer
	31 May 1812	Rebecca, daughter of Henry and Dina Mayer, Non-Catholics, age 20 Sponsors: Francis and Catherine Hopp
20 May 1812	2 June 1812	Susan, daughter of George and Susan Fenstermacher Sponsors: Henry and Susan Kass
21 May 1812	11 June 1812	Mary Barbara, daughter of John and Mary B. Kunss Sponsors: George and Elisabeth Kunss
18 April 1812	14 June 1812	John, son of Joseph and Catherine Mohr Sponsors: John Eckenrod and Anna Felix
9 December 1812	14 June 1812	Mary, daughter of James and Susan Shlosser Sponsors: Francis and Elisabeth Hartmann
7 May 1812	14 June 1812	Elisabeth, daughter of James and Elisabeth Becker Sponsors: Thomas and Catherine Zweyer
13 May 1812	14 June 1812	Mary, daughter of Francis and Eva Eichorn Sponsors: Paul Erntzen and Mary Leckis

Date of Birth	Date of Baptism	Names of Those Baptized
28 May 1812	5 June 1812	Isaac, son of Thomas and Mary Queen Sponsors: Joseph Rohr and Mary M'Farthy
3 June 1812	12 July 1812	Catherine, daughter of Ernest and Madeline Klee Sponsors: James and Catherine Hartmann
30 April 1812	12 July 1812	Elisabeth, daughter of Adam and Susan Huver Sponsor: Eva Fricker
18 June 1812	17 July 1812	Juliana, daughter of Peter and Christine Erb Sponsors: P. Erntzen and Juliana Kunss
7 August 1812	9 August 1812	Twins of George and Barbara Sigfrid Sponsors: (for Salome) James Felix and Catherine Rohr, (for Mary) the godmother was Mary Felix
3 June 1812	30 August 1812	John, son of John and Barbara Beaver Sponsors: Philip and Elisabeth Henrich
31 July 1812	13 September 1812	Salome, daughter of Christian and Elisabeth Eckenrod Sponsors: James Grett and Barbara Eckenrod
12 August 1812	20 September 1812	John, son of John and Elisabeth Coblet Sponsors: James and Mary Els
20 September 1812	1 November 1812	Henrietta, daughter of Maurice and Catherine Budde Sponsors: Anthony Shorp and Catherine Shmidt
24 September 1812	1 November 1812	Margaret, daughter of John and Mary Egg Sponsors: Joseph Egg and Mary Bauer
14 September 1812	15 November 1812	John, son of Solomon and Anna Egg Sponsors: John and Caroline Egg
21 September 1812	29 November 1812	Anna, daughter of James and Juliana Dum Sponsors: Andrew Grett and Mary Dum
1 September 1812	11 October 1812	Catherine, daughter of Michael and Elisabeth Hart Sponsors: Charles Clee and Catherine Hartmann
28 November 1812	13 December 1812	Rebecca, daughter of Charles and Madeline Sigfrid Sponsors: James Felix and Barbara Sigfrid
20 November 1812	13 December 1812	John George, son of George and Catherine Repplier Sponsors: John and Mary Allgayer
1 November 1812	26 December 1812	Elias, son of Augustine and Anna Reichert Sponsors: Joseph Keffer and Elisabeth Reichert
4 January 1813	8 January 1813	Judith, daughter of Philip and Elisabeth Grett Sponsors: Peter Egg and Judith Grosskopp
31 December 1812	13 January 1813	Joseph, son of John and Anna Covely Sponsors: Joseph Bachman and Mary Fort
31 December 1812	8 March 1813	Anna, daughter of Daniel and M. Margaret Eck Sponsors: Peter and Madeline Eck

Date of Birth	Date of Baptism	Names of Those Baptized
8 March 1813	9 March 1813	Anna Rachel, daughter of James and Mary Hauss Sponsors: John and A. Elisabeth Els
[?] December 1812	21 March 1813	Mary Anna, daughter of John and Anna Ganss Sponsors: Louis and Barbara Katzenmayer
13 December 1812	21 March 1813	Henry, son of Simon and Elisabeth Seifert Sponsors: Francis and Eva Eichhorn
19 March 1813	22 March 1813	Sarah Anna, daughter of Frederick and Catherine Shmidt Sponsor: Anna Mintzen
5 March 1812	23 March 1813	Elisabeth, daughter of William and Catherine Traut Sponsors: James Sigfrid and Elisabeth Hart
26 February 1813	23 March 1813	Anna, daughter of Thomas and Catherine Zweyer Sponsors: Andrew and Madeline Hopp
7 December 1811	24 March 1813	David, son of James and Elisabeth Gilbert Sponsors: Joseph and Anna Mary Shnabel
23 February 1813	26 March 1813	Henry, son of William and Sarah Minzen Sponsors: Henry Missimer and Sarah Jones
1 February 1813	26 March 1813	Anna Mary, daughter of James and Mary Malzberger Sponsor: Catherine Malzberger
11 March 1813	27 March 1813	Juliana, daughter of Anthony and Sarah Rufner Sponsors: Paul Erntzen and Barbara M'Dowel
9 December 1812	4 April 1813	Michael, son of Samuel and Susan Hartmann Sponsors: Michael and Catherine Grett
13 April 1813	20 April 1813	John, son of Peter and Madeline Egg Sponsors: John and Eva Egg (grandparents)
11 April 1813	20 April 1813	Elisabeth, daughter of James and Madeline Kemp Sponsors: John Rohrbach and Mary Madeline Kemp
12 April 1813	16 May 1813	Elisabeth, daughter of Nicholas and Margaret Kass Sponsors: John and Elisabeth Walker
18 February 1813	22 May 1813	Anna Mary, daughter of Benjamin and Elisabeth Haass Sponsor: Catherine Obold
25 February 1813	23 May 1813	Anthony, son of Joseph and Margaret Sigfrid Sponsors: Anthony and Eva Martin
7 January 1813	24 May 1813	Rebecca, daughter of Michael and Elisabeth Felix Sponsors: George and Barbara Sigfrid
16 January 1813	30 May 1813	John, son of Andrew and Esther Grett Sponsors: John Becker and Susan Grett
25 October 1812	30 May 1813	Elisabeth, daughter of John Nicholas Zweyer and Elisabeth Zweyer Sponsors: Philip and Elisabeth Henrich

Date of Birth	Date of Baptism	Names of Those Baptized
30 May	1 June 1813	George, son of Neal and Susan Boyle Sponsors: George Arenz and Elisabeth D. Seifert
21 May	2 June 1813	Henrietta, daughter of James and Susan Rohrbach Sponsors: James and Madeline Kemp
22 December 1812	6 June 1813	Aaron, son of John and Albertine Egg Sponsors: Nicholas Hammerstein and Margaret Miller
25 April 1813	6 June 1813	John William, son of James and Mary Els Sponsors: John and Elisabeth Els
5 May 1813	13 June 1813	Daniel, son of George and Catherine Binder Sponsors: Martin and Barbara Felix
	4 July 1813	Sarah Anna, daughter of Andrew and Sarah Shindler Sponsors: Joseph Bachmann and Brigid Sweetmann
18 June 1813	11 July 1813	William, son of Anthony and Catherine Felix Sponsors: George and Barbara Sigfrid
16 June 1813	12 July 1813	John, son of John and Barbara Ebert Sponsors: Andrew and Margaret Shimfessel
12 February 1813	8 August 1813	Anna, daughter of William and Madeline Ganss Sponsors: Charles Clee and Anna Felix
30 May 1813	8 August 1813	Madeline, daughter of Daniel and Elisabeth Grett Sponsors: Adam and Madeline Wummer
1 August 1812	15 August 1813	Litta, daughter of Philip and Barbara Gruber[8] Sponsors: Henry and Elisabeth Covely
24 July 1813	29 August 1813	Andrew, son of Andrew and Sarah Byrns Sponsors: Thomas and Madeline Dum
15 October 1812	12 September 1813	Susan, daughter of John and Susan Kass Sponsors: John Kunss and Elisabeth Kass
	15 September 1813	Shedericus, son of Abraham and Mary Green[9] Sponsor: Catherine Reichert
14 August 1813	19 September 1813	David, son of Joseph and Mary Bachmann Sponsors: Henry and Elisabeth Covely
11 September 1813	19 September 1813	Elisabeth, daughter of John and Barbara Kemp Sponsors: Charles and Elisabeth Rohr
9 September 1813	1 October 1813	Nathan, son of Peter and Rosina Bauer Sponsors: Paul Erntzen and Mary Bauer
4 September 1813	8 October 1813	Anna, daughter of Michael and Margaret Shnabel Sponsors: Joseph Egg and Mary Shnabel
26 September 1813	10 October 1813	Edward, son of Anthony and Eva Merten Sponsors: James Felix and Catherine Rohr

---

8 Supplevi omissa super Littam, filiam, etc. The priest baptizing notes that he supplied at this date everything omitted from the baptism given in danger of death earlier.

9 Sedeur from the Book of Numbers may have been a biblical name used at this time.

Date of Birth	Date of Baptism	Names of Those Baptized
7 September 1813	10 October 1813	Mary, daughter of John and Elisabeth Rittner Sponsors: James and Mary Roger
7 February 1813	10 October 1813	Margaret, daughter of George and Anna Keesy Sponsors: John and Mary Allgayer
15 September 1813	10 October 1813	Edward, son of William and Sophia Rohr Sponsors: Joseph and Margaret Allgayer
7 August 1813	10 October 1813	Mary, daughter of John and Mary Kass Sponsors: Anthony and Catherine Felix
1 August 1813	10 October 1813	Juliana, daughter of John and Barbara Beaver Sponsors: Michael Hartman and Mary Arentz
13 July 1813	10 October 1813	Ernest, son of Ernest and Madeline Clee Sponsors: Michael and Elisabeth Hartmann
31 October 1812	11 October 1813	Thomas, son of John and Elisabeth Bryan Sponsors: Christian and Elisabeth Eckenrod
6 September 1811	11 October 1813	Elisabeth, daughter of George and Mary Fuchs Sponsors: Joseph and Catherine Mohr
9 September 1813	15 October 1813	Sarah, daughter of John and Catherine Grett Sponsors: John George Spring and Catherine Shmid
27 October 1813	30 October 1813	Anna, daughter of James and Elisabeth Zweyer Sponsors: Thomas and Anna Dum
3 July 1813	31 October 1813	Anna, daughter of Christopher and Anna Beaver Sponsors: James and Madeline Kass
17 September 1813	7 November 1813	Margaret, daughter of Anthony and Catherine Reichert Sponsors: Joseph and Catherine Burkard
2 October 1813	7 November 1813	John, son of Andrew and Elisabeth Kunss Sponsors: John and Catherine Kunss
[?] September 1813	21 [?] 1813	Sarah, daughter of Joseph and Eva Reppert Sponsors: Joseph Kemp and Mary Reppert
[?] November 1813	5 December 1813	John, son of John and Elisabeth Waker Sponsors: Daniel Shnabel and Therese Kunss
3 November 1813	12 December 1813	Justus, son of Joseph and Elisabeth Sigfrid Sponsors: James Felix and Elisabeth Shmidt
25 October 1813	12 December 1813	Litta, daughter of James and Barbara Shnabel Sponsors: Joseph Keffer and Elisabeth Reppert
6 August 1813	11 December 1813	Bernard, son of Bernard and Elisabeth Hart Sponsors: James Sigfrid and Mary Zweyer
2 November 1813	13 December 1813	Adam, son of Adam and Madeline Wummer Sponsors: Philip and Madeline Shmidt
19 November 1813	26 December 1813	Daniel, son of John and Philippina Wingert Sponsors: John Jlain and Mary M'Farthy.
[?] October 1813	24 January 1813	John Joseph, son of John and Madeline Shlosser Sponsor: Joseph Shlosser (Grandparent)
3 January 1814	20 February 1814	Catherine, daughter of Christian and Catherine Clemmer Sponsors: James Jlain and Sarah Kemp

245

Date of Birth	Date of Baptism	Names of Those Baptized
28 February 1814	11 March 1814	Mary Dorothy, daughter of Joseph and Margaret Allgayer Sponsors: John and Mary Allgayer
27 January 1814	18 March 1814	Elisabeth, daughter of John and Susan Keffer Sponsors: Michael and Elisabeth Hartmann
20 February 1814	18 March 1814	James, son of James and Susan Shlosser Sponsors: James and Catherine Hartmann
5 February 1814	20 March 1814	Litta, daughter of John and Theresa Glassmeier Sponsors: Daniel and Margaret Egg
27 February 1814	20 March 1814	John, son of Peter and Christine Erb Sponsors: John Kuhnss and Catherine Adam
16 February 1814	20 March 1814	Anthony, son of M. Budde and Catherine Sponsors: Anthony and Catherine Shorp
1 February 1814	27 March 1814	James, son of John and Mary Neuer Sponsors: John and Anna Shnabel
[?] December 1813	28 March 1814	Anna, daughter of James and Elisabeth Becker Sponsors: Joseph and Madeline Becker
24 March 1814	28 March 1814	Thomas, son of James and Juliana Dum Sponsors: Thomas and Madeline Dum
8 February 1814	16 April 1814	Joseph, son of Joseph and Christine Lambert Sponsors: Joseph and Margaret Allgayer
12 December 1813	17 April 1814	Esther, daughter of Michael and Esther Grett Sponsors: Ernest and Madeline Clee
1 December 1813	17 April 1814	Henry, son of Christian and Elisabeth Eckenrod Sponsors: Henry and Mary Hartmann
22 February 1814	17 April 1814	Joseph, son of George and Barbara Eyerson Sponsors: Joseph Keffer and Mary Eckenrod
19 March 1814	17 April 1814	Sarah Anna, daughter of James and Mary Roger Sponsor: Mary Leckis
5 November 1813	1 May 1814	Mechtilde, daughter of James and Elisabeth Gilbert Sponsors: Joseph Rohr and Mary Shnabel
29 March 1814	11 May 1814	Sarah, daughter of John and Madeline Seifert Sponsor: Madeline Seifert
11 February 1814	18 May 1814	Joseph, son of John and Elisabeth Sterling Sponsors: Joseph and Elisabeth Shindler
20 January 1814	18 May 1814	John, son of Joseph and Elisabeth Shindler Sponsors: George and Anna Keesy
30 March 1814	22 May 1814	Elisabeth, daughter of John and Catherine Burgy Sponsors: Philip and Elisabeth Henrich
[?] April 1814	22 May 1814	Andrew, son of Joseph and Madeline Seifert Sponsors: Andrew and Madeline Hopp
27 April 1814	30 May 1814	John, son of John and Catherine Adam Sponsors: John and Barbara Kemp
[28?] March 1814	29 May 1814	Louis, son of William and Anna M. Gobele Sponsors: John B. and Mary Gobele

Date of Birth	Date of Baptism	Names of Those Baptized
9 May 1814	12 June 1814	Mary, daughter of William and Catherine Fricker Sponsor: Eva Fricker
21 April 1814	12 June 1814	Elisabeth, daughter of Peter and Sarah Rittner Sponsors: Peter and Barbara Rittner
[?] June 1814	29 June 1814	Sarah, daughter of John and Susan Shell Sponsor: Salome Kuhns
[?] June 1814	31 July 1814	Catherine, daughter of Nicholas and Elisabeth Shweyer Sponsors: Joseph and Elisabeth Henrich
23 June 1814	4 September 1814	Charles, son of John and Mary Egg Sponsors: John and Catherine Grett
[?] May 1814	11 September 1814	Anna, daughter of Michael and Elisabeth Keech Sponsors: James Walter and Mary Shindler
27 February 1814	23 September 1814	Mary, daughter of James and Mary Adam Sponsors: Daniel and Catherine Shnabel
[?] September 1814	5 October 1814	Samuel, son of Jonathan and Mary Grosskopp Sponsors: Michael and Margaret Shnabel
[?] September 1814	6 October 1814	Mary, daughter of William and Catherine Traut Sponsors: Joseph Zweyer and Mary Kass
[?] July 1814	9 October 1814	Henry, son of Joseph and Eva Wingart Sponsors: Philip and Barbara Gruber
[?] September 1814	30 October 1814	Sarah, daughter of Andrew and Esther Grett Sponsors: Thomas and Anna Dum
[?] September 1814	1 November 1814	John, son of Henry and Elisabeth Covely Sponsors: John and Elisabeth Covely
18 April 1810	2 December 1814	Anthony, son of Anthony and Catherine Shutt Charles, born 6 March 1814 Sponsors: (for Anthony) Adam and Barbara Zweyer (For Charles) Henry and Susan Kass
1 December 1814	18 December 1814	Twins of John and Barbara Kemp Sponsors: (for Edward) John Clemmer and Elisabeth Reichert (For Aaron) Bartholomew and Elisabeth Coblet
12 November 1814	18 December 1814	Mary Anna, daughter of George and Elisabeth Kuntz Sponsors: James Jlain and Susan Shmidt
8 June 1814	18 December 1814	Joseph, son of Joseph and Eva Reppert Sponsors: Joseph and Catherine Burkard

Document

The Goshenhoppen Registers; Fifth Series

Baptisms, 1815-1819

Date of Birth	Date of Baptism	Names of Those Baptized
30 December 1814	6 April 1815	Anna, daughter of James and Madeline Kemp Sponsor: Anna Christina Kemp, widow.
5 September 1814	26 March 1815	William, son of Thomas and Elisabeth York, Non-Catholic Sponsors: John and Barbara Kemp
20 March 1814	9 April 1815	Caroline, daughter of Simon and Elisabeth Seifert Sponsors: William and Sophia Rohr
29 March 1815	12 April 1815	Philip, posthumus son of Philip and Madeline Shmidt Sponsors: Andrew Grett and Catherine Obold[10]
5 February 1815	13 April 1815	Henrietta, daughter of Anthony and Eva Martin Sponsor: Eva Fricker
12 March 1815	15 April 1815	David, son of James and Madeline Kass Sponsors: James and Barbara Kass
14 April 1815	15 April 1815	Lita, daughter of Peter and Madeline Egg Sponsors: James and Madeline Kass
24 December 1814	15 May 1815	Michael, son of Abraham and Mary Hofman Sponsors: Daniel Coblet and his wife
18 April 1815	30 April 1815	Solomon, son of Valentine and Madeline Dum Sponsors: George and Margaret Hopp
24 April 1815	2 May 1815	Mary, daughter of Philip and Elisabeth Grett Sponsor: Mary Kass
16 January 1815	14 May 1815	Samuel, son of John and Albertine Egg Sponsors: Anthony and Catherine Shorp
27 March 1815	14 May 1815	Sophia, daughter of James and Mary Els Sponsors: William and Sophia Rohr
16 April 1815	14 May 1815	William, son of John and Elisabeth Cobele Sponsors: Joseph and Catherine Burkard
18 March 1815	14 May 1815	Henry, son of Joseph and Catherine Burkard Sponsors: John and Philippina Wingert
9 March 1815	21 May 1815	Mechtilde, daughter of Ernest and Madeline Clee Sponsors: John Hartmann and Henrietta Bruckman
12 April 1815	21 May 1815	Anna Christine, daughter of George and Catherine Binder Sponsors: Michael Hartmann and Sophia Binder

10 Priest baptizing notes that he supplied the Ceremonies of Baptism at this time. It appears that baptism was given on the date of birth, 29 March 1815.

Date of Birth	Date of Baptism	Names of Those Baptized
12 May 1815	21 May 1815	Theresa, daughter of Francis and Eva Eickhorn Sponsors: Martin and Barbara Felix
25 April 1815	21 May 1815	Joseph Mark, son of George and Catherine Repplier Sponsors: Joseph and Margaret Allgayer
14 November 1813	22 May 1815	Joseph, son of John D. and Rachel Kruger Sponsors: Anthony and Eva Merten
1 May 1815	22 May 1815	Clara, daughter of Michael and Elisabeth Hart[mann] Sponsors: James and Catherine Hartmann
15 April 1815	25 May 1815	Caroline, daughter of Andrew and Sarah Shindler Sponsors: Joseph Bachman and Mary Coble
23 May [?]	4 June 1815	Eleanor, daughter of Charles and Elisabeth Rohr Sponsors: John Clemmer and Sarah Rohr
27 October 1814	11 June 1815	William, son of John and Anna Ganss Sponsors: Sebastion and Catherine Allgayer
26 May [?]	11 June 1815	James Sebastian, son of Joseph and Margaret Allgayer Sponsors: John Lambert and Anna M. Allgayer
5 May 1815	12 June 1815	Nelly Anna, daughter of Adam and Esther Kreisher Sponsors: Joseph Keffer and Nelly Rodenburger
12 March 1815	6 July 1815	Mary, daughter of William and Sarah Minzen Sponsor: Anna Minzen
15 June 1815	9 July 1815	Catherine, daughter of Anthony and Catherine Felix Sponsors: James Felix and Catherine Reichert
3 October 1812	24 October 1812	Elisabeth, daughter of James and Elisabeth Conrad Sponsors: George and Anna Tutt
June 1815	24 July 1815	Anna, daughter of Daniel and Elisabeth Reinzel Sponsors: James and Mary Arentz
9 October 1814	25 July 1815	John, son of George and Anna Keesy Sponsors: John and Elisabeth Sterling
19 July 1815	30 July 1815	Anna, daughter of John and Mary Never Sponsors: James and Elisabeth Becker
28 May 1815	6 August 1815	Enoch, son of Augustine and Anna Reichert Sponsors: Joseph Rohr and Elisabeth Rohrback
	20 August 1815	Henry, son of Andrew and Elisabeth Kuhns Sponsors: Lawrence Illein and Juliana Kuhns
8 May 1815	20 August 1815	Anna, daughter of Solomon and Anna Egg Sponsors: Joseph and Mary Glassmayer
Age 19	10 September 1815	Sarah, daughter of Job and Anna Harvey, Non-Catholics Sponsors: Ernest and Christine Clee

Date of Birth	Date of Baptism	Names of Those Baptized
20 August 1815	10 September 1815	Sarah, daughter of Samuel and Susan Hartman Sponsors: Michael Hartman and Catherine Hartman
11 September 1815	15 October 1815	Mary Anna, daughter of John and Margaret Shnabel Sponsors: Joseph Shnabel and Judith Miller
13 July 1815	29 October 1815	Elias, son of John and Barbara Beaver Sponsors: James and Mary Arentz
20 September 1815	12 November 1815	Sarah, daughter of James and Barbara Shnabel Sponsors: James and Mary Roger
10 October 1815	12 November 1815	Uriah, son of William and Sophia Rohr Sponsors: Simon and Elisabeth Seifert
11 November 1815	14 November 1815	Catherine, daughter of John and Elisabeth Ruttner Sponsors: James Ruttner and Catherine Reichert
20 May 1815	17 November 1815	James, son of James and Agatha Eisenhauer Sponsors: Thomas and Catherine Sigfrid
6 October 1815	18 November 1815	Esther, daughter of Daniel and M. Margaret Egg Sponsor: Mary Kass
6 September 1815	26 November 1815	Mary Eva, daughter of Matthias and Elisabeth Kass Sponsors: John and Eva Shonebruck
31 October 1815	3 December 1815	Aaron, son of John and Philippina Wingart Sponsors: John Quickly and Elisabeth Reichert
6 November 1815	31 December 1815	James, son of James and Juliana Dum Sponsors: George and Margaret Hopp
26 May	31 December 1815	Mary, daughter of George and Mary Gernand Sponsors: Thomas and Madeline Dum
2 November 1815	31 December 1815	Mary, daughter of James and Elisabeth Zweyer Sponsors: Adam and Eva Reichert
6 December 1815	1 January 1816	Joseph, son of John and Catherine Burgy Sponsors: Nicholas and Susan Grett
24 January	10 February 1816	Adam, son of James and Susan Rohrback Sponsors: Adam and Barbara Zweyer
21 January	9 March	Elisabeth, daughter of Charles and Helen Sigfrid Sponsors: Anthony and Catherine Felix
13 January 1816	10 March	William, son of Charles and Sarah Clee Sponsors: Michael and Elisabeth Hartmann
26 January 1816	10 March	Mary, daughter of Peter and Sarah Ruttner Sponsors: John and Mary Allgayer
22 September 1815	10 March	Susan, daughter of James and Susan Shlosser Sponsor: Elisabeth Hartmann
4 February 1816	13 March	Samuel, son of James and Elizabeth Felix Sponsors: Joseph and Regina Shmidt
7 June 1814	17 March 1816	Sarah, daughter of James and Madeline Wagner Sponsor: Margaret Shorp

Date of Birth	Date of Baptism	Names of Those Baptized
13 February 1816	17 March	Margaret, daughter of Nicholas and Margaret Kass Sponsors: George and Elisabeth Kunss
10 February 1816	31 March	Sara, daughter of Nicholas and Elizabeth Zweyer Sponsors: Philip and Catherine Burgy
11 February 1816	7 April 1816	Peter, son of Peter and Christine Erb Sponsors: Andrew and Susan Kaltenbach
2 February 1816	10 April 1816	Samuel, son of Anthony and Catherine Reichert Sponsors: Joseph and Catherine Burkard
8 March	15 April 1816	John, son of Joseph and Eva Reppert Sponsors: Joseph Keffer and Barbara Reppert
19 March 1816	21 April 1816	Joseph, son of Christopher and Susan Beaver Sponsors: Michael and Mary Madeline Hartmann
	21 April 1816	Manuel, son of Daniel and Elisabeth Grett Sponsors: Philip Obold and Sarah Lambert
16 March 1816	21 April 1816	Michael, son of James and Mary Roger Sponsors: Anthony and Catherine Felix
10 January 1816	21 April 1816	George, son of John and Anna Felix Sponsors: Anthony and Eva Merten
13 March	23 April 1816	Anthony, son of William and Catherine [Fricker?] Sponsors: John and Eva Miller
22 April 1816	24 April 1816	Anna, daughter of George and Barbara Sigfrid Sponsors: Martin and Barbara Felix
4 April 1816	21 April 1816	Louis, son of Joseph and Catherine Mohr Sponsors: Louis Eckrodt and Mary Eckrodt
27 March	5 May 1816	Maurice Franklin, son of Maurice and Catherine Budde Sponsors: John and Elisabeth Shorp
[?] January 1816	5 May 1816	John Frederick, son of Peter and Mary Samson Sponsors: Frederick and Elisabeth Miller
19 December 1816	5 May 1816	Sarah, daughter of James and Mary Malzberger Sponsor: Sarah Jones
2 April 1816	23 May	James, son of James and Mary House Sponsors: John Rohrbach and Madeline Reichert
20 March	9 June 1816	John, son of John and Susan Keffer Sponsors: John and Barbara Kemp
30 April 1816	9 June 1816	Sarah, daughter of Michael and Mary Hartmann Sponsors: Joseph Grett and Sarah Kemp
29 April 1816	9 June 1816	Sarah, posthumous daughter of Michael and Esther Grett Sponsors: Joseph Keffer and Barbara Grett
25 April 1816	9 June 1816	Catherine, daughter of Michael and Elisabeth Felix Sponsors: Anthony and Catherine Felix
20 May	16 June 1816	Mary Anna, daughter of Joseph and Mary Egg Sponsors: Peter Daubert and Anna Bauer

Date of Birth	Date of Baptism	Names of Those Baptized
11 June 1816	28 June	Sarah, daughter of Michael and Mary Shmidt Sponsor: Salome Kunss
22 April 1816	30 June 1816	Samuel, son of John and Madeline Grett Sponsors: Nicholas and Susan Grett
16 May 1816	30 June 1816	Elisabeth, daughter of Thomas and Anna Dum Sponsors: George Arentz and Elisabeth Seifert
17 November 1815	11 July 1816	John Adam, son of John Adam and Madeline Wummer Sponsors: Christian and Elisabeth Grett
16 May 1816 1816	11 July 1816 1816	Anna Margaret, daughter of Sebastian and Catherine Kissel Sponsors: John Adam and Madeline Wummer
13 June 1816	14 July 1816	Peter, son of James and Barbara Felix Sponsors: Anthony and Eva Merten
5 July 1816	21 July 1816	William, son of John and Elisabeth Walker Sponsors: John and Catherine Kunss
14 July 1816	10 August 1816	Samuel, son of Joseph and Madeline Seifert Sponsors: Joseph and Elisabeth Seifert
29 May 1816	15 August 1816	Henry, son of William and Anna Covely Sponsors: Henry and Elisabeth Covely
22 February 1816	18 August 1816	David, son of John and Madeline Sheckman Sponsors: Stephen and Madeline Reppert
26 May 1816	18 August 1816	Henry, son of John and Anna Egg Sponsors: John and Charlotte Egg
[?] July 1816	1 September 1816	George, son of John and Mary Egg Sponsors: John Bauer and Elisabeth Egg
15 July 1816	1 September 1816	Caroline, daughter of John and Catherine Grett Sponsors: George and Elisabeth Kunss
28 August 1816	24 September 1816	Joseph, son of James and Madeline Kass Sponsors: Paul Erntzen and Catherine Bauer
15 December 1815	29 September 1816	Charles, son of Thomas and Catherine Zweyer Sponsors: Andrew and Madeline Hopp
17 July 1816	30 September 1816	Mary Anna, daughter of Neal O'Boyle and Susan Sponsors: James and Juliana Dum
8 August 1797	6 October 1816	Anna, daughter of Anthony and Elisabeth Denis[11] Sponsors: John and Charlotte Egg
1 August 1816	13 October 1816	John, son of Ernest and Madeline Klee Sponsors: John and Barbara Kemp
14 July 1816	13 October 1816	William, son of Joseph and Christine Lambert Sponsors: William and Sophia Rohr
14 September 1816	3 November 1816	Anthony, son of Joseph and Catherine Burkard Sponsors: Anthony and Catherine Reichert

---

11 Anna Denis renewed consent with John Laurence Egg on the same day of her Baptism; Cf. *Records*, Vol. II, p. 205. (Page 213, this volume.)

Date of Birth	Date of Baptism	Names of Those Baptized
7 April 1816	10 November 1816	Sara Anna, daughter of John and Elisabeth Sterling Sponsors: Charles and Madeline Sigfrid
28 May 1795	11 November 1816	Philippina, daughter of Josue and Sarah Moon[12], Non-Catholics Sponsors: James and Elisabeth Felix
13 September 1816	10 November 1816	Joseph, son of Henry and Anna Missemer Sponsors: William Minzen and Catherine Shmidt
20 October 1815	11 November 1816	Peter Charles, son of Stephen and Elisabeth Orth Sponsors: Peter and Catherine Orth
1 November 1816	8 December 1816	Margaret, daughter of Philip and Catherine Windbiegler Sponsors: James Grett and Elisabeth Hartmann
4 December 1816	3 January 1817	David, son of John and Catherine Henrich Sponsors: Peter and Madeline Egg
21 December 1816	14 January 1817	Louise, daughter of John and Sarah Lambert Sponsors: James and Dorothy Lambert
11 January 1817	17 January 1817	Samuel, son of Bernard and Elisabeth Hart Sponsors: James Sigfrid and Mary Press
8 January 1817	26 January 1817	Joel, son of Joseph and Juliana Shnabel Sponsors: John Shorp and M. Catherine Shnabel
4 March 1817	22 March 1817	Samuel, son 'of Peter and Susan Egg Sponsors: Peter and Madeline Egg
3 January 1817	22 March 1817	Margaret, daughter of John and Catherine Hess Sponsors: Francis and Catherine Hopp
[?] February 1817	23 March	Mary, daughter of James and Elisabeth Becker Sponsors: Adam and Eva Reichert
18 October 1816	23 March 1817	Rebecca, daughter of George and Mary Gernand Sponsor: Elisabeth Seifert
11 January 1817	23 March	Catherine, daughter of Philip and Catherine Burgy Sponsors: Frederick and Catherine Reninger
24 February 1817	30 March	Paul, son of Benjamin and Margaret Egg Sponsors: John and Charlotte Egg
4 February 1817	30 March	Elisabeth, daughter of Andrew and Elisabeth Kunss Sponsors: John Bauer and Juliana Kunss
8 April 1817	13 April 1817	Catherine, daughter of William and Sophia Rohr Sponsors: George and Catherine Repplier
19 March 1817	13 April 1817	Elisabeth, daughter of John and Barbara Kemp Sponsors: Joseph and Elisabeth Sigfrid
15 February 1817	13 April 1817	Henry, son of Anthony and Catherine Felix Sponsors: James Ruttner and Catherine Sigfrid

12 On the day of her baptism, Philippina was married to Andrew Shmidt. Cf. *Records*, Vol. II, p. 205. (Page 213, this volume.)

Date of Birth	Date of Baptism	Names of Those Baptized
25 March 1817	13 April 1817	Anna, daughter of Peter and Sarah Ruttner Sponsors: James Ruttner and Catherine Reichert
14 March 1817	13 April 1817	Mary Margaret, daughter of Anthony and Anna Waters Sponsors: Solomon Felix and Mary Leckis
2 April 1816	14 April 1817	James, son of Daniel and Elisabeth Swimler Sponsor: Madeline Keffer
14 December 1816	14 April 1817	Margaret, daughter of Adam and E. Kreisher Sponsor: Margaret Mayer
15 January 1817	15 April 1817	Margaret, daughter of John and Madeline Shlosser Sponsors: Joseph and Catherine Shlosser
4 April 1817	16 April 1817	Joseph, son of Andrew and Philippina Shmidt Sponsors: Joseph and Regina Shmidt
7 April 1817	17 April 1817	Joseph, son of James and Madeline Kemp Sponsors: Joseph Zweyer and Elisabeth Rohrbach
8 January 1817	20 April 1817	Elisabeth, daughter of John and Sarah Melchior Sponsors: John Kuntz and Elisabeth Bock
4 May 1817	10 May 1817	Charles, son of Joseph and Margaret Allgayer[12a] Sponsors: James and Dorothy Lambert
[?] April 1817	11 May 1817	Samuel, son of George and Catherine Binder Sponsors: John and Barbara Kemp
24 March	11 May 1817	Benjamin, son of James and Barbara Shnabel Sponsors: James and Elisabeth Felix
22 February 1817	13 May 1817	Elisabeth, daughter of Samuel and Catherine [Umben..?] Sponsors: Joseph and Margaret Obold
24 May	26 May 1817	Elisabeth, daughter of George and Elisabeth Kunss Sponsors: Caspar and Susan Shmid
21 April 1817	7 June 1817	Joseph, son of William and Catherine Trout Sponsors: Joseph Zweyer and Mary Preiss
23 April 1817	8 June 1817	Mary Anna, daughter of George and Barbara Eyerson Sponsors: Christian Eckrod and his mother, a widow
1 May 1817	8 June 1817	Joseph, son of Simon and Elisabeth Seifert Sponsors: Joseph and Catherine Seifert
25 June 1817	27 June 1817	Catherine, daughter of James and Mary Adam Sponsor, Catherine Adam, aunt of the infant
9 May 1817	29 June 1817	Daniel, twin son of Valentine and Madeline Dum Sponsors: James and Sabina Dum

12a The priest baptizing mentions that he supplied the Ceremonies of Baptism for Charles Allgayer, indicating the Baptism itself, perhaps in case of necessity, had been performed sometime earlier. Probably on the 4 May, the day of birth.

Date of Birth	Date of Baptism	Names of Those Baptized
9 May 1817	29 June 1817	Sarah, one of the twins, daughter of the above Sponsors: George and Mary Gernand[13]
9 May 1817	1 July 1817	James, son of Thomas and Elisabeth Georg, Negro Sponsors: Adam and Eva Reichert
5 June 1811	1 July 1817	Anna, daughter of James and Anna Mary Guth Sponsor: Rosine Reichert
18 March 1813	1 July 1817	Juliana, daughter of the same [James and Anna Guth] Sponsor: Barbara Weinmann
8 July 1815	1 July 1817	Margaret, daughter of the same [J. & A. Guth] Sponsor: Madeline Reichert
21 January 1817	1 July 1817	Mary Madeline, daughter of the same [James and Anna Guth] Sponsors: Adam and Mary Reichert[14]
5 January 1812	6 July 1817	Joseph, son of John and Catherine Hudens Sponsors: Joseph Bachmann and Madeline Reichert
30 April 1816	6 July 1817	Elisabeth, daughter of the above [John and Catherine Hudens] Sponsors: Andrew and Susan Kattenbach
23 June 1817	14 July 1817	Samuel, son of Samuel and Susan Hartmann Sponsors: James and Catherine Hartmann
25 May 1817	14 July 1817	John, son of James and Elisabeth Eisenhauer Sponsors: Joseph and Elisabeth Sigfrid
22 June 1817	15 July 1817	Jonathan Joseph, son of Peter and Rosine Bauer Sponsors: Joseph Zweyer and Madeline Egg
17 July 1817	12 August 1817	Appollonia, daughter of Michael and Elisabeth Hartmann Sponsor: Elisabeth Hartmann
[?] 1817	31 August 1817	Esther, daughter of James and Susan Shlosser Sponsors: James and Elisabeth Becker
[?] July 1817	14 September 1817	Charles, son of Charles and Sarah Clee Sponsors: James and Catherine Hartmann
19 June 1817	19 September 1817	Elisabeth, daughter of William and Sarah Minzen Sponsor: Anna, wife of Henry Missemer
24 July 1817	21 September 1817	Joel, son of Augustine and Anna Reichert Sponsors: Charles and Elisabeth Rohr
29 July 1817	21 September 1817	Clara, daughter of Andrew and Sara Shindler Sponsors: John Quickly and Mary Ford
3 September 1817	5 October 1817	Jonathan, son of Solomon and Anna Egg Sponsors: John and Catherine Grett

---

13 Priest baptizing states, in case of the twin Sarah, that he supplied the Ceremonies of Baptism on this day.
14 In the case of Mary Madeline Guth, the priest baptizing states that on this day, 1 July, 1817, he supplied the Ceremonies of Baptism.

Date of Birth	Date of Baptism	Names of Those Baptized
	2 October 1817	In the home of Peter Maison near Philadelphia, I, [Paul Erntzen], baptized the three daughters of Peter Maison and his spouse: Catherine born 26 May, 1813; Christine Anna, born 23 June, 1815; Josephine Angela Therese, born 26 May, 1817. The Godfather of all three was John Alphonse Maison, Catholic, brother of Peter Maison.
18 September 1817	11 October 1817	Ruben, son of Joseph and Mary Egg Sponsors: Joseph and Agatha Egg
27 August 1817	12 October 1817	William, son of Joseph and Eva Wingart Sponsors: William and Sophia Rohr
23 August 1817	12 October 1817	Rebecca, daughter of Michael and Mary Hartmann Sponsors: John Sigfrid and Catherine Kemp
	12 October 1817	Joseph, son of Joseph and [ ] Sigfrid Sponsors: Joseph and Margaret Allgayer
25 August 1817	19 October 1817	James, son of Daniel and Mary Margaret Egg Sponsors: Simon Adam and Madeline Egg
22 August 1816	19 October 1817	Samuel, son of James and Elisabeth Gilbert Sponsors: Joseph and Juliana Shnabel
13 May 1817	9 November 1817	Henry, son of Anthony and Eva Merten Sponsors: Anthony Felix and Catherine Kemp
27 May 1817	9 November 1817	Anna, daughter of Henry & Catherine Lemmon Sponsors: Solomon Felix and Mary Leckis
16 September 1817	9 November 1817	Nicholas, son of John and Barbara Beaver Sponsors: P. E. [Paul Erntzen] and Madeline Baumann
27 September 1817	9 November 1817	Anna, daughter of John and Susan Keffer Sponsors: James and Barbara Shnabel
22 October 1817	9 November 1817	George Sebastian, son of George and Catherine Repplier Sponsors: Sebastian and Catherine Allgayer
31 October 1817	26 November 1817	Catherine, daughter of William and Catherine Fricker Sponsors: John and Mary Franz
4 October 1817	28 November 1817	Susan, daughter of George and Catherine Vogely Sponsors: John and Philippina Wingert
20 September 1817	30 November 1817	Catherine, daughter of John and Catherine Burgy Sponsors: Philip and Catherine Burgy
13 November 1817	30 November 1817	Frederick, son of John and Catherine Reninger Sponsors: Frederick and Catherine Reninger
23 November 1817	30 November 1817	John, son of Daniel and Elisabeth Dillon Sponsors: George and Margaret Hopp
9 September 1817	1 December 1817	Joseph, son of James and Elisabeth Zweyer Sponsors: Adam and Mary Reichert
25 September 1817	1 December 1817	Daniel, son of James and Juliana Dum Sponsors: Thomas and Madeline Dum

Date of Birth	Date of Baptism	Names of Those Baptized
16 January 1814	7 December 1817	William, son of John and Catherine Whulen Sponsors: John B. and Mary Coblet
11 October 1817	7 December 1817	Mary Anna, daughter of Joseph and Mary Backman Sponsors: William and Anna Covely
3 November 1817	27 December 1817	Charles, son of John and Anna Egg Sponsors: Peter and Madeline Egg
18 December 1817	1 January 1818	Juliana, daughter of George Henry and [ ] Shuchler Sponsors: Joseph and Margaret Allgaier
12 December 1817	1 January 1818	Mary, daughter of James and Elisabeth Felix Sponsor: Anna Mary Felix
27 October 1817	2 January 1818	Mary, daughter of Andrew and Margaret Grett Sponsors: Joseph and Margaret Obold
15 June 1817	11 January 1818	Catherine, daughter of Michael and Litta Roggers Sponsors: James and Catherine Waghon
9 January 1818	13 January 1818	Joseph, son of Joseph and Elsabeth Sigfrid Sponsors: Paul Erntzen and Sarah Kemp
5 December 1817	18 January 1818	Joseph, son of Steward and Mary Simpson Sponsors: Joseph and Catherine Burkard
13 December 1817	18 January 1818	Clara, daughter of Charles and Elisabeth Rohr Sponsors: John and Sarah Melchior
? January 1818	2 February 1818	Richard, son of John and Sarah Rohrbach Sponsors: Richard Rohr and Elisabeth Rohrbach
? June 1818	9 February 1818	Michael, son of Thomas and Sarah M'Callen Sponsors: Anthony and Catherine Felix
11 November 1817	17 February 1818	Mary, daughter of John and Susan Shell Sponsors: Maurice and Catherine Buddee
28 January 1818	17 February 1818	Mary Anna, daughter of Maurice and Catharine Buddee Sponsors: Joseph Kemp and Margaret Shorp
1 February 1818	1 March 1818	Reuben, son of John and Sarah Melchior Sponsors: Christian and Catherine Clemmer
10 November 1799	23 March 1818	Madeline, daughter of Samuel and Sophia Hottel, non-catholics [15] Sponsor: Catherine Adam, Sen.
2 March 1818	25 March 1818	Mary Anna, daughter of John and Mary Quickly Sponsors: Joseph Bachman and Elisabeth Reichert
28 October 1817	29 March 1818	Daniel, son of John and Mary Neuer Sponsors: Adam and Mary Reichert
10 March 1818	29 March 1818	Mary, daughter of Adam and Mary Reichert Sponsors: Adam and Eva Reichert
11 December 1817	29 March 1818	Mary Anna, daughter of Andrew and Madeline Wenzel Sponsors: Aloyzius [ ] and Elizabeth Becker

---

15 Interesting, for verifying the date of birth of Madeline Hottel, which is blotted in the Register, to find that on November 12, 1818, she married Paul Adam. Cf. *Records*, Vol XI, No. 2, p. 207. ✳

*Page 215, this volume.

Date of Birth	Date of Baptism	Names of Those Baptized
17 March 1818	29 March 1818	Susan, daughter of Thomas and Anna Dum Sponsor: Susan Grett
2 March 1818	30 March 1818	David, son of John and Madeline Grett Sponsors: Helen Baumann and Susan Grett
30 March 1818	7 April 1818	Aaron, son of John and Juliana Bauer Sponsor: Paul Kunz and Catherine Bauer
3 March 1818	12 April 1818	Susan, daughter of Charles and Helen Sigfrid Sponsors: Francis and Eva Eichhorn
22 October 1817	24 May 1818	Jonah, son of Henry and Anna Balinger Sponsors: Matthias and Catherine Rohr[16]
23 May [1818]	30 [May] [1818]	Peter, son of Peter Riedner and Elizabeth Felix Sponsor: Peter Riedner, Sr.[17]
15 May [1818]	31 May [1818]	Joseph Jeremiah, son of Joseph Rohr and Margaret Speitel Sponsors: Richard Rohr and Sarah Kemp
22 May [1818]	31 [May] [1818]	James Reuben, son of Peter Erb and Christine Kuntz Sponsors: Charles and Elizabeth M'Entire
1 May [1818]	31 [May] [1818]	Mary, daughter of John Miller and Christine Barky Sponsors: James Barky and Barbara Heever
11 April [1818]	31 [May] [1818]	Joseph, son of Philip Barky and Catherine Reininger Sponsors: Joseph Barky, for whom Philip Henry acted as proxy, and Mary Barky.
9 June [1818]	12 July [1818]	William, son of Anthony Reickart and Catherine (Eltz) Sponsors: Henry Dolhauer and Margaret Reickart
20 May [1818]	12 July [1818]	Elizabeth, daughter of John Melon and Sarah Burk Sponsors: Christian and Catherine Clemmer

1818—*In Reading*[18]

2 July [1818]	18 September [1818]	Sylvester, son of Philip Windbichler and Catherine Hartman Sponsors: Philip Hartman and Catherine Hartman
10 March [1818]	13 September [1818]	Mary Elizabeth, daughter of Joseph Eirenzen and Mary Catherine Eckenrode Sponsor: Elisabeth Eckenrode

---

16 These two entries and written on a scrap of paper and have been inserted in the book loosely. They are in the handwriting of Father Paul Erntzen, and are the last entries in his hand. For convenience, they have been inserted here in their proper chronological order.

17 This entry, the first in a new hand, shows a considerable change of method in the inscribing of the record. Thus, where Father Erntzen mentions only the first name of the mother, the new priest gives the full maiden name. The year is likewise no longer written in each entry. It is possible that these entries are in the hand of Father Maximilian Rantzau, who is certainly the author of the entries after 13 September 1818 (date of baptism), but the ink is quite different and the handwriting so irregular that it is not possible to say with certainty.

18 This is the first entry which is certainly in the handwriting of Father Maximilian Rantzau. The indication of the place of baptism appears hereafter and evidently applies to all of the entries which follow it, until a new place indication is made. These place indications appear at times in the column headed *Dies Generationis*; at times in the column *Dies Regen*, and sometimes are written across the page in the column where the names of those baptized are entered. They have been uniformly set across the first two columns in this printing of these records.

258

Date of Birth	Date of Baptism	Names of Those Baptized
27 August [1818]	12 September [1818]	William Francis, son of William Rohr and Sophia Atsper Sponsors: Francis Eichhorn and Eva Eichhorn
14 July [1818]	18 September [1818]	Mary Anna, daughter of John Felix and Anna (Joh?) Sponsors: Anthony Felix and Catherine Merthen
10 July 1817	14 September [1818]	Matthew, son of Stephen Ort and Elisabeth Roland Sponsors: Peter Ort and Charlotte Roland

In Goshenhoppen

1 September [1818]	19 September [1818]	Mary Elizabeth, daughter of John Louis Berton and Utilia Madeline Miller Sponsors: Joseph Hurber and Mary Anna Hurber
5 July 1818 in Haycuk	27 September 1818	Isaac, son of William Heny and Peggy Helopart Sponsors: Michael and Elisabeth Heny
22 May 1818	27 September 1818	Elisabeth, daughter of John Kohl and Elisabeth Hoffman Sponsors: James and Elisabeth Kohl
27 September 1817	27 September 1818	Jonathan, son of Jonathan Lettelmeyer and Theresa Kunzen Sponsors: James and Elisabeth Kohl
14 September 1818	27 September	Cecilia, daughter of Anthony Grieser and Margaret Shop Sponsors: Joseph Heny and Elisabeth Bock
24 October	27 September	Joseph, son of John McEntee and Sara McKarty Sponsors: John and Polly McKarty
28 May	27 September	James, son of James Honig and Theresa Gardener Sponsors: Francis Carty and Peggy Honig
11 weeks old	27 September	Joseph, son of Frederick Baumgartner and Sara Fock Sponsors: Martin Sichar and Madeline Shmith
[8] May	27 September	Veronica, daughter of Andrew Gasman and Anna Kayserin Sponsors: Nicholas and Mary McKarty
6 September [?]	4 October	Judith, daughter of John Eck and Polly Berndt Sponsors: Henry and Susan Kass

In Reading

7 October	11 October	Anna, daughter of Anthony Felix and Catherine Martin Sponsors: Solomon and Polly Felix
3 October	12 October	Elisabeth, daughter of Joseph Stocker and Catherine Burgard Sponsors: Martin and Barbara Felix

In Orwigsburg, Skulkill County

26 March 1814	14 October	John, son of William Kassely and Mary Fennigen Sponsor: Thomas McDonald

Date of Birth	Date of Baptism	Names of Those Baptized
5 years old	14 October	Margaret, daughter of Daniel McColligen and Mary McFergen Sponsor: John Kelly
27 January 1814	15 October	Martin, son of Henry Leman and Catherine Felix Sponsor: I, Maximilian Rantzau
21 January 1811	Same day [15 October]	Mary, born of same parents Sponsor: Mary Fennigen
19 April [1818]	15 October [1818]	William, son of Neal O'Boil and Susan Dollinger Sponsors: James Borget and Peggy Renninger
16 May [1818]	18 October [1818]	Joseph, son of Christopher Bever and Susan Bayren Sponsors: Nicholas and Susan Grett [non-Catholic]
1 September [1818]	18 October [1818]	Solomon, son of Nicholas Schwayer and Elisabeth Borgeson Sponsors: Philip and Elisabeth Henrich

In Goshenhoppen

20 September [1818]	1 November [1818]	Henry, son of John Wingart and Philippine Coble Sponsors: John and Mary Coble
23 June [1818]	1 November [1818]	Jeremiah, son of William Coble and Anna Bachman Sponsors: Henry Dolhower and Catherine Julens
23 September [1818]	3 November [1818]	Rachel, daughter of Aegidius Bower and Madeline Eck Sponsors: James Eck and Anna Bower

In Reading

8 weeks old	3 November [1818]	William, son of Conrad Wirned and Ludgardis Noper Sponsors: Anton Noper and Mary Anna Leman
17 [February ?] [1819]	7 March 1819	James, son of John Huhs and Catherine Henrich Sponsors: Henry Dolhower and Madeline [?][19]
4 February [1819]	7 March [1819]	John, son of Gabriel Albubtz and Apollania Gertbachery Sponsors: Francis Pfluam and Catherine Adam
22 September [?	7 March [1819]	Susan, daughter of Andrew Koons and Elizabeth Mester Sponsors: Matthew Case and Elizabeth Koons
26 February [1819]	8 March [1819]	Henry Reuben, son of Paul Koons and Catherine Bauer Sponsors: Henry Coverly and Anna Bauer
13 February [1819]	8 March [1819]	Emil, son of Charles McIntire and Elisabeth Cole Sponsors: George Shenfelter and Juliana Cole

---

19 This is the first entry in a new hand. No identification has been made of the priest responsible for the few entries which extend to May 5, 1819.

Date of Birth	Date of Baptism	Names of Those Baptized
9 April 1819	5 May 1819	Jerome, son of Andrew Shindler and Sarah Jones Sponsors: Christian and Catherine Clemer
18	10 March 1819	Samuel, son of Joseph Eck and Mary Bauer Sponsors: Peter Bauer and Anna Eck[20]
[?] November 1818	10 May 1819	John Aaron, son of John Snabel and Margaret Miller Sponsors: [?] and [?] Miller
18 November 1818	9 May 1819	John, son of Joseph Hennick and Mary Weber Sponsors: Michael and Helen Hennick
18 October 1818	9 May 1819	John, son of Fridolinus Miller and Joan Nieman Sponsors: Sylvester Joseph and Regina Rigelin
4 [?] 1819	9 May 1819	Daniel, son of Matthew Heinick and Susan Snyder Sponsors: T. McCarty and Mary Anna [Geog?]
[?] November 1818	9 May 1819	Rebecca, daughter of John McCarty and Mary McCarty Sponsors: Peter McCarty and Rebecca McCarty
[?]	11 May 1819	Elizabeth, daughter of Nicholas Buck and Susan Heinech Sponsors: Nicholas and Madeline Buck
[?] February 1819	11 May 1819	Susan, daughter of Philip Hamerstein and Catherine Melchoir Sponsors: Elizabeth Buck
[?]	11 May 1819	Elisabeth, daughter of Peter O'Connor and Mary Buck Sponsors: Nicholas and Madeline Buck
[?]	22 August 1819	[Denis?], son of Joseph Rohr and Margaret[?] Sponsors: Joseph and Julian Rohr

In the year of Our Lord 1819, in the month of September, on the 12th day, I, Thomas Praniewitz, baptized an infant, born on the 18th day of June by the name Elisabeth, the father Simon Schlacht, the mother, Madeline. The sponsors were George Kuns with Elisabeth. All from Goshenhoppen.

In the year of Our Lord 1819, on the 19th day of September, I, Thomas Praniewitz, baptized an infant born on the ninth day of the same month, by name Simon, the father Simon Adams and the mother Catherine. The sponsors were Paul Adams with Madeline.

In the year of Our Lord 1819, on the 19th day of September, I, Thomas Praniewitz, baptized an infant born on the 20th day of August, by name Rebecca, the father John Tenesser, the mother Catherine. The sponsors were Matthew Sauber with Catherine Tenesser. From Folgner Schwan. All of the parish of Coschenhopensis.

In the year of Our Lord 1819, in the month of September, on the 26th day, I, Thomas Praniewitz, baptized an infant, born on the 14th day of May, by the name Michael, the father Adam Reichert and the mother, Mary. The Sponsors were Adam Reichert and Eva Reichert. At Massillum.

---

20 This entry is signed by Father Shenfelder, and is the first in his hand. Entries by Father Shenfelder continue until August 22, 1819. It will be noted that these entries cover practically the same period as those of the preceding priest. It is probable that both priests were working on the mission, using Goshenhoppen as their headquarters, and transcribing their baptismal entries on their return.

In the year of Our Lord 1819, on the 26th day of September, the above priest baptized an infant born on the 2nd day of July by the name Joseph. The father James Dum and the mother Juliana. The Sponsors were James Elay and Catherine Hob. At Massillum.

In the year of Our Lord 1819, on the 26th day of September, the above priest baptized an infant, born on the first day of April, 1818, by the name Samuel, the father Thomas Zweem, the mother Catherine. The Sponsors were George Hop with Margaret. At Taunschrip.

In the year of Our Lord 1819, on the 26th day of September, the above priest baptized an infant born on the 19th day of May, by name Catherine, daughter of James Miller, the mother Christine. The Sponsors were Philip Barge with Catherine. At Winzer (Sc ?).

In the year of Our Lord 1819, on the 11th day of May by the Rev. Schenfelter were baptized infants, by name Susan and Leah, born [?]. The father, John Bever and the mother Barbara Great. The Sponsors were John Great and Madeline Great.

In the year of Our Lord 1819, on the 10th day of May, by the same priest, was baptized James, born on the 21st day of November, 1818, the father John (? ger), the mother Catherine. The Sponsors were Thomas [?] Dolhamer with Margaret Reainger.

In the year of Our Lord 1819, on the 9th day of May, by the same priest was baptized Elisabeth, born on the 19th day of April. The father Andrew [?], the mother Madeline Shubin. The Sponsors were John [Relt?] and Rosalie Reicherd.

In the year of Our Lord, 1819, on the 9th day of May, by the same priest, was baptized Catherine, born on the 7th day of November, 1818. The father Daniel Dille, the mother Elisabeth Hop. The sponsors were James Elim and Catherine Hop.

--- A ---

Aaf, Elizabeth 93,98
  Magdalen 98
  Theodore 98
  Theodoric 93,98
Ackermann, Barbara 27
Adam, Abraham 231
  Catharine 156,160,
    164,191,198,199,202,
    204,207,210,211
  Catherine 224,231,
    232,235,238,246,254,
    260
  Catherine (Sr.) 257
  Elisabeth 224
  Elizabeth 139
  James 207,224,231,
    232,247,254
  John 152,166,168,176,
    191,198,204,207,224,
    232,235,238,246
  Mary 164,168,188,198,
    207,227,231,232,247,
    254
  Paul 164
  Sabina 210,231
  Simon 103,139,147,
    148,152,160,164,191,
    198,204,207,210,211,
    216,239,256
  William 235
Adams, --- 43
  Anna M. 48,55,72,82
  Anna Maria 62,69,108
  Anna Maria Kupser 119
  Anna Mary 52
  Catharine 35,41,61,
    69,87
  Catherine 261
  Elizabeth 26,102,103
  James 77
  John 61
  John James 96
  Mary 61
  Paul 215,261
  Simon 32,48,61,69,77,
    87,96,105,108,119,
    215,261
Affer, --- 24
  Francis 38
  Mary Ann 38
  Mary Ann Eva 38
Aggy, Henry 229
  Madeline 229
  Susan 229
Aitz, James Frederich
  139
Albrecht, John 238
  Justina 167
  Justine 238
Albubtz, Gabriel 260
  John 260
Alexander, Catharine 150
  Margaret 150
  Solomon 150

Algayer, Jacob 215
  Joseph 26
Algeier, Sebastian 154
Algeyer, Catharine 141
  Elizabeth 141
  Sebastian 141
Allen, Eleanor 67
  John 67
  William John 67
Allgaier, John 214
  Joseph 257
  Margaret 257
  Sebastian 211
Allgayer, Anna M. 249
  Anthony 151
  Catharine 151
  Catherine 225,227,
    228,229,233,249,256
  Charles 254
  James Sebastian 249
  John 211,224,233,239,
    241,242,245,246,250
  Joseph 224,227,228,
    233,234,236,238,245,
    246,249,249,254,256
  Louise 236
  Margaret 224,227,228,
    233,234,236,238,245,
    246,249,254,256
  Mary 242,245,246,250
  Mary Dorothy 246
  Sebastian 151,207,
    210,225,227,228,229,
    233,256
  Sebastion 249
  William 228
Allgeier, Anna Mary 165
  Catharine 155,159,
    165,188,192,205
  Joseph 205
  Sebastian 155,165,
    192,205
Allgeyer, Catharine 170,
    175,190,193,195,196,
    200,202,204
  George 175
  James 207
  John 193,202
  Joseph 170,172,190,
    196,200,202
  Margaret 196,202
  Mary 200
  Sebastian 170,175,
    183,190,193,195,196,
    200,202,204,205
Allsman, Anna Maria 144
  Anna Mary 144
Allwein, Catharine 94
  Conrad 94,105
Aloin, Catharine 207,213
  Conrad 207,213
  Elizabeth 207
  John 213,230
  John (Sr.) 207
  Madeline 230
  Mary Margaret 230
  Ph. 213

Aloine, Catharine 211
  Conrad 211
  Magdalen 181
  Theresa 211
Altendorff, Mary Eva 101
Alter, A. M. 7
  A. Margaret 9
  Caspar 7,9,11,12
  Catharine 6,9
  Christina 9,12
  Eva 11,12
  John Martin 6,11
  Martin 9,12
  Simon 12
Altgayer, Barbara 54
  Catharine 71,79,87
  John Michael 50
  Joseph 71
  M. Ann 48
  Sebastian 54,68,71,
    79,87,109
Altkayer, Catharine 33
  John Michael 31
Andres, Christian 137,
    142
  Jacob 142
  Mary 137,142
  Peter 137
Angst, Catherine 241
  Daniel 208,235,241
  Elizabeth 208
  Mary 235,241
  Mary Casa 235
Anselm, Mary 31
Arens, --- 155
  Elizabeth 137,164,
    167,170,176,193,196,
    206,207,184
  George 171,194,200,
    203,206,236
  Jacob 151,152,159,
    163,166,167,168,170,
    173,181,182,190,202
  James 137,184,207
  John 152,162,164,167,
    170,176,181
  John Jacob 138
  Joseph 153,166,170,
    176,182
  M. 207
  Magdalen 168,182
  Margaret 138,159,166,
    168,170,173,181,182,
    184,190,200,203,218
  Mary 167,200,202
  Peter 173,191,205
Arents, Elizabeth 199
  George 199
  George Adam 80
  Henry Peter 60
  Jacob 35,43,104
  James 47,49,60,74,80
  John 43
  Joseph 53
  Margaret 43,47,49,53,
    60,74,199
Arentz, George 210,230,

Arentz (cont.)
  252
  James 69,96,213,249,
    250
  Magdalen 69
  Margaret 69,213,230
  Mary 213,249,250
  Philip Caspar 96
Arenz, George 218,244
  Jacob 146,217
  Margaret 146,229,231,
    232
  Margaret Egg 218
  Mary 200
Arnold, Catharine 213
  Christina 181
  Christine 213
  Elizabeth 179,181
  Eve 202,213
  George 4,8
  Herman 213
  James 213
  John 179,181,202,213
  Margaret 8
  Mary Elizabeth 202
  Peter 213
Arrentz, Mary 245
Arrold, Catharine 146
  Peter 146
Ashborn, --- 132
  Catharine 170
  George 170
  Jesse 170
Ashburn, --- 132 ·
  Catharine 163,189
  Elizabeth 163
  Joseph 189
  William 163,189
Ashburner, --- 132
  Jacob 154
  Sara 154
  William 154,180
Atsper, Sophia 259
Auf, Flizabeth 46
  Frederic 46
  Magdalen 98
  Theodoric 46,93

  --- B ---

Bachman, Anna 176,226,
    260
  Barbara 226
  Elizabeth 176
  Ferdinand 226
  Henry 176
  John 176,226
  Joseph 209,239,242,
    249,257
  Louis 239
  Martin 226
  Mary 214,239
Bachmann, Anna Elizabeth
    175
  Barbara 12
  Catherine 225
  Clara 175
  David 244
  Elizabeth 230
  Henry 175
  Joseph 240,244,255
  Mary 240,244
Back, Apollonia 209
  Elizabeth 209
  Leonard 209
Backman, Joseph 257

Backman (cont.)
  Mary 257
  Mary Anna 257
Balinger, Anna 258
  Henry 258
  Jonah 258
Barge, Philip 262
Barky, Christine 258
  James 258
  Joseph 258
  Mary 258
  Philip 258
Barth L. (Rev.) 128,215
Bauer, Aaron 258
  Aegidius 238
  Agidius Michael 154
  Anna 188,251,260
  Catharine 164,215
  Catherine 252,258,260
  Christine 213
  David 188
  Egidius 214
  Elizabeth 149,152,
    154,155,160,213
  George 149,152,154,
    155,160,180,181
  Henry 233
  John 158,178,212,214,
    215,252,253,258
  Jonathan Joseph 255
  Joseph 213
  Juliana 258
  Madeline Elisabeth 228
  Mary 212,242,244,261
  Nathan 244
  Peter 154,158,164,
    168,188,192,197,198,
    201,212,214,228,233,
    237,244,255,261
  Reuben 237
  Rosina 164,168,214,244
  Rosine 188,192,197,
    198,201,212,214,228,
    233,237,255
  Samuel M. 198
  Solomon Jacob 201
Bauman, John 112
  Peter 112
Baumann, Anna Magdalen
    159
  Elizabeth 147
  Helen 258
  John 147,159
  Madeline 256
  Magdalen 147
  Susan 205
Baumgartner, Frederick
    259
  Joseph 259
Baur, Anna Maria 85
  Catharine 39,42,99,106
  Catherine 78
  Elizabeth 52
  Francis 52,105
  Henry 27
  John 39,102
  John Jacob 114
  John James 27
  Leonard 27,113,114,117
  Mary 52,59
  N. 113
Bauss, Jacob 203
Bayren, Susan 260
Beaver Anna 236,245
  Augustine 230
  Barbara 224,230,236,
    242,245,250,256
  Christopher 206,217,

Beaver (cont.)
  234,245,251
  Conrad 206
  Elias 250
  John 206,224,230,234,
    236,242,245,250,256
  Joseph 251
  Juliana 245
  Margaret 206
  Mary 234
  Nicholas 256
  Samuel 217,224,234
  Susan 234,251
  Susanna 217
Bebers, --- 24
Becher, Elizabeth 16
Bechtel, --- 215
Bechtl, A. Mary 11
Beck, John 15
Becker, Anna 246
  Anna Mary 30
  Catharine 16
  Elisabeth 241,246,
    249,253,255
  Elizabeth 4,26,154,
    211,219,257
  Elizabeth Mary 4
  Eva 38,104
  George 113
  Jacob 219
  James 211,241,246,
    249,253,255
  John 30,52,69,70,83,
    84,154,243
  Joseph 246
  M. Magdalen 84
  Madeline 246
  Margaret 51,80,105,108
  Mary 154,253
  Michael 232
  Simon 3,4,12
Beitelmann, A. M. 7
Benden, Sara 202
Bender, Adam 6
  Anna 139
  John Adam 5
  John Peter 6
  Margaret 6
Bennen, Anna 169,185
  John 169,185
  Paul 169
Benner, Anna 148
  John 148
Benton, Elisabeth 235
  Elizabeth 209
  Helen 209,235
  J. 209
  Jonathan 196,209,235
  Mary 196
  Nelly 196
  Th. 209
Berger, Barbara 40,43
  Magdalen 182
Bergleit, Joseph 214
Bergmann, John 115
Bergmans, Christopher
    113
Beringer, Madeline 228
  Magdalen 191
  Mary Elizabeth 191
  Mary M. 198
  Mary Magdalen 198
  Mathias 191,198,228
Berlis, Barbara 151
Berndt, Polly 259
Bernen, John 145
  Maria 145
  Peter 145

Berner, John 178
Bernheiser, Jacob 202
  James 226
  Margaret 202,226
Bernt, Frederick 209
  John 233
  Margaret 209
  Mary 209
Berton, Elizabeth 155
  Esther 155
  John Louis 259
  Mary Elizabeth 259
  Thomas 155
Betz, Catharine (Sr.) 70
Beutelman, Leonard 13
Beven, Henry 148
Bever, Christopher 260
  Conrad 41
  Henry 139
  John 262
  Joseph 260
  Leah 262
  Margaret 41
  Susan 262
Beverts, --- 24
  Catharine Margaret 73
  Conrad 73
  Magdalen 103
  Margaret 73
  Margaret Eckenroth 111
Bevertz, --- 24
  Anna Magdalen 84
  Anna Margaret 64,66
  Christian 82
  Christopher 55
  Conrad 37,44,47,55,
    61,64,66,82,86,92
  Henry 37
  John 82,92
  John George 44
  Magdalen 87,102,102
  Margaret 37,47,55,61,
    82,86,92
  Mary Magdalen 30
Bewerts, Catharine 14,15
  Conrad 17
  Henry 11
  John 11
  M. Ottilia 11
  Sara Catharine 7
Bewertz, --- 24
Beyer, Susan 206
Beyler, Balthasar 215
Bibers, --- 24
  Conrad 30
  Magdalen 30,102
  Mary Magdalen 30
Biberts, --- 24
Bieger, Magdalen 62
Bies, Mary 179
Billich, Arnold 56,70
  John Arnold 87
  Mary Barbara 56
  Petronilla 56,70
Binder, Anna Christine
    248
  Catherine 244,248,254
  Daniel 244
  George 210,244,248,254
  Samuel 254
  Sophia 248
  Theresa 210
Bischof, Charlotta 7
  Paul 7
  Peter 7
Bischoff, Anna Mary 33
  John 17
  Mary 36

Bisping, Henry 17
Bisschof, Charlotte 35
  Elizabeth 47
  Mary 35
  Mary Charlotte 28
  Maurice 56
  Peter 28,35
  Philip James 35
  Simon 28
Bisschoff, Anna Barbara
    43
  Elizabeth 38
  John 43
  Mary 38
  Peter 115
Bisschop, Peter 113
  Simon 113
Blainy, Ann 6
Blany, Ann 8
Blany, Ann 9,10
  Anna 5
  Catharine 5
  Edmund 5,6,10
Blayny, Ann 3
  Edmund 3
  John 3
Bluhm, Anthony 46
  Anthony (Jr.) 29
  Anthony (Sr.) 28
  Barbara 29
  Mary Catharine 29
  Peter 29
Boatman, Bernard 163
  Catharine 163
  John 163
Boch, Elizabeth 93
Bock, --- 12
  Anna Margaret 142
  Apollonia 13
  Appollonia 235
  Barbara 64
  Catharine 46,64,140,
    144,145,152,152,210
  Elisabeth 254,259
  Elizabeth 32,40,46,
    55,64,74,91,95,97,
    99,140,142,143,146,
    207,210
  Jacob 148
  James 40
  John 55
  John Caspar 143
  Joseph 13,142,143,
    146,150,177
  Joseph Leonard 140
  Katharine 179
  Leonard 13,98,138,
    142,146,152,177,210
  Magdalen 91,148,152,
    153,213
  Mary 99,207,213
  Mary Apollonia 146
  Mary Magdalen 142,149
  Nicholas 13,16,30,32,
    33,46,55,64,74,80,
    91,95,99,102,142,
    148,149,152,153,178,
    207,213,214
  Nicholas John 148
  Nicolas 40
  Susan 148
Bohm, Daniel 229
Bohr, Elizabeth 151
  Joseph 151
Bomer, Adam 182
Bond, Charte 159
  John 159
  Samuel 159

Borge, Joseph 87
Borgeson, Elisabeth 260
Borget, James 260
Both, Catharine 149,155
  Elizabeth 149
  Elizabeth Ann 155
  Eva 28,47
  Eva Catharine 28
  Jacob 149,155
  John 28,44,45,113
  John Adam 105
  John Leonard 113
  Mary 52
Botman, Benjamin 171
  Bernard 170,188
  Catharine 170,171,188
  Margaret 170
Botmann, Bernard 155
  Catharine 155
  Mary Ann 155
Bott, Anna Maria 199
  Catharine 161,170,
    199,226
  Catherine 236
  Elisabeth 236
  Jacob 161,170,199
  James 226,236
  John 236
  Margaret 226
  Susan 236
  William 161
Bottman, Bernard 149
  Catharine 149
  Mary Magdalen 149
Bouer, Elizabeth 157
  George 157
Bower, Aegidius 260
  Anna 260
  Rachel 260
Boyle, George 244
  James 238
  John 233
  Neal 233,238,244
  Susan 233,238,244
Bradley, William 60,109
Brady, N. 32
Brand, Fred. 66,80
  Frederick 72,73,75,
    77,106
  M. Magdalen 75
  Magdalen 66,72,73
  Peter 106
Brant, Frederic 46
Braun, --- 132
  Agnes 107
  Andrew 60,64,66,73,
    78,88,94,96,108,119,
    120,138,141,148,150
  Catharine 60,158
  Francis 73
  Henry 96
  John 120
  John Conrad 66
  Joseph 138
  M. Barbara 78
  Magdalen 119
  Margaret 88
  Mary Ann 148
  Rachel 60,66,73,94
  Regina 60,73,94,138,
    141,148,150
Brawn, --- 132
  Andrew 150
  Regina 150
Bre, Michael Anthony 165
Brechtel, N. 49
Breier, Elizabeth 150
Breitenbach, --- 24

Breitenbach (cont.)
  Susan 27
Brenner, Joseph 43
Brennig, M. Eva 90
Brestal, Charles 148
  Joseph 148
  Mary Ann 148
Brettes, Catharine 140
Breyer, Elizabeth 179
Brick, Elizabeth 139
Bricker, Ann Elizabeth 3
  Barbara 3
  John 3
Brodbeck, Margaret 14
Brown, --- 132
  --- (Dr.) 7
  Andrew 154,161
  Catharine 157,189
  John 161,174
  Magdalen 154
  Margaret 171,174,175
  Regina 154,161
  William 174
Bruck, --- 24
  Anna M. 69
  Anna Margaret 140
  Catharine 140,146
  Elizabeth 166,174
  George 158
  Henry 166,174
  John 169,185
  Joseph 69,119
  Magdalen Margaret 166
  Maria 85
  Mary 72,73,95,146,
    158,166,169,174,185
  Mathias 183
  Matt. 78,110
  Matthew 146
  Matthias 69,70,72,73,
    75,85,95,119,140,
    158,166,169
  Peter 174
  Theresa 95
Bruckman, Henrietta 248
Bruckner, Adam 12
  Magdalen 9,12
Brucks, --- 24
  Anna Maria 53
  Henry 52
  Maria 56
  Mary 52
  Matthias 52,53,56,106
Brucx, --- 24
  Mary 50,63
  Matthias 50,63
  Peter 63
Brugarth, Philip 177
Brunner, Anna Mary 16
Bryan, --- 83
  Cherry 182
  Elisabeth 228,245
  Elizabeth 190,195
  James 12
  John 190,195,228,245
  Mary Catharine 190
  Philip 228
  Thomas 245
Buchart, Martin 117
Bucher, A. Barbara 8
  Elizabeth 8
  Peter 8
Buck, --- 12
  Apollonia 181
  Barbara 159,180
  Christian 170
  Elizabeth 155,158,
    162,163,164,169,170,

Buck (cont.)
  171,174,176,180,181,
  185,189,189,201,204,
  213,261
  George 194
  Henry 189
  Jacob 158,162,163,170,
    171,174,183,189,204
  John 160,162,164,166,
    169,170,171,176,181,
    192
  John Nicholas 157
  Joseph 155,158,161,
    162,164,165,166,170,
    171,181,185,189,194,
    195,198
  Leonard 158,164,169,
    176,189,213
  Madeline 261
  Magdalen 157,166,171,
    189,192,193
  Mary 164,169,174,189,
    190,193,261
  Mary Magdalen 171
  Nicholas 157,164,166,
    169,171,174,180,181,
    183,189,192,204,261
  Rebecca 176
  Rosina 161,162,164,
    165,166,170,171
  Rosine 189,194,195,198
  Salome 162,164,166,
    169,170,171,176,192
  Sara 213
  Susan 158,163,170,
    171,174,189,198
Budde, Anthony 246
  Antoninus 219
  Catharine 219
  Catherine 242,246,251
  Fr. Anthony 210
  Henrietta 219,242
  M. 219,246
  Maurice 210,219,242,
    251
  Maurice Franklin 251
Buddee, Catherine 257
  Mary Anna 257
  Maurice 257
Buger, Christopher 83
  Magdalen 79,83,109
Buker, Jacob 142
  John 142,148,149
  John Thomas 149
  Mary 142,149
Bur---, Catharine 94
  Jacob 94
Burchard, Gertrude 34,
    40,44
  James 34
  John 40
  Martin 34,40,44,115,
    118
Burchart, Cornelius 116
  Gertrude 55,60,62,65,
    71,91
  John Joseph 91
  John Peter 71
  John William 79
  M. Magdalen 62
  Mart. 55,60
  Martin 62,71,79,91,120
  Philip 62,65
  William 120
Buregy, Anna Maria 147
  Jacob Joseph 147
  Joseph 147
Burgard, Catherine 259

Burger, Anna Mary 32
  Joseph 32
  Michael 32
Burgie, Anna Maria 142
  John 142
  Joseph 142
Burgy, Anna M. 203
  Anna Maria 158
  Anna Mary 240
  Catharine 205,240
  Catherine 246,250,
    251,253,256
  Christina 158
  Christine 215
  Elisabeth 246
  Elizabeth 192,201,207
  John 196,207,209,240,
    246,250,256
  Joseph 158,165,197,
    203,206,209,212,215,
    227,237,240,250
  Madeline 236
  Magdalen 215
  Margaret 203
  Mary 165,197,209,212,
    215,227,237
  Mary Barbara 165
  Philip 212,251,253,256
Burk, James 185
  Joseph 184,185
  Mary Elizabeth 184
  Rosina 185
  Sarah 258
Burkard, Anthony 252
  Catharine 194,203
  Catherine 229,236,
    241,245,247,248,251,
    252,257
  Catherine Sophia 229
  Christian 214
  Elisabeth 236
  Esther 214
  Gertrude 193,217
  Henry 248
  John 194
  Joseph 194,203,229,
    236,241,245,247,248,
    251,252,257
  Martin 193,217
Burke, Anna Maria 151
  Joseph 151
  Philip 151
Burkhard, Catharine Mar-
    garet 164
  Dorothy 185
  Gertrude 26,164,205
  John George 158
  John Phillip 26
  Joseph 205
  Magdalen 158,164
  Martin 26,164,185,205
  Mary Eve 150
  Peter 185
  Philip 158,164
Burkop, John 193,212,
    218,232
  Juliana 193,218,232
  Mary 193
Burkopp, Elizabeth 199
  Frederick 189
  John 182,189,199
  Juliana 189,199
Busch, Maria 93
  Mary 138
Bush, Henry 190
  Magdalen 190
  Margaret 190
  Mary 153

Bussch, Anna Maria 112
Buttler, James 7
  Mary 7
  William 7
Butz, Anna Sophia Ju-
    liana 82
  Anthony 89
  Augustine 73
  Catharine 64,67,69,
    73,75,81,87,90,93,
    109,110,150,155
  Charles 95,121
  Christ. 90,94
  Christian 64,66,69,
    78,120
  John Henry 64
  John William 63,69,
    70,73
  Joseph 89
  Laurence 118
  Lawrence 70
  Magdalen 63,65,70,73,
    78,95,120
  Maria 89,112
  Mary 65
  Mary Magdalen 84
  William 82,83,84,95,
    108,118,121
  William Peter 63,118
Byrner, Andrew 240
  Salome 240
Byrns, Andrew 244
  Sarah 244

--- C ---

C---, Ernest 227
  Mary 227
Calver, Patrick 4
  Philip 4
Cammel, Regina 84,119
  William 225
Canada, Anna 81
Canceler, Elizabeth 6
  George Ernest 9
  John 3,6,9
  Mary 6,9
  Sara 3
Candel, Regina 148
Canner, John 139,151
  Mark 151
  Mary 139,151
  Paul 139
Carass, Christina 169
  John 169
  Salome 169
Carcy, Thomas 6
Cardy, --- 132
  Ann 12
  Catharine 5
  Edward 5,8,12,16
  John 12
  Nicholas 16
  Patrick 5,12,15
  Thomas 5,8,12
Carens, Christina 152
  John 152
Carlin, Anna 105
Carr, Ann 151
  Anna 179
Carroll, Ann 17
  Dominus 123
  John (Bishop) 130,131
Carter, Edward 66
Carty, --- 44,105
  Albertina 33,50,51,

Carty (cont.)
  58,65,67,69,72,73,
  95,96,97,98
  Catharine 33,45,47,
  54,82,90,92,94,95,
  96,97,113
  Ed. 68
  Edward 13,26,27,28,
  29,32,33,34,35,36,
  43,45,49,50,51,52,
  53,54,55,56,57,58,
  59,60,61,65,67,71,
  73,74,97,101,107,
  108,110,113
  Elizabeth 45,95,99
  Francis 259
  John 90,92,96
  M. Salome 51
  Margaret 71
  Mary 69
  Mary Albertina 69
  Mary Ann 40
  Nicholas 24,33,50,51,
  57,58,65,67,69,72,
  73,75,78,80,82,84,
  87,89,90,91,92,93,
  94,95,96,97,98,99,
  101,109
  Nicholas (Jr.) 71,90
  Th. 82
  Thomas 99
Case, Matthew 260
Cassely, Michael 219
Castelah, Mary 10
  Pierce 10
  Sarah 10
Catugn, Thomas 10
Cauffman, Mary 67
Cauffmann, Joseph 67
Causse, J. B. (Rev.) 127
Cavely, Daniel 240
Cawlvert, Margaret 6
  Patrick 6
  Philip 6
  William 6
Cecily, Mary 55
Chaffet, Catharine 37
  Henry 37
  Michael 37
Chateau, A. Barbara 8
  Catharine 8
  M. Eva 8
  Nicholas 8
Chaudmont, Anna Mary 165
  Anthony 159
  Elizabeth 159
Chaudron, John Simon 131
  Joseph Elizabeth Ju-
    lius 131,173
Chaumon, Anna Maria 73
  Elizabeth 73
  John 73
Chaumont, Anna M. 89
  Anna Maria 66
  Anna Maria Fricker 113
  Catharine 89
  Elizabeth 73
  John 66,89
  John Bernard 53
  Joseph 39,89,113
  M. Catharine 39
Chaussee, Claudine Fran-
    coise 131
Chevain, Catharine 162,
  168,194
  Elizabeth 194
  Magdalen 168
  Peter 162,168,194

Chevain (cont.)
  Valentine Peter 162
Chevin, Catharine 176
  Peter 111,176
Christ, Barbara 106
Clark, Anna ·195
  Henry 195
  James 195
  John 195
  Patrick 195
  Rachel 195
  William 216
Clee, Charles 212,238,
  239,242,244,250,255
  Christine 189,212,249
  Elizabeth 210
  Ernest 189,210,212,
  238,245,246,248,249
  John 189
  Madeline 238,245,246,
  248
  Mechtilde 248
  Sarah 250,255
  William 238,250
Clemer, Catherine 232,
  261
  Christian 151,152,
  179,232,261
  George 232
  Mary 152
Clemmer, Catharine 158,
  164,167,170,174,189,
  193,209
  Catherine 236,238,
  245,257,258
  Christian 158,164,
  164,167,170,174,189,
  193,209,213,236,238,
  245,257,258
  Elizabeth 158,209
  James 214
  John 167,247,249
  Joseph 174
  Samuel 193
  Sarah 238
Clerk, John 164
  Mary Eve 164
  William 164
Closkey, M. Magdalen 80
Cobele, Anna Catharine
  Philippina 87
  Anna Maria 98
  Bartholomew 88,99
  Catharine 87
  Daniel 87,98
  Elisabeth 248
  Henry Daniel 98
  John 78,87,91,233,248
  John James 87
  Madeline 233
  Maria 87
  Mary 233
  William 248
Coble, Bartholomew 231
  Daniel 235
  Elisabeth 231,233
  Henry 233
  Jeremiah 260
  John 175,233,260
  Joseph 233
  Mary 249,260
  Mary Anna 235
  Philippine 260
  William 260
Coblet, Anna 225,226
  Bartholomew 155,191,
  193,195,203,204,205,
  206,225,247

Coblet (cont.)
  Catharine 165,165,
    170,191,195,196,198,
    200,204
  Catherine 234
  Charles 225
  Daniel 151,161,183,
    188,194,195,198,204,
    205,212,248
  Elisabeth 234,242,247
  Elizabeth 194,195,
    197,200,203
  Eva 151
  Helen 225,226
  Henrietta 234
  Henry 195,197,198,
    200,234
  John 157,161,164,165,
    169,171,172,183,191,
    194,195,197,198,200,
    205,234,242
  John B. 257
  Joseph 158,199,225
  M. Anna 198
  Martin 226
  Mary 151,161,165,183,
    188,204,212,225,257
  Mary Ann 155,161,195
  Mary Anne 205
  Philippina 191,192
  William 225,226
Cognway, John 10
  Margaret 10
  Mary 10
Cole, Christina 96
  Elisabeth 260
  Juliana 260
Comins, Anna 7
  Michael 2,7,8,9
  Sarah 8
  Thomas 7
  Timothy 2
Conaugh, David 12
  Coners, Judith 2
Connelly, Catharine 24,
    53
Connely, Bernard 8,10
  Brigid 8
  Mary 10
  Peter 8
Conner, Anna 157,161,
    165,171,189,198,203
  Anna Maria 189
  Catharine 165
  John 157,161,165,171,
    172,189,198,203
  Margaret 171
  Mary 157,198
  Paul 198
Connolly, Bernard 201
  Catharine 201
  John 201
  Mary 201
Connor, Peter 213
  Rose 213
  Thomas 7
Conrad, Elisabeth 249
  James 249
Cooper, Benigna 56
  Francis 51,52,53,54,
    56,57,58
Cornyn, Dominick 227
  Margaret 227
Corrent, Fairis 28
  Rose 28
  Samuel 28
Covely, Aaron 238
  Anna 240,242,252,257

Covely (cont.)
  Bartholomew 208,229,
    238
  Catharine 208
  Catherine 238
  Daniel 208,220
  Elisabeth 226,229,236,
    238,240,244,247,252
  Elizabeth 208,220
  Ferdinand 240
  H. 209
  Henry 208,210,211,
    220,226,227,230,236,
    240,244,247,252
  John 208,214,220,226,
    238,240,242,247
  John B. 209,214
  Joseph 242
  M. An. 208
  Mary 209,225,226,238,
    240
  Mary Ann 220
  Mary Anna 240
  Mary Catherine 240
  William 240,252,257
Coverly, Henry 207,260
Cramer, Joseph 174
  Mary Magdalen 174
  Veronica 174
Crames, Johanna 12
Cred, Andrew 138,139,
    140,147
  Barbara 147
  Catharine 140,141,144
  Elizabeth 140,144
  John 140,144,147,148
  Joseph 144
  Magdalen 139,147
  Mary 140
  Mary Elizabeth 148
  Mary Susan 138
  Michael 141,144,148
  Nicholas 138,147
  Nicholas Andrew 140
  Susan 138,147
  Susanna Barbara 141
Cremer, Anna Maria 102
  Anna Maria Gertrude 47
  Elizabeth 38,152
  Mary Ann 94
  Mary Catharine 38
  Matthias 38,47,84,94,
    101
Cremers, Joanna 140
Creutzer, Anna M. Grand-
    jean 111
  Anna Maria 84
  Maria 92
Crone, Mary Eva 57
Croner, John George 57
  Margaret 57
  Rebecca 80
Crossby, Farrel 3
  Thomas 3
Crunewald, Catharine 44
Cunius, John 205

--- D ---

Dabber, --- 24
  Andrew 63
  Elizabeth 74
  John Henry 63
  Maria 63
Dabre, Barbara 142
Daily, Charles 29

Daily (cont.)
  Helen 29
  Margaret 29
  Mary 29
Danckel, Eva 80
  Jacob 105
  James 3
Daner, Christina 13
Dapper, Andrew 51,71,210
  Barbara 51
  Catharinne 71
  Christian 51,90
  Elizabeth 90
  George 210
  Jacob 202
  Margaret 210
  Maria 71
  Mary 51,202
Daren, William 166
Darham, Johanna 98
Darnay, James 8,9,15
  Rose 8,9
Darsey, Charles 11
  Daniel 11
  Elizabeth 11
Daubert, Peter 251
Dauny, John 200
  Margaret 200
  Thomas 200
de Barth, Louis (Rev.)
    128,129
de La Grange, Joseph E.
  G. M. 131
Delkamm, Henry 139
  Mary Eve 139
Dellecan, Henry 145
  Mary Charlotte 145
  Mary Scharlotta 145
  Susan 145
Delvaux, Nicholas (Rev.)
    125,127,128,129,130,
    135,149,152,179,221
Demand, George 17
de Montulle, Marraine
  Made. Marie Louise
    Julienne Barrone 131
Demuth, Anna Catharine
    67
  Catharine 78,110
  James 67
  M. Catharine 67
Denis, Anna 213,252
  Anthony 252
  Elisabeth 224,252
  Elizabeth 196
  John 196,224
  Mary 196
  Mary Juliana 224
  Onan 3
Dennes, Catharine 147
  Catharine Elizabeth
    147
  John 147
Dennis, Catharine 173
  Elizabeth 173
  John 173
Dens, Conrad 220
Depre, --- 86
  Andrew 27,68,110
  Barbara 37
  Christina 108
  Eliz. 86
  Elizabeth 73,74
  James 27,37,73,74,
    108,184
  M. 71,82
  Margaret 81,95,107
  Mary Barbara 37

268

Derham, Catharine 65
Johanna 111
John 65
De Ritter, John Baptist
(Rev.) 1,12,13,14,
17,20,101,102,122
Derr, James 67
John 67
Margaret 67
Dever, Charles 156
De Vologe, Aime Jean
Gerbier 131
Blanche Jeanne Marie
Louise 131,155
dewald, Anna 140
Dgg, Mary 205
Dideraff, John 38
Diderich, John 185
Diederich, Catharine
202,208
Elizabeth 208,217
John 208
Dienes, Elizabeth 192
John 192
Mary Barbara 192
Dieterichs, Elizabeth 97
John 97
Dietrich, Catharine 59
George 75
Mary Eva 32
N. 32
Dietrichs, Elizabeth 97
John 97,121
Maria 121
Mary 97
Dille, Catherine 262
Daniel 262
Dillinger, Susan 229
Dillon, Daniel 214,256
Elisabeth 256
John 256
Johnson 214
Sara 214
Doeri, George Peter 9
James 4,6,9
John 4
Doffee, Dorothy 99
Dolhamer, Thomas 262
Dolhauer, Henry 258
Dolhower, Henry 260
Dollhagen, Elizabeth 191
Henry 191
Mary Barbara 191
Dollhauer, Anna 227,233
Barbara 197,231,238
Catharine 202
Helen 238
Henry 197,202,214,
218,219,231,238
Litta 231
Mary Barbara 202,218
Mary Philippina 197
Dollinger, Susan 260
Dollingers, Catharine
139
Dom, --- 155
Anna Elizabeth 199
John 199
Joseph 199
Domm, Elizabeth 138,
142,145,146
Jacob 138
Joseph 142
Mary Elizabeth 142
Michael 138
Philip 146
Rosina 138,139,142,143
Thomas 142,145,146

Donahew, Thomas 9,10
Dorm, Anna 5
Catharine 3,5,9
John 3,5,9
Margaret 9
Dorret, Mary 156
Neal 156
Dorst, Frederick 107
Dossert, Susanna 178
Dotendorf, Jacob 162
John Andrew 162
Mary Theresa 162
Dotendorff, Dorothy 175
John 175
John Andrew 168
Theodore 168
Theresa 168,175
Dresen, Mary 150
Drexel, --- 13
Anthony 64,108
Catharine 64
James 64
Dries, --- Maria 109
Driess, Mary 83
Drollinger, Catharine
110
Dubon, Lawrence 14
Duf, Anna 97,98
Catharine 97
Cornelius 97
Margaret 97
Samuel 97
Duffy, Daniel 99
Dugan, Mary 156
Dum, Anna 225,240,242,
245,247,252
Anna Elisabeth 225,226
Caspar 154,164,169,
181,182
Catharine 154
Daniel 254,256
Elisabeth 252
Elizabeth 152,162,
164,168,181,191,194,
200,206,208,210
Eva 164,181,182
George 200
Jacob 152,173
James 210,240,242,246,
250,252,254,256,262
John 225,226,229
Joseph 191,199,262
Juliana 240,242,246,
250,252,256,262
Madeline 227,229,233,
235,236,241,244,246,
248,250,254,256
Magdalen 173,191,196,
200
Margaret 236
Mary 154,238,242
Mary Eva 169
Rosina 181
Sabina 254
Sarah 255
Solomon 248
Susan 258
Thomas 164,168,182,
182,196,202,203,205,
206,208,210,227,228,
229,233,235,240,244,
245,246,247,250,252,
256,258
Thomas (Jr.) 206,207
Valentine 162,168,
173,182,191,196,200,
208,209,229,236,241,
248,254

Dunckel, Jacob 120
Dupont, Petronilla 87
Durr, John 78
Margaret 78
Duval, Francis 132,217
Dwen, William 166

--- E ---

Eber, Margaret 139
Ebert, Barbara 244
Elizabeth 211
John 244
Ebrers, Catharine 177
Eccorod, --- 132
Adam 142
Barbara 142
Elizabeth 138,139,142
George 139
Henry 138,142
James 139
Magdalen 177
Mary Catharine 142
Mary Elizabeth 138
Eck, --- 24
Abraham 150
Agatha 90,94,150
Anna 30,242,261
Anna M. 68,92,99
Anna Maria 68,92,99,
111
Barbara 147
Catharine 54,75,77,
82,96,108,112,139,
143,152,153,155
Charlotte 150
Conrad 30
Daniel 80,138,242
Dorothy 139,152
Elizabeth 93,99,138,
139,141,143,178
Eva 138,152,155,179
James 260
John 26,30,49,54,61,
67,80,102,106,109,
112,116,139,143,150,
151,152,155,178,179,
259
John (Jr.) 64,92
John Baptist 49
John Joseph 153
John Peter 26
Joseph 46,64,68,80,
82,90,94,99,143,150,
156,261
Judith 259
Juliana 143
M. 72,90
M. Margaret 90,242
Madeline 242,260
Magdalen 30,49,54,
112,116,142,143,148,
153,178,179
Margaret 63,108,151
Maria 83
Mary Elizabeth 141
Mary Eva 26,96,178
Mary Magdalen 26
Mary Teresa 30
Peter 98,99,137,147,
152,153,155,179,242
Samuel 261
Theodore 69,141,147,
153
Veronica 54,116
Eckenrod, Anna Elisabeth

269

Eckenrod (cont.)
238
Anna Margaret 182
Barbara 211,242
Catharine 200
Christian 234,242,246
Christopher 182,199
Elisabeth 233,238,
242,246
Elizabeth 200,208,
211,214
Francis 238
George 169
Henry 208,211,213,
214,233,238,246
John 200,214,241
Magdalen 213
Margaret 199,200
Mary 169,246
Mary Barbara 169
Mary Catharine 208
Peter 169
Salome 242
Stephen 182
Eckenrode, Elisabeth 258
Mary Catherine 258
Eckenrodt, --- 132
Anna Margaret 165
Benjamin 201
Charles 193
Christian 157,214
Christopher 165,173,
199,205
Daniel 158
Elisabeth 224,228
Elizabeth 162,168,175,
190,194,196,199,214
George 158,193,205,224
Henry 162,168,175,
190,194,195,199,214,
224,228
Jacob 194
John 192,205,214
John Henry 162
Magdalen 157
Margaret 157,168,173,
196,199,205
Mary 158,173,192,193,
196,201,205,207,214
Mary Elizabeth 192
Michael 199
Peter 173,175,192,
196,201,205
Susan 228
Eckenrot, Catharine
Elizabeth 148
George 148
Mary 148
Eckenroth, --- 111
Adam 28,97
Anna Barbara 35,41,
54,70
Anna Catharine 88
Anna Margaret 46,64,
66,76,83,84,95
Anna Maria 88
Anna Mary 28
Barbara 28,61
Catharine 46,62,102
Catharine Scandal 46
Christ. 46,84,95
Christian 60,82,83,
97,110
Christopher 55,70,74,
76,88,110
Conrad 61
Elizabeth 28,30,37,
42,76,97,102

Eckenroth (cont.)
Elizabeth (Jr.) 47
Elizabeth Margaret 33
Eva 46
Eva Mary 33
George 36,40,41,47,
66,88
Henry 28,35,41,43,45,
46,52,54,56,61,70,
76,111
John 7,8,35,88
John Adam 84
Joseph 42
M. 44
M. Barbara 52
M. Elizabeth 54,82,
84,91
Margaret 7,8,88,97,111
Peter 28,33,46,76
Eckerod, --- 132
Anna Magdalen 141
Eckerott, --- 132
Elizabeth 146
Henry 146
Louis 146
Eckorod, --- 132
Christian 141
Mary 141
Eckrod, Christian 254
Eckrodt, Christian 210
Elizabeth 210
Henry 210
Louis 251
Mary 251
Eckroth, Anna Margaret
17
Catharine 11
John 11
Margaret 11
Edelblut, Anna Catharine
120
Catharine Elizabeth 65
James 65,87
John Ferdinand 87
NN. 120
William Peter 65
Egen, Elizabeth 137
Egg, --- 24
Aaron 244
Agatha 172,183,190,
192,201,208,209,212,
216,256
Albertine 244,248
Aloitina 191,196,201,
217,226,235
Andrew 196
Ann 249
Anna 35,104,191,219,
235,242,252,255,257
Anna Maria 137
Anthony 189
Benjamin 164,253
Carolina 242
Catharine 104,106,
108,166,183,206,211
Catherine 231,235
Charles 247,257
Charlotte 157,164,173,
192,199,201,206,208,
213,231,235,252,253
Daniel 201,206,206,
219,227,231,237,246,
250,256
David 202,217
Dorothy 157,172,182,
184
Elisabeth 252
Elizabeth 34,184,189,

Egg (cont.)
194,201
Esther 173,235,250
Eva 36,137,191,219,243
George 172,252
Henry 252
Jacob 160,196
James 216,256
John 31,34,36,37,39,
43,44,49,108,157,
164,172,173,182,183,
184,191,192,196,199,
201,202,204,206,208,
209,213,217,226,231,
234,235,237,242,243,
244,247,248,252,253,
257
John (Jr.) 50
John (Sr.) 16,206,
218,219
John George 157
John Laurence 157,
213,252
John Peter 36
Jonathan 255
Joseph 48,51,62,74,
157,164,172,183,190,
192,201,208,209,212,
216,226,242,244,251,
256
Leah 226
Lia 201,216
Lita 248
Louisa 172,191,196,
201,217
M. Margaret 219,227,
231,237,250
Madeline 226,227,232,
236,238,243,248,253,
253,255,256,257
Magdalen 34,37,43,
157,158,160,166,168,
172,175,182,183,188,
191,196,202,211,212,
214,217
Margaret 166,194,206,
218,227,242,246,253
Maria 182
Mary 108,137,158,166,
214,237,242,247,251,
252,256
Mary Agatha 157,164
Mary Anna 251
Mary Barbara 201
Mary Elizabeth 160,
168,189,192,216
Mary Eva 44
Mary Magdalen 16,39,
201
Mary Margaret 256
Paul 168,191,199,217,
253
Peter 29,157,158,160,
166,168,172,175,188,
191,192,196,202,205,
206,207,208,211,212,
214,217,220,226,227,
232,236,237,238,242,
243,248,253,257
Peter (Sr.) 215
Rachel 238
Robert 226
Ruben 256
Sabina 43,158,160,172
Salome 208,227,232,237
Samuel 220,248,253
Solomon 208,235,242,
249,255

270

Egg (cont.)
Susan 220,253
Theodore 53,160,168,
189,194,216
Theresa 206
Veronica 164,166,183
Ehrman, Henry 30
John 16,30,102
Mary Cecelia 30
Eichhorn, Andrew George
233
Eva 232,233,233,243,
258
Francis 205,232,233,
243,258,259
Eichorn, Eva 230,241
Eve 197,201
Eve Helen 201
Francis 197,201,204,
241
J. F. 230
John Francis 230
Mary 241
Mary Ann 197
Eickhorn, Eva 249
Francis 249
Theresa 249
Eierson, Anna 202
John 202
Thomas 202
Eimold, Peter 16
Eirenzen, Joseph 258
Mary Elizabeth 258
Eisemann, Christian 193
Frances 193
Susan 193
Eisenhauer, Agatha 238,
239,250
Anna 238
Elisabeth 255
James 238,239,250,255
John 255
Eisenmann, Christian
147,197
Salome 197
Susan 147,197
Elay, James 262
Elim, James 262
Ellz, Margaret 215
Els, A. Elisabeth 243
Ann Elizabeth 165
Anna Elisabeth 228
Anna Elizabeth 140,
141,155,161,183
Anthony Jacob 198
Catharine 139,145,
150,179,193
Elis. 190
Elisabeth 237,244
Elizabeth 99,150,151,
157,176,181,188,203,
207
Henry 150
Henry John 140
Jacob 143,144,150,
157,160,161,169,174,
176,181,183,189,193,
196,198,200
James 207,208,235,
239,242,244,248
John 79,84,91,99,141,
150,151,155,161,165,
176,179,181,183,188,
190,199,200,203,207,
228,233,237,243,244
John Frederick 69
John Henry 64,176
John Jacob 140

Els (cont.)
John William 244
Juliana 198,203,224,
232
M. Elizabeth 69
M. Frederica 69
M. Magdalen 198
Magdalen 174
Margaret 169
Mary 169,172,176,183,
189,196,200,219,235,
239,242,244,248
Mary Juliana 141
Mary Magdalen 157,193
Sophia 169,193,194,
195,197,207,226,228,
248
Sophia Maria Juliana
79
Sophy 207
Susan 228,233
Eltz, Catherine 258
Ely, Anna Margaret 168
Embs, John Paul 142
Juliana 142
Valentine 142
Emmery, Andrew 182
Elizabeth 182
Emms, Joseph 169
Juliana 169
Valentine 169
Ems, Anna Maria 148
John 193
Juliana 148,151,193
Valentine 148,178,193
Engel, Catharine 181,
188,193,194,199,219
Elias 194
Henry 181,188,194,199
Mary 181
Sara 199
William 188
Engelhard, Andrew 6
Walburga 6
Erb, Christine 201,208,
217,226,229,232,237,
242,246,251
George 226
James Reuben 258
John 201,217,246
Juliana 242
Mechtilde 237
Peter 201,206,208,
217,226,229,232,237,
242,246,251,258
Theresa 232
Erman, Catharine 34,53,
107
John 33,34
Joseph 53
M. Cecilia 34
Mary Cecilia 33
Ermann, Catharine 108
M. 107
Maria 104,105,106
Mary 49,55,59
Erntzen Paul (Rev.) 125,
128,129,130,131,132,
133,134,152,156,162,
163,164,168,169,187,
188,191,194,198,199,
201,207,221,222,223,
225,230,231,232,239,
240,241,242,243,244,
252,256,257,258
Esselin, George 4
Ettinger, Andrew 208
Anna 208

Ettinger (cont.)
Catharine 208
Catherine 228
Frederick 208
John 228
Everard, Elizabeth 79
Philip 79
Everling, Anna Catharine
86
Henry 86
Eyan, Anna 211
George 211
John 211
Eyerson, Anna 214
Barbara 246,254
George 246,254
John 214
Joseph 214,246
Mary Anna 254
Eysehuden, Catharine 152
Eysenbeiss, Mary 81
Eysenhutt, Catharine 89,
104
Eysenmann, Christian
144,177
Jacob 144
Susan 144

--- F ---

Faller, John 17,29,36
Farmer, Ferdinand (Rev.)
13,17,20
Fasser, Charles 68
William 68
Fe, Anna 86
Febinger, Catharine 212
Frederick 212
Margaret 212
Federer, Elizabeth 227
Feels, Elisabeth 227
James 227
Litta 227
Felix, Anna 176,212,
241,244,251,259
Anna M. 70
Anna Margaret 77
Anna Maria 49,61
Anna Mary 172,175,
230,239,257
Anthony 79,188,189,
193,196,198,199,207,
215,226,229,230,232,
233,234,237,240,244,
245,249,250,251,253,
256,257,259
Barbara 61,70,77,162,
165,175,182,188,189,
212,214,234,244,249,
251,252,259
Catharine 48,70
Catherine 229,230,
232,233,234,237,240,
244,245,249,250,251,
253,257,260
Daniel 189
Elisabeth 238,243,
251,253,254,257
Elizabeth 170,189,193,
206,209,213,250,258
Eva 236,238
Eve 175,209
George 251
Henry 253
Jacob 175
James 209,212,213,

Felix (cont.)
241,242,244,245,249,
250,252,253,254,257
John 48,251,259
John Anthony Nicholas
240
Margaret 226
Martin 70,77,109,175,
188,189,209,212,214,
234,244,249,251,259
Mary 211,212,235,238,
242,257
Mary Anna 259
Michael 170,189,193,
238,243,251
Nicholas 32,40,48,49,
61,70,77,79,106,172,
175,182,211,212,218,
226,230,239
Nicholas Laurence 32
Peter 252
Polly 259
Rebecca 243
Regina 77
Samuel 170,250
Sarah 234
Solomon 214,254,256,
259
Stephen 40
William 244
Felue, John 106
Felur, John 106
Fennigen, Mary 259,260
Fenstermacher, Anna Mary
234
George 207,234,241
Susan 234,241
Fernan, Maria 97
Fernandez, John 15
Ferry, Bernard 212
Ferstermacher, Anna 227
George 227
Susan 227
Fick, Anna Regina 5
Jodoc 5
Mary Susanna 5
Fiderer, Catharine 47,87
James Michael 47
Peter 65
Stephen 40,47,65,86,87
Finck, Adam 109
Agnes 56,69
Anna M. 56
Benjamin 83
Catharine 37,62
Conrad 33,37,62
Conrad Andrew 45
Elizabeth 69
Henry 59,72,79,83,109
John 62,72
John Adam 70
John Michael 107
Magdalen 62,72,79
Mary Christina 37
Nicholas 56,69
Fine, Anna 173,183
Elizabeth 173,183
John 173,183
Fink, Catharine 45,213
Conrad 45
Henry 213
John 213
Magdalen 213
Fischer, Agnes 14
Andrew 70
Anna Barbara 46
Anna M. 70
Anna Margaret 84

Fischer (cont.)
Anna Maria 59,94,139
Anna Mary 52
Catharine 59
Elizabeth 98,111
James 46
Joseph 46,52,59,70,
84,94
Mary Barbara 52,102
Fischwasser, Rosina 138
Rosine 183
Fisher, Catharine 42
Henry 43
Joseph 43
Fitzcharroll, Elizabeth
5
Gerald 5
John 5
Patrick 5
Flaharty, Frances 10
Margaret 10
Flauer, --- 132
Anna Maria 141,151
Catharine 138,141,
146,148
Christopher 141,151
John 138,141,146,148
Joseph 141
Magdalen 141,151
Flemenn, Jerome 137
Mary 137
Rosina 137
Flennigen, Charles 126
Flood, Anna Catharine 77
Bernard 77
Mary 77
Flower, --- 132
Andrew 176
Anna 156
Anna Mary 224
Catharine 65,88,155,
163
Christopher 98,111,
156,163,170,176,200
Henry 40,43,48,56,65,
88
James 224
John 88,155,163,224
John Henry 43
Joseph 48,210,229,
230,241
Louis 241
Louis Henry 99
Magdalen 98,156,163,
170,176,200
Margaret 43,88,102
Peter 155
Rachel 43
Rebecca 241
Rose 88,99
Rosina 40,48,65
Samuel 163
Thomas Christopher 56,
200
William 163
Focht, --- 234
Daniel 194
Fock, Sara 259
Foelix, Anna Maria 141
Leonard 143
Nicholas 141
Regina 141
Fort, Mary 242,255
Fortman, Charles Leopold
182
Margaret 172
Fortmann, Charles 167
Charles Joseph 195

Fortmann (cont.)
Charles Leopold 195
Margaret 195,207,219
Fowler, Edward 62,110
Elizabeth 62
Peter 62
Thomas 62
Foy, Henry 68
James 68
Sarah 68
Frambachs, James (Rev.)
21,103
P. 13
Frantz, Elizabeth 8
Eva M. 8,12
Jacob 7,8,12,15
James 3,5,9
Mary Apollonia 3
Nicholas 16
Simon 12
Franz, John 207,256
Franzel, Eva 154
Fraul, Anna M. 39,79,109
Anna Maria 105
Maria 67
Fredder, Anna Mary 13
Henry 13,17,24
Frendenberger, Conrad
116
Fretter, Anna Mary 30
Henry 24,27,28,29,30,
35
Fricker, --- 207
Anna Maria 113
Ant. 79
Anthony 27,29,33,37,
39,41,50,77,90,99,
141,185,251
Antony 42
Catharine 97,145,162,
163,205
Catharine Albertina 97
Catharine Elizabeth 33
Catherine 247,251,256
Eva 79,90,99,141,165,
183,225,242,247,248
Eva Mary 77
Eve 170,174,175,176,
196
Frances 31,48
George 97,111,161
Henry George 27
John 16,90
John Frederic 42
Joseph 59,80,87,90,97,
145,151,162,163,205
M. Catharine 39
M. Theresa 50
Magdalen 99
Margaret 37,39,41,42,
50
Mary 247
Mary Anne 43
Mary Eva 77
Mary Salome 26
Mary Salome Kohl 102
Mary Teresa 30
Nicholas 80,205
Salome 13
Theresa 89,98,107
Thomas 50
William 90,209,247,
251,256
Frickert, Anthony 149
Catharine 142,152
Eva 149
Eve 149
George 142

Frickert (cont.)
John 152
Joseph 142
Frickerts, Mary Eve 148
Fricklinger, Christian
59
Friderer, Catharine 214
Stephen 214
Friderich, George Rei-
nold 3
Philip 3
Fridrich, A. Barbara 8
Barbara 15
Fries, Bernard 111
Mary 97
Fromm, Francis (Rev.)
126
Frydenberg, Eve 216
Fuchs, Anna Mary 29
Elisabeth 245
George 245
Mary 245
Fues, Dorothea 8
Dorothy 10
John 8,10
Margaret 8
Fuhler, Ulric 106
Fuss, A. Catharine 11
Catharine 78,86,104
Dorothy 11
George Adam 31
John 11,31,50,62
John Adam 104
Futterer, Stephen 35
Futtner, Joseph 58

--- G ---

G---, Anna Philippina
224
Barbara 224
Philip 224
Gaas, Salome 185
Gabriel, John 81
Mary Magdalen 81
Gaddy, --- 133
Elizabeth 137,142
George 142
Gajner, Edward 184
Gainer, Edward 112
Gallacher, William 224
Gallejar, Barbara 145
Gallon, Andrew 31
Anna Margaret 62
John Joseph 31,48,88,
96
Joseph 62
Margaret 48,88,96
Gans, Catharine 138,
149,171
John 138,149,163,171
John William 149
William 138
Ganss, Ann 194
Anna 197,198,224,229,
236,243,244,249
Catharine 198
Catherine 224,227,229
Elisabeth 229,239
Ernest 227
George 175,191,194,
197,232,237
John 175,191,194,197,
198,224,229,236,243,
249
Madeline 232,237,244

Ganss (cont.)
Magdalen 175,194,197,
198,236
Mary 224,227,239
Mary Anna 243
Samuel 237
Sara 191
William 197,227,239,
244,249
Gantz, Balthasar 107
Balthaser 105
Jacob 105
John 105
Garden, Edward 4
Thomas 5
Gardener, Theresa 259
Gartner, Margaret 14
Gaschet de Lisle, Regina
Frances Genevieve
Charlotte 132,173
Joseph Louis 132
Gasman, Andrew 259
Veronica 259
Gassawer, Catharine 194
John 194
Gassner, Caspar 11
Edward Daniel 11
Elizabeth 11
Martin 9
Gatringer, Elizabeth 7
Gauch, Mary 80
Gaucker, Ann 39
Anna 93
Anna Barbara 44,51,
55,67,75,138
Anna Maria 61,98,115
Anna Mary 48
Barbara 48,59,61,141,
144,153,154
Catharine 75
George 150
James 83
John 39,44,48,51,55,
59,61,67,75,78,81,
82,83,93,98,104,111,
115,137,138,141,144,
150,153,154
John George 138
John Peter 55
Joseph 51,154
Louis 39
Marina 137
Michael 144
Gauckler, George 6
John George 4,10
Gauger, Anna Christina
166
Barbara 156,161,180
Elizabeth 166,185
John 156,158,166,180,
185
Mary 158
Peter 158,185
Gayde, William 154
Gayner, Elizabeth 219
Gede, Margaret 190
Sophia 190
William 190
Gehry, Eve 216
Martin 196,201
Mary 196,201
Mary Catharine 196
Geidlinger, Catharine 16
Geiger, A. M. 12
A. Mary 8
John Henry 8
Matthew 7,8,11,12
Simon 12

Geisler, Luke (Rev.) 20,
39,104
Geisweiler, Catharine
138
Henry 138
Philip 138
Gellhoff, Sophia 156
Geog, Mary Anna 261
Geogen, Margaret 145
Georg, Elisabeth 255
James 255
Thomas 255
Gererd, Catharine 188
John 188
Margaret 188
Gergel, Henry 169
Joanetta 169
Geri, Eva Bernard 26
Philip 26,114
Philip James 26
Gerich, Eva 105
Maria 93
Mary 80
Mary Eva 26
Phil. 26
Gernand, George 250,
253,255
Mary 250,253,255
Mary Magdalen 220
Rebecca 253
Gerschweiler, Catharine
55,59,69
John 59
John Michael 83
Louis 55
M. Elizabeth 69
Philip 55,59,69,83,107
Gerstweiler, Catharine
195
Catherine 226,228
Elisabeth 232
Elizabeth 182,208
Frances 232
John 162,174,195,208,
232
Louis 154
Mary 208,232
Michael 199,208,232
Philip 151,195,226,228
Susan 151
Gersweiler, Andrew 144
Catharine 144
Philip 144
Gertbachery, Apollania
260
Gervais, Charles Nicho-
las 132
Gery, Elizabeth 143,171
Elizabeth Eva 157
Jacob 191
John 146
Joseph 164
Martin 145,146,151,
157,164,171,191,236
Mary 145,146,151,157,
164,171,191,236
Philip 143,178,185
Sara 143
Thomas 236
Geth, Anna Mary 178
Geven, Catharine 149
Gever, Catharine 143
Peter 143
Rosina 143
Geyde, George 172
Sophia 172
William 172
Geyer, Anna Margaret 97

Geyer (cont.)
  Conrad 26,113
  Mary Elizabeth 26
  Mary Eva 26
Geyger, Catharine Fre-
  derica 90
  Conrad 90
  Philippina 90
Gibbins, Ellen 34
  Frances Margaret 41
  Helen 41
  James 27,34,41
  Mary 27
Gibsen, Catharine 145
  George 148
  Henry 145
  Joseph 144
  Margaret 138,146
  Mary 178
Gibson, Anna 200
  Catharine 35,37,41,44,
  48,56,60,63,68,70,
  72,88,96,98,151,152,
  154,156,157,158,180,
  181,183,197,201,231
  Catherine 237
  Christina 168,170,
  171,238
  Christine 190,194,
  200,206,210,224,228,
  231,237
  David James 237
  Elisabeth 236
  Elizabeth 167,175,210
  Fr. 92
  Francis 6,34,35,41,
  49,116,190
  Frank 5,6,9,10,12,14,
  15
  George 41,180
  Gertrude 164,171,173,
  183
  Henry 6,9,14,15,35,
  37,41,44,48,56,60,
  62,63,65,68,70,72,
  81,82,88,96,98,102,
  149,153,165,167,175,
  180,183,193,197,201,
  205,207,216,231,237
  John 98,201,206,237
  Joseph 48,150,153,
  158,168,170,171,190,
  194,197,200,200,210,
  224,228,231,237,238
  M. Barbara 82
  M. Gertrude 65
  Margaret 5,6,8,9,28,
  34,35,71,86,88,98,
  100,138,184,194
  Margaret Elizabeth 175
  Maria 102
  Mary 27,171
  Rachel 88,96
  Regina 28,41,78,108
  Salome 231
  Susan 167
Gilbert, Daniel 234
  David 243
  Elisabeth 234,243,
  246,256
  James 207,234,243,
  246,256
  Mary 207
  Mechtilde 246
  Nicholas 207
  Samuel 256
Gilgert, Adam 212
  Elizabeth 212

Gilgert (cont.)
  Jonas 212
Gincken, Louis 151
Girard, John 50
  Mary 50
Given, Peter 149
Givin, Catharine 149
Glass, Anna Catharine 34
  James 34
  Mary 29
Glassmayer, Joseph 249
  Mary 249
Glassmeier, Catharine
  206
  John 206,246
  Litta 246
  Peter 206
  Theresa 246
Gless, Ann 38
  Anna 38
  George 43
  James 38,41
  John George 38
  Mary Agatha 41,41
Gling, Mary 146
  Peter 146
  William 146
Gluin, Patrick 151
  Thomas 151
Gobele, Anna M. 246
  John 218
  John B. 246
  Louis 246
  Magdalen 218
  Mary 218,246
  William 246
Godfrey, Henry 73
Golding, John 167
  Sara 167
Good, Catharine 202
  Jacob 202
  John 202
Gording, Catharine 194
  John 194
  Theresa 167,181
Gordon, John 89
  Maria 89
  Rachel 83,101
  Sarah 89
Gotz, Catharine 29
Grandjean, Anna M. 111
Grass, Catharine 28,34,
  42,48,57
  Christopher 28,34,42,
  48,57
  Elizabeth Catharine 42
  John 48
  Magdalen Catharine 57
  Mary Barbara 34
  Regina 28
Great, Andrew 151
  Barbara 262
  Catharine 149
  Jacob 149
  John 262
  Madeline 262
  Michael 149
Green, Abraham 219,244
  Frederick 187,219
  Magdalen 109
  Margaret 60
  Mary 219,244
  Sedeur 244
  Shedericus 244
Greenewald, Barbara 163
  Catharine 195
  Jacob 195
  Joseph 163

Greenewald (cont.)
  Mary Ann 163
  Susan 195
Greenvald, Jacob 159
  Joseph 159
  Mary 159
Greenwald, Anna Mary 167
  Barbara 180
  Jacob 155
  John 155
  Joseph 167
  Magdalen 167
  Mary 155
  Mary Ann 173
  Peter 173
  Philip Joseph 173
  Susan 155
Greeser, Anthony 157
  Rachel 157
Gret, Andrew 154,155,
  158,161,167,168,189,
  205
  Anna 153
  Barbara 167,196
  Catharine 166,168,172,
  190,191,192,194,205
  Charles 196
  Christian 154
  Christina 163
  Christine 190,195
  Daniel 194,196,197
  David 190
  Elizabeth 158,161,
  164,168,183,189,192,
  195,196,204,205
  Esther 191
  Eva Margaret 166
  George 163
  John 153,159,162,164,
  165,166,169,171,183,
  190,191,192,194,196,
  204,205
  John Adam 156,161,190
  Joseph 153,163,164,
  190,195
  Magdalen 158,159,160,
  162,163,165,168,171
  Mary 170
  Mary Elizabeth 153,
  159,162
  Mary Magdalen 167
  Michael 153,158,166,
  173,191,192
  Nicholas 153,156,159,
  166,194,196
  Philip 183,195,196,204
  Samuel 161
  Sara 195
  Solomon 168
  Susan 153,156,159,166,
  181,194,195,196,205
  Susan Barbara 184
Grett, Andrew 27,40,45,
  62,70,75,79,93,94,
  99,100,109,202,203,
  208,211,212,213,215,
  218,228,230,232,233,
  242,243,247,248,257
  Andrew (Jr.) 74,88,107
  Andrew (Sr.) 71
  Ann 208
  Ann Elizabeth 37
  Anna 230
  Anna Barbara 75
  Anna M. 107
  Anna Maria 201
  Barbara 62,111,206,
  224,229,234,251

Grett (cont.)
Barbára 62,111,206,
224,229,234,251
Caroline 252
Catharine 54,56,66,
75,85,87,99,184,188,
200,209
Catherine 226,232,239,
243,245,247,252,255
Charles 229
Christian 212,252
Christine 227
Daniel 93,199,200,
202,203,206,208,209,
228,229,235,237,239,
244,251
David 258
Elias 233
Elisabeth 227,228,
229,231,233,235,237,
238,239,242,244,248,
251,252
Elizabeth 13,62,70,
74,88,93,95,100,188,
199,202,208,211,212,
213
Esther 200,224,235,
237,239,243,246,247,
251
Eve 212
George Adolph 27
Henry 200
J. Adam 229
James 79,233,235,242,
253
John 13,28,31,37,43,
62,65,104,108,188,
199,200,202,205,206,
208,209,211,212,213,
226,227,229,231,232,
235,236,238,239,243,
245,247,252,255,258
John (Jr.) 207
John (Sr.) 206
John Adam 70,201,217
John James 31
John Paul 239
Jonathan 200
Joseph 202,205,224,
227,232,251
Judith 242
M. 208,229
M. Magdalen 74,75
Madeline 244,252,258
Magdalen 40,62,66,70,
71,83,94,112,216
Manuel 251
Margaret 257
Mary 201,227,235,248,
257
Mary Anna 239
Mary Madeline 235
Michael 37,56,66,75,
76,85,87,95,107,184,
200,208,220,224,235,
237,238,239,243,246,
251
Nicholas 85,206,208,
212,213,215,224,250,
252,260
Philip 202,229,237,
242,248
Philip (Jr.) 206
Salome 202,235,237
Samuel 213,228,252
Sarah 245,247,251
Solomon 213
Susan 203,206,208,

Grett (cont.)
212,213,224,236,243,
250,252,258,260
Theresa 209,226,229,
231,234,237,239
Grieser, Ant. 86
Anthony 34,83,259
Cecilia 259
Eliz. 86
Elizabeth 83
Griesmeyer, Anna Mary 7
Simon 7,12
Susanna 7
Griff, Catharine 84
Griffin, Catharine 104
Patrick (Jr.) 49
Griffith, Catharine 34
Mar. 105
Patrick 31,105
Griffonson, Catharine 27
Grill, Eve 196
John 196
Sara 196
Griser, Anthony 167,181
Elizabeth 164,176
Rachel 167
Grismeyer, M. Agnes 9
Simon 9
Susanna 9
Grist, Catharine 84
Groner, John George 40
M. Margaret 40
Mary Catharine 40
Groskop, Abraham 231
Paul 207
Groskopff, A. Margaret 8
Anna Mary 8
James 8
Jacob 15
Grosskopp, Jonathan 211,
212,247
Judith 242
Margaret 212
Mary 247
Samuel 247
Gruber, Barbara 233,244,
247
Henry 96
John 233
Litta 244
Margaret 90,96
Philip 233,244,247
Valentine 90,96
Grubler, Anna 103
Gruenwald, Philip Joseph
30
Grun, Magdalen 109
Margaret 60
Grunenwald, Eva 142
Grunewald, --- 86
Anna Barbara 30
Anna Margaret 70
Anna Maria 53,116,152
Anna Mary 32
Barbara 35,44,47,53,
55,56,70,71,85,89
Elizabeth 16,85
Jacob 143
James 35
Jerome 32
John 17,30,35,44,47,
53,56,70,82,85,116,
118,152,178
Joseph 148,152
M. Barbara 52,56
Mary Ann 148,178
Peter 143
Philip Joseph 148

Grunewald (cont.)
Rosina 143
Susan Mariana 143
Grunewalt, Andrew Jacob
147
Jacob 147
Susan 147
Gruser, Ant. 86
Ant. (Jr.) 57
Anthony 38,49,54,58,
89,91,96,104,106,
108,109
Anthony (Jr.) 47,59,69
Elizabeth 38,54,58,
95,106
Rachel 89,91,96
Regina 91
Gruss, Jacob 103,112
Grusser, Anthony 13,35,
37,101
Catharine 80,105
Elizabeth 13,35,37,
40,80
Gruver, Barbara 191,
197,204
Elizabeth 197
Mary 191
Philip 191,197
Gubernator, Joanna 156,
157
John Laurence 24,111,
156
Laurence 24,70,87,98,
112,155,156,161
Lawrence 156,157
Guereti, Edmund 3
Guery, George 152
Martin 152
Philip 152
Guibson, Henry 3,4,14
Guill, Patrick 11
Peter 11
Gust, Henry 4
Mary Magdalen 4
Rosina 4
Guth, Anna 255
Anna Mary 255
James 255
Juliana 255
Margaret 255
Mary Madeline 255
Gutlan, Joseph John 102
Guttmann, John 178
Gutz, Antonia 103
Gyrven, Judith 126

--- H ---

Haass, Anna Mary 243
Benjamin 243
Elisabeth 243
Haffer, John Georgius
172
Haffner, Barbara 61,66,
149
Catharine 42,61
Conrad 149
Elizabeth 109
Frederic 42,45,50
Frederick 61,66,107
John Michael 66
Susanna 65
Ursula 27
Hagaty, Margaret 233
Patrick 233
Rachel 233

Hagenbuch, James 236
Margaret 236
Hagety, Francis 238
Patrick 238
Rachel 238
Hahn, Catharine 210
John 210
Hailmann, Catharine 108
Haiss, M. Catharine 50
Mary 50
William 50
Hall, William 4
Halter, Andrew 9
Anna Eva 9
Caspar 9
Catharine 59
James 59
M. Eva 8
Margaret 59
Hamerstein, Andrew 27
Philip 261
Susan 261
Hamilton, John 100
Hammerstein, Albertina
73
Andrew 57,65,73,81,
89,107,137,143,151,
182,204
Anna Barbara 57,59,65
Anna Margaret 57
Barbara 73,137,143,
151,182,191,201,204
Catharine 89,98,176,
204
Catharine Elizabeth 65
Elizabeth 137
Louisa 182
M. Barbara 89
M. Magdalen 81
Margaret 81,89,121,181
Nicholas 98,244
Philip 143
Handlon, --- 5
John 12
Matthew 8,10,12
Rachel 12
Handly, Margaret 195
Thomas 195
Hansel, Margaret 154
Hanss, Benjamin 239
Catherine 239
James 239
John James 239
Mary 239
Harken, James 225
Harkens, James 225
Hart, Bernard 235,239,
245,253
Catherine 242
Elisabeth 235,239,
240,242,243,245,253
John 239
Michael 242
Samuel 253
Hartman, Angela 81
Barbara 179
Catharine 51,165,170,
202,209,210
Catherine 224,234,
250,258
Charles 161
Elisabeth 224,239
Elizabeth 175
Francis 16,36,81,101,
108,112,114,163,170,
175,183,224
Francis Joseph 34
Franz 152

Hartman (cont.)
George 152
Henry 170
Jacob 153,165,170
James 92,210
John 44,71,152,161,238
John David 153
John Peter 163
Madeline 225,226
Magdalen 29,170,185,
207
Margaret 165,168,207
Margaret Hammerstein
121
Mary 112,163,165
Mary Magdalen 31
Michael 47,54,81,111,
114,121,165,168,207,
208,210,234,237,239,
245,250,256
Michael Hoffman 29
Philip 258
Polli 152
Polly 152
Samuel 224,250
Sarah 250
Simon 81
Susan 161,250
Hartmann, Abraham Fre-
derick 66
Angela 59,66,92,208
Anthony Michael 148
Appollonia 255
Barbara 16,80
Catharine 47,76,85,
95,98,105,107,144,
148,160,190,197,202,
208,213
Catharine Frederica 94
Catherine 231,232,
241,242,246,249,255
Clara 249
D. 208
Daniel 92
Elis. 214
Elisabeth 241,245,
246,249,250,253,255
Elizabeth 80,102,139,
190,197,201,210
Fr. 214
Francis 38,59,66,84,
92,105,107,139,146,
190,197,201,208,210,
214,241
George 84
Henry 246
Jacob 139,144,148,
160,190,197
Jacob Frederick 140
James 63,85,89,98,
212,213,231,232,241,
242,246,249,255
John 59,66,94,98,140,
147,197,212,213,229,
248
John Joseph 139
John Peter 197
Joseph 146
M. Magdalen 89
Magdalen 63,76,102,
160,191,192,195
Margaret 84,99,213,234
Mary 146,214,246,251,
256
Mary Elizabeth 190
Mary Madeline 251
Mary Magdalen 28,147
Mich. 84

Hartmann (cont.)
Michael 56,59,89,99,
102,112,199,206,213,
234,243,245,246,248,
249,250,251,255
Rebecca 256
Samuel 194,243,255
Sarah 251
Susan 140,147,243,255
Hartranfer, Mary 139
Harvay, Catharine 9
Harvey, Anna 212
Anna 249
Catharine 12
Catherine 11
Job 212,249
Sara 212
Sarah 249
Harvy, Catharine 8
Harzel, Eve 208
Henry 208,233,241
Margaret 241
Ruben 241
Hasser, John Georgius
172
Hauck, Andrew 27
George 27,34
Jacobina 27,34
John George 34,39
Mary Jacobina 39
Matthias 39
Haug, Christian 3,4
Simon 4
Haupt, Dorothy 84
Frederick 84
Hauss, Abraham 172,183
Anna Elizabeth 203
Anna Rachel 243
Frances 189
Jacob 172,173,183,
189,193,203,218
James 234,243
John Jacob 218
Mary 189,193,203,234,
243
Mary Rose 234
Veronica 172,183
Hecht, William 15
Heever, Barbara 258
Heilbron, J. Carolum
(Rev.) 127
Hein, Henry 14
Magdalen 14
Heinech, Susan 261
Heinick, Matthew 261
Heins, John Peter 29
Heitsman, Anna Barbara
49
John George 41
N. 49
Heitsmann, Agatha 38
George 38
James 38
John George 38
Heitz, --- (Widow) 81
Anna Barbara 67
Eva Wagner 121
Michael 105,116,121
Heitzmann, John George
43
John William 43
Helbron, John Baptist
Charles (Rev.) 123,
124,125,126,127,128,
129,134,137,177
Peter (Rev.) 123,124,
125,126,127,128,129,
130,137,138,145,149,

Helbron (cont.)
171,177,179,182,183,
221
Helbronn, Peter (Rev.)
123,124,125,130
Helffer Apollonia 7,8,
10,11
Christ. 81
John Maurice 10
John Wendelin 5,10,11
Mary Apollonia 3,4,6,
81
Wendel 6,7,8,15
Wendelin 3,4,5
Heller, Magdalen 191
Helopart, Peggy 259
Henley, Elizabeth Bar-
bara 40
Henly, Anna Martha 40
Dennis 40
Hennick, Helen 261
John 261
Joseph 261
Michael 261
Hennrich, Conrad 149
Henrich, Anna Magdalen
66
Anna Maria 75,95,203
Barbara 13,70,72,79,
100,147,149,151,156,
161,163,173,185,191,
199,204
Catharine 173,202,
211,215
Catherine 232,253,260
Christian 17,30,33,
35,36,37,40,44,45,
46,47,48,49,50,51,
53,54,56,57,59,60,
61,61,62,63,64,66,
67,68,69,70,71,72,
76,78,79,82,83,84,
86,88,91,92,94,95,
97,98,99,100,102,
103,104,105,108,109,
111,141,147,154,184,
185,205,207
Christian (Jr.) 60,74
Christian (Sr.) 69,74
Christopher 16
Conrad 149
David 253
Elisabeth 229,231,
232,237,242,243,246,
247,260
Elizabeth 40,50,61,
68,75,76,79,88,93,
95,100,105,109,138,
147,154,159,183,189,
191,193,196,198,201,
202,205,209,210,215
Eva Catharine 138
Eva Mary 33,103
Francis Joseph 156
George 185
Jacob 193
John 43,54,56,66,68,
70,72,74,79,83,83,
95,100,106,109,142,
147,149,151,156,163,
173,185,189,191,200,
211,215,236,238,253
John Adam 51,164,199
John George Conrad 142
Joseph 50,147,156,
166,167,183,189,196,
202,232,237,247
M. Barbara 74

Henrich (cont.)
M. Margaret 46,64,88
Magdalen 35,40,50,51,
52,59,60,66,67,74,
83,108,109,154,161,
162,167,205
Margaret 36,47,54,55,
57,74,103,108
Maria 103
Mary 31,193,207
Mary Barbara 66,74,142
Mary Magdalen 60,81,
154,184
Peter 81
Phil. 95,103
Philip 31,50,61,68,
74,75,76,88,93,100,
105,138,159,183,193,
201,205,207,210,211,
215,229,231,237,242,
243,246,260
Philip Adam 159
Henrichs, Anna Maria
Elizabeth 149
Christian 149
Elizabeth 141,142
Henrick, Elizabeth 198
Joseph 198
Henrith, John 78
Henry, John 219
Philip 258
Hentzing, Margaret 159
Heny, Elisabeth 259
Isaac 259
Joseph 259
Michael 259
William 259
Henziger, Barbara 180
Jacob 180
Margaret 180
Herb, Angela 84,108,139
Engel 152
Susan 92
Herbst, Mary Anna 225
P. 172
Peter 162,225
Richard 219
Ther. 172
Theresa 162,225
Hering, Susan 158
Herp, Catharine 15
Hert, Christopher 98
Elizabeth 41,70
Frederic 70
Frederick 84,98
John 41,70,71,75
John Frederick 75,84
M. Elizabeth 75
Magdalen Margaret 41
Mar. Elizabeth 71
Hess, Catherine 253
George 85,92
George James 92
Jeremiah 182
John 182,253
Margaret 182,253
Maria 92
Hickey, Susan 7
Hild, Albertina 68,74,80
Anna Cecilia 33
Catharine 30,33,58,
59,77,87,94,103
Frederic 80
John 68
Joseph 33,37,41,45,
46,58,59,68,74,80,
87,105,108,109,114
Joseph (Jr.) 52

Hill, Christina 71
Jeremias 71
Mary 183
Susan 71
Hinderleiter, Catharine
209
Elizabeth 209
Mathias 209
Hirtsman, George 31
John 31
Mary Catharine 31
Hob, Catherine 262
Hock, Anna 178
Joanna 142
Juliana 178
Hoenig, Catharine 145
Elizabeth 177
Eva 154
Helen 145
John 150
John Henry 140
Magdalen 150
Michael 145,178
Simon 177
Hoenigs, Catharine Helen
147
Mary Magdalen 177
Michael 147
Hoff, Magdalen 218
Mary 205
Susan 208
Hoffman, Abraham 212
Catharine 14
Catharine 29
Christine 212
Elisabeth 259
Elizabeth 82
James 5
Margaret 14,67
Martin 29
Michael 14,29,44,51,
212
Hoffmann, --- 25
Catharine 53,180
Catharine Barbara 77
James 100
John 77
Louis 67
Margaret 77
Michael 77
Hoffmeister, Elisabeth
229
George 229
Juliana 229
Hofman, Abraham 248
Catharine 36,37,73,
93,154,159
Christina 100
James 100
John 62
John Henry 154
Magdalen 36,117
Mary 248
Michael 36,37,73,100,
117,154,248
Michael (Sr.) 93
Hofmann, Catharine 59,
118
John 77,91
Margaret 89
Michael 91
Hogan, Edward 11
Mary 11
Sarah 11
Hogener, Elizabeth 9
John Peter 9
Hogner, Elizabeth 14
Peter 14

Holler, Catharine 107
Holstein, Anna M. 121
  Anna Maria 38
  Anna Mary 32
  George James 32
  Maria 94
  Mary Barbara 61
  Michael 32,61
  Michael (Jr.) 61,62
Honig, Anna 171
  Anna Maria 153,161
  Anna Mary 153,161,175
  Anthony 53,55,89,96,
    101,106,107,159,181
  Apollonia 84
  Catharine 33,54,61,
    90,162,181,182
  Catherine 230
  Eleonor 169,176
  Elizabeth 33,91,96,
    99,160
  Eva 45,79,106
  Helen 153,157,161,
    162,171,172,176,189
  Jacob 26,33,167,174,
    181,182,189
  James 54,55,96,98,259
  John 89,153,167,169,
    171,176
  John Joseph 54
  Joseph 45,162,164,
    171,182,189
  M. 230
  M. Eva 39
  Magdalen 98,189
  Margaret 153
  Mary 153,171,174
  Mary Salome 26
  Michael 89,94,157,
    161,162,171,172,176,
    189,230
  Peggy 259
  Petronella 171
  Salome 89,101
  Sara 159
  Sarah 96
  Simon 66,92,95,153,
    161,175
  Susan 157
  Theresa 174,189
Hookey, --- 12,13
Hoop, Andrew 147
  Andrew Francis 147
  Catharine 147
  George 147
  Margaret 147
Hop, Andrew 150
  Catharine 152
  Catherine 262
  Christina 150,152
  Elisabeth 262
  George 150,152,262
  Margaret 150
  Mary 152
Hopkins, James 15
Hopp, Andrew 147,173,
    176,182,184,190,193,
    200,209,217,229,230,
    235,241,243,246,252
  Anthony 169,241
  Catharine 158,161,165,
    166,169,170,181,182,
    190,193,199,203,209
  Catherine 224,230,
    241,253
  Christina 152,153,
    158,165
  Elitta 217

Hopp (cont.)
  Elizabeth 165,193,
    214
  Elizabeth Margaret
    147,184
  Fr. 214
  Francis 161,169,181,
    182,190,193,203,214,
    241,253
  Francis Anthony 199,
    216
  George 145,146,147,
    150,162,166,169,173,
    178,182,190,193,194,
    197,198,199,200,206,
    210,214,216,224,228,
    231,235,241,248,250,
    256
  John 235
  John George 144,199
  Joseph 165,228
  Litta 200
  Madeline 229,230,235,
    241,243,246,252
  Magdalen 147,153,162,
    173,176,181,184,190,
    193,200,209,216
  Margaret 147,150,162,
    166,169,173,190,193,
    194,197,198,199,210,
    214,216,217,224,228,
    231,235,241,248,250,
    256
  Mary 166
  Susan 193
Horn, Ann Margaret 43,37
  Anna Mary 38
  Caspar 38
  Elizabeth 37,84
  George 43
  John 38
  John George 29,37
  John Peter 29
  M. Magdalen 43
  Philip 38
Hornberger, Barbara 121
Hornecker, John 106
  Mary 106
Hostmann, --- 25
Hottel, Madeline 257
  Samuel 257
  Sophia 257
Houcki, Elizabeth 27
House, James 251
  Mary 251
Huber, Catharine 29
  Mary 138
  Mary Ann 35
Huck, Anna 151
  Anna Mary 48
  Johanna Margaret 39
  John 34,39
  John James 55
  Joseph 62
  Juliana 34,37,39,48,
    55,62,218
  Magdalen 141
  Paul 16,17,34,37,39,
    48,55,62,218
  Susanna Margaret 34
Hucki, Anthony 86
  Anthony 13,43,75,108
  Catharine 13,45,47,
    75,80,84,87,90,108
  Catharine Kleyss 13
  Elizabeth 13,27,39,
    40,42,45,108
  J. George 82

Hucki (cont.)
  John George 13,86
  Juliana 62
  Mary Juliana 29
  Nicholas 13,35,38,39,
    40,42,43,45,58,63,
    67,73,78,84,86,90,
    104,110
  Paul 29,62
Hudel, Magdalen 215
Hudens, Catherine 255
  Elisabeth 255
  John 255
  Joseph 255
Hughes, Ann 192
  Catharine 192
  John 192
Huhs, James 260
  John 260
Humm, Mary 189
Hundsmann, Louis 159
  William 159
Hunsberger, Catharine
    199,205
  Catherine 224,231,
    237,237
  Elias 224
  James 237
  John 199
  Litta 231
  Peter 199,205,224,
    231,237
Huoben, Joseph 215
Hurber, Joseph 259
  Mary Anna 259
Huth, Benedict 76
  Catharine 93
  Elizabeth 76,93
  George 76,86,93
Huver, Adam 176,182,
    192,196,202,217,229,
    235,235,239,242
  Anna 176
  Elisabeth 239,242
  Francis 174,178,182,
    202,209,224,239
  Helen 235
  James 224
  John 182,192,196,200,
    209,229,239
  Jonathan 196,217
  M. Ann 209
  Mary 224
  Mary Ann 182
  Mary Anna 224
  Susan 176,192,196,
    202,229,235,239,242
  Susanna 217
  Thomas 192

--- I ---

Ihlein, John 202
Ilain, Catharine 211
  Fr. Louis 211
  Francis 214
  Francis Louis 218
  Juliana 214
  Laurence 214
  Louis 150
  Margaret 214
  Mary Magdalen 211
  Matthias 150
Ilein, Catharine 143,
    148,211
  Catharine Regina 141

Ilein (cont.)
Daniel 138
Elizabeth 152
Fr. 211
Francis 138,143,148,
  178
Francis Louis 144
Jacob Isidord 144
Jacob John 143
James 211
John 143,145
John Anthony 178
Joseph 138,141
Juliana 144
Magdalen 138
Margaret 141
Marina 138
Mary Magdalen 148
Matthias 150
Illain, Anna Mary 166
Catharine 159,162,164,
  167,172,173,175,185
David 167,185
Elizabeth 158,166,
  167,191,197
Francis 162,164,167,
  172,173,175,185
Francis Louis 159
George 159
John 158,166,167,191,
  197,202
Joseph 158,159,166
Juliana 162
Magdalen 158
Margaret 166
Mary 201
William 175
Illein, Francis 153
John Peter 153
Lawrence 249
Immel, --- 12
Eva Mary 4
Irish, Frances 100
Isinger, Augustine 34,40
Elizabeth 34,40
M. Elizabeth 83
Margaret 121

--- J ---

Jacks, Michael 15
Jedel, Anna Margaret 30
Jhlein, John 230
Jlain, Catherine 231,232
Francis 231,232
James 236,239,245,247
John 245
Madeline 238
Joh, Anna 259
Johns, Edward 68
Emaus 179
Joseph 68
Johnson, Edward 9
John 4
Mary 10,12
Patrick 4,9,10
Jones, Amos 156
Anna Maria 219
John Amos 156
Mary 174,193,210,240
Sarah 243,251,261
Julein, Joseph 98
Magdalen 98
Margaret 98
Julens, Catherine 260
Julii, --- 86

Jund, Anna Maria 106
Jung, Ann 29
Anna 79
Anna Christina 29
Catharine 115
Eva 94
Ferdinand 29,115,117
John 29
John Adam 79
Joseph 94
Mary 81
Mary Johanna 29
Jutz, Anthony 36,103
Catharine 36
John Anthony 36

--- K ---

Kaeffer, --- 132
Anna Maria 138,148
Anthony 138
Jacob 148
Joseph 145,148
Magdalen 148
Martin 138,148
Regina Catharine 148
Kaeiffer, Peter 179
Kaes, Barbara 151
Catharine 155
Jacob 151
John 151,155,179,180
Magdalen 151,152,179
Margaret 155,179
Peter 151,152,155,179
Kaiffer, --- 132
Barbara 151,152
Catharine 152
Jacob 149
Joseph 179
Magdalen 151
Kall, Dennis 212
Elizabeth 212
Kaltenbach, Andrew 251
Susan 251
Kamperling, Anna Maria
  104
John 55,104
John George 55
Kan---, M. Eva 86
Kaner, Mary 139
Kanner, John 137,179
Kapus, Christine 232
Lothaire 208
Lothar 232
Karmick, Patrick 3
Karpf, Adam 146
Margaret 146
Kas, --- 24
Anna Margaret 30
Peter 30
Peter Anthony 30
Kass, --- 24
Anna M. 69
Anna Margaret 50,70,
  162,206
Anna Maria 190
Barbara 142,167,175,
  192,207,248
Caspar 40
Catharine 162,167,168,
  173,190,198,211
Catherine 225,232
Charles 237
Daniel 188,190,216
David 220,248
Elisabeth 225,229,

Kass (cont.)
  237,243,244,250
Elizabeth 157,158,
  162,168,174,192,197,
  202,211
Eva 96
Henry 64,167,174,189,
  192,197,198,225,226,
  229,233,237,241,247,
  259
J. 210
Jacob 112,142,158,
  162,167,192,202,220
Jacob Peter 143
James 79,91,175,207,
  211,225,245,248,252
John 146,157,162,167,
  173,184,190,192,198,
  207,211,225,229,230,
  232,236,237,240,244,
  245
John George 236
John Peter 202
Joseph 72,173,236,252
M. Barbara 211
Madeline 229,245,248,
  252
Magdalen 155,158,159,
  160,168,184,188,192,
  196,201,202,206,220
Margaret 40,45,56,58,
  63,64,68,72,78,80,
  92,162,181,190,197,
  203,211,216,227,230,
  236,243,251
Maria 85,94
Mary 56,112,167,168,
  192,198,229,232,236,
  237,238,240,245,247,
  248,250
Mary Barbara 158,211
Mary Eva 250
Mary Magdalen 45
Mary Margaret 162,
  198,206
Mathias 181,192,197,
  202,225,229
Matthias 50,157,168,
  174,237,250
Nicholas 78,190,197,
  203,216,227,230,236,
  243,251
Paul 202
Peter 31,38,40,43,45,
  47,49,50,56,58,61,
  63,64,68,70,72,78,
  80,89,92,112,140,
  142,158,159,160,162,
  168,181,184,188,192,
  196,201,202,206,207
Philip 229
Solomon 232
Susan 198,203,226,
  229,232,233,236,237,
  241,244,247,259
Kassely, John 259
William 259
Kasser, Joseph 140
Kattenbach, Andrew 255
Susan 255
Katzenmayer, Barbara 243
Louis 243
Katzenmeyer, Barbara 236
Peter 236
Kauffman, Joseph 67
Mary 67
Kauffmann, Anna 77
Barbara 77

279

Kauffmann (cont.)
Joseph 77
M. Eva 17
Kay, Barbara 142
Jacob 142
John 146
Peter 142
Kayserin, Anna 259
Keating, Jean 131
Keech, Anna 247
Elisabeth 247
Michael 247
Kees, Anna Margaret 140
Carl 140
John 140
Margaret 137
Peter 137
Keesy, Anna 233,245,
246,249
George 233,245,246,249
John 249
Margaret 245
Mary 233
Keetch, Elisabeth 224
James 224
Michael 224
Kefer, John Philip 43
Mary Eva 43
Matthias 43
Keffer, --- 25,92,107,
132
A. Dorothy 10
Ann M. 106
Ann M. (Jr.) 86
Anna 256
Anna Catharine 51
Anna Eva 33,34
Anna Madeline 224
Anna Maria 99
Anna Maria Barbara 197
Anthony 237
Barbara 34,36,38,46,
47,51,67,71,85,91,
94,106,110,114,115,
153,154,157,159,163,
175,180,190,197,218,
224
Bernard 94
Catharine 47,55,115,
155,180,192,196,202
Christina 159,163,171
Christine 192,201
Daniel 196
Eleanor 241
Elisabeth 246
Elizabeth 30,80,91,
112,120,159
Eva 51,60,102
Eva Rose 99
Francis Joseph 38,201
George 163,233
Jacob 153,170,180,
190,194,195,197,219
Jacob (Sr.) 219
James 90,95,97,224,
228,233,237
John 30,36,51,82,153,
180,192,194,197,202,
205,225,228,237,241,
246,251,256
John George 171
John George Michael
137
John James 78,228
John Joseph 86
John Louis 33,67
John Peter 4,224
Joseph 34,153,159,163,

Keffer (cont.)
171,192,196,201,205,
242,245,246,249,251
Louis 41,66,94,102,106
M. Barbara 59,71
M. Elizabeth 60,91,
94,99
M. Eva 71,78
M. Magdalen 84
Madeline 224,228,233,
237,254
Magdalen 66,90,94,97,
98,155,170,190,194,
195,197,219
Martin 31,38,44,82,99
Mary 94,118
Mary Barbara 28,36
Mary Elizabeth 99
Mary Eva 31,33,36,38
Mary Magdalen 28,31
Matt. 94
Matthew 4
Matthias 33,51,60,71,
78,82,84,91,99,102,
111
Michael 237
Peter 16,28,32,34,36,
38,46,47,51,59,67,
71,80,85,91,98,99,
107,114,115,120,121,
139,154,159,163,175,
180,190,197,219
Regina 30,36
Samuel 194
Susan 41,153,194,197,
202,228,237,241,246,
251,256
Kefter, A. M. 10
Matthew 10
Keiffer, Magdalen 149
Keisling, Sebastian 181
Barbara 31
Frances 31
Jacob 15
John 31
Kelly, John 182,260
Kelsey, Anna 8
Bartholomew 8
Kemmel, Regina 71,111,
151
Kemp, --- 134
A. Xt. 190
Aaron 247
Anna 43,60,72,85,140,
145,180,181,248
Anna Barbara 154
Anna Catharine 195
Anna Christina 37,
159,166,175,204,248
Anna Christine 190,228
Anna Christine (Sr.)
228
Anna Margaret 86
Barbara 164,167,171,
189,190,196,197,199,
201,212,213,219,231,
234,235,236,238,239,
244,246,247,248,251,
252,253,254
Catharine 82,85,90,
92,139,155,180,190
Catherine 256,256
Christine 202
Edward 247
Elisabeth 226,239,
243,244,253
Elizabeth 91,97,98,
147,158,180,191,195,

Kemp (cont.)
200,219,238
Frederic 171
Frederick 160,180,189
George 151,152,165,
166,170,171,172,183,
188,189,191,195,200,
204,226,238,239
Jacob 164,165,190,
191,193,200
James 85,206,226,228,
234,238,243,244,248,
254
John 37,43,50,60,72,
85,86,98,100,145,
147,148,150,151,152,
153,159,164,165,166,
167,171,175,178,180,
181,189,190,195,196,
197,199,201,202,204,
213,218,219,226,228,
231,234,235,236,238,
239,244,246,247,248,
251,252,253,254
John (Jr.) 213
John Frederick 72
John George 50
John William 140
Joseph 99,201,226,
231,240,245,254,257
M. 95
M. Magdalen 43
Madeline 226,234,238,
243,244,248,254
Magdalen 153,191,200
Margaret 148,154,228
Martha 238
Mary 201,228,236,240
Mary Catharine 155
Mary Madeline 243
Mary Magdalen 159,213
Matthias 150,155
Salome 234,239
Salome Elizabeth 171
Sara 212,213
Sarah 245,251,257,258
Susan 153,165,181
Susanna 50,60
Kemper, John 143,144
John Jacob 139
Kemperling, Anna Maria
115
Anthony 99
Barbara 64
Elizabeth 75
John 64,75,97,107,115
M. Cecily 64,75,99
Mary 97
Keppert, Magdalen 194
Keragan, Johanna Crames
12
Manasses 12
Manus 12
Thomas 12
Kerck, Bridget 10
Mary 10
Kerenz, John 96
Margaret 96
Kerlin, Bridget 166
Edward 166
Eleonor 166
Kesner, Catharine 140
Henry Adam 140
John 140
Kester, --- 25
Matthias 45
Keycher, Ignatius 30
Mary Elizabeth 30

Khun, Joseph 72
Margaret 39
Kich, Michael 200
Rose 200
Kick, Elizabeth 200
Kieffer, Susan 158
Kieh, Rose 200
Kientz, Albertina 106,
109
Anna Margaret 99
Anna Maria 75,89,97,
99,100
Catharine 59,68,80,109
George 67,75,80,89,
91,97,99,100,107,109
James 89
John 68
John George 100
M. Magdalen 75
Magdalen 46,77,80,89,
106
Margaret 60,74
Mary Eva 39
Matthias 39,50,60,118
Michael 16
Kiesel, Catharine 172,
190,191,197,203,212,
215
Catherine 233,235,241
Elizabeth 212
Jacob 203
John 191
Magdalen 197
Mary 233
Sarah 241
Sebastian 172,190,
191,197,203,212,215,
233,241
Kiesig, Anna 229
Elisabeth 229
George 229
Kiesling, Catharine 163,
167
Elizabeth 163
Sebastian 163,167
Kiesy, Anna 197,202
Catharine 197
George 197,202
William 202
Kiler, John 215
Kill, George 3
Philip 3
Killenberger, Adam 31
George Adam 28
James 31
Kins, Anna Maria 140
George 140
Kirchenman, Magdalen 150
Kirschweiler, Andrew 30
Catharine 30
Kissel, Anna Margaret
252
Catherine 252
Sebastian 252
Klee, Anna Elisabeth 234
Anna Elizabeth 84,119
Catherine 242
Charles 224
Christina 74,78,100,
145,207
Ernest 100,145,207,
234,242,252
Ernest Frederick 78
Frederick 74
Henry 145
Hilary 84,119
Hiliard 71
James 74

Klee (cont.)
John 252
John Adam 75,119
John Hilary 75,119
Madeline 234,242,252
Margaret 234
Nicholas 78
Regina 75,119
Regina Kemmel 111
Klein, Elizabeth 206
Philip 206
Kleintop, John 49,53
M. Eva 49,53
Kless, George 31
Kleyss, Catharine 13
Elizabeth 13
Klitz, Anthony 93
Mary Catharine 93
Kluzki, Anthony 80
M. Magdalen 80
Knauer, Charlotte 150
Knaus, Charlotte 80
Kobele, Mary 137
Koble, Anna Eva 141
Anna Maria 144
Anna Mary 144
Barbara 177
Bartholomew 139,144,
184
Daniel 141,144,148
Eva 144
Jacob 144
James 184
John 143
John Augustus 141
Margaret 150
Mary 148
Mary Ann 139
Mary Ann Helen 148
Mary Juliana 141
Koblets, Margaret 150
Koch, A. Maria 7
Adam 9
Anna Mary 9
Anna Mary 9
Catharine 142
Dorothy 142
Frederick 9
Henry 7
John Adam 7
John Henry 142
Kohl, Abertina 2,45,78,
102
Anthony 47
Apollonia 16
Barbara 2,13,57,58,
64,82
Bernard 46,51
Catharine 46,47,51,
56,58,59,67,68,69,
91,94,97,142,143,
170,173,189,194
Elisabeth 259
Eliz. 160
Elizabeth 29,32,38,
42,45,51,52,60,83,
91,96,104,163,164,
167,171,188,192
George 2,10,13,16,28,
33,38,39,58,64,65,
97,142,170
George Bernard 10,47,
52,58,59,67,68,69,
80,91,94,105
George James 83
George Philip 143
Jacob 106,163,164,
167,171,188,189,189,

Kohl (cont.)
192,194,204
James 40,51,56,60,91,
95,96,163,259
John 57,173,259
John Anthony 142
John George 6,82
John James 74,78,80
John Michael 26
Joseph 13,26,30,45,57,
65,74,81,82,93,95,
107,201,204,207,
214
M. Apollonia 6
M. Barbara 65
M. Salome 45
Margaret 65,74,163,
204,207,214
Maria Barbara 65
Mary Barbara 38
Mary Magdalen 192
Mary Salome 102
Michael 16,94,216
Nicholas 207
Salome 16
Kohler, Elizabeth 153
Jacob 153
Nicholas 153
Kohlman, P. Paul (Rev.)
222
Kohn, George 16
James 102
Kolb, John 164,181
Magdalen 164
Margaret 16
Peter 164
Konlen, Denis 7
Honora 7
Patrick 7
Koons, Andrew 260
Elizabeth 260
Henry Reuben 260
Paul 260
Susan 260
Korb, Adam 97,175
Anna Christina 175
Catharine 97,206
Margaret 175
Krafft, --- 25
Anna Catharine 10
Anna Maria 62
Catharine 35
Elizabeth 43,62,73,
84,85,97
Frederick 10
James 73
John George 10,52
John Samuel 97
Magdalen 35,39,85
Magdalen Elizabeth 48
Michael 10,35,39,43,
48,52,62,73,84,85,
97,103
Michael Henry 43
Simon John 48
Kraft, Michael 102
NN. 120
Kramer, Elizabeth 98,158
Joseph 67,183
M. Catharine 67
Magdalen 158
Mathias 183
Matt. 67
Matthias 67,158
Krast, --- 25
Kraus, Charlotte 92
Christiaan 92
Gertrude 17

281

Krebler, Anna Maria 102
Krebs, Jacob 14
Kreisher, Adam 249,254
  E. 254
  Esther 249
  Margaret 254
  Nelly Anna 249
Kreiss, Catharine 59
  Joseph 59
  Martin 59
Krell, Anna 167
  Jacob 167
  John 167
  Sara 167
  William 167
Kremer, Elizabeth 177
  George 145
  Juliana 98,150
  Mary 145
  Mary Apollonia 146
  Matthias 145,146
Kremers, Juliana 178
Kreyss, Catharine 65
  Martin 65
  William Peter 65
Krippel, Mary 169
  Matthew 169
Kroner, John George 53
  Margaret 53
  Matthias 53
Kropf, Anna Maria 61
  Anthony 54
  Claudina 40,54,61
  George Tobias 40
  John Joseph 26
  Peter 26,40,54,61
Kruger, John D. 249
  Joseph 249
  Rachel 249
Krupser, Jacob 102
Kugler, John 73
Kuhn, --- 28
  Andrew 46
  Anna Barbara 3,7,9
  Anna Catharine 12
  Anna M. 46
  Anna Margaret 26,38,66
  Anna Maria 83,89
  Anna Mary 38
  Barbara 102,103
  Bartholomew 77
  Catharine 9,10,11,27,
    36,42,47,54,59,62,
    66,75,89,126
  Elizabeth 66,95,99,178
  Eva 15,33,34,41,46,
    56,80,83,85,91,102,
    103,120,161
  Eva Margaret 31
  Eva Maria 3
  Eva Mary 3
  Eve 185
  George 3,7,9,11,75
  George James 10,96
  George Joseph 88
  Henry 3,9,11,12,17,36,
    38,46,47,52,54,64,
    66,67,73,75,79,88,
    96,106,107,108,142
  Henry Matthias 73
  Jacob 26,32,33,102,
    103,105,108
  Jacoh 16
  James 47,53,57,64,68,
    101
  John 3,4,6,7,9,14,15,
    23,34,35,36,42,47,
    54,59,62,64,66,68,

Kuhn (cont.)
    75,89,98,99,100,102,
    105,106,107,116
  John George 15
  Joseph 54,66,69,72,
    78,80,84,88,89,90,
    91,92
  Judith 99
  M. Margaret Magdalen
    46
  M. Odilia 79
  M. Ottilia 9
  Magdalen 34,50,57,68,
    82,86,108
  Marg. 7
  Margaret 3,7,9,11,12,
    17,34,39,64,66,67,
    69,73,75,79,96,104,
    115,142
  Maria 84,85
  Mart. Jos. 86
  Mary 32,35,36,41,43,
    70,106
  Mary Eva 103
  Mary Magdalen 52,68,
    142
  Matthias 52,53,55,57,
    105
  Michael 33,34,41,46,
    56,82,91,108,161,198
  Odilia 26
  Robert 85
  Theresa 59,64,68,99,
    100
Kuhns, Andrew 249
  Catharine 49,53,58,
    62,140
  Elisabeth 249
  Elizabeth 31,43,43,53
  Henry 249
  Joanna 140
  John 31,49,53,58,62,
    140
  John Adam 49
  Juliana 249
  Margaret 62
  Mary 58
  Salome 247
  William 31,43
Kuhnss, John 211,246
Kuhnz, Elizabeth 31
Kuhz, John 210
Kun, Henry 137
  John Michael 139
  Margaret 179
  Teresa 137
Kuns, Anna Mary Juli-
  ana 137
  Barbara 169,199,202,
    203
  Catharine 137,145,152,
    156,157,162,168,180,
    181,190,201,205,207
  Christina 206
  Christine 190
  Elizabeth 157,181
  George 137,261
  John 38,137,145,156,
    162,167,168,174,181,
    190,196,199,201,202,
    203,205,206,207
  John Jacob 145
  Magdalen 197,199,173
  Marina Maria 137
  Mary 165,181
  Paul 162
  Salome 156
  Susan 203

Kunss, Andrew 209,239,
  245,253
  Barbara 237,238,239
  Catharine 209,210,214
  Catherine 226,237,
    239,245,252
  Elisabeth 238,239,
    241,245,251,252,253,
    254
  George 210,226,241,
    251,252,254
  John 209,210,212,214,
    226,237,238,239,241,
    244,245,252
  Joseph 226,238
  Judith 238
  Juliana 214,242,253
  Litta 239
  Mary B. 241
  Mary Barbara 218,241
  Salome 252
  Therese 245
Kunstler, Anna Elizabeth
  92
  Christ. 89
  Christopher 92
  Margaret 92,205
Kuntz, Andrew 152
  Catharine 43,67,72,
    94,149
  Christian 89
  Christine 258
  Elisabeth 247
  Elizabeth 84
  George 215,247
  Helen 94
  John 43,67,72,84,89,
    94,104,149,152,254
  John Henry 67
  Joseph 84
  Mary Anna 247
  Paul 215
  Susan 72
  Theresa 149
Kunz, Barbara 231,235
  Catharine 206,209,
    209,212,215
  Catherine 231
  Christina 206
  George 215,232,236
  John 206,209,212,215,
    219,231,235
  John (Sr.) 207
  Joseph 209,215,232,
    235,236
  Juliana 230
  Mary Barbara 219
  Paul 258
  Salome 237
  Susan 209,235
  Theresa 212,232
Kunzen, Theresa 259
Kupser, Anna Maria 119
  Anna Mary 52
  Barbara 58
  Catharine 41,42,47,52,
    58,67,73,84,99,115
  Elizabeth Theresa 84
  Jacob 34,103,115
  James 41,42,47,52,58,
    67,73,77,84,94,101
  John James 94
  M. Elizabeth 67
  Magdalen 47,82,101
  Simon 103,104
Kuss, George Adam 31
  Henry 45
  John 45

Kunss (cont.)
Magdalen 45
Peter 31

--- L ---

Lafleur Catharine 59
Catharine 90
George 78
Henry James 59
John 59,78,90,106
Valentine 90
La Fleur, Catharine 52,
  65
John 52,65,99
Louis Henry 99
Laibig, Henry 28
John 28
Lamberg, Antony 139
Lambert, Anna 239
Anna M. 199,236
Anna Margaret 62
Anna Maria 199
Anna Mary 237,241
Benjamin 189
Christina 239
Christine 233,246,252
Dorothy 72,78,83,88,
  138,141,144,147,149,
  163,195,199,202,205,
  224,235,236,239,253,
  254
Eleanor 199
Elias 194
Elisabeth 239
Jacob 138,141,144,
  147,149,159,189,194,
  195,199,202
James 72,78,83,88,163,
  170,205,209,215,224,
  235,236,239,253,254
John 88,141,199,226,
  233,249,253
Jonathan 170
Joseph 197,233,239,
  246,252
Louise 253
Margaret 163,190,197,
  205
Mary 170,189,193,194,
  199,215,233
Mary Anna 224
Mechtilde 226
Peter 172,199,205,
  226,232,239
Samuel 232
Sara 215
Sarah 251,253
Seraphinus 141
Susan 199,226,232,239
William 149,239,252
Lamberton, Seraphinus
  141
Lambin, Anna Margaret 42
Anna Maria 32,42,47,52
Anna Mary 61
Catharine 47
Christopher 32,36,42,
  47,52,58,61,102
George James 36
James 32
John 52
M. Ann 58
Mary Ann 36
Matthew 58
Lambing, John Anthony

Lambing (cont.)
  142
Lampert, Anna Margaret
  62
Dorothy 62,72
James 62,72
John James 72
Lang, Apollonia 9,11
James 9,11
Mary Apollonia 4
Langbe, Mary 163
Mary Barbara 163
Langbein, Anna M. 71,96
Anna Maria 78,81
Ant. 86
Anthony 97
Christopher 58,71,78,
  81,89,96,102
Joseph 83
M. Ann 58
M. Barbara 71
Matthew 58
Michael 78
Nicholas 96
Peter 62
Langby, Anna Mary 189
Christopher 189
Langford, Frances 7
Langhammer, Ann Mar. 45
Barbara 45
George 42,45,48,105
George Michael 48
M. Barbara 48
Lantz, Anna 3
James 3
Lantzel, George 47
Lanzel, George 40
Lanzinger, James 74
Nicholas 74
Salome 74
Largbe, Christopher 163
Larkin, John 2
Lasl, Elizabeth 101
Laub, John Michael 14
Regina 14
Laurence, Elizabeth Re-
  gina 131,132
Laurentii, Anna Maria
  140
Joseph 140
Mary 138
Mary Apollonia 138
Moritz 138
Laurenz, Joseph 177
Laurers, Maurice 139
Lawrenz, Jacob 140
Laydon, James 6
Maurice 6
Leaf, Catharine 192
George 174,192,240
Lechler, Anthony 10
George Ernest 4,8,9,10
John 4
M. Magdalen 8,10
Martin 8
Leckis, John 214
Mary 214,226,241,246,
  254,256
Lecky, Mary 228
Ledermann, John 16
Leehoffer, Johanna Ca-
  tharine Albertina 4
Ursula 4
Lehmon, Anna Maria 194
Catharine 194,197
Catherine 229,238
Henry 194,197,229,238
John 238

Lehmon (cont.)
Mary Elizabeth 197
Lehr, William 211
Leibig, Gertrude 42
John 17,42
Leonard 42
Leitig, Christina 158
John 158
Mary Magdalen 158
Leman, Henry 260
Martin 260
Mary 260
Mary Anna 260
Lemmon, Anna 256
Catherine 256
Henry 256
Lemons, Catharine 189
Henry 189
John 189
Lentzinger, Catharine 90
Jacob 108
James 38,45,51,56,63,
  90,102
John 45
M. Salome 56
Mary Barbara 38
Mary Salome 38,51
Salome 63
Lenzinger, Elizabeth 32
Jacob 29,32
James 63
M. Magdalen 63
Mary Salome 32
Nicholas 74
Salome 63
Leonard, Margaret 15
Leop, Charles 172
Charles Bernard 172
Leopold, Charles 172
Charles Bernard 172
Leple, Laurence 75,77,
  99,108
Lawrence 32
Margaret 75,77,99
Lepler, Lawrence 32
Lepple, Laurence 99
Margaret 99
Lery, Anna Margaret 2
Derby 2
George Henry 2
Lestrange, James 11
Lettelmeyer, Jonathan
  259
Leutner, Anna Margaret
  27
Anna Mary 33
Barbara 33
Eva Barbara 27
Matthias 27,33
L'eveille, Joseph 111
Leydecker, Simon 36
Leydekker, Simon 28
Lichhorn, Francis 161
Liess, Susan 208
Linch, John 115,116
Linnert, Margaret 6
Litzenger, Leonard 85
Magdalen 85
Litzinger, Anna Maria
  50,72
Anna Maria Schmitt 121
Anthony 82
Catharine 32,37,103
Henry 37,43,50,105
John 55
John James 48
John Leonard 64
Leonard 30,32,37,39,

Litzinger (cont.)
 42,47,48,50,55,64,
 72,82,101
Maqdalen 30,32,37,42,
 47,48,50,55,64,72,
 116
Simon 32
Lochler, Henry 103
John 103
Lochner, Eva 103
Loggeri, Philip 35
Lonberg, Mary 211
Michael 211
Lora, Catharine 210
Christine 210
Henry 210
Lorentz, Anna Barbara 4,
 157
Barbara 5,11
Catharine 157
Henry 13
Jacob 10
James 6
John Wendelin 5
Joseph 11,16,17,157
M. Eva 8
Mary 13
Maurice 4,5,6,10,11,
 13,15,16,17
Maurice (Jr.) 77
Wendel 16,17
Lorenz, Ann 29
Anna Catharine 31
Anna Maria 45,53,61,
 140
Apollonia 54,69
Barbara 33,82
Catharine 55
Christian 61,69
Eva 45,83
Eva Rose 84
George 91
Jacob 31,113
John 36,54
John Wendel 16
Joseph 26,28,45,48,
 53,86,87,102
Joseph (Jr.) 85
M. Apollonia 84
M. Eva 50,55
Martin Stephen 44
Mary 50,138
Mary Ann 44,48,92
Mary Apollonia 38
Mary Eva 36,50
Maurice 16,33,38,44,
 50,54,61,69,81,84,
 91,139
Wendelin 36,45,50,55
Lorschbach, Catharine 64
Henry 64
John 63
Magdalen 63
Loscher, --- 65
John 55,76
N. N. 49
Loughery, Philip 35
Love, Louis 215
Luckenbihl, Ursula 4
Lusl, Elizabeth 101
Luth, Elizabeth 95
Frederick 95
Henry 95
Luther, Anna M. 121
Henry 121
Margaret 97
Lutz, --- (Widow) 183
Daniel 208

Lutz (cont.)
Elizabeth 142
Frederick 91,142,208
James 208
M. Elizabeth 91
Mary Elizabeth 208
Lydon, Margaret Linnert
 6
Lynch, John 115
Lynn, Anna 35
Hugh 35
Mary 35

--- M ---

Mac---gan, Patrick 81
MacAlister, Elizabeth
 110
Macarty, Nicholas 26
Maccarty, Catharine 57
Edward 39
John 57
MacCarty, Albertina 89
Margaret 89
Mary 95
Nicholas 81,85,89
Thomas 95
MacDivet, Catharine 44
Michael 44
MacGuchin, Henry 76
John 76
Machel, Adam 81
Anna 59
Catharine 81
Christopher 32,59,72
Joseph 32
Magdalen 32
Magdalen 59
MacHill, Anna Maria 63
Arthur 63
Margaret 63
Mary 63
MacKarmick, David Pa-
 trick 5
Johanna 5
Martha 5
Patrick 5,6
Mackel, Adam 143
Christopher 143
Elizabeth 143,146
George 146
Joseph 143,146
Magdalen 146
Maria 143
Thomas 143
MacKuki, James 96
Maclaski, Mary 35
MacLone, Elizabeth 90
MacMalone, Catharine 24,
 91
Elizabeth 24,91
Lothi 24,25,91
MacMalowne, Laughlin 25
Lothi 25,82
Loughy 25
Mary 82
Madin, Elizabeth 10
Margaret 7
Patrick 7,10
Sarah 7,10
Maerten, James 103
Margaret 103
Magdalen, M. 43
Magdanel, Edmund 14
Michael 3
Magel, Adam 153

Magel (cont.)
Christopher 38,43,49,
 153
Daniel 153,160
David 153
Elizabeth 38,143,153
George 153,160
Jacob 153
Magdalen 38,49,153,160
Maria 97,143
Mary 160
Peter 153
Susanna 49
Thomas 143
William 160
Magloski, Henry 29
Margaret 29
Magorni, Michael 35
Magudiens, Catharine 2
Mary 2
Patrick 2
Maguin, Henry 3,17
Margaret 3
Mary 3,17
Mair, David 5
Helena 7
John 11
Lawrence 3,5,11
Mary 5,7
Maison, Adam 81
Catharine 223
Catherine 256
Christine Anna 223,256
Elizabeth 72
John Alphonse 223,256
Josephine Angela The-
 resa 223
Josephine Angela The-
 rese 256
Peter 59,72,81,223,256
Majus, --- 86
MaKarmick, Elias 3
Makarmick, Patrick 3
Malone, Laughlin 25
Malsberger, Catharine
 35,43
Jacob 35
James 43
Malzberger, Anna Mary
 243
Catharine 189,202
Catherine 243
Elizabeth 196
Ernest 189
George 196
Jacob 156,189,196,
 202,205,233,243,251
Joseph 196,205,232,233
Margaret 205
Mary 189,196,202,233,
 243,251
Sarah 251
Marien, Anna Elizabeth
 174
Marks, Anthony 165
Charlotte 165
Thomas Anthony 165
Marlip, Susan 152
Martin, Anthony 29,209,
 238,240,241,243,248
Catharine 193,194,
 199,207,209,219
Catherine 241,259
Ellen 29
Eva 111,238,240,241,
 243,248
Henrietta 248
Henry 29

Martin (cont.)
J. H. E. 193
John 194,209,217
Joseph 207
Marty, Jacob 152
John 152
Margaret 152
Marx, Anthony 54
Eva 54,62
Thomas 54,57,62,120
Matheis, Apollonia 177
Catharine 146
John 137,143
Maria 143
Martin 146
Mary Magdalen 143
Mathes, Margaret 103
Mathews, Mary 215
Matis, Marten 103
Mattes, Anna Maria 191,
201
George 173,185
John 158,173,185,191,
201,202,220,227,232,
234
John Elias 191
Mary 158,173,185,202,
218,227,232,234
Mary Sarah 227
Susan 202,207
Wilhelmina Dorothy 175
Matthes, Ann M. 69
Anna M. 45
Anna Maria 80
Anna Mary 166
Apollonia 36,98,99
Catharine 36,44
Elizabeth 97,100
James 31,35,46,52,53,
89,97,100,103,105
John 77,80,99,111,166
M. Catharine 99
Marg. 86
Margaret 29,32,35,36,
44,77,103,104,105,
119
Mart. 44
Martin 36,115
Mary 51
Nicholas 119
Matthew, Catharine 97
Matthys, Catharine 28
Joseph 28,113
Martin 28,113
Maurer, John 5
M. Catharine 5
Maxfield, Catharine 7,12
Isabella 12
James 12
Margaret 7
Mayer, Adolph 37
Anna Mary 37
Caspar 3,6
Catharine 32,35,45,
200,204
Dina 241
Dinah 210
Elizabeth 204
Francis Michael 35
George 200,204
George Adolph 27
Henry 210,241
Joseph Caspar 3
Magdalen 206
Margaret 254
Michael 35
Peter James 6
Rebecca 210,241

Mayer (cont.)
Simon 42,45,104
Mayler, Catharine 27
Mary 27
Robert 27
McAgane, Frank 5
M'Bright, B. 210
M'Callen, Michael 257
Sarah 257
Thomas 257
M'Canna, Charles 194
Martha 174
Mary 174,194
Michael 174,194
M'Canny, Mary 172
Matthias 172
William 172
McCardy, Ann 8
Catharine 3
Nicholas 3
Patrick 8
Thomas 4,8
M'Carr, Bridget 212
Francis 212
Henry 212
McCarthy, --- 132
M'Carty, --- 132,133
Abner Paul 171
Albertina 159
Aloitina 156,162
Catharine 176
Edward 156,180
Elizabeth 142,153,
156,164,168,169,171,
173,175,176,181,188,
192,214
Francis 156
John 153,154,156,160,
164,168,169,171,173,
175,177,181,192,214
Joseph 164
Louisa 156,168,169,
171,172,174,176,182
Margaret 166
Mary 160,168,173,174,
175,176,192,214
N. 155,181
Nicholas 139,153,156,
159,162,168,169,171,
172,173,174,175,176,
181,182,188,204
Peter 168
Sally 160,181
Salome 155,160
Sara 160
Thomas 160,166,170,
173,174,176,193,230
Unity 168
Unity Juliana 160
McCarty, --- 132
Catharine 147
Edward 16,72
Elizabeth 150,152
John 145,152,261
John William 146
Louisa 162
Margaret 99
Mary 261
Nicholas 99
Nicholas Megaddy 137
Patrick 15
Peter 214,261
Rebecca 261
T. 261
Thomas 207
McClaughlen, Gaudentia
10
John 5,10

McCloskey, Henry 29
Margaret 29
Mary 35
McColligen, Daniel 260
Margaret 260
M'Cormick, Hugh 226
Mary 226
Philip 226
McCray, Catharine 10
John 9,10
M'Cu, Guess 156
M'Cue, Denis 193
McDeed, Philip 17
McDoffee, Daniel 99
McDonald, Thomas 259
M'Donnel, James 230
M'Dowel, Barbara 243
McEntee, John 259
Joseph 259
M'Entire, Charles 192,
214,258
Elizabeth 258
M'Farthing, Andrew 198
Catharine 198
Daniel 198
Eve 198,200,207
John 198,200
M'Farthring, Eve 212
John 212
Mary 212
M'Farthy, Catharine 161
Eva 161
John 161
Mary 242,245
McFergen, Mary 260
McGaddy, --- 133
M'Gill, James 210
Mary 210
M'Gorgan, Elisabeth 227
John 227
William 227
M'Gullery, James 163
Mary 163
M'Gurgan, John 195
McIntire, Charles 215,
260
Emil 260
McKarty, John 259
Mary 259
Nicholas 259
Polly 259
Sara 259
M'Manus, Bernard 238
Catherine 238
Mary 238
MeCardy, --- 133
Catharine 147
Elizabeth 147
John 147
Mecarty, --- 133
Elizabeth 150,152
John 152
Salome 151
Thomas 151
Meccle, Elizabeth 177
Mechl, Anna Elizabeth 92
Mechle, Louis 37
Mary Elizabeth 37
Mechler, Anna Elizabeth
92
Meck, Catharine 200
George 200
Marian 16
Meckel, Elizabeth 185
Margaret 151
Meckeler, --- 24
Barbara 64
Meckl, --- 24

285

Meckler, --- 24
Anna Margaret 105
Barbara 77
Elizabeth 49,69
Elizabeth 75
M. Barbara 91
Margaret 77
Mary Barbara 112
Megaddy, --- 133
Elizabeth 139
John 145,177
John William 146
Margaret 146
Nicholas 139
Meikle, Elizabeth 150
Meinick, Daniel 261
Meister, Balthasar 209,
237
Elizabeth 209,237
Madeline 237
Magdalen 209
Melchior, Catharine 154
Elisabeth 254
George 4
Jacob 164
John 213,254,257
Magdalen 161,171,175,
189
Mary 154,164
Mary Ann 189
Michael 154,161,164,
171,177,189
Nicholas 4
Reuben 257
Sara 171
Sarah 254,257,257
Susan 161
Melchoir, Catherine 261
Melcker, John 150
Michael 150
Melon, Elizabeth 258
John 258
Mensch, Adam 206
Margaret 206
Mary Elizabeth 104
Susan 206
Merkel, Barbara 191
Benjamin 191
John 191,204
Merten, Anthony 214,
224,238,244,249,251,
252,256
Edward 244
Eva 244,249,251,252,
256
Henry 256
Merthen, Catherine 259
Meschel, Adam 58
Anna 58
Elizabeth 58
Mester, Elizabeth 260
Metz, John 173
Mary 173
Mary Elizabeth 173
Meyer, A. M. 5,7,9,12
Anna Mary 10
Caspar 72,81,117
Catharine 5,72,107
Clara 149
Elizabeth 205
John 3,5
John Frederick 81
John James 10,72
Mary 3,5
Mary Ann 29
Mary Elizabeth 205
Ottilia 9,10
Simon 205

Michat, John 110
Michel, --- (Rev.) 31
Henry 2
Miclaine, Catharine
Elizabeth 24,53
Lochely 24,25,53
Mild, Catharine 121
Charles 121
Mild---, Charles 111
Miller, Anna 41,160,
164,215
Anna Catharine 167
Anna M. 45,53
Anna Maria 39,63,160
Anna Mary 37,45,55,162
Barbara 44,183
Catharine 28,31,32,
39,40,46,49,53,58,
72,105,156,180
Catherine 262
Christian 214,262
Daniel 215
Elisabeth 226,251
Elizabeth 31,39,44,
55,67,102,155,163,
167,171,174,192,199,
210,211,213
Eva 251
Frederick 155,167,
174,192,199,210,211,
213,226,251
Fridolinus 261
George 160,205,215
George James 32
Gertrude 192
Henry 26,36,39,63
Jacob 164,174,183,192
James 44,262
John 37,39,41,49,104,
215,251,258,261
John Frederick 199
John George 40
John Michael 39
John William 67
Judith 250
Juliana 213
M. Magdalen 72
Magdalen 207
Margaret 26,211,215,
244,261
Martin 41,104
Mary 53,55,56,210
Mary Barbara 155
Michael 31,44,55
Nicholas 28,40,156,
160,164,215
Peter 46
Philip 37,45,53,63,
72,121
Salome 107
Susan 226
Theobald 31,32,46,58,
102
Theodore 39
Utilia Madeline 259
William 183
Milty, Anna 229
Minder, Burchard 180
Catharine 180
Frederic 180
Susan 180
Minimay, John 9,12
Mary 9
William 12,35
Minime, Anna 4
John 4
Martha 4
Minsen, John 179

Mintz, John 240
Mary 240
Mintzen, Anna 243
Mintzer, Joseph 218
Mintzers, Catharine 144
Minzen, Ann 201
Anna 230,233,237,249
Elisabeth 255
Henry 243
Mary 249
Sarah 243,249,255
William 201,230,237,
243,249,253,255
Minzer, Anna 210,240
Engelbert 240
Sara 210
Sarah 240
William 210,240
Missemer, Anna 253,255
Henry 253,255
Joseph 253
Missimer, Henry 243
Misteli, Alois (Rev.)
221
Mitchel, Catherine 225
Michael 225
Yeomy 225
Mogel, Maria 97
Mogorni, Anna Mary 35
Daniel 35
Mohr, Albert 208
Catharine 208
Catharine 241,245,251
John 241
Joseph 208,241,245,251
Louis 251
Molitor, Anna Martha 4
Elizabeth 9
John 4,8,9
Mollin, Margaret 152
Molsberger, Anna M. 77,
85
Catharine 43,51,60,
73,92
George 92
James 43,51,60,73,85
John 51
John George 60
Margaret 85
Susanna 73
Moltzbeger, Catharine
144
Jacob 144
Joseph 144
Moltzberger, Catharine
177
Jacob 169
John 169
Mary 169
Monroy, Henry 40
Rebecca 40
Moon, Josue 213,253
Philippina 213,253
Sara 213
Moor, Anthony 49
James 49
Sophia 49
Morgan, Ann 9
Catharine 7,9,12
Francis 9,10,15
Frank 12
M. Elizabeth 12
Moritz, Anna Mary 36
Morloch, Magdalen 45,48
Michael 45,47,48
Morpheu, Edward 10,11,12
Morphey, Edmund 11
Mottin, Margaret 152

Moulier, Catharine 14
  Martin 14
Mulcastor, John 6
Mullen, Catharine 139
Muller, Anna 154
  Anna Mary 29
  Catharine 146,150
  Charlotte Elizabeth 7
  Christian 146,151
  Daniel 154
  Elisabeth 238
  Eva 151
  Eva Margaret 29
  Frederick 150,179,238
  Isaias 178
  Jacob 150
  John Henry 14
  M. Magdalen 7
  Magdalen 150
  Margaret 150,151
  Mary 146
  Michael 16
  Nicholas 154
  Paul 7,14
  Peter 146
  Philip 29
  Sophia 238
Mundan, Abraham 231
  John 231
  M. Margaret 231
Munzer, William 196
Murphay, John 7
Murphi, Catharine 29
  Edward 29
Mutard, Catharine 167,
  182
  Frederick 182
  Magdalen 182
Muthard, Frederick 184
Muthards, Magdalen 184
Muthardt, Frederick 137
  John George 137
Muthart, Anna Maria 63,
  87
  Catharine 54
  Frederic 46,54
  Frederick 63,71,76,
  87,98
  James 46,76
  John 71
  M. Barbara 98
  Magdalen 46,54,56,63,
  71,87,89,98
Mutthart, Frederick 144
  Magdalen 144
  Mary Magdalen 144
Mygaddy, Albertina 139
  Nicholas 139
Myler, Anna Mary 36

--- N ---

Nagel, Adam 106
  Barbara 155
Nester, Andrew 103
  Catharine 81,103,112
  Frederick 72,81,120
Neuer, Catharine 173
  Daniel 257
  Elizabeth 191
  Eva Mary 169
  James 246
  John 169,173,182,191,
  195,201,235,241,246,
  257
  John Adam 225

Neuer (cont.)
  Joseph 225
  Magdalen 201
  Maria 139
  Mary 169,173,191,195,
  201,225,235,241,246,
  257
  Philip 195
  Susan 235
Neuman, Henry 63
  James 63
Never, Anna 249
  John 249
  Mary 249
Nieman, Joan 261
Noel, Catharine 120
  Ignatius 117,120
Noper, Anton 260
  Ludgardis 260
Norbeck, Catharine 68,
  72,108,117
  Daniel 73
  Elizabeth 196
  Eva Rose 84
  Henry 27,39,52,60,71,
  72,81,84,102,108,
  109,110,118,176,194,
  196
  Henry (Sr.) 70
  Jac. Jacobus 82
  James 35,53,60,71,
  103,104,106,118
  John 41,44,54,55,59,
  63,68,76,77,84,108,
  120
  John Henry 71
  John James 27,48
  M. Anna 52,60
  M. Magdalen 53
  Magdalen 63,63,109
  Margaret 27,80,82,103
  Maria 71,82
  Mary 49,60,103,106
  Mary Ann 27,60
  Mary Apollonia 77
  Mary Magdalen 63
  Rosina 59,63,68,76
  Rosine 194,196
  William Peter 84
Norbudy, Henry 14
  John Daniel 14
  Mary 14
Nordbeck, Margaret 103
Normand, Johanna 8,9
  John 8,9
  Joseph 9
  Richard 8
Noulen, Ann 9
  Denis 9,11
  Honora 9,11

--- O ---

Oberdorf, Abraham 210
  Christine 210
  John 210
Oberholser, Mary 159
O'Boil, Neal 208,260
  William 260
Obold, Catharine 213
  Catherine 243,248
  Elisabeth 239
  Elizabeth 219
  John 217
  Joseph 163,203,213,
  219,230,239,254,257

Obold (cont.)
  Margaret 163,203,213,
  230,239,254,257
  Philip 163,213,251
Obolt, Anthony 177
Oboltz, Anthony 177
O'Boyle, Mary Ann 252
  Neal 252
  Susan 252
O'Connor, Elisabeth 261
  Peter 261
Odere, Debora 194
  John 194
  Patrick 194
O'Donnel, Edward 154
  Elizabeth 154
  John 154
  Neal 154
Oeckkenrodt, Elizabeth
  154
  Henry 154
  John Louis 154
Oeltz, John 63
Ofer, --- 24
  Francis Joseph 48
  Frank 68
  M. Ann 48
  M. Elizabeth 68
  Mary Ann 68
Offer, --- 24
  Francis 30
  Francis Joseph 30
  Frank 51
  Magdalen 51
  Mary Ann 30,51
Ohrendorf, Christian 93
Onan, Denis 3,6,9,10
  Mary 6
  Rebecca 3,6,10,12
O'Nayl, Catharine 5
  Judith 14
  Thomas 5
O'Neal, Hugh 157
O Neal, Anna 182
O'Neill, John 60
Onel, Henry 60
  John 60
Opold, Catharine 167
  Elizabeth 156
  George 191
  John 159
  Joseph 156,159,167,
  168,171,191
  Margaret 156,167,168,
  171,191
  Mary Margaret 159
Oppolt, Elizabeth 85
Orendorff, Christian
  156,178
  Christina 156
  Eva 156
  John 181
  Mary 156
  Matthias 156
Ort, Matthew 259
  Peter 259
  Philip 168
  Stephen 259
Orth, Anna Catharine 168
  Anna Margaret 168
  Catharine 192
  Catherine 253
  Elisabeth 253
  Mary Catharine 202
  Peter 168,192,202
  Peter Charles 253
  Sebastian Peter 192
  Stephen 253

Osenbacher, Eva Mary 160
John 160
Overbeck, Anna Mary 170
Owings, Robert 104

--- P ---

Palm, John 34
Pannen, John 151
Joseph 151
Pantan, Jonathan 182
Nelly 182
Susan 182
Paul, Anna Maria 84
Pawlitz, Jacob 3,8,15
Michael 3
Penington, Daniel 84
M. Anna 84
Perant, Margaret 79
Peraut, Margaret 79
Peter, Barbara 16
Peyl, Anna 177
Pfeffer, Anna Maria 157
George 157
Pfluam, Francis 260
Philipps, Charles 230
Margaret 230
Mary 230
Philips Anna 230
Charles 230
Mary 230
Pike, Henry 71,85
Johanna 71
John 85
Martha 71
Piri, Philip 29
Pisbing, John Henry 11
Plank, Elizabeth 191
Jacob 191
John 191
Plock, Susan 207
Popp, Abraham 42
Poth, Adam 148,154
Catharine 148,151
Elizabeth 149
Mary Eve 148
Pott, Catharine 146
Peter 146
Power, Anna 95
Catharine 95
James 95
John 95
Nicholas 8
Rachel 95
Samuel 95
Praniewitz, Thomas
(Rev.) 222,223,261
Preiss, Mary 254
Press, Mary 253
Pulton, Barbara 9
Charles 5,9,12
Ruth 5,9,12
Pusert, Eleanor 10
Putta, Catharine 155
Peter 155
Putz, John William 52,
107
Magdalen 52
Mary Sophia 52
Pycke, Henry 85
John 85

--- Q ---

Queen Catharine 183
Catharine Philippina
192
Daniel 235
Henry 217
Henry Daniel 195
Isaac 242
James 227
John 188
Mary 192,195,227,235,
242
Thomas 183,188,192,
195,204,227,235,242
Quickly, John 250,255,
257
Mary 257
Mary Anna 257

--- R ---

Ramstone, Frances 208
Rankings, Jacob 183
Rantzau, Maximilian
(Rev.) 128,215,222,
258,260
Rapp, Joseph 32
Ursula 32
Ratschar, Magdalen 142
Rauch, Peter 138
Reainger, Margaret 262
Rebbert, Barbara 140
Catharine Elizabeth
144
Joseph 140
Magdalen 140,144
Stephen 140,144
Redener, James 215
Redert, Elizabeth 131
Reese, Barbara 212
John 212
Reeser, Andrew 232
Sybil 232
Refshneider, Catharine
205
Elizabeth 205
Henry 205
Sophia 205
Reich, Adam 138
Elisabeth 228
Eva Catharine 138
Reichard, Adam 155
Anna Elizabeth 155
Anthony 131,179
Elizabeth 155,215
John 155
Mary Eve 155
William 131
Reichart, Adam 85
Anna Mary 69
Catharine 93
John 80
John Adam 64,69,95,109
John Philip 95
M. Eva 69,85
Mathias 16
Michael 85
Stephen 80,93
William 93
Reicharts, Helen 86
Reicher, Adam 214
Eve 214
Magdalen 214
Reicherd, Catharine 150

Reicherd (cont.)
John 150
Reichert, A. 205
Ad. 208
Adam 142,148,159,161,
167,168,173,176,182,
190,206,207,209,214,
215,217,225,236,241,
250,253,255,256,257,
261
Anna 237,242,249,255
Anna Juliana 203
Anna Mary 237
Anthony 157,161,172,
188,193,196,198,199,
203,220,228,235,240,
245,251,252
Augustine 209,224,
231,237,242,249,255
Barbara 169
Catharine 141,143,
144,145,150,157,161,
164,166,167,172,185,
188,190,193,194,196,
198,199,203,209,220
Catharine Christinne
148
Catharine Lydia 194
Catharine lidia 194
Catherine 224,225,228,
229,235,240,244,245,
249,250,251,252,254
David 198
Elias 242
Elisabeth 228,236,
239,242,247,250,257
Elizabeth 151,190,
193,200
Enoch 249
Esther 235
Eva 142,159,161,167,
168,206,225,236,250,
253,255,257,261
Eve 148,176,190,206,
214,217
Frances 190
George 228
Henry 172
Joel 255
John 101,141,144,145,
150,161,164,166,167,
169,172,185,190,194,
198,199,200,206,209,
220,224,228,229,231,
232,234
John Augustine 141
John Henry 157
John Jacob 161
John William 140
Joseph 145,208,210,
233,234
Madeline 251,255
Magdalen 168,209
Margaret 172,190,245
Mary 140,145,146,150,
166,182,188,193,255,
256,257,261
Mary Catharine 196
Mary Eve 173
Mary Magdalen 166
Matthias 162
Michael 191,198,200,
201,206,217,261
Paul James 231
Philip 195,200,203,
206,225,227,231,233,
235,237
Reuben 237

Reichert (cont.)
Rosalie 262
Rosina 142,241
Rosine 255
Salome 191,199
Samuel 251
Sophia 240
Stephen 140,145,146,
193
Susan 200,203,225,
227,231,233,235,237
Thomas 169
William 185
Reickart, Anthony 258
Margaret 258
William 258
Reider, Anna M. 38
Fr. Joseph 38
Susanna 38
Reiffenberger, Elizabeth
8
Reiger, Anna Margaret 33
George Simon 33
John Simon 33
Reimel, John 214
Magdalen 214
Reininger, Catherine 258
Reintz, Anna Maria 139
Rosina 139
Valentine 139
Reintzel, Conrad 112
Reinzel, Anna 249
Anna Maria 146
Catharine 146
Daniel 249
Elisabeth 249
Felton 146
Reisel, Martin 8,15
Reiser, Michael 10
Reisinger, Elizabeth 204
Reisner, Benjamin Jacob
145
Catharine 145
John 145
Reiss, David 6
Elizabeth 6
Sara 168
Valentine 6
Reiter, Anna Mary 26
James 72
Reitmeyer, Margaret 165
Mary 165
Relt, John 262
Remstone, Frances 202
Phenenna 193
Reninger, Anna Mary 180
Catharine 160,164,168,
170,194,198,203,212
Catherine 229,235,
240,253,256
Christine 229
Elizabeth 194
Frederick 160,164,
168,170,180,194,198,
203,212,229,235,240,
253,256
George 198
Henry 173
Hethe 194
James 235
John 160,256
Joseph 168
Mary 203
Salome 240
Wendel 194
Renninger, Catharine 173
Frederic 173
Peggy 260

Reppert, --- 105
Anna 162,203
Anna Barbara 190
Anna Catharine 90
Anna Christina 86
Apollonia 77
Barbara 151,238,239,
251
Catharine 68,171,190,
205
Catharine Elizabeth
144
Catherine 239
Christina 76,95
Daniel 9
Elisabeth 245
Eva 245,247,251
James 11,76,95
John 76,155,180,190,
239,251
John James 97
Joseph 140,211,245,
247,251
Litta 231
M. Apollonia 91
Madeline 231,239,252
Magdalen 92,162,170,
190,197,199,200,203,
205,211
Margaret 170
Mary 155,245
Mary Apollonia 4,16
Mary Barbara 26
Mary Catharine 26
Melchior 16
Peter 190
Rose 77,108
Sara 197
Sarah 245
Stephen 4,9,11,26,68,
86,90,92,97,121,151,
155,162,170,190,203,
205,211,231,239,252
Ursula Barbara 86
Repperts, Magdalen 147
Stephen 147
Repplier, Anna Catharine
217
Anna Catherine 227
Catharine 192,193,
202,217
Catherine 227,230,
232,233,236,238,242,
249,253,256
Eva Louise 232
George 163,175,188,
192,193,202,204,217,
227,230,232,233,236,
238,242,249,253,256
George Sebastian 256
John George 242
Joseph Mark 249
Mary 202
Mary Sophia 193
Theresa Margaret 238
Repport, Madeline 226
Reynart, Barb. 86
Rhor, Eva Margaret 143
Mary 143
Nicholas 143
Theresa 149
Richard, Catharine 215
Richer, Martin 181
Mary 181
Richerd, Elizabeth 151
Stephen 151
Richert, Elizabeth 190
John 150

Richert (cont.)
Mary 150
Ridgens, John 5,6
Margaret 10
Mary 5,6,10
Samuel 5
Riedacker, Jacob 16
Riedner, Peter 258
Peter (Sr.) 258
Riegel, Daniel 205
Riffel, --- 25
Agatha 46,74,80,82,
99,109
Anna Barbara 9
Anna Magdalen 51
Anna Maria 102
Augustine 40,117
Barbara 72,74,90
Bernard 71,94,97,111
Catharine 8,15
Catharine Barbara 58
Catharine Elizabeth 34
Christina 9,34,40,95
Daniel 51
Elizabeth 51,56,85
Elizabeth Henrich 109
George 57,58,60,72,
74,78,82,85,90,93,
94,97,110
George Jacob 36,105,
117
George James 39,41,
56,69,85
George James George 51
Jacob 10,15
Jodocus 103,104
John 77,94
John Jodocus 35,103
John Joseph 43,51,56,
58,60,62,69,77,105,
106
Joseph 51,53,62,63,
64,72,73,85,105
Magdalen 74
Margaret 51,58,60,63,
69,72,73,85,97
Maria 32
Mary 103
Mary Catharine 15
Mathias 17
Matthew 9
Matthias 31,34,40,67,
69,85,90,92,95,109,
111,117
Matthias (Jr.) 52,57,
82
Melchior 51,74,90,97
Riffels, Mary Agatha 150
Rigelin, Regina 261
Sylvester Joseph 261
Rilay, Ambrose 3,14
Hugh 6
Judith 3,5
M. Margaret 5
Thomas 6
Riles Charles 9,10,15
Elizabeth 9
Sarah 9
Riley, Charles 6
John 6
Sarah 6
Ristel, --- 25
Bernard 13
Christina Danner 13
George 63
Matthew 13
Ritner, Barbara 34,40
Ritshi, Anna Margaret

Ritshi (cont.)
  234
  Catherine 229
  Joseph 229,234
  Margaret 229,234
Ritshy, John 224
  Joseph 224
  Mary 224
Rittener, Jacob 151
  Peter 151
Ritter, John Baptist
  (Rev.) 18,19,20,21,
  22,23,25,26,27,42,
  62,63,74,76,81,91,
  93,96,100,101,102,
  104,106,107,109,110,
  112,116,118,119,121,
  122,124
Jo'es Bapt'a (Rev.)
  107
Joanne Baptista (Rev.)
  76
  Philip 104
Rittner, Anna M. 45
  Anna Maria 192
  Barbara 40,114,141,
  144,159,165,172,192,
  224,247
  Catharine 53
  Elisabeth 245,247
  Elizabeth 165,211
  Eva 141,144,165
  George 172
  Jacob 151
  John 141,209,245
  John Joseph 141
  Joseph 53,114,159,
  184,224
  Joseph Peter 144
  M. Barbara 105
  Mary 245
  Michael 47,48
  Peter 141,144,159,
  165,172,175,192,209,
  210,224,247
  Regina 114
  Sarah 247
  Simon 159
Rochol, Joseph 236
Rode, Michael 27
Rodenburger, Nelly 249
Rodger, James 211
  Michael 211
  Sara 211
Rodt, Christian 207
  Eva 182
  Eve 171
  John 182
Roger, James 245,246,
  250,251
  Mary 245,246,250,251
  Michael 251
  Sarah Anna 246
Rogers, Anna 89
  James 46
  John 46
  M. Margaret Magdalen
  46
Rogert, Mary 205
Roggers, Catherine 257
  Litta 257
  Michael 257
Rohr, Agatha 208
  Angela 237
  Anna 209,231,233
  Anna M. 59,118
  Anna Margaret 29
  Anna Maria 29,48

Rohr (cont.)
  Anna Mary 13,36
  Catharine 70,81,84,
  87,109,110,140,142,
  144,156,162,172,184
  Catherine 242,244,
  253,258
  Charles 209,244,249,
  255,257
  Clara 257
  Daniel 155
  David 194
  Denis 261
  Edward 245
  Eleanor 249
  Elisabeth 244,249,
  255,257
  Elizabeth 211
  Eva Margaret 143
  Frances 36,96
  George 174
  Henry 70
  John 59,81,118,184,
  199,209,214
  John Charles 140
  John Martin 13
  Joseph 79,88,96,137,
  140,144
  Joseph 144,147,153,
  155,161,167,172,182,
  184,190,194,198,199,
  201,207,208,209,211,
  212,214,228,233,235,
  237,242,246,249,261
  Joseph (Sr.) 211
  Joseph Jeremiah 258
  Jul. 211
  Julian 261
  Juliana 88,96,137,
  144,153,155,161,167,
  172,190,194,198,199,
  201,207,209,212,214,
  228,233,235,237
  Justina 87
  Litta 228
  M. Agatha 95
  M. Barbara 88
  Magdalen 87
  Margaret 140,144,151,
  178,261
  Martin 13,29,36,48,
  59,88,110,118,119
  Mary 165,174,196,199,
  208,226,232
  Mary Ann 144
  Matthias 45,79,87,95,
  110,140,142,144,151,
  156,162,172,184,190,
  258
  Nancia 151
  Nancy 151
  Nicholas 35,65,81,109,
  110,155,165,174,196
  Richard 210,213,258
  Richard James 167
  Salome 155,241
  Sara 214
  Sarah 249
  Sophia 190,232,234,
  237,245,248,250,252,
  253,256
  Theresa 48,149,162
  Uriah 250
  William 201,207,209,
  215,232,234,237,245,
  248,250,252,253,256,
  259
  William Francis 259

Rohrbach, Anna 236
  Christina 153,179
  Elisabeth 254,257
  Eliz. 181
  Elizabeth 170
  Frederick 228
  George 179,181,200,207
  Henrietta 244
  Jacob 170,181,191,
  193,200,204,214,228,
  236,238,244
  John 243,251,257
  Richard 257
  Sarah 257
  Susan 170,189,191,200,
  214,228,236,238,244
Rohrback, Adam 250
  Elisabeth 249
  Jacob 189
  James 250
  John 214
  Susan 193,250
Rohrs, Elizabeth 140
Roland, Charlotte 259
  Elisabeth 259
Roosberry, Mary 15
Rorbusy, Magdalen 63
Rosch, Henry 108
Rose, Anna Margaret 29
  Anna Mary 35
  Elizabeth 35,42,43
  James 35,42,43
Roselly, John (Rev.) 128
Rosetty, John (Rev.) 215
Rosner, Anna Barbara 107
  Anna Elizabeth 66
  Barbara 81
  Catharine 26,54,58,
  59,66,74,92
  John 45,47,52,58,59,
  66,74,83,92,108
  John Joseph 74
  Joseph 26,54,59,65
  Magdalen Eva 83
  Simon 92
Rossner, John 43
Roth, Michael 102
Rottman, Elizabeth 140
Rottmann, Bernard 140
  Catharine 140
Rudolf, Stephen 31
Ruffener, Adam 12
  Anna Mary 32
  Catharine 32
  George Adam 32
  Jo. M. Eva 8
  M. Barbara 8,12
  Philip 32
  Simon 8,12
Ruffner, --- 25
  Anna 86
  Anna M. 89
  Anna Margaret 26,44,
  196
  Anna Maria 75
  Anthony 53,171
  Barbara 53,64
  Catharine 38,41,44,
  46,49,53,58,61,75
  Chr. 94
  Christian 26,31,36,
  38,46,49,53,54,56,
  58,64,68,72,75,79,
  84,89,92,93
  Elizabeth 77,79,84
  Eva 53,58,61,73,84,181
  George 94
  George Adam 44,54,58,

Ruffner (cont.)
61,72,73,80,89,94,
104,121
Henry 38,46
John 49
M. 86
M. Eva 49,53,72,77
M. Magdalen 73
M. Odilia 49,53,58,
64,68,89,93
Magdalen 68
Margaret 80,171,176
Maria 80,94
Mary 54,58,61,72,73,
86,112,137
Mary Barbara 41,61
Mary Odilia 31
Odilia 36
Peter 31,38
Philip 27,38,41,46,
53,58,61,62,72,73,
75,77,79,84,106,171,
176,181,196,204
Simon 27,36,41,44,49,
53,58,64,75,84,94,
104,112,121
Rufner, Anthony 243
Juliana 243
Sarah 243
Ruhl, Conrad 92
Frederick 84,92,138
M. Anna 84
Margaret 92
Salome 138
Rupel, Elisabeth 230
George 230
Margaret 230
William 230
Rupell, John 230
Margaret 230
Rupert, Apollonia 104
Ruple, James 230
Margaret 230
Ruppel, Anna Maria 32
Barbara 32,55
Georg. 86
George 86
Jacob 32,145
John 49
John James 55
John William 55
Mary 140
Ruppels, Barbara 37
Ruppert, Magdalen 197
Stephen 197
Rupple, Anna 166
Anna Maria 160
Barbara 160,171
Catharine 162
Elizabeth 160,162
George 160,162,182
Jacob 160,166,174
John 160,162,174
Joseph 160,171,180
Margaret 166
Mary 174
Mary Barbara 163
Pegge 160
Peggy 160
Rebecca 174
Sarah 171
William 160
Russ, Elizabeth 34,42
James 34,42
Rustner, --- 25
Rutshi, Anna Elisabeth
240
Joseph 240

Rutshi (cont.)
Margaret 240
Ruttner, Anna 254
Anna Maria 79
Barbara 58,71,73,210
Catharine 66,68,80,109
Catherine 250
Elisabeth 238,250
James 250,253,254
John 68,238,250
John Michael 66
Joseph 53,54,55,71,
73,79,80,111
M. Barbara 80
Mary 250
Michael 68,80
Peter 65,210,250,254
Sarah 238,250,254
Ryan, James 10

--- S ---

Saintgerard, Joseph 79
St. Jean, Anthony 46
Louis 46
Samson, Gene 210
Jenny 210
John Frederick 251
Mary 251
Paul 210
Peter 210,251
Sanders, Anna Mary 31
Margaret 15
Peter 31
Sanderson, Ann 15
Sands, William 7
Sanneffert, Mary Barbara
153
Philip 153
Sauber, Matthew 261
Sauevert, Catharine 190
Joseph 190
Sara 190
Sauffert, Catharine 153
Joseph 153
Magdalen 153
Sauter, Christina 7,11
Philip 7,11
Simon 7
Sauvert, Barbara 162,168
Catharine 168,172,
174,206
Daniel 197,206,227
Elisabeth 227
Elizabeth 206
John 174,182,197,202,
235
Jonathan 197
Joseph 168,172,174,
202,206,208
Madeline 235
Magdalen 174,197,202
Mary Barbara 156
Mary Magdalen 168
Philip 156,162,168,235
Samuel 202
Sara 190
Solomon 162
Susan 156
William 174
Savage, Henry 6
Scandal, Catharrine 46
Schaeffer, Margaret 9
Schafer, John 52
Susanna 52
William 52

Schaffer, --- 25
Adam 106
Anna Margaret 59
Dorathy 109
Elizabeth 29
John William 55
Susan 44
Susanna 29,55,59
William 29,32,37,42,
44,56,59
Schall, Sara 178
Schamfessel, Elizabeth
32
John Louis 32
Schappert, Nicholas 15
Scharg, Catharine 110
Scharp, Andrew 179
Joseph 179
Mary 179
Schartel, Catharine 73
Rosina 73
Schartl, --- 94
Schaster, --- 25
Schedler, Michael 139
Schenfelter, --- (Rev.)
262
Scheven, Catharine 146,
148
Peter 146,148
Schif, Joseph 28
Schiff, Joseph 31,34
Schiffer, Mark 4,6
Schiltz, Mary Barbara 27
Schimfassel, Andrew 141,
146
Andrew Jacob 147
Anthony 141
Catharine 142
Ludovic 142
Margaret 141,146,147
Mary Barbara 146
Schimmplemmer, Rosina
138
Schimpfasel, Catharine
146
Louis 146
Schimpfassel, Andrew 144
Mary 144
Schimpfessel, Andrew 51,
56,65,75,80,90,105,
108
Catharine 60,83,151
John George 56
John Michael 50
Louis 50,51,55,59,60,
80,83
M. Catharine 80
M. Elizabeth 65
Margaret 51,55,56,65,
75,90
Margaret Barbara 75
Peter 90
Schimpfessl, Catharine
107
Elizabeth 111
M. Elizabeth 69
Schindler, Henry 106
Schinmfassel, Mary
Elizabeth 138
Schlauer, Cecily 101
Schlaut, Anna Maria 56
Schlings, Thomas 100
Schlosser, Anna 238
Anna M. 53
Anna Margaret 48,72
Anna Maria 150
Anna Maria Margaret
140

Schlosser (cont.)
Anna Mary 72
Anna W. 91
Catharine Anna 110
Catherine 224
Elizabeth 193
Francis Joseph 193
George 53,193
George James 72
John 142,154
Joseph 48,53,70,72,
  91,97,138,141,150,
  193,224
M. Margaret 48
Magdalen 83,111
Mary 138
Schluys, Thomas 78,100
Schmid, Barbara 140
Catharine 143
Elizabeth 143,145,147
Eva Catharine 146
Eva Mary 142
George 140
Jacob Caspar 145
Jacob Peter 143
John 139,145
Joseph 143,145
Mary 145
Mary Catharine 140
Philip 17,144,146
Regina 145
Ursula 143
Schmidd, Eva 149
Schmids, Anna 141,145
Cosmas 141,145
John 141
Juliana Seraphina 141
Margaret 141
Mary Ann Barbara 145
Schmidt, --- 132
A. Barbara 7
Andrew 139
Anna Martha 4
Barbara 17
Caspar 145
Catharine 9,137
Elizabeth 145,147,148
Eva Mary 7,9
Henry 149
John 4,14,147
John Adam 56,102
John George 13
Joseph 137,139
M. Eva 6
Margaret 56
Mary Eva 30
Michael 137
P. 28
Philip 9,15,148
Philip Joseph 144
Regina 139
Ursula Zip 13
Schmit, --- 132
Caspar 30
Catharine 151
Joseph 151
Schmith, Caspar 152
Catharine 149
Gertrude 151
Henry 149
Joseph 149
Schmitt, --- (Widow) 86
Anna 105
Anna Barbara 82
Anna Maria 76,121
Anthony 107,115,117
Caspar 39,40,69,88,
  96,184

Schmitt (cont.)
Catharine 81,82,88,
  98,102,117,184
Elizabeth 45,88,96,105
Frederick 117
George 96
Gertrude 43,65,81,104
Henry 52
James 74,119
Johanna 98
John Adam 39,44,48,
  52,62,75,79,80,82,
  102,103,115,119
John Adams 74
John James 82
John Joseph 98
John Melchior 34
John Michael 47
John William 67
Joseph 63,88,94,98,
  100,111,112
Margaret 35,36,39,44,
  48,52,62,65,74,75,
  79,80,96,102,103,
  104,115
Mary 67
Mary Dorothy 39,115
Michael 115
Nicholas 24,97,98,
  111,112
Ph. 103
Phil (Jr.) 103
Philip 30,31,32,34,
  35,36,37,40,43,47,
  103,115,117
Philip (Jr.) 38
Regina 98
Rose 115
Ursula 30,34,47
William 67
Schnab, Michael 149
Schnabel, Andrew 33,34,
  41,44,46,50,56
Eva 33,34,41,56,80
John 50
Joseph 93,112
M. Eva 44,50
Magdalen 152
Maria 93
Mary Elizabeth 33
Michael 112,138
Rosina 41
Schnabell, Elizabeth 138
Jacob 142
John 145
Joseph 138,145
Magdalen 145
Mary 145
Schnable, Joseph 69
Schnaebels, Magdalen 142
Schneider, Elizabeth 47
John 38,43,56
John George 40
Mary 43,47,56,73
Peter 56
Theodore (Rev.) 1,2,
  12,13,14,17,18,19,
  76,110,116,122,132,
  135,221,223
Theodorus (Rev.) 20
Schoenebruck, Caspar
  142,151
Catharine 151
John Caspar 143
Margaret 139,142,143
Schoenfelder, D. (Rev.)
  222
Schoffer, Mary Magdalen

Schoffer (cont.)
  178
Schommo, Andrew 144
Anthony 144
Elizabeth 144
Schonebruch, Andrew 57
Anna Elizabeth 89
Caspar 57
Margaret 57
Schonebruck, Anna Eliza-
  beth 92
Anna Margaret 49
Caspar 49,69,77,91,
  92,93,94,96,105,112
Elizabeth 69
Jacob 199
James 77
John 49
Margaret 69,91,92
Mary Barbara 91
Schonebruek, Caspar 225
Schonenbusch, Caspar 38
Schoner, Anna M. 35
Anna Maria 43,105
Catharine 85
Schonfessel, Catharine
  35
Louis 35
Mary Ann 35
Schorb, --- 32
Adam 47,54
Andrew 47
Anna 29,111
Anna Elizabeth 54
Anna Maria 84,110,138
Anna Mary 31
Barbara 54
Elizabeth 40,94,142,
  145
Frances 31,34
John 94,101,142,145
John Adam 40
Joseph 29,142
Joseph Andrew 29
M. Anna 84
Margaret 145
Mary Magdalen 94
Stephen 40
Schorck, Catharine 86
Schos, Susan 177
Schot, Catharine 67
Joseph 67
Philip 67
Schott, John William 145
Peter 145
Sophia 145
Schreik, Apollonia 16
Schroder, Maria 89
Schror, George 55
Schrunck, Elizabeth 45
John William 41
Louis 41
M. Elizabeth 51
Mary Eva 45
William 45,51
Schuhmacher, Anna Mary
  37
Catharine 100
Christian 37
Christian Joseph 37
Schuhmacker, Anna Maria
  48
Christian 48
M. Dorothy 48
Schuhmann, Adam 37
Andrew 27,37,104
Barbara 37
Christopher 27,36,37,

Schuhmann (cont.)
  39,41
  Conrad 37
  Elizabeth 37
  John 37
  Mary Elizabeth 39
  William 37
Schul, M. 101
  Mary 94
Schumacher, Anna Mary 33
  Christian 33
Schumann, Andrew 34
Schussler, Catharine 5
  Henry 5
  John George 5
Schwager, Anna Magdalen
  11
  John Peter 15
  Peter 11,15
  Wolffgang Adam 11
Schwartz, Agnes 3
  Anna Maria 150
  George James 3
  John 3,14
  Margaret 150
  Philip 150
Schwartzmann, Andrew 6
  Anna Maria 6
  John 6
  John George 3
Schwarz, --- 132
Schwayer, Nicholas 260
  Solomon 260
Schwitman, John Charles
  140
Schwittman, John 139,144
  Joseph Reichardus 144
  Margaret 144
Schwittmann, --- 132
  John 145,178
  Joseph Richard 144
  Margaret 144,145
Schwitz, Anna Magdalen
  15
Schwob, Anna Elizabeth
  184
Scnabells, Rosina 145
Scorb, Salome Elizabeth
  138
Scot, Petronilla 30
  William 30
Scott, Sara 210
Sebold, Anna 208
  Catharine 218
  Catherine 235
  John Jacob 218
  John James 235
  Nicholas 208
  Peter 208,218,235
Sedli, Jonas (Judge) 28
Seelli, Jonas (Judge) 28
Seely, D. 46
Seibert, Catharine 5,6,
  15
Seifert, Andrew 246
  Caroline 248
  Catharine 210
  Catherine 254
  Elisabeth 243,248,
    250,252,253,254
  Elisabeth D. 244
  Henry 243
  John 228,246
  Joseph 210,213,246,
    252,254
  Madeline 228,246,252
  Magdalen 213
  Philip 210

Seifert (cont.)
  Samuel 252
  Sarah 246
  Simon 243,248,250,254
Seiffert, --- 25
  Anna Maria 114
  Elizabeth 108
  Matth. 58,71
  Matthias 108
  Philip 111
Seigfried, --- 46
Seissloff, M. Elizabeth
  8
Seistert, --- 25
Semigoter, Catharine 143
  Peter 143
Sep, Margaret 71
  Michael 71
  Regina 71
Settel, Elizabeth 79
Seyvert, Catharine 144
  Joseph 144
  Philip 144
Seywert, Catharine 148
  John Benjamin 148
  Joseph 148
Shaefer, Anthony 232,
  236,237
  Catharine 213
  Christine 232
  Henry 213
  John 230
  Joseph 236
  M. Madeline 232,236,
    237
  Margaret 230
  Mary 230
  S. 230
  Susan 230
Shafer, Christina 208
  Eleonor 162
  John 160,162,163,172
  Mary 162,163,172
  Susan 172
  William 160,163,172
Shaffner, Anna 240
Shand, Margaret 225
Shaver, Susan 162
  William 162
Shaw, Denis 17
  Johanna 11
Shay, Edward 8
  Eleanor 8
  John 8
Shea, --- (Dr.) 126
Sheckman, David 252
  John 252
  Madeline 252
Shed, John 213
Shehea, Eleanor 10
Shell, Catharine 209
  Catherine 239
  James 209
  John 209,239,247,257
  Mary 257
  Sarah 247
  Susan 239,247,257
Shenfelder, --- (Rev.)
  261
Shenfelter, George 260
Shepperd, James 112
Shere, Anna 157
  Daniel 157
  George 157
Sherf, Eve 211
  James 211
Shevein, Mary Elizabeth
  154

Shevein (cont.)
  Peter 154
Shimfessel, Andrew 207,
  211,244
  Margaret 211,244
  Mary 207
  Peter 207
Shimpfessel, Elisabeth
  236
  Peter 208,236
Shindler, Andrew 176,
  189,230,232,235,238,
  239,240,244,249,255,
  261
  Caroline 249
  Clara 255
  Elias Jonas 230
  Elisabeth 246
  Elizabeth 172
  Esther 235
  Jacob 189
  Jerome 261
  Joseph 232,246
  Mary 189,200,232,239,
    247
  Sara 189,255
  Sarah 227,230,235,
    239,240,244,249
  Sarah Anna 244
Shippen, John 226
Shlacht, Elisabeth 261
  Madeline 261
Shlacht, Simon 261
Shlosser, Anna Maria 193
  Anna Mary 163,170
  Catharine 170
  Catherine 254
  Charles 198
  Charles Francis 190
  Elizabeth 198
  Esther 255
  George 198
  George Stephen 200
  James 229,241,246,
    250,255
  John 162,163,170,181,
    190,198,200,229,235,
    238,245,254
  John Joseph 245
  Joseph 163,170,181,
    229,245,254
  Madeline 229,235,238,
    245,254
  Magdalen 163,170,190,
    198,200
  Margaret 254
  Mary 163,181,212,241
  Susan 229,241,246,
    250,255
Shmid, --- 132
  Caspar 220,254
  Catherine 245
  Elisabeth 240
  Elizabeth 155
  George 155
  Susan 220,254
Shmidt, --- 132,231
  Andrew 213,253,254
  Angela 201
  Anna Margaret 199
  Barbara 158,160,165,
    174,189,194,199,216,
    225,232,238
  Caspar 157,160,165,
    167,170,181,188,193,
    201,210,211,212,226,
    236
  Catharine 153,157,159,

Shmidt (cont.)
165,174,181,190,194,
195,196,201,203,211
Catherine 225,230,233,
236,237,242,243,253
Charles 174
Christian 180,182
Christina 165
Elisabeth 229,234,
239,245
Elizabeth 156,160,
163,168,171,172,189,
190,194,195,196,197,
206,210,212
Frederic 196
Frederica 237
Frederick 174,192,
201,230,237,243
George 158,159,160,
165,171,174,175,189,
192,194,199,212,216,
225,232
Henry William 196
Jacob 190
John 160,162,169,174,
188,190,195,201,214,
225,233,236,240
John Adam 159
John Frederick 174
Joseph 159,162,165,
167,171,200,212,213,
250,254
Juliana 236
Litta 236
Madeline 233,240,245,
248
Madeline Eva 233
Magdalen 182,191,197,
203,211
Margaret 165,233
Mary 165,169,174,193,
194,196,202,225,229,
232,236,252
Mary Anna 229
Mary Catherine 230
Mary Magdalen 180
Michael 165,169,174,
181,196,202,229,232,
236,238,252
Phil. 219
Philip 156,163,172,
181,189,190,191,197,
203,206,217,219,233,
240,245,248
Philip (Jr.) 206
Philippina 254
Regina 162,167,171,
212,213,250,254
Sarah 232,252
Sarah Anna 243
Sus. 212
Susan 157,160,165,
167,170,188,193,201,
206,210,211,212,226,
236,247
Thomas 168,180,195,202
Ursula 159,181
Shmith, Madeline 259
Shnabel, A. Maria 188
Aegidius Andrew 192
Andrew 153,154,167,
173,175,176,180,182,
183,192,196,200,207,
210,216,227
Ann 195
Anna 175,191,192,198,
227,234,244,246
Anna M. 226

Shnabel (cont.)
Anna Margaret 166
Anna Maria 192
Anna Mary 243
Barbara 159,162,165,
167,171,175,190,195,
200,212,224,228,234,
239,245,250,254,256
Benjamin 254
Catharine 167,173,
176,192,196,216
Catherine 247
Daniel 207,211,234,
234,235,245,247
Elizabeth 175,180,
195,196,207
Eva 153,182,183,207
Henry 234
Jacob 159,162,167,
171,175,180,182,190,
195,200,218
James 205,224,228,
234,236,239,245,250,
254,256
Joel 253
John 158,162,165,175,
183,191,192,195,198,
211,227,234,241,246,
250
John Peter 224
Joseph 153,157,166,
188,192,197,207,211,
213,226,228,234,243,
250,253,256
Judith 234
Juliana 253,256
Leah 226
Litta 245
M. 197
M. Catherine 253
Margaret 165,173,176,
191,192,197,212,218,
226,236,237,239,244,
247,250
Mary 157,159,166,171,
176,207,211,213,227,
234,244,246
Mary Anna 250
Mary Catharine 188
Mary Eve 175,180,192,
218
Mary Susan 226
Mary Theresa 153
Michael 154,159,165,
173,176,180,183,191,
192,197,207,212,218,
226,236,244,247
Paul Andrew 197
Rosina 154,158
Sarah 250
Shneider, --- 132
Catharine 169,175,189
Daniel 169,175,189
Jacob 169
Margaret 189
Peter 175
Shnieringer, John 169
Susan 169
Shoenebruck, Caspar 139,
180
Shonebruck, Andrew 162,
165,175,183,195,201
Barbara 174
Barbara 189
C. 210
Caspar 158,160,161,
166,168,183,189,199,
201,202,203,205,206,

Shonebruck (cont.)
208,209,241
Caspar (Jr.) 198,205
Elizabeth 165,167,
182,183
Eva 232,250
Jacob 193,201
James 206,233
John 171,175,182,232,
250
Joseph 161
Madeline 233
Magdalen 195,201
Margaret 158,160,161,
166,168,183,189,199,
201,202,203,205,206,
208,209,232,233,241
Mary 175
Mary Ann 192
Mary Barbara 196,205
Rosina 171
Solomon 195
Susan 201
William 233
Shonebruek, Andrew 225
Catherine 225
Eva 225
James 225
John 225
Madeline 225
Susan 225
Shop, Margaret 259
Shorb, Margaret 158
Shorp, Anthony 211,220,
242,246,248
Catharine 210,220
Catherine 246,248
Elisabeth 251
Elizabeth 159,160,211
John 160,210,211,251,
253
Joseph 159
Margaret 250,257
Rebecca 210
Simon Lazarus 160
Shots, Anthony 194
Catharine 194
John 194
Shott, Anthony 174
Catharine 174,175
John George 174
Joseph 174
Mary 174
Peter 174
Philip James 174
Shreer, Adam Daniel 161
Catharine 161,209,215
George 209
John George 161
Shroer, Catharine 166
John George 166
Mary 166
Shubin, Madeline 262
Shuchler, George Henry
257
Juliana 257
Shudder, Mary 154
Peter 154
Shuppert, Anna Mary 165
Shurp, Anthony 153
Elisabeth 232
Elizabeth 153,168,
185,189,195,196,203
John 153,168,185,189,
195,196,203,232
John William 154
Joseph 154,185
Lazarus 203

Shurp (cont.)
Mary Elizabeth 154
Philip 195
Simon Lazarus 185
Solomon 189
Shutt, Anthony 201,217,
229,247
Catharine 201,217
Catherine 229,247
Charles 247
Henry 229
Jacob 201
James 217
Shwarz, --- 132
Francis Philip 161
John 154
Margaret 154,157,161
Philip 154,161
Philip Michael 157
Shweyer, Catherine 247
David 236
Elisabeth 231,236,247
John Nicholas 207,231
Joseph 231
Nicholas 236,247
Sibert, John Felix 184
Sichar, Martin 259
Sicken, Gertrude 47
Siegfrid, Barbara 147
Joseph 147
Siegfried, Andrew 179
Barbara 150
Catharine 151
Joseph 150,177
Juliana 151
Mary 150,151,152
Mary Agatha 179
Sigfrid, Agatha 157,
184,197,198
Andrew 16,184,197,218
Anna 251
Anna Maria 198
Anna Mary 226
Anthony 243
Barbara 157,161,172,
174,176,188,191,193,
194,198,199,201,209,
214,226,233,242,243,
244,251
Catharine 143,188
Catherine 234,239,
250,253
Charles 209,242,250,
253,258
Daniel 233
Elisabeth 226,234,
239,245,250,253,255
Elizabeth 193
Elsabeth 257
Eva 16,161,168
Eve 172,175,188,189,
192,204,205
George 16,156,165,
172,174,176,182,188,
191,193,194,198,226,
233,242,243,244,251
Helen 250,258
Jacob 159,167,180
James 209,243,245,253
John 143,172,209,211,
256
John Michael 16
Joseph 167,180,184,
193,206,226,234,239,
243,245,253,255,256,
257
Justina 180,182
Justus 245

Sigfrid (cont.)
Madeline 242,253
Magdalen 159
Margaret 226,239,243
Mary 143,180,239,242
Michael 180,182
Philip Charles 143
Rebecca 242
Salome 242
Susan 159,167,258
Thomas 234,250
Sigfried, --- 39,40,41,
59,80,99
Agatha 30
Agathan 42,97
Andrew 30,37,42,51,71
Anthony 87
Barbara 79,83,88,89,
92,110,111
Catharine 44,45,49,
52,55,56,64,71,79,
95,105,109,110
Catharine Elizabeth 33
Francis Joseph 48
George 29,33,52,104,
119
John George 52
John Michael 29,33,
34,40,42,48,52,71,
76,92,96,109,121
Joseph 30,86,96
Juliana 70
Justina 29,33,34,42,
48,52,61,73,79,83,87
M. 88
M. Agatha 71,95
Margaret 99
Mary 51,61,77,88,97,
109
Mary Agatha 37
Mary Ann 29
Mary Catharine 42
Mary Eva 42
Michael 55,57,61,64,
65,71,73,78,79,83,
86,87,89,93,100,110,
111
Thomas 61
Simpson, Joseph 257
Mary 257
Steward 257
Sires, Michael 212
Smidt, Caspar 179
Eva 179
Philip 179
Ursula 179
Smith, David 12
Elizabeth 11,12
John 15
Patrick 11,12
Philip 11
Snabel, Jacob 157
John 261
John Aaron 261
Snyder, Susan 261
Sommer, Adam 8,9,11
John Adam 9
John Henry 11
Spaeth, Adam 9
Spahn, Anna Margaret 87
M. Elizabeth 97
Mark William 87
William 97
Spang, Susan 205
Speitel, Margaret 258
Spengler, Adam 215
Catharine 4,6,8,15
Christ. 215

Spengler (cont.)
Elizabeth 215
George 4
Mary Eva 3
Peter 3
Spies, Anna Magdalen 11
Catharine 11
Wolffgang 11
Spring, Anna Catharine
50,53
Anna M. 50
Anna Maria 70,160
Anna Mary 205
Barbara 40,54,57,63,
64,83,95
Barbara Keffer 110
Catharine 41,46,56,
63,67,70,73,78,83,
92,100,154,157,201,
202,204,205
Catherine 234,241
Charles 199
Conrad 41,87,95,142
George 57,63,106,164,
205
J. 193
Jacob 83,154,157,195,
201,204
James 28,41,46,50,53,
54,56,63,67,70,73,
77,78,86,92,100,104,
205,225,226
John 50,78
John Adam 86
John George 40,44,
100,104,245
Joseph 55,78,199,205
M. Barbara 57,106,109
M. Margaret 46
Margaret 164,204
Mary Barbara 28,56,58
Susan 199
Susan Catharine 164,
195
Susan Catherine 225,
226
Staab, A. Catharine 12
Adam 11,12
Catharine 7,9,11
Eva Catharine 7
George Adam 9
John Adam 7,14
Staal, Eva 179
Stagle, Anna 6
Matthew 6
Melon 6
Stahl, Adam 28,79,102
Anna Maria 49,79,83,
106
Anna Mary 17,26
Barbara 107
Bernard 79
Cathalina 47
Catharine 42,49,53
Eva Mary 79
James 53
Joseph 31,39
Margaret 39
Michael 16,31,39,49
Regina 48
Stahler, Adam 36,54,64,
103,160,204
Catharine 36,160
Charles 226
Christian 59,193,195,
199,202,204,226,231,
241
Elizabeth 54

295

Stahler (cont.)
 Eva Maria 64
 Eva Mary 160
 F. Joseph 225
 John Adam 51,59,103
 Joseph 225
 Judith 241
 Margaret 193,195,199,
  202,226,231
 Mary 36,51,54,59,204,
  231
 Mary Elizabeth 156
 Rebecca 202
 Salome 199
 Susan 195,225
Stal, Catharine 148
Stalt, Elizabeth 76
Stalten, Benedict 76
Stalter, Anna Maria 140
 Apollonia 140,146
 Henry 140,146,177
 John 146
Stand, John 145
 Juliana Margaret 141
Standt, John 141,147
 Juliana Margaret 141
Stantigel, Anthony 79
 Matthias 79
Starr, Daniel 117
Stasy, Ann 10
 Matthew 10
Stattler, Henry 108
Stengler, Barbara 15
Sterling, Bartholomew
 229
 Elisabeth 229,234,
  240,246,249,253
 Elizabeth 203
 Henrietta 234
 John 203,206,229,234,
  240,246,249,253
 Joseph 246
 Sara Anna 253
Steward, Bernard 150
 Daniel 209
Stewart, Daniel 208
 David 235,236,240
 Juliana 235,236,240
 Litta 240
 Reuben 236
Steyerwald, A. Marg. 10
 M. Catharine 10
Sthaler, Catharine 95
Stocker, Elisabeth 259
 Joseph 259
Stockschlager, A. Martha
 5
 John 5
 John Adam 5
Stockschleger, A. Martha
 6,10
 John 6,10
 M. Apollonia 10
 Mary Clara 15
Stoll, Edward 101
 Elizabeth 112
 Erhard 217
 Eva 28
 Eva Margaret 29
 Eve Margaret 217
 Margaret 42,83
Stollawerk, Jane Gene-
 vieve 131,132
 John Genevieve 131
Stott, Erardus 150
 Margaret 150
Strack, Anna 94
 Catharine 171,175,

Strack (cont.)
 188,200
 Daniel 175,192,200,
  202,226
 Elisabeth 226
 Elizabeth 175,188,
  192,200,202
 Henry 159,171,175,
  180,188
 John 192
 Susan 202
 William 76,94,159
Strauss, Anna Elizabeth
 81
Strautenbach, Antony 139
 Barbara 139
 John 139
Streebe, Elizabeth 171
 George 171
 Mary 171
Striby, George 181
Stricker, Eve 189
Stroback, Anthony 230
 Catherine 230
Strohm, Anna Maria 114
Strubbel, --- 24
 Elizabeth 64
Strubel, --- 24
 Anna Sophia Juliana 82
 Charles 101
 Magdalen 90
 Maria Anna 90
 Peter 90
Strubl, --- 24
 Anna Catharine 87
 Anna Sophia Juliana 82
 Catharine 94
 M. Catharine 87
 Mary Sophia 52
Strunck, Anna Maria 179
 Barbara 120
 Catharine 92
 Elizabeth 68,92,141,
  179
 Eva 178
 Henry 68
 John 100
 M. Elizabeth 60,86,100
 Margaret 86
 Mary Elizabeth 145,146
 Mary Eve 146
 Philip 78,138,151,179
 William 60,68,78,79,
  86,92,100,101,112,
  120,139,141,145,146,
  179
Strunek, Philip Charles
 143
Strung, Eva Margaret 143
Strunk, Agatha 159,161
 Elizabeth 60,91
 Gertrude 154,159
 John William 154
 M. Gertrude 60
 Mary 159
 Mary Elizabeth 154
 Philip 159,161,168
 William 60,91
Strupel, John Henry 70
 Magdalen 70
 Peter 70
 William Peter 65
Struppel, --- 24
 Catharine 78,120
 Charles 88,95,101
 Henry 73
 John Daniel 73
 M. Elizabeth 73,77,109

Struppel (cont.)
 M. Magdalen 84
 M. Sophia 79
 Magdalen 70,90
 Peter 63,65,70,90,109
 William Peter 84
Stumpf, Anna Mary 15
Stumpff, Christopher 9
Sulivan, Daniel 11
 Eleanor 27
Sullivan, John 32
 Rebecca 32
 Solomon 32
Sutten, Martin 169
 Sara 169
 William 169
Swartz, Margaret 151
 Philip 151
Sweetman, --- 132
 Brigid 244
 Clara 164
 John 95,97,156,160,
  164,182,185,218
 Joseph Richard 218
 Margaret 156,164,182,
  218
 Pegge 160
Sweetmann, John 90
Sweikert, David 189
 Magdalen 189
 Susan 189
Sweyer, Anna Mary 227
 Elisabeth 227
 John Nicholas 227
Swimler, Daniel 254
 Elisabeth 254
 James 254
Swoab, Magdalen 152
Swuitman, --- 132
 Bridget 151
 John 151

--- T ---

Tapper, --- 24
 Andrew 39,42,43,46,
  57,63,82,103
 Anna M. 42
 Anna Maria 39,82
 Anna Mary 46
 Barbara 78
 Catharine 71
 Christian 51,78
 Elizabeth 26,36,39,
  42,78,90,91,94,103
 James 57
 John 42,46,78,82,91,94
 John Henry 63
 Magdalen 103
 Margaret 82
 Maria 63
 Mary 57,82
Taubetsen, Magdalen 180
Tenes, Magdalen 156
Tenesser, Catherine 261
 John 261
 Rebecca 261
 Elizabeth 166
 John Frederick 166
 John Henry 166
 Veronica 166
Thomasen, Mary 151
Thompson, Mary 151
Thorn, John 175
Thornbach, Catharine 49
 Nicholas 49

Thum, Ann M. 69
  Caspar 33,40,45,55
  Catharine 111
  Eva 33,40,45
  Eva (Jr.) 45
  Joseph 45
  M. 109
  M. Eva 57
  Magdalen 40
  Maria 111
  Mary Elizabeth 55
  Mary Eva 55,83
  Peter 111
  Rose 111
  Th. 83,109,112
  Thomas 46,56,61,66,
    79,80,83,105
  Valentine 33
Thumm, Eva 95
  Mary Eva 109
Toy, James 7
Trapper, Elizabeth 88
Traut, Catherine 237,
    243,247
  Elisabeth 243
  Mary 247
  Rachel 237
  William 237,243,247
Tren, John 111
Treu, John 111
Trolling, Susan 179
Trout, Catherine 254
  Eve 209
  George 209
  Joseph 254
  William 209,254
Tuf, Anna 98
  Cornelius 98
  John 98
  Mary Ann 98
Tutt, Anna 249
  George 249
Twicker, Anthony 155
  Eva 155

--- U ---

Ufer, --- 24
  Balthasar 44
  Francis 41,58
  Frank 44,83
  John 83
  John Adam 58
  M. Anna 86
  Mary Ann 41,44,58
  Susan Juliana 41
Uhlein, Elizabeth 55,206
  Fr. 105
  Francis 64,110,112,182
  Francis Louis 156
  John 75,82,93,97,99,
    206
  Joseph 72,75,101
  Juliana 156,182
  Laurence Agnellus 156
  Margaret 101
  Mary 206
  Mary Cecily 107
  Ursula 105
  Valentine 33,117
Ulmer, Frederic 57
Ulrich, Adam 31
  Barbara 10
  Catharine 31,106
  John Francis 10
  John George 11

Ulrich (cont.)
  John Michael 31
Umben..., Catherine 254
  Elisabeth 254
  Samuel 254
Umbenhauer, Samuel 213
Ursenbach, Catharine 156
  John 156
  Mary Elizabeth 156
Usden, John 85
  Susanna 85
  William 85
Utzman, A. M. 12
  Albertina 2,6,9,12
  Goerge 2
  John 2,4,5,6,9,12,14
  Margaret Apollonia 6
  Sarah 12
Utzmann, A. M. 10

--- V ---

Vaeth, Adam 9,11
  Elizabeth 9
  Magdalen 11
  Magdalen Bruckner 9
Varendorf, Anna Mary 214
Vaughen, James 237,239
Victor, John 215
Villar, John George 11
  M. Eva 11
Vingart, Elizabeth 206
  John 197
  Mary Elizabeth 198
  Philippina 197
Vogely, Catharine 191,
    194,197,198,204
  Catherine 256
  Elizabeth 194
  George 191,194,197,
    198,204,205,256
  John 204
  Mary 191
  Sara 197
  Susan 256

--- W ---

Wack, Elizabeth 210
  Frederick 210
  Martin 210
Waehtwein, John 140
  Mary 140
  Matthias Joseph 140
Wagener, Israel 203
  James 232
  Mary 203,232
  Philip 232
Waghen, James 209
Waghon, Catherine 257
  Jacob 199
  James 206,207,257
Wagner, Anna M. 63
  Anna Maria 38
  Catharine 58,81
  Catherine 227
  Eva 81,105,121
  Ferdinand 24,111
  James 250
  John 227
  John Baptist 38
  Madeline 250
  Magdalen 58
  Mary 227

Wagner (cont.)
  Mary Salome 50
  Matth. 63
  Matthias 38,50,58
  Salome 90,108
  Sarah 250
Waker, Elisabeth 245
  John 245
Walburger, Anna Mary 14
Walker, Agatha 97
  Daniel 77,81,88,100,
    120,151,211
  Elisabeth 243,252
  Elizabeth 220
  George Christian 66
  Gertrude 88,211,217
  Henry 81
  Jacob 139
  John 77,151,211,220,
    243,252
  Maria 85
  Mary 70
  Mary Ann 139
  Mary Juliana 70
  Susanna 66,118
  William 66,70,77,85,
    88,97,100,109,118,
    252
  William Bartholomew 88
Walltrich, Mary Magdalen
    14
Walsh, Anna 230
  Catherine 230
  Elisabeth 230
  Richard 230
Walter, Catharine 74,175
  Frances 68,210,233
  George 175
  Henry 175
  Jacob 175
  James 63,68,68,74,
    110,119,185,247
  John 40,104,210
  Joseph 6,175,232,233
  Margaret 68,105,175
  Mary 210
  Mary Ann 41
  Nicholas 39,103
Walton, George 89
  John Joseph 89
Wanghan, Jacob 189
Wanner, Mary Ann 102
Wans, Abraham 138
  George 138,148
  Mary 138,148
Wants, John George 103
Wantz, George 55,109,
    141,146
  John 146
  John George 33,42,52,
    56
  Maria 141
  Mary 146
  Peter 103
Waters, Anna 254
  Anthony 212,254
  Margaret 212
  Mary Margaret 254
Watter, John 193,200
  Mary 193,200
Watters, Joseph 202
Weaver, Anna 182
  Catharine 182
  Jacob 182
Webel, Frederick 137
Weber, Andrew 165
  Anna Catharine 77
  Caspar 139

297

Weber (cont.)
Elizabeth 74
James 77
John Henry 146
John James 119
Magdalen 67,74,93,165
Margaret 83
Mary 261
Mary Barbara 93
Mary Magdalen 139,146
Mathias 215
Matthias 67,74,79,83,
93,108,109,139,146,
165
Weegllain, Daniel 185
Weibel, Anna Catharine
31
Anna M. 75,87
Anna Margaret 110
Anna Maria 51,139
Anna Mary 48
Barbara 38,81,83,115,
150
Catharine 105
Elizabeth 26,104,105
Elizabeth Catharine 46
Eva 55,108,111
John 29,54,55,59,60,
108,142
Joseph 50,76,93,139
M. Barbara 78
M. Eva 87,93,94
M. Theresa 76
Margaret 60,70,76,93,
139,142
Mary 60
Mary Barbara 104
Mary Margaret 60
Regina 44
Susanna 38
Valent. 61
Valentine 36,39,117,
118
Weible, Barbara 82
Weidener, Jesse James
231
Lazarus 231
Madeline 231
Weider, Anna Margaret
137
Weidner, Anna Margaret
40
Weiler, Christina 104
Weinmann, Barbara 255
Weirich, James 207
Magdalen 207
Weisbecher, Catharine 26
Weisenburg, Catharine
197
Jacob 197
Weismiller, --- 62
Anna Maria 51
Catharine 33
Elizabeth 34,41,43,
78,79,179
Eva Margaret 102
Gertrude 79
M. Elizabeth 51
M. Eva 45
Mary Elizabeth 26
Philip 26,43,51
Susanna 40
Weismuller, Elizabeth
139
Susan 139
Weiss, Susan 205
Weissemburg, Mary 200
Weissenburg, James 229

Weissenburg (cont.)
Margaret 229
Weissenburger, Anna M.
68
Catharine 68
Christian 105
Jacob 105
James 68
M. Catharine 106
Welcher, --- 132
Welcker, Anna Maria
Helen 148
Henry Stephen 140,184
Jacob 148
James 184
John Jacob 140
Magdalen 140,148,184
Peter 52
Welken, Anna Elizabeth
179
Welker, --- 132
Elizabeth 191
Gottlib 185
Helen 91
Jacob 166,169
John 170,191
John Jacob 154,157
John James 86
John Theophilus 86
Joseph 169
Magdalen 154,157,169
Mary Barbara 118
Mary Magdalen 166,185
Peter 118
Theophilus 79,86,217
Weller, Elizabeth 204
Welsch, Conr. 86
Conrad 63,85,92,120
Elizabeth 32,85,120
James 83,87,91
John 32
Juliana 120
Martha 85
Welsh, Sarah 14
Wenamer, Bernard 168
Elizabeth 168
Wenarmer, Bernard 182
Elizabeth 182
Wenig, Anna 113
Catharine 102
George 113
Wennerich, James 236
John 236
Susan 236
Wentzel, Catharine 7,11
John William 7
Simon 7
Theodore 11
William 8,11
Wenzel, Andrew 257
Madeline 257
Mary Anna 257
Sophia 154
Werner, Andrew 149
Catharine 149
Westemayer, John 71
M. Odilia 71
Westemeyer, John 75
Oldilia 75
Westermayer, John 75
Odilia 75
Wetzler, Mary Catharine
26
Weuer, Maria 139
Whulen, Catherine 257
John 257
William 257
Wiber, Matthias 57

Wichhorn, Eva 259
Widder, John Adam 49
Wider, Anna 106
Anna Margaret 44
Elizabeth 53,66,78
Eva 53
John 69
Margaret 48,52,57,79,
88,108
Mary Elizabeth 79,153
Wieder, Ann M. 46
M. Elizabeth 82
Wild, Valentine 15
Wilder, Elizabeth 108
Wildt, Valentine 15
Will, Margaret 212
Willheim, Eva 162
Williams, Peter 80
Windbichler, Philip 258
Sylvester 258
Windbiegler, Catherine
253
Margaret 253
Philip 213,253
Windeler, Frances 235
Francis 241
John 235,241
Juliana 235
Louise 241
Winek, Caspar 183
Wineyard, Elizabeth
191,195
John 195
Joseph 195
Philippina 195
Wingart, Aaron 250
Elisabeth 228,231
Elizabeth 192,198,
201,203,204,206,209
Eva 227,228,231,241,
247,256
Helen 209
Henry 247,260
John 198,203,204,206,
224,228,234,239,240,
250,260
Joseph 192,200,204,
206,207,209,227,228,
231,241,247,256
Juliana 240
Mary Elizabeth 198
Philippina 198,203,
224,228,234,239,240,
250
Philippine 228
William 234,256
Wingert, Anna Elizabeth
67,75
Daniel 245
Helen 234
John 245,248,256
Joseph 67,75
Philippina 245,248,256
Susan 75
Theresa 67
Wirned, Conrad 260
William 260
Wolf, Abraham 213
Catharine 213
Elizabeth 213
Wolflinger, Bernard 9
Wolter, Frances 208
Joseph 208
Wulsin, Mary 30
Wummer Adam 172,190,
194,197,201,217,227,
232,236,241,244,245
Elizabeth 194

298

Wummer (cont.)
  George 190
  Jacob 217
  James 227
  John 172
  John Adam 252
  Madeline 227,232,236,
    241,244,245,252
  Magdalen 172,190,194,
    197,201,217
  Margaret 197
  Mary 201
  Samuel 232
Wurf, Eva 90,91
  Michael 91
  Peter 90,91,120
Wurff, Anna Maria 83
  Peter 80,83
Wurst, Anna Maria 83
  Peter 83
Wurtzer, Elizabeth 68
  Eva 68,72
  George 68,72,86,90
  John 90
  Regina 72

--- Y ---

Yedler, Thomas 32,33
Ylain, Elizabeth 152
  John 152
  Joseph 152
York, Elisabeth 248
  Thomas 248
  William 248

--- Z ---

Zatip, Catharine 151
Zenner, David 149
  Elizabeth 149
  Mary Elizabeth 149
Zerfass, Catharine 108
Zerly, Eve 212
  James 212
  Louis 212
Zettelmayer, Jonathan
  212
Zeyer, Claudina 26
Ziegefuss, Catharine 108
Ziegenfuss, Anna Eliza-
  beth 66
  Catharine 83
Zieger, Catharine 28
  Melchior 28
Ziegler, Catharine 13,
  34,114
  John Melchior 34
  Magdalen 208
  Melchior 13,114
Zimmermann, George 14
Zimmermartin, --- 134
Zinck, Anthony 16
Zing, Catharine 147
Zinn, Susanna 53
Zip, Apollonia 31,37,46
  Eva 13
  George 13,114
  Joseph 31,37,46
  Margaret 71
  Mary Elizabeth 37
  Mary Eva 114
  Matthias 31
  Michael 71

Zip (cont.)
  Ursula 13
Zipp, Anna Catharine 53
  Apollonia 40,53
  George 114
  Joseph 16,40,53
  M. Elizabeth 40
  Margaret 71
  Michael 71
Zweem, Catherine 262
  Samuel 262
  Thomas 262
Zweier, Adam 138
  Anna 139
  Anthony 138
  Balthasar 138
  Barbara 138
  Catharine 208
  Mary 138,139
  Mary Ann 138
  Mary Elizabeth 138
  Thomas 139
Zweyer, --- (Widow) 110
  Adam 68,83,89,92,111,
    150,157,192,209,235,
    237,247,250
  Agatha 179
  Anna 243,245
  Anna M. 64,96,99
  Anna Maria 55,96,98,
    145,195
  Anna Mary 162
  Anthony 65,71,83,87,
    92,93,96,99,109,125,
    143,150,179
  Balthasar 29,44,49,
    99,109,141,142,143,
    148,150,156,180
  Balthassar 48
  Barbara 192,209,235,
    237,247,250
  Benjamin 235
  Catharine 65,71,75,93,
    141,150,165,208,209
  Catharine Frances 64
  Catherine 241,243,252
  Charles 252
  Daniel 83,201
  Elisabeth 224,231,235,
    240,243,245,250,256
  Elizabeth 150,180,
    195,199,251
  Elizabeth Magdalen 143
  Eva 42,45,46,52,68
  Frances 199
  George 115,143,180,
    181,224
  James 89,206,224,231,
    235,240,245,250,256
  John 42,45,52,86,104,
    189
  John Adam 45
  John Anthony 145
  John Balthasar 148
  John George 29
  John Nicholas 243
  John Thomas 52,71
  Joseph 30,38,39,41,45,
    51,55,62,65,75,86,
    93,110,141,157,165,
    193,199,201,208,209,
    236,247,254,255,256
  Juliana 41,48,62,65,
    93,180,210
  Julianna 17
  Justina Elizabeth 83
  M. Anna 83
  M. Apollonia 98

Zweyer (cont.)
  M. Juliana 93
  M. Margaret 99
  Magdalen 143
  Maria 87
  Mary 40,125,143,148,
    165,179,180,181,201,
    206,208,209,229,231,
    245,250
  Mary Agatha 16
  Mary Ann 156
  Mary Juliana 29,156
  Mary Magdalen 46
  Mathias 195,199
  Matthias 55
  Nicholas 251
  Sara 251
  Solomon 240
  Stephen 17,40,46,55,
    64,83,98,145,180,181
  Thomas 71,75,89,96,
    148,149,156,165,182,
    189,192,201,206,209,
    210,231,241,243,252
Zweyers, --- 30

--- no surname ---

---, --- 43,159,178,226
  Abigail 28
  Adam 86
  Aloyzius 257
  Andrew 262
  Anna 176
  Anna Barbara 140
  Anna Catharine 11
  Anna Elizabeth 28
  Anna Louise 230
  Anna Mary 224
  Catharine 37,57,200
  Catherine 225,232,262
  Cecily 65,73
  Charles 92
  Christina 7,176
  Christopher 232
  Cornelius 5
  Daniel 52,99
  David 4
  Edward 11
  Elias Paul 231
  Elisabeth 224,225,
    226,231,261,262
  Elizabeth 85,160,167,
    176
  Esther 196
  Eva Helena 6
  Felicitas 28,34,49
  Frederick 104
  George 65,107,224,229
  Henry 224,225
  Isaac 9
  Jacob 167
  James 5
  John 4,34,86,165
  John Michael 31
  Joseph 38,200,203
  Julii Ann. Margaretha
    12
  Louis 28,49,55,65,73,
    85
  M. Dorothy 39
  M. Elizabeth 111
  Madeline 232,260,261
  Margaret 262
  Margaret Elizabeth 7

--- (no surname, cont.)
  Mark 49
  Mary 160
  Mary Madeline 224
  Maurice 231
  Michael 196
  Patrick 5

--- (no surname, cont.)
  Peter 231
  Petronilla 69
  Rachel 12
  Rosina 34
  Salome 55
  Sarah 9,85

--- (no surname, cont.)
  Simon 48
  Susan 146,196
  William Solomon 224
---ger, Catherine 262
  James 262
  John 262

CPSIA information can be obtained at www.ICGtesting.com
Printed in the USA
LVOW13s1953261213

366997LV00006B/37/P